THE BIOPSYCHOSOCIAL APPROACH TO THE PATIENT

THE BIOPSYCHOSOCIAL APPROACH TO THE PATIENT

Chase Patterson Kimball, M.D.
Professor of Psychiatry and Medicine
and Professor in the College
University of Chicago
Chicago, Illinois

WILLIAMS & WILKINS
Baltimore/London

Made in the United States of America

Library of Congress Cataloging in Publication Data

Kimball, Chase Patterson
The biopsychosocial approach to the patient.
Includes bibliographical references and index
1. Medicine and psychology. 2. Sick—Psychology
I. Title. [DNLM: 1. Patients—Psychology.
2. Physician—Patient relations. 3. Nurse—Patient relations. W62 K49b]
R726.5.K5 616'.001'9 80-18022
ISBN 0-683-04616-0

Composed and printed at the
Waverly Press, Inc.
Mt. Royal and Guilford Aves.
Baltimore, MD 21202, U.S.A.

For

Lisa Giddings
Allison Easton
Susan Chase
Jamie Giddings

PREFACE

Thinking about Patients

The Basis of Objectivity:

This book is intended as a verbal introduction to the person as a patient. It is intended to supplement the experience of the student in her or his early orientation to the patient and the environments of care. The emphasis is on the experiential and the phenomenological. The student does not enter the world of the patient without experience. He or she has had previous experience with illness and the institutions within which illness develops and is treated. This illness may have been of oneself or of one's family or close friends. He or she may have been sensitized to the phenomenon of illness at a more distant and abstract level as relating to problems in health care delivery, costs, world-wide famines, and epidemics. The student comes with considerable experience that has sensitized, perhaps prejudicially, her in her approach to illness, patients, and the institutions of their care. An awareness of these experiences and the feelings, attitudes, reflections, and knowledge that they have engendered is an important first step in the individual's experiencing and objectification of illness in the patient. This previous experience of individuals, of illness, and of issues in medicine and health serves the student in good stead and has fostered the growth of intuitive processes that are both essential and useful in the practice of medicine. However, the power of intuition is only generative. Once aroused, it requires rigorous objectification, review, and testing as to whether and to what extent it applies in the present situation.

Of Evolution: The Author

This book derives from my own experience as a student, physician, and teacher in attempting to understand the experience of illness in the patient and its effect on the family and individuals who treat it in the different environments of illness. Intimately related with this attempt has been one of identifying the multifacets of illness as they can be viewed by social, psychological, and biological perspectives, in short the Biopsychosocial Approach. This interest and approach has been fostered by a number of my teachers along the way, including Duncan Clark, M.D., Professor of Community Health and Environmental Medicine at the State University of New York, Downstate Medical Center; Ellsworth L. Amidon, M.D., Professor of Medicine, University of Vermont; Kerr L. White, M.D., Chairman and Professor of Epidemiology and Community Medicine, University of Vermont (currently Deputy Director, Division of Health Sciences, the Rockefeller Foundation, New York); George L. Engel, M.D., and his associates, Arthur H. Schmale, M.D., William L. Greene, M.D., Professors of Medicine and Psychiatry in the Medical Psychiatric Liaison Program, University of Rochester; numerous colleagues within the American Psychosomatic Society, perhaps especially Herbert Weiner, M.D., Myron Hofer, M.D., Professors of Psychiatry at the Albert Einstein School of Medicine in New York, and Mickey Stunkard, M.D., Professor of Psychiatry at the University of Pennsylvania. Seminal influences in my thinking have come from my many friends and teachers in the European Society for Psychosomatic Research and the Japanese Psychosomatic Society. Major perspectives and especially the provision of time and a "clinical laboratory" have been the responsibility and contribution of my chairmen, Daniel X. Freedman, M.D., Professor of Psychiatry; Alvin R. Tarlov, M.D., Professor of Medicine; and my colleagues in the division of Social and Behavioral Sciences, University of Chicago. This unusual and precious university community has contributed to a deepening richness of the effect of the social and economic on health care and its delivery through Odin Anderson, Ph.D., Director of the Center for Health Administration Studies, and of ethical issues through James Gustafson, Ph.D., Distinguished University Professor of Theology at the university. I owe much to Heinz Kohut, M.D.,[1] Professorial Lecturer, teacher and friend. A dedication to the written word as it relates to a contemporary society and its events has been the heritage of my father, Reginald Stevens Kimball, and the sustaining influence of Anne Giddings Kimball, my wife.

Of Evolution: The Book

What has evolved in this book is an attempt to identify approaches to the patient that are useful in generating objective data through which to understand the individual's illness experiences through one or more conceptual schemes. These schemes are viewed as tentative and have value only to the extent that they are useful. Usually, several conceptual approaches are necessary to grasp enough of an understanding of a patient's illness to treat not only the illness but also the patient with the illness and to relate to the affected others in the illness circle, i.e., family, colleagues, friends, and other professional attendants. Medicine, an eclectic discipline, has borrowed from many over the centuries and to various extents forged these into an approach that is more medicine's than those from which it has borrowed. These borrowed concepts and terminology have gradually taken on an identity and specificity of their own within the context of medicine and serve as ways of thinking about the patient, his illness, and his treatment. For example, in the first section of the book, we shall consider interviewing not as an inquisition, but rather as the process of relating with a patient with the objective of understanding both the patient and her illness experience. In thinking about relationships between individuals in a dyadic professional relationship, we borrow from psychoanalytic studies the concepts of transference and countertransference between patient and physician or nurse. In talking with our patients, we identify emotions and the defenses serving to cover them and/or the repressed conflicts that they attempt to conceal. Central to almost all of the disciplines from which we borrow is a developmental approach, fundamental to Western thought, embracing the idea of antecedents, predicators, causes, determinants of events, and the observations of them that we make in the present. At the same time, we note that both our observations and our formulations based on them are frequently skewed by our preferred orientations. In an effort to obviate this predilection as much as possible, we attempt to clarify our observations and descriptions of things as neutrally and as matter of factly as possible, in phenomenological terms, separating the observation distinctly from a later formulation and conceptualization. These later processes are only attempts to illuminate one or more facets of the "objectified and neutral" object as a means of getting a handle on it, a grasp so that through one means or another we can attend to it. In this sense, a symptom is never biological, psychological, or social in and of itself. The latter are only ways of thinking about the symptom. Within each of these orientations, we can further focus our ways of thinking about the symptom to the extent to which each further defines a particulate aspect of the symptom and leads to a pragmatic approach, i.e., the alleviation of the symptom. At the same time, one must beware that alleviation of the symptom through this approach does not always answer such abstractions as cause or effect. This documentation of the relationship demands a different approach based on limited variables, statistical methodologies, and experimental situations.

Thus, there are many useful ways of thinking about the symptom using social, psychological, and biological perspectives. More complex is thinking about the interrelationships of these approaches. Can each be legitimately interrelated with the others in terms of cause and effect? Oftentimes, this is quite appealing. Frequently, it leads to explanations that seem to be pragmatic both in the alleviation of the symptom and in preventing its recurrence either in the same organism or another. In these situations, our thinking becomes pleasantly concrete. More often, such simplistic relationships do not hold up, or they hold up only on the basis of a common association but do not get at the essence or mechanism of the relationship. Thus, we need to proceed with caution and rely upon a more basic laboratory study of the relationships between variables. These are being performed by substantive investigators who have the capacity to proceed both analytically and elegantly, if minutely, in making and defining these associations.

On Development:

The early chapters suggest that behavior has been approached through many perspectives, some of which are useful in viewing the ill patient. These are most often used in parts, in bits and pieces as they suit a specific observation. The clinician becomes comfortable with a number of these as they fit his style and experience and borrows smaller bits and pieces of other approaches for explaining other observations. In one way or another, clinicians use the concept of personality, usually as identifying characteristic patterns of behavior (defenses) by which patients handle emotions and the underlying conflicts generating them. We may use rather traditional labels as are suggested in Chapter 4 (The Patient's Personality), or we may use behavior patterns similar to those raised by Thomas et al.[2] in their work with children or Friedman and Rosenman's[3] identification of behavior pattern type A in coronary artery disease-prone patients. These are globally conceptualized patterns. There are other approaches to behavior that, although not unrelated to personality, are at a more particulate level. These include biological markers and largely biological variables stressed by Herb Weiner[4] and Carolyn Thomas,[5] respectively. Piaget[6] stresses cognitive development as an approach to understanding behavior. Others, such as Konrad Lorenz,[7] emphasize the effect of early life experience in the concept of imprinting. Together with other approaches, these emphasize the nature-nurture controversies that have always been with us. As clinicians, our position has characteristically been that of integrationists adhering to both concepts as each helps address an aspect of illness.

The Environments of Illness:

A useful approach to behavior that is indigenous to illness is that which is addressed in the second section, Phases of Illness. There is a point in time between well-being and illness, characterized as the illness onset situation. Most often, it is identified retrospectively; occasionally, it is viewed concurrently and knowingly. It is a time when the prodromata of illness may be noted by the individual: the first vague symptoms of discomfort, of apprehension. It may occur at a time of considerable personal uneasiness resulting from social and environmental factors. These may be viewed as putting the patient at risk. Once illness develops, depending upon its severity, it is treated in different environments of care, which in turn affect illness behavior. These vary from the home visit through doctors' offices, emergency rooms, inpatient special care environments, and convalescent and rehabilitative environments. Within these environments, there are complementary expectations, tasks, and obligations of patients and members of the health professions. Our hypothetical patient is brought through these environments.

The third section addresses itself to selected illnesses and the environments of care in which they are treated as examined by the author's experience. Many of the observations noted can be extrapolated and/or modified for patients with illnesses other than these, who are treated in specialized environments that require specific knowledge if optimal care is to be provided. Clinical research in this area is critical for excellence in patient care.

The Case Method:

The fourth section of the book suggests the use, through several case reports, of the clinical case model of teaching, utilizing the concepts of interviewing, behavior, and specific illness situations identified in the preceding sections.

Inasmuch as this book is an outgrowth of teaching, it is only fitting that it is dedicated to my students of the past, present, and future. Little, if any of it, would ever have come to fruition without the steadfast nurturance of Mrs. Carol Ann Al-Barazi, my secretary of 10 years.

References

1. Kohut, H. *The Restoration of the Self.* New York, International Universities Press, 1977.
2. Thomas, A., Chess, S., and Birch, H. G.: The origin of personality. Sci. Am. *223:* 102, 1970.
3. Friedman, M., and Rosenman, R. H.: Overt behavior pattern in coronary disease: Detection of overt behavior pattern A in patients with coronary disease by a new psychophysiological procedure. J.A.M.A. *173:* 1320, 1960.
4. Weiner, H.: Psychobiological markers of disease. Psychiatr. Clin. North Am. *2:* 227, 1979.
5. Thomas, C. B.: *The Precursor's Study. IV. A Prospective of a Cohort of Medical Students.* Baltimore, Johns Hopkins University Press, 1977.
6. Piaget, J.: *The Development of Thought: Equilibrium of Cognitive Structure.* New York, Viking Press, 1977.
7. Lorenz, K.: *King Solomon's Ring.* New York, T. Y. Crowell, 1952.

ACKNOWLEDGMENTS

Appreciation is expressed to the following for their kind permission granted to me to publish modified versions of papers previously published in journals or books:

American College of Physicians (*Annals of Internal Medicine*)
American Psychiatric Association (*American Journal of Psychiatry*)
Brunner/Mazel Publishing Company (*Psychiatric Medicine*, G. Usdin, M.D., Editor)
Elsevier-North Holland Publishing Company (*General Hospital Psychiatry*; *Psychosomatic Medicine*)
Greenwood Publishing Company (*Psychiatry in Medicine*)
Little, Brown and Company (*Basic Psychiatry for the Primary Care Physician*, Harry S. Abram, M.D., Editor)
Medical Insight Publishing Company (*Medical Insight Journal*)
C. V. Mosby Publishing Company (*Heart and Lung Journal*)
W. B Saunders Company (*Medical Cinics of North America*)
Thanatology Foundation (*Journal of Thanatology*)
University of Ottawa (*Psychiatric Journal of the University of Ottawa*)

Appreciation is also expressed for the support of the following:

American Heart Association (Grant-in-Aid 68-778) 1968–1971; United States Public Health Service, Department of Health, Education and Welfare:

HEW—Epidemiology and Community Resources in the Care of the Chronic Sick (5 A07 AH 00178-05) 1968–1972

HEW—Undergraduate Intracultural Mental Health Training (1 T21 MH 12385-03) 1970–1973

HEW—Training Grant for Teaching of Psychiatry to Non-Psychiatric Physicians (1 T21 MH 10466-06) 1968–1972

HEW—National Health Service Corps/Chicago Externship (PHS D 21-MB-1518303) 1975–1980

National Institute of Mental Health:

NIMH—Psychiatry—GP Special Training (5 T01 MH 07797-18) 1967–1980

NIMH—Liaison Psychiatry Fellowship Program in Primary Care (5 T01 MH 07795-19S2) 1978–1985

NIMH—Undergraduate Psychiatry Training (2 T02 MH 06002-20) 1966–1977

NIMH—Medical Student Psychiatric Education (5 T02 MH 14580-02) 1977–1982

CONTENTS

PART ONE
THE PERSON AS PATIENT

PART TWO
PHASES OF ILLNESS; REACTIONS TO ILLNESS; IMPRESSIONS OF ENVIRONMENTS AND SITUATIONS; TASKS OF PATIENTS AND DOCTORS

PART THREE
SELECTIVE STUDIES OF ILLNESS: ON RELATIONSHIPS

PART FOUR
USING THE CLINICAL CASE METHOD IN THE BIOPSYCHOSOCIAL APPROACH

PART 1

THE PERSON AS PATIENT

CHAPTER 1

On Approaches: Interviewing

Interviewing is not new to us. We have been interviewing and being interviewed all of our lives. It is the basic process of communication between individuals, a process of relating, of being known and of getting known, of finding out and of being found out. One does not interview, does not find out, without being found out. It is a two-way process, one of hearing and being heard, of seeing and being seen, of feeling and being felt, sometimes of touching and being touched. It is a process of intimacy, a process of intrusion and invasion, which is invited, permitted, and granted. This permission, often more implicit than explicit, is given in a sense of mutual trust, expectation, and hope.

As such, interviewing is bound by codes of honor, based on trust and expectation. It is a private relationship, a trusted and confidential relationship. What is communicated, observed, felt, and exposed is a privileged communication, a sacred trust to be guarded and protected. These communications are not easily transferred, certainly not without permission, and even then only sparingly and specifically. So even at the beginning, even before the observations and the data begin to flow, we have the first principle of interviewing, that of confidence and confidentiality, of privacy and privilege. This principle is daily transgressed, abused, ignored, and violated.

Even before the interview begins, a stage is set for its subsequent drama. There has developed in the principals, the identified patient and the identified interviewer, expectations that are both realistic and fantasied, founded and unfounded. Presumably the patient is in need of assistance. He or she may have been in such need for a long time. He has tried various home remedies and advice from parents, relatives, friends, the lady upstairs, the nurse around the corner, or the shopping center drugstore. He has gotten the name of the physician from a friend or the telephone book. The name comes not without a description, an impression. What kind of name, what kind of doctor, what kind of woman or man, with what kind of expertise, of what appearance, and of what demeanor. The physician, as she takes the call or he glances over his appointment schedule, has more or less information about the soon-to-be patient. She has had a description from a referring physician or nurse, a privileged and sanctioned communication. He has taken a bit of data over the telephone, heard a voice, identified sex, age, and complaint, and formed an impression based on fact and fantasy.

The interview has begun. The initial relationship has taken place. The impressions made set a stage that may be erroneous and may need to be rearranged and reformulated.

Interviewing is simple. It is a conversation. It is based on curiosity, interest, inquisitiveness, and perhaps a basic voyeuristic instinct. We want to find out. We are sanctioned to find out by society which licenses us and by the patient who gives us permission. We begin with the ticket of admission, the *complaint,* the hurt: why the patient comes to us. The complaint, the symptom once defined, is the focal point of the relationship, the basis of the contract. The interview begins, returns to, and frequently ends with the symptom or its redefinition. But we soon find the symptom does not exist in isolation. It is a part of a person, indeed in the present situation the most important part of the patient. As such it is all wrapped up in the space and identity of the patient. This patient is not only a patient with a hurt, this patient is a hurt patient; he sees himself and is seen as a hurt or sick patient. So we need to know not only of the hurt and of the patient, but also of the hurt or "altered" patient. Thus, as we begin our analysis of the symptom—*what* is the complaint, *when* did it begin, *where* did it begin, *what* was it like, and *how* was it for the patient—we are beginning to find out *who* the patient is. As we listen to the patient's own words as she describes her complaint, we begin to know through our ears, eyes, nose, and fingers something about the patient. She is of a certain age, obviously of a certain appearance, married or unmarried, perhaps a mother, who works at this or that. These are orienting and identifying characteristics. They trigger off a set of associations in terms of illnesses for which she may be at risk, the phase of life she may be in, and its related social and psychological processes. These will need to be listened for, verified, ruled in or out. But they are in our mind. They cannot be ignored or they will inevitably work their way, however erroneously, into our thinking. So, like the symptom, we need to begin to know *who* the patient is, *where* she was when the symptom began, with *whom* she was, *what* was going on, the time *when* she first experienced the symptom, and *how* things were for her at that time.

By now, the doctor and patient have sampled enough of each other's selves, personalities, backgrounds to try to adjust an optimal and effective communication style. Are both physically comfortable? Is there privacy? Should a significant other be present, such as a relative, or nurse? Are the two emotionally in tune? Are specific things needed to put the patient at ease—turning off a tape recorder, not taking notes, specific disarming statements, a joke? How much direction will be needed in getting the data? How much refocusing, review, reshaping of the data? Are the doctor and patient on the same wavelength? Are they using the same language, albeit English? Is the doctor using a lot of medical terms, polysyllabic words, and complex sentences while the patient uses only one- and two-syllable words and simple sentences? Are there difficulties in the physician's or the patient's comprehension? Is the patient having difficulties in his orientation, memory, attentive and abstractive processes? Does this relate to his illness, mood, anxiety? Do these need to be investigated or ameliorated before we can get on with the interview? Can we really do all we need to do now, or should we do this in bits and pieces, allowing the patient time to go at his own pace and to rest in between?

So early in the interview, we have to make some estimate of the mental status, the cognitive processes of attention, concentration, memory, orientation, and abstractive ability, both of the patient *and* of ourselves. Sometimes we are sharper than at other times, sometimes we are preoccupied, tired, bored, fatigued, angry, hungry, uncomfortable, satiated. Is this the time to listen, to hear, to feel, to do all that an interview requires?

Thus with the analysis of the symptom, its breakdown into the more particulate factors and vectors of its description, we are also doing the same for the patient. While we are separating out one from the other, we are simultaneously finding something out about the relatedness of the two and perhaps, ultimately, *why this symptom at this time in this individual,* the ultimate goal of our analysis and the root of our therapy. An early part of interviewing is directed at a process of *clarification,* first clarifying the nature of the symptom in terms of a precise description, time, duration, intensity, quality, location; then we can begin the *identification* of who and what kind of individual this patient is. A *relationship* is established: the interview is in full swing and therapy has begun. The patient has found someone to *talk* with, to whom she can express her concerns, fears, and anxieties, to *listen* and help *focus* and *clarify* more objectively what is going on. The relationship gives structure and *support*. Initial expectations are being met. Things are a little clearer. Perhaps the problem can be found and treated. The doctor seems interested in not only the problem but the patient and her comfort. She is in a relaxed and private environment. Uninterrupted time is provided. She has become familiar with the environment and has identified its colors, order, smells. She has learned something of the physician, that he or she is a person of certain shape, size, color, and tastes.

As the interview progresses from the global to the particulate, as it begins to focus on more precise description and detail, it takes on an order of its own in terms of the specific doctor and patient and their relationship. Beginning in the present, and usually with the symptom, it moves back and forth in time, the patient leading, the doctor following, clarifying descriptions here, ordering sequences there, noting the patient's language, expressions, and feelings throughout. As the interview progresses, the physician begins to mold the data into a mutually agreed upon form. He does so by brief *summations* of the complaint, of the setting in which it occurred, with whom the patient was, where the patient was, what else was going on—all the while allowing the patient to add, change, revise, amend, or emend this feedback. This summation brings order and tangible dimensions and, hence, substance to the problem, allowing for increasingly objective approaches which will be followed during the subsequent examination and diagnostic and therapeutic procedures.

By now we have an identifying statement, our patient is of certain age, sex, race, ethnicity, marital status, student or work status, religious affiliation, with a complaint identified in his or her own words. We can follow this in our notes with a description of what the complaint is all about, when it began, how it began, where it began, and what has occurred up to the present time.

As we begin to order our thoughts during and after interviewing, we begin to focus on roots and origins, again of the symptom, of the patient, and of the patient with the symptom. Has she ever had anything like this in the past? Has anyone else in the family or whom she has known? When? What was it like? What happened? Has she had other illness? What were these? When were these? What were they like? So we begin to get a past history, first a medical history, then a bit of social history, and, at some point, a bit of developmental history. This is more or less organized as we obtain it. Most of its organization comes about through our summations and in our dictated or written report, an essential motor act of the physician as he gives concrete expression to his thoughts in word and deed. A chronological past history is useful as we note the relationship of illnesses to ages and reflect upon the possible meaning of these *life events* to that phase of development, for example, how it related to the mother-child relationship in the first year of life, to the interpersonal and social tasks of later stages of development, or to the present life phase of the patient. We want to know something of psychological development and difficulties as well as the possible effect of these on how the patient accepts, reacts, and copes with her present illness.

Similarly, we address the facts and events of family life, the health and illnesses and deaths of parents, grandparents, children, spouse. This provides us with both *biological* and *psychological markers* of disease and illness that will influence our thoughts about our patient and her symptoms. It will also give us a view of present life *supports* in terms of significant others as we order these along with social structures: work, friends, organizations. These return our attention to the present social field and our analysis of the factors going on and the relationship of these to the patient's problem—its onset, precipitation, and identification—and to treatment and eventual resolution.

Thus our predilection to our subsequent organization of the data will give some structure to our thinking about what we want to know about our patient, why we want to know it, for what purpose and how it will direct our diagnostic and therapeutic activities. While we are busy with our objectification, clarification, supportive measures, we are very much into the therapeutic relationship through this attentiveness. We are also very much into our physical examination, as we note the patient's color, posture, eyes, lips, teeth, facial expression, neck, pulsating neck arteries and veins, chest, hands, legs, and fingernails during the interview. As we correlate our observations with one another, we begin to note *relationships* of events in time and place that give insight into our patient's problem. We also bring explanation and, with this, education to the individual regarding his body and mind, his health and illness, his care and treatment.

As we begin to think and rethink about our patient and what he has told us, of what we have observed, heard, seen, smelt, and felt; of how this fits with our past and emerging experience; as we think and rethink this, as we write our summaries and formulations, while we eat lunch, drive home, talk with colleagues, dream; we make new associations, perhaps find a new connection, think of a new procedure to do. Thus, our interview continues and evolves. Our patient has become an extension of our experience and offers a new dimension to our thought and practice. In his uniqueness, we see him and his illness. As we accumulate from experience the uniqueness of others, patterns of similarities emerge which will help us with other patients. These will be of illness and disease patterns, of personality and behavioral profiles, of social and environmental factors. Thus the patient we see today becomes a part of our internal textbook that we will use tomorrow. The value of that textbook will depend upon the shaping of ourselves, not only cognitively, but affectively, socially, and ethically as a skillful instrument of interviewing, which is the beginning of a therapeutic relationship.

CHAPTER 2

Interviewing and the Meaning of the Symptom

OVERVIEW

The interview process of clinical medicine as the basic tool of accumulating the data essential for diagnosis and as the vehicle for the therapeutic process is discussed. For diagnostic purposes, the physician should approach the presenting complaint or symptom of the patient as a translator who will attempt to interpret the somatic, social, and psychological meanings of that symptom by participating in a specific interview methodology that will allow for the free flow and unbiased production of the requisite data. The symptom itself identifies the final common pathways that the body uses for manifestation of its feelings, reactions, and behavior, including illness, and whether these represent responses to the internal or external milieu in which the organism exists. The relationship that develops during the interview process and how this in itself is therapeutic for the patient—as it contains most of the primary ingredients of psychotherapy: support, ventilation, and clarification—is also discussed.

Interviewing

Interviewing may be considered the basic science of clinical medicine. It is the vehicle through which all data and evaluations regarding the patient's condition are obtained, whether these be for the purpose of research or therapy. The interview process as it is communicated to students of medicine is rarely made the subject of scientific scrutiny

---

Modified version (and reproduced with permission) of article from Annals of Internal Medicine *71*: 147–153, 1969; copyrighted by the American College of Physicians.

and objectivity, despite the fact that interviewing is basic to clinical investigation and diagnosis and, with the physical examination, helps determine the decisions upon which laboratory studies are based.

For the purpose of this chapter, interviewing is defined as the process of evaluating the individual through all the modes of observation, short of laboratory procedures. It includes three fundamental objectives: (1) developing a *relationship* with the patient; (2) finding out what is *wrong* with the patient; and (3) establishing the basis for the subsequent therapy of this condition. These processes occur throughout the interview and are only arbitrarily isolated for more objective consideration.

The contract that is made between the patient and the doctor creates a specific relationship. This contract may change as the physician assesses the patient's complaint, but initially it is quite simple. The patient (usually) voluntarily comes to the doctor with a complaint about himself, most often about his body. He hurts, and he seeks alleviation of this hurt. The doctor, by self-profession and the mandate given him by society, is identified as the individual who relieves hurts. To do this he is expected to use his skill to discover: (1) what the hurt is and (2) the cause of the hurt in order to (3) offer relief from the hurt. This is the implicit and explicit nature of the contract. For the contract to be honored, the physician's primary objective must be to *understand* the hurt. To do this he needs to translate from the private, idiosyncratic language and expression of the patient to the universal language with which he is familiar. It is my contention that a symptom cannot be viewed as a medical, surgical, or psychiatric symptom *per se* but as a symptom in its own right belonging to a specific individual. The task of the physician is to interpret the symptom in terms of the specific patient so that he can identify as objectively as possible the processes and mechanism giving rise to the symptom.[1]

Hence, the doctor is first and foremost an *interpreter*.[2] But he is a multilingual interpreter whose interpretation of the symptom depends upon his knowledge of several languages. In this discussion we can identify these "languages" as those of somatic medicine, psychological medicine, and the social and environmental sciences. In the traditional framework of medicine, many students become reasonably adept in interpreting symptoms into possible pathological processes based on anatomical-physiological mechanisms. Most are less adept or totally untrained in identifying the psychological or social (or environmental) significance of a symptom.

THE INTERVIEW METHOD

The Symptom in the Patient

The interview method[3] as described below is the essential tool by which analysis and synthesis of the various aspects of the patient's problems may be accomplished by the physician. To be effective, the physician (interpreter) conducting the interview needs to have developed the fundamental grasp of the languages in which he will attempt to make the translations. The doctor's contract with the patient begins with the translation of the symptom into its organic, psychological, and social components in order to identify *what is going on* so that he can institute therapy. This is done through an open-ended, partially directed interview technique that allows the patient to identify and discuss his symptoms *in his own way and words*. The doctor's lead is by some general introductory question identifying the patient as existing in a time and place and in a certain condition. A statement such as "how are you" or "how are you feeling" generally suffices in making this opening (see Appendix). From there on, the doctor follows the lead of the patient, listening to and noting what is identified by the patient and in what context. When the patient's spontaneous reply ceases or the physician discerns that it has become irrelevant to the patient's identified complaint, it is the physician's task to direct the conversation back to the complaint as unobtrusively as possible. In this way the doctor is accomplishing several tasks: (1) By allowing the spontaneous flow of the patient's conversation, and hence his associations, the physician is alert to identify what may be the significant organic, environmental, and psychological components of the symptom. (2) By returning to and sticking to the patient's complaint, he is always in tune and rapport with the patient's request for help. (3) The physician begins to construct a framework for the symptom, identifying it as existing in a time-and-space relationship.

Following the journalist's lead, he identifies the five W's—What, Where, When, (with) Whom, Why—and the How of the symptom. Expanded, these are as follows:

1. What is the precise nature of the symptom? What is its quality, intensity, quantity?
2. Where is the symptom in terms of the patient's body? Does it radiate, change location? Also, where is the patient when he experiences this symptom?
3. At what time is the symptom experienced: What is its frequency, duration, pattern?
4. With whom is the patient when the symptom is experienced? How does it affect the relationship with that person?
5. Why? What is the meaning of the symptom organically, psychologically, socially?
6. How is the symptom for the patient? What is his reaction to it?

Thus, the task of clarifying very specific characteristics of the complaint is achieved. At the same time, by permitting the patient to present the material in his own way, the doctor can begin to identify other things going on in the life of the patient which will be important in his assessment and treatment of the patient's complaint. The following case will serve as an illustration:

> A 38-year-old white insurance executive, recently transferred to a new territory, is seen in the emergency room complaining of substernal pain of sudden onset and of increasing intensity radiating down the left arm (similar to that experienced by his father 5 years earlier, prior to the latter's death), which occurred when the patient was frantically attempting to extinguish a fire ignited in his new home by his 6-year-old retarded son, who had obtained matches left carelessly around by the patient's wife.

We should suspect that this man was having an acute myocardial infarction. But, we would also note a number of other vexations and frustrations in his life that might be of major significance in suggesting the differential diagnosis, as well as in the subsequent treatment of this man, regardless of what becomes substantiated as the major underlying pathological process. In this case, the possible organic interpretation of the pain is relatively simple. However, in accumulating this information in the emergency room in a few minutes, several other important identifications were made, not by the interrogator's direct question, but by allowing the patient to describe his problem in his own way. Not only do we have a man who is upset and anxious about his pain, but we have a man who may be anxious and upset about his recent job change and his new home, who may be aggravated at his wife about far more than matches, and who may never have accepted the death of his father 5 years ago (a speculation that is increased by our noting the patient's tears when he related this) nor the retardation of his son. We begin to suspect that this pain, whether or not it identifies specific organic pathology, serves to communicate the helplessness[4] the man feels in the present environmental field[5] that has forced several unresolved conflicts into his awareness.

Corroboration of the hypotheses suggested by these data requires further investigation in subsequent interviews. The pertinence of the social and psychological data obtained in the context of this interview is not its separateness from the patient's complaint, but rather its direct relevance to the very interpretation of the symptom, as well as to what will be indicated for the effective treatment of the patient. It is this relevance that is often obscured or missed when case histories are arbitrarily compartmentalized into medical, social, and psychiatric sections.

As the symptom is *clarified*, the spontaneous productions of the patient in response to nonspecific or neutral stimuli given by the physician provide essential data that can be interpreted into medical, social, or psychological significances on the basis of how and when they are introduced by the patient. Whatever is introduced by the patient becomes pertinent to the physician's further exploration, if he suspects its relevance to the patient's complaint.[6] The fact that a patient begins to describe his symptoms as occurring whenever he visits his mother-in-law is much more important than knowing for another patient whose symptom has no such relationship but is elicited in a perfunctory social history that the latter despises his mother-in-law. It is the relationship of the data to the spontaneous thoughts or associations of the patient to his complaint that identifies for the physician what data are signficant.

The Patient with the Symptom

In addition to analyzing the symptom for its identifying and directional value as to what is going on with the patient, attention must also be given to the reaction of the patient to the symptom. What are his anxieties, fears, and fantasies as to the meaning of the symptom? To what other life experiences does he associate it—that is, what are his subjective interpretation and feelings about the symptom? Has he ever had such a complaint before? Has he known others with this complaint? Why does he think he should have acquired such a complaint? What old anxieties has it evoked? Are there other memories, conjured up by the patient in association to it, which in turn contribute or resurrect their own emotional responses independent of those generated by the current crisis? Does the individual experiencing a crushing chest pain believe this is "just punishment" for some real or imaginary wrong for which he must suffer and perhaps die? Does it recall the pain endured by his nephew who died from leukemia or the myocardial infarction that his father sustained? In a man who has had a recent business failure, does it feel as if the whole world is "crushing down" on him? This is the private or idiosyncratic or personal signature that we all give to our sensory experiences.[7, 8]

Consider also the meaning of the communicative aspects of the symptom! How does it affect and what is its message to those individuals significant to the patient in the environment, both as intended and unintended by the patient? Does it serve as a nonverbal communication to another individual or group in an ongoing dialogue to which the physician is only the most recent witness? Such questions only serve to emphasize that our feelings are frequently manifested through the expression of physical complaints or symptoms, as is corroborated by such expressions as, "you give me a pain in the neck," "it gets me right here" (as the patient points to the gut), "my heart cries for you." These examples emphasize how, in clarifying a symptom, it is necessary to listen for the very words with which the symptom is described.

As the interview progresses, the past medical history, the life style, and the environmental milieu of the individual spontaneously unfold with little need for pursuit on the basis of specific questioning. As the symptom is identified as relating to a particular life crisis, organ system, social milieu, or all of these, the physician focuses his and his patient's attention on further examination of the identified process. He may do this by suggesting that the patient explain this or that in greater detail. Using such terms as "I don't understand," "can you explain that," "anything else," or just "and" often helps the patient continue without the therapist interjecting or contaminating the patient's story by his own ideas as expressed in specific questions or by assuming that he has a grasp of the patient's situation before he has exhausted the available data, that is, description by the patient.

Nonverbal Aspects

Although much of the preceding emphasis on interview technique has concerned a verbal exchange that occurs between the therapist and patient, it is important that we do not ignore senses other than the auditory one in a discussion of the interview process. Indeed, many cues for the direction of the interview derive from other sense modalities. Not only what and how a patient says something in verbal accents are important, but the facial accents with which he punctuates these expressions are significant. These are noted by scrutinizing aspects of the patient's nonverbal behavior.[9] Simultaneously, we must be cognizant of how our own reactions as therapists, nonverbally as well as verbally, provide positive and negative—that is, encouraging or inhibiting—feedback to the patient during the interview and hence affect the patient's own censoring processes and thereby interfere with the spontaneity desired. How the patient sits, what he does with his hands and feet, and so forth at different times during the interview alert us to specific behavioral reactions that may give a clue to the underlying feelings of anxiety, agitation, and pleasure, which we will become interested in correlating with the verbal remarks.

Awareness of the patient's general appearance and deportment often gives us an immediate impression of the individual that the subsequent interview will either corroborate or discredit. This appearance may lead to distinct and immediate impressions about the patient's organic, social, or psychological processes, or all of these. Awareness of the mask-like facies in the patient with Parkinson's syndrome, of the facial expression in some depressions and in grief, and of the moon-like facies of the

Cushingoid patient gives the physician clues for investigation. This observational process can be extended to the patient's clothes, his bed, and the surrounding room. An ordered as opposed to a disordered personal environment will lead to certain formulations about the patient's condition that will later have to be substantiated by additional data. The physician cannot always make a sharp distinction between data obtained in the interview session in contrast to data from the physical examination proper. Detection of phenomena through all sensory modalities from the earliest point of contact may assist the physician in channeling the flow of the interview without interfering with the patient's spontaneity and in directing his subsequent formal examination.

Therapy in the Interview

The therapeutic aspects of the interview process occur largely through the relationship that is established between the parties of the interview—the physician and the patient—*and* the analysis of this relationship by the physician. The reactions (transferences) of the patient to the physician and the reactions (countertransferences) of the physician to the patient need to be identified. When the physician identifies and understands these he is then in a position to direct the relationship in such a way as to best help the patient. As the dynamic interview and the relationship continue, the physician begins to detect the patient's defenses (commonly identified as resistance, denial, projection, identification, intellectualization, rationalization, and so on). With increasing appreciation for the *life style*[10] of the patient, the physician is able to formulate impressions of the individual's *personality style*[11] or characteristic way of interacting with others in the environment. Identifying specific feeling tones or affects—such as flatness, depression, happiness, sadness, anger, or euphoria—or specific peculiarities of establishing relationships serves to make the physician cognizant of the background in which the major conflict is reflected. These background feeling tones assist the physician in his arduous task of trilingual interpretation as well as provide cues for him to project himself actively into the interview relationship.

Another function of the physician in the therapeutic process of the interview is his role as a *clarifier* and *objectifier* of the patient's complaint. This is the essence of the therapeutic process, for when the patient and physician understand what is going on, therapy can be instituted and often takes care of itself.[12]

Out of the relationship and the clarification, the feeling of support and the knowledge that the doctor is both competent and cares are created for the patient. In giving the patient the opportunity to present his story in his own way, the physician is allowing him to ventilate. Thus, three of the four basic tenets of psychotherapy[13–15] occur in the interview process identified here: ventilation, clarification, and support. Only interpretation leading to insight is omitted as an essential part of every interview. Insight, however, may occur spontaneously as a part of the interview in the process of symptom clarification. In addition, the educational aspect of the interview tending toward clarification and objective identification as to what is going on helps to allay the diffuse anxiety that the unknown presents to humans, both individually and collectively. In performing this, the doctor fulfills his ancient role as teacher.

Termination of the Interview

An essential feature of any interview, regardless of its duration, is how it is terminated. A convenient method of closure is summarization. This allows the physician to: (1) arrange the data that he has gathered into some meaningful framework; this may be done according to a chronological sequence, although other models may be more appropriate for a specific patient's problems; (2) modify, add, delete, or amend the information so summarized; and (3) reaffirm with the patient the nature of the contract. A corollary to summarization is that it also sets the stage for the physician and patient to arrange for the next step in the relationship, that is, when and what will be the nature of the next meeting? "Where do we go from here?" What further procedures are to be done? What is "our" thinking at this time, and so on.

References

1. Feinstein, A. R.: *Clinical Judgment*, p. 24. Baltimore, Williams & Wilkins, 1967.
2. Welt, L. G.: The medical journal—Forum for the translator (Editorial). Am. J. Med. Sci. *255:* 11, 1968.
3. Engel, G. L.: *Psychological Development in Health and Disease*, p. xxxiii. Philadelphia, W. B. Saunders, 1962.
4. Schmale, A. H., Jr.: Relationship of separation and depression to disease. Psychosom. Med. *20:* 259, 1958.
5. Grinker, R. R.: *Psychosomatic Research*, pp. 158–161. New York, W. W. Norton, 1953.
6. Morgan, W. L., Jr., and Engel, G. L.: *The Clinical Approach to the Patient.* Philadelphia, W. B. Saunders, 1969.
7. Engel, G. L.: "Psychogenic pain" and the pain-prone patient. Am. J. Med. *26:* 899, 1959.
8. Szasz, T.: *Pain and Pleasure.* New York, Basic Books, 1957.
9. Mahl, G. F.: Some clinical observations on nonverbal behavior in interviews. J. Nerv. Ment. Dis. *144:* 492, 1967.
10. Meyer, A.: *The Common-Sense Psychiatry of Dr. Adolf Meyer*, A. Lief, editor, p. 418. New York, McGraw-Hill, 1948.
11. Shapiro, D.: *Neurotic Styles*, p. 1. New York, Basic Books, 1962.
12. Freud, S.: Preface. In *The Faith of the Counsellors*, P. Helmos. New York, Schocken Press, 1966.

13. Colby, K. M.: *A Primer for Psychotherapists*, chapters 6 and 7. New York, Ronald Press, 1951.
14. Garrett, A.: *Interviewing: The Principles and Methods*. New York, New York Family Welfare Association of America, 1942.
15. Gill, M. M., Newman, R., and Redlich, F. C.: *The Initial Interview in Psychiatric Practice*. New York, International Universities Press, 1954.

Appendix to Chapter 2

The following list of questions is appended to convey an idea of what subject matters may be opened for discussion and how they may be approached by the interviewer. Although this list of questions is composed on the basis of recorded interviews, it is in no way meant to be used in and of itself or as a checklist. Any of these questions is legitimate as a question only when the subject to which it refers has been introduced in a specific context by the patient.

1. How are you?
2. How are you feeling?
3. What brought you to the hospital?
4. Can you tell me a bit about that?
5. And, what else?
6. Anything more?
7. Anything else?
8. So—(this is what you have described)—Is there anything more?
9. When did it all begin?
10. When was the last time that you were completely well?
11. What was the first thing that you recall that made you aware that things were not (just) right?
12. And before that?
13. So (you noticed this sequence of events)? Anything else?
14. Besides you, who else is at home? (Usually after the patient has spontaneously introduced such a person into the dialogue.) Besides you, there is at home your wife and . . . ?
15. Anyone else?
16. So, at the time you first experienced this symptom, you were with —,—,—?

17. And your relationship with him (her, them) is?
18. Your friend is-----?
19. Do you know anyone else who has experienced a similar symptom?
20. Have you ever had anything similar to or like this before?
21. What are some of your thoughts as to what is (has been) going on with your health?
22. What is it like (the symptoms, illness, etc.) for you?
23. How has it been (the illness) for you?
24. How has this (illness) affected your life (your work, family, plans)?
25. Your work is----? (Usually after the patient has spontaneously introduced this subject.)
26. This (your work) involves----?
27. You have been doing this (work) for how long?
28. You find this (work) easy, compatible, interesting, enjoyable, hard, unsatisfactory, boring, dull, etc.?
29. Have you noticed any changes in this work recently (employer, production techniques, new colleagues, decreasing interest or ability)?
30. What other kinds of work have you done?
31. Which of these were most compatible, interesting, successful, etc.?
32. How do you think this (work) affects your (present) health?
33. Your wife (significant relative, child, husband, mother, father, sister, brother)—How is she (he)? (After spontaneously introduced into the interview by the patient.)
34. How does she (he) feel about your illness (disability)?
35. You have been married how long?
36. This (marriage) has been (good, bad, great, up and down, etc.)?
37. Can you describe this (marriage) a bit?
38. You say that everything has been fine, except for---? Can you explain this?
39. When you married, you expected----?
40. How has it (marriage) been?
41. Sexually, you find that----?
42. And now (sexually)?

43. What would you say has been the most irritating (best, worst, etc.) thing about your relationship with---(key relative)?
44. Your children (parents) are?
45. They (parents, children) see you how often?
46. You feel that these relationships are---?
47. With which one are you closest?
48. Can you describe this relationship?
49. What has been your greatest satisfaction (dissatisfaction) with your children (parents)?
50. Such as---?
51. Your closest friend is---?
52. You enjoy what kind of relationship with him (her)?
53. Your (mutual) interests are---?
54. What is it that you find in common?
55. How do you get along together?
56. Do you find that it is easy for you to enter into and maintain friendships?
57. How would you describe your associations with others?
58. In the past, your health has always been---?
59. Other than for (these illnesses) your health has been---?
60. What would you say has bothered you most about your health in the past?
61. As a child, your health was---?
62. You first noticed a change in your health when---?
63. Your growth during childhood and adolescence was---?
64. Periods (menses, menarche) occurred when?
65. You were prepared for this (menarche) how?
66. Your reaction to this was---?
67. With your menses, you noticed (have noticed, notice)---?
68. This changed how after your first (sexual experience, marriage, pregnancy)?
69. You first began to go with girls (boys)---?
70. Your early relationship(s) with girls (boys) (was, were)?

71. Since marriage, you have noticed what changes in your relationship with your wife (husband)?
72. As you understand what your problem (health) is now, what adjustments do you see your having to make in the future?
73. How do things look to you for the future?
74. What do you see for yourself in the future?
75. You see yourself having to make certain adjustments, changes in your way of life?
76. Your concern about your health has left you with what other considerations (family, business, future)?
77. What thoughts do you have about your illness?
78. And its (illness) outcome?
79. What are some of your thoughts about (your) death?
80. Have you thought about the possibility of your death (dying)?
81. How do you see this (dying) as affecting others (children, spouse, parents)?
82. What plans have you made for your (business, children, spouse) in the event of your death?
83. After this (illness, present crisis) is over, what are your plans?
84. What are some of your long-term ambitions, goals, desires?
85. For the future, you are most concerned about----?
86. You identify (see) yourself in the future as doing---?
87. After you have recovered from this acute episode, you see what if any changes for your life in the future?
88. Your understanding of your illness has led you to what thoughts (conclusions) about its development (cause, precipitation, etc.)?
89. Other members of your family who have experienced similar (symptoms, illness, etc.) are---?
90. Their (his, her) health has been (was, is)---?
91. Are there particular diseases that you have noted that run in your family?
92. Hmmm?
93. Uh-huh?
94. Yes?
95. Then, you see this (identifying some specific point) as---?

96. After grade school (high school, college, medical school), you did---?
97. Some of your other ambitions (goals, skills, enterprises) have been---?
98. In summary, then, you see your symptoms or complaint (what) as developing (when) while you were at (where) engaged in doing (activity) with (whom). And that the nature of these symptoms was (what) and was perceived by you as (how). These have persisted (changed, been intermittent, etc.) since (when) but have been particularly severe (when) in the following circumstances. You have noted some relief by doing (activity) and exacerbation under these (circumstances). You have noted that (your father) had a similar complaint when (he) was in his middle age and have wondered if this is the same condition. In addition to your present complaint, you have noted (what else) and have had in the past the following illness noted under the following (circumstances). Most recently, you have been engaged in (this business) but before that you did (this), living (where)? At this time, you see yourself with these objectives?
99. My (as the physician) plans now are to do these studies in order to evaluate this symptom for this possibility. This will entail---. I will be seeing you again---.
100. Do you have any questions about this (plan)?

CHAPTER 3

The Person as Patient: Thinking about Patients

Another way of thinking about patients other than in terms of symptoms and signs or even specific personalities is in terms of whom they remind you. This, of course, is a matter of approximation. It has several advantages. It begins at the basic level of emotions. You like or you don't like. There is something that attracts you or repels you. There is something that reminds you of Aunt Tilly, or so and so's mother-in-law, perhaps even your own. Now, there is no question but that these are biasing and, left on this basis, lead to all kinds of countertransferences, i.e., we begin to relate to this person, or aspects of this person, as though they *were* Aunt Tilly or our mother-in-law. Nevertheless, once we make this observation and allow ourselves to bring it further into focus, we will be able to raise the question for ourself, "Just what is it in this person that reminds me of Aunt Tilly?" Or, "Why Aunt Tilly rather than Aunt Sarah?" This leads us to further observations and objectification of the specific factors, not only about Aunt Tilly, but about ourselves and especially about the potential relationship with this patient who reminds us of Aunt Tilly. It allows us to become more aware of ourselves and, hence, to monitor ourselves in the reality of our relationship with this patient, who is not Aunt Tilly and really has only a few characteristics of Aunt Tilly.

Not only is this a more natural operation in the pursuit of getting a sense of or grasp on this individual, but it allows us to individuate similarities and differences before we jump into more traditional classifications of traits, behavioral patterns, and personalities, which all too easily become stereotypes casually passed onto our confreres as labels of pejorative potential in the charts of our patients.

So for the moment, while we are first getting to know our patient, let us stick with what comes most easily and naturally, at least as long as we remain aware that it is our associations which are working, not the patient's. After all, the patient does not have the faintest idea who Aunt Tilly is or that we are even thinking of her. This is quite a natural process. We have been meeting other people all of our lives and trying to find words by which we can make some sense of them to ourselves and to describe them to our mothers and others when they invariably ask, "What is she like?" Such a question almost demands a comparison with another individual: hair the color of Jane's, a shape like Peggy's, your smile, a personality like Fawcett's. A picture is conjured up, albeit often at variance with reality. However, beneath this there are certain facets of the description that bear further examination if we want to get to essential elements which may help us relate to our patient in our efforts at diagnosis and treatment. We do this all the time: "Mr. S. in 308 is a lot like that old man who was in 315 a month ago; you know who I mean. Not only do they look alike, but they have the same way of talking. They're cute; they both kind of pretend they don't understand, but they're really sharp underneath. But it's sure difficult getting them to settle down at night." Vague as this may sound, there is a lot of communication in this between those individuals who have cared for both of these gentlemen. Beneath this, we can begin to identify more specific traits and factors that help us get closer to the similarities *and* dissimilarities, how these affect our relationships, and the special alterations in our communicative style to adjust to their specific needs. So much of this is done automatically, without objectification, that we have to force ourselves to sit back and try to describe this patient as a person before we go on to focus on the disease process.

In our thinking about patients, the knowledge that has been given us by the referring physician, the admitting office, or the floor nurse will influence us greatly. It will set off a train of thought, prejudgments if you would, which will need to be brought forward in our mind so that they can be ruled in or out. Next will be written referrals or reports from other physicians or hospitals; then the patient's appearance, including of whom she reminds us, her approximate age, race and/or ethnic background, sex, and complexion and the specific disease associations these may trigger off; the posture, the dullness or brightness of eye, the slowness or rapidity of reply, the use of hands, the constant movement of feet, the worried look of the spouse in the background. These are the early observations *and* biases. They remain the latter until each is brought to the forefront, objectified, and tested out. Each is of potential significance. They need to be shed of their prejudgment associations by ruling in or out on the basis of substantive and focused particulate observation. In this way, the patient emerges as a person in her own right, different from Aunt Tilly or the mother-in-law. The early part of this process is that of intuition, the kind of instant recognition on one level or another that cuts through, gets a hold of the essence of the individual, and sets in motion within us a whole series of responses that are automatic in our communicative processes with our patient. Intuition can take us a long way in the right *or* wrong direction. Without making ourselves aware of our intuition and valuing it, we shall fail to test it, risking being led astray, while taking our patient with us.

As we become more comfortable with specific terminology relating to specific traits, defensive mechanisms,[1] "types" of patient's reactions to illness,[2] and, ultimately, classical personality styles[3, 4] and behavioral pattern,[5] we can adopt them so long as we are certain that they and their implications are understood by those with whom we communicate. It is especially important that we eschew their becoming pejorative labeling that assures a common automatic response on the part of our colleagues or ourselves in our relationships with the patient. Such labeling is merely a shorthand communication to ourselves and others of common patterns which will need to be more individually identified for our specific patient in terms of how they affect her illness and its care.

The Relative

While we are at it, our snap identifications of what makes patients tick is rapidly extended to the relatives of our patient, on the basis of even less obervation. To an extent, the relative is sometimes seen as an inconvenience. It is one more person to be listened to and to relate to. It takes time. Even more so, it takes attention and concern. The relative becomes a person in his or her own right. As such, she or he has feelings which will "out," which will need to be communicated and listened to, before we are going to get the other kinds of information that we want about the primary patient. So the relative may be seen as an obstacle between us and our primary concern, the patient. The relative often needs her or his own relationship with the patient. Whatever its nature, how it is handled by the physician has therapeutic potential for both patient and relative.

With the family, there are two basic principles: First, an interview with a patient is never complete until at least one other family member is interviewed. Most frequently, this is the spouse, mother, or child of the patient. Second, in interviewing the relative, the initial query is: "How are you?" The frequent response to this question is an invariable one: "Let me tell you how I am... (in a sense)... I have had it up to here!" The setting for this conversation, as that with the identified patient, is important. It needs to be private, quiet, and comfortable. It takes time, patience, attention, and emotional interaction. It becomes apparent that illness is not in the patient alone, but also *in* the family, existing as a meaningful entity between the patient-family and physician. Often if there is one relative, there are sometimes others, some of whom will demand, if not need, equal time. The physician will need to exercise his judgment as well as his emotions in these encounters.

What we have been talking about are human encounters. These are social interactions, although they occur around the phenomenon of illness. These are person-to-person relationships, first and foremost. Overlayed upon them are the objectives and tasks of patient on one hand and physician on the other. This overlay obviously imposes and creates its own expectations, which are different in the sets of the recipient and the provider. But the initial relationship is on the basis of person to person. The extent to which this can be kept in perspective by the frequently harassed and overburdened physician will depend upon his capacity for compassion and humility. These difficult terms are perhaps best exemplified in terms of the physician who can give a sense to his patient that "We are in this together; I just as easily could be, and certainly may be at some time in the future, in the situation you are." This is not mock humility. This is an existential reality and the basis of empathy.

References

1. Freud, A.: *The ego and mechanisms of defense.* In *The Writings of Anna Freud,* vol. II (revised edition). New York, International Universities Press, 1966.
2. Kahana, R., and Bibring, G.: Personality types in medical management. In *Psychiatry and Medical Practice in a General Hospital,* N. E. Zinberg editor. New York, International Universities Press, 1964.
3. Shapiro, D.: *Neurotic Styles.* New York, Basic Books, 1965.
4. Fairbairn, W. R.: *Psychoanalytic Studies of the Personality.* London, Tavistock Publications, 1952.
5. Friedman, M., and Rosenman, R. H.: Overt behavior pattern in coronary disease: Detection of overt behavior pattern A in patients with coronary disease by a new psychophysiological procedure. J. A. M. A. *173:* 1320, 1960.

CHAPTER 4

The Patient's Personality

OVERVIEW

This chapter represents a conceptualization of several different personality styles which are of value to the physician in formulating an overview of the patient as a person. An attempt has been made to limit these to a relatively small number of fairly distinct types in order that the physician working with general medical patients may more easily identify the features that polarize more toward one than another type. The value of differentiating these styles is the effectiveness it affords the physician in objectifying a characteristic style, which will orient his own approach to the patient in his attempt to assist him. In no way are these verbal groupings meant to be either pejorative or diagnostic in and of themselves. There are formulations suggested by others which have merit, but I have found the six outlined here of pragmatic value to students and general physicians (partly because of their common usage). The physician who learns to objectify a style for his patient will no doubt in time begin to formulate his own favorite groupings that he finds helpful in working with patients.

In this chapter we are concerned with objectifying that aspect of the interview process that we have called relationship. We attempt to demonstrate how a physician, in assisting a patient who has come to him for help, can facilitate the interview by identifying the individual's characteristic emotional, defensive, cognitive, and conative patterns according to one of six styles: obsessive, suspicious or paranoid, hysterical, impulsive, depressive, and infantile. These entities are descriptively presented *not as diagnostic entities* in a psychopathological sense, but rather as life styles toward one of which each of us as individuals polarize. The advantage to the physician of making himself objectively aware of both his own and his patient's style is discussed in terms of facilitating the interview process from the standpoint of both data collecting and therapy.

PERSONALITY STYLES

Personality styles may be regarded as the result of an exaggeration of one or several normal defense patterns that have become fixed and stereotyped responses to external or internal processes that cause individuals to experience unpleasure, usually anxiety. More recently, the unpleasure associated with a depressive reaction has been conceived also as a basic affect state against which the organism defends.[1] These responses to anxiety and depression serve to bind these experiences in such ways as to maintain homeostasis, helping to keep the unpleasant emotions generated around conscious or unconscious conflicts in check. When these conflicts come too close to the conscious life of the patient, thereby causing the experience of unpleasure, or the unpleasure generated from actual experience in the conscious life becomes too great, the individual defends against these affects by erecting or utilizing those defensive patterns which have been useful in the past. These patterns, for our purposes, may be viewed as derived from the genetic predispositions and the learned epigenetic experiences of the individual. These patterns may be considered pathological when they are overdetermined in response to the initiating stimulus, resulting in behavior which is maladaptive for the biological and/or social adjustment of the individual. The individual, reacting to any consciously or unconsciously determined affect of displeasure with a stereotyped, nonselective, rigid set of defenses, may be considered as demonstrating a psychoneurosis. The characteristic defenses utilized by the individual on a repetitive basis in response to stress will serve to identify the neurotic style of the individual. All individuals may be considered as possessing life styles characteristic of and polarizing more closely toward one rather than another neurotic pattern. However, so long as these are effective in maintaining an homeostasis that is not maladaptive for the individual in the majority of his life experiences, they are not considered pathological. It is when they are used inappropriately at unsuitable times that they no longer serve adaptively for the individual and opt for his disharmony with life in terms of his own inner tranquility and of his interaction with the environment. At the same time, it is pertinent to recognize that these styles may serve as a protection against a less adaptive state and further disintegration of the ego.

It is possible to hypothesize an almost infinite number of more or less specific neurotic patterns based upon the various combinations and permutations of basic defenses. However, several investigators[2,3] have identified various styles that seem more basic than others and which are pragmatically useful for the clinician, from the standpoint of both diagnosis and therapy. These are: (1) the obsessive-compulsive, (2) the suspicious or paranoid, (3) the hysterical, (4) the impulsive, (5) the depressive, and (6) the infantile.

The Defenses

Characteristic verbal means whereby the individual attempts to allay or modify the experience of anxiety or depression that occurs in response to conscious external and unconscious internal processes are called defenses. There are a large number of these, of which the following are presented and grouped for identification and definition:

1. Denial, suppression, and repression all refer to processes utilized by the individual in attempting to eliminate from the conscious life either feelings or thoughts that usually give rise to unpleasant affect. They may be thought of as being somewhat on a continuum varying from a deliberate conscious effort to an unconscious process of which the individual is aware. For clarity and use, these terms should necessarily require an object or identification of what affect or conflict is being so handled. In other words, an individual may deny an event such as illness by: (1) a flat statement to the contrary; (2) a failure to acknowledge either to himself or others that he experiences any affect relating to that event; or (3) acting as if there are no consequences to the event, despite a verbal acknowledgment of it. Suppression is a more or less conscious effort to keep from thought an incidence which causes the experience of discomfort. Repression is used to identify several mechanisms whereby the conflict that could give rise to a feeling of displeasure is neither consciously identified nor accepted.

2. Intellectualization and rationalization refer to specific maneuvers which the individual utilizes in order to avoid experiencing the intensity of the affect associated with actual or (thought of) uncomfortable events. He attempts to do this by binding the event in so many verbal explanations that he is often able to convince himself (possibly through autosuggestion) that there is no need for further concern about this event.

3. Displacement and projection identify means by which the individid-

ual attempts to rid himself of either the affect associated with a conflict or the actual conflict by attributing it to another event or identifying it as actually the responsibility of another individual.

4. Reversal of affect occurs when the individual attempts to deny the real affect experienced in relation to a conflict and to demonstrate or suggest that he is feeling the opposite emotion.

5. Introjection is considered a primitive means of coping with a conflict and emotion. The individual fails to identify objective existence of the conflict apart from the rest of his life and, instead, incorporates it and elevates it as the central concern of his life to which all of his actions are related. In other words, the individual comes to represent or be the actual conflict or situation which has caused discomfort. In doing so, he may be said to become the affect by acting it out, thereby losing his own autonomous ego functioning.

6. On the other hand, sublimation represents the most sophisticated process whereby the libidinal energies associated with usually sexual and aggressive conflicts or events are directed or channeled toward activities and concerns which are adaptive for the individual's security and welfare.

7. Obsessive and compulsive mechanisms are those whereby the organism attempts to deny or repress conflicts and the affects around these by involved, worrisome thought processes or often complex, ritualistic physical activity (as a means of expiating the conflict). What is obsessed or acted out is only symbolic of the repressed conflict.

8. Regression is a kind of mental withdrawal and retreat from the use of more sophisticated defense processes to more primitive ones. The term is essentially an ambiguous one, inasmuch as it refers to both psychological and behavioral processes which do not necessarily correlate with one another.

A galaxy of other terms identifies both psychological processes and/or behavior representing them. To a large extent, any activity of the individual may be interpreted as representing a psychological mechanism serving to bind the affect associated with an unconscious conflict and/or as a means of keeping the conflict from the conscious life of the individual. When these fail, the individual may be so flooded with the affect associated with them that he can no longer pursue life-facilitating activity but must seek refuge in an increasing distortion of reality or the external world in order to escape from the tortures of uncomfortable affect and unacceptable thoughts. Neurotic styles, when characterized by increasing rigidity of thought and action, represent combinations of defense mechanisms which have become so formalized and stereotyped and so pervasive in the life of the individual that they no longer serve the specific defense purpose for which they were originally intended, but are used indiscriminately by the individual in his interaction in life, thereby becoming inefficient and maladaptive.

Obsessive-Compulsive

The individual with an obsessive-compulsive personality is frequently hard working, conscientious, industrious, and perfectionistic. His habits are marked by orderliness and stereotypy and his work by rigidity and inflexibility. He cannot accept change, which in the face of his patterns may become even more rigid and stereotyped. Things have to be just so. There needs to be a place for everything and everything needs to be in its place. Until this is so, he cannot sit back and rest. Since things are never just right, because the obsessive is always thinking about something that needs doing, he is always busy. Even when he is sitting still, he needs to somehow be doing two things at once. If he is looking at television, he is also doing something with his hands. When he listens to music, his thoughts are far afield, "worrying" about something that he is planning or that needs doing. In all that he does there is a sense of urgency, a driven need to get things done and over with, while at the same time his perfectionism may drive him to exact repetition until things are the way they should be. There is only one way, one method, one perfection not so much dictated by the individual but by his conscience or superego that seems to have moved in, dominating and directing his every action. Such emphasis on an idealized perfection frequently interferes with productivity. The inflexibility and inability to deviate prevents innovation. On the other hand, this individual may do extremely well performing technical tasks requiring unswerving attention to detail and rigid adherence to procedure. As long as there is work to be done, a task, anything that will provide a structure for him to organize and direct his activities, he is able to bind his underlying anxieties by compulsive activity. His style of thinking is stimulus bound, dogmatic, and opinionated and seems unresponsive to anything anyone else may say. This is not necessarily because it is disagreed with, but more likely because of an inability to countenance or hear anything that will distract the thought sequence set in motion. Such an interference would upset everything, resulting in chaos and anxiety. When not in absolute control of his environment, when not at home or in a familiar and secure work situation, a pervasive sense of uneasiness is experienced that leads to a stilted social manner and posture, lacking in spontaneity, and burdened with perfunctoriness which is made only more acute by the individual's self-awareness. Although often opinionated and dogmatic in responding to peripheral issues, the individual, when confronted by a problem central to his own life, is plaqued by doubts, reservations, and deliberateness that lead to indecisiveness, failure to act, frustration, and, finally, anxiety or depression with the awareness of one's inadequacy, missed opportunity, and resulting loss. The lack of a sense of self is everywhere apparent as this person attempts—always unsuccessfully—to adopt one role and then another which, in his continual search for absolute perfection, he disregards because of the failure of any to satisfy his superego demands. He never does anything exactly because he wants to, but rather because he should. This style serves to weave a web in which the individual is eternally entrapped and which prevents him from ever doing anything of his own in his own right; hence, it assures that he will never achieve any real satisfaction or gratification.

The more entrenched and formidable these patterns become, the more maladaptive they are, tending to result in increasing purposeless and goal-less activity. The importance of recognizing these styles is their prevalence in a general medical population. At a time of illness and the resulting increased anxiety, such patterns usually become exaggerated. The physician realizing this can assist his patient in overcoming the anxiety by working with him in structuring his illness experience in ways which reinforce the patient's need for control. A precise outline of what is wrong, what needs to be done, and when it will be done frequently accomplishes this with gratifying results for both patient and physician. When these patterns become so formidable as to interfere seriously with the social and domestic functioning of the individual, there is generally a need for further exploration and treatment by a psychiatrist. At times of increased stress, these patients may exaggerate latent phobias that may respond to conditioning therapies, if treated early.

Suspicious or Paranoid

The suspicious or paranoid individual is best characterized by the single word "suspicious." He is at every moment on the watch for the overt or covert insult, slight, or potential threat to himself and the world that he has built around him. Such a style attempts to protect him from his sense of vulnerability and penetration. His fear of violation demands that he be ever on alert and guard against all manner of attacks from all sides at all times. To this end, he scans word and picture, deed and talk, the slightest movement or sound in his perceptual sphere for the personal message that it may have for him. The fear and its underlying wish that he might be slighted or otherwise selected for vulnerability or honor is projected outward onto the environment, which is always viewed as menacing and hostile. At the same time that there is an omnipresent fear of external control, the paranoid individual exercises intense internal control. There is a lack of spontaneity in his behavior, which leads to a loss of affective expression. Constant preoccupation with autonomy leads to a constriction and narrowing of behavior. Rigidity and intentionality characterize external behavior, which is always calculated and frequently gives the impression of being feigned or imitative. Whether the individual gives an external appearance of furtiveness, constriction, and suspicious apprehensiveness or of aggressive edginess and arrogance, bordering on the megalomanic, or of rigid preoccupation, the quality of hypervigilance is ever present. Beneath these facades, almost always hidden from public view, is extreme hypersensitivity and feelings of shame and inadequacy which the externalized projections have been erected to shield. The paranoid position is both a psychological and a physical one. The individual is in a continuous state of mobilization in preparation for an emergency. In this defensive vigilance, there is continual muscular tension. In situations in which the predisposed individual is threatened with real or fantasied injury, these usual modes of perception are exaggerated, leading to a loss of a sense of proportion and to behavior out of context with the social situation. Delusions may occur which dramatize the internal fear of the individual. At the same time, there is a frightening intactness and internal logic to the delusion that may escape the unsuspecting physician and may only be detected after talking with the patient's relatives and family. When threatened by physical injury or discomfort, the paranoid patient's anxieties and defenses are at a high level. At these times, he will view the environment with even more than his usual suspicion and will need very simple, direct explanations from all those working with him about what is wrong, what is to be done, and how it will be done. Even then, the physician and staff should be prepared for constant criticism and antagonism by the patient. Understanding that an acutely anxious and sensitive individual exists beneath this facade will tend to alleviate the countertransference and passive-aggressive tendencies aroused in the staff in response to these projections.

Hysterical

The basic mechanism of the hysterical personality is repression of underlying conflicts resulting in emotions that are often out of context and always out of proportion to the environmental or social stimulus. The hysteric lives his life by reacting to stimuli with affect, projecting theatrical, seductive (promising more than what is delivered), and exhibitionistic presentations of himself. However, a single affect is rarely sustained, and the general mood is one characterized by fleetingness and lability. At times, especially around issues or incidences likely to give rise to affects of displeasure, the hysteric seems unconcerned. This style, the affectual facade, the lack of sustained presentation, has caused investigators to note the apparent shallowness of the hysteric's behavior and to suggest an underlying sense of inadequacy and core of depression or emptiness. The affectual style is matched by an equally superficial cognitive style. This is one characterized by a global approach to events, which are grasped in their totality by visual impressions rather than by careful and detailed analysis. There is an incapacity for intense or persistent intellectual activity, and an exaggerated tendency for distraction, vagueness, and suggestibility. There is an obliviousness to factual detail and an inability to describe things with sharp definition and precision, which contributes to an impression of naivete, incredulity, and deficient intelligence. Ideas are not developed but are seemingly pulled out of the air or materialize as hunches, and they are presented in their initial form as accomplished fact. There seems to be a failure in the ability of the hysteric to work through any thought or problem according to traditional logic. It is suggested that the purpose of this mode of behavior and cognition is to deliberately prevent the individual from taking a look at himself and to shield him from an awareness of the underlying emptiness and uncertainty which he only vaguely feels. Such an individual, confronted with catastrophic environmental situations or physical difficulties, reacts in characteristic dramatic ways, often marked either by exhibitionism or indifference. The hysteric may not be able to summon the necessary attitudes for the remediation of problems. The hysteric may need reassuring guidance of the physician. This is best done in a matter-of-fact manner suggesting certainty and allowing for the dramatic, although medically irrelevant, productions of the patient. These patients do not require precise and detailed descriptions of their illness. In fact, they may often become extremely uncomfortable when such attempts are made. The physician's attention may need to be focused more on confronting the denial utilized by the patient in regard to his illness, which may interfere with diagnostic procedures or therapy. This denial may require the ingenious efforts of the physician to convince the patient through processes that defy logical explication.

Impulsive

The impulsive style is one in which there is an impairment of normal feelings of deliberateness and intention. Individuals with this handicap seem to act on impulse, whim, or urge. Action is unplanned and instantaneous, abrupt and discontinuous. It is as though there is a short circuit between stimulus, whether arising internally or externally, and response. Impulsive activity is not limited to the small and inconsequential acts of life but to monumental and frequently catastrophic ones, such as robbing a bank. The incriminated individual may offer the seemingly shallow but matter-of-fact explanation, "I just felt like it," without any show of affect. However, on closer scrutiny, it would seem as if the act itself may be a way of handling an affect that is only dimly perceived, never documented. It would also seem that these persons have a low tolerance for frustration or tension. It may be hypothesized that these individuals lack a discriminatory perception of a range of emotions and, when feeling a vague discomfort, strike out in a way that often seems antisocial. This has led many to view impulsive individuals as lacking in development of superego or conscience, but, on closer scrutiny, one is struck with the professed rigidity and conformity to the prevailing moral and social code, even in the face of contradictory behavior. This pattern is also reflected in the concrete and passive thinking that is manifested. Behavior is explained in terms of having been made to do the inappropriate act by the simple mechanism of projection. Because an urge to do something has been felt, this is offered as the complete explanation for the act. Their concerns rarely extend beyond the immediate boundaries of their own existence. There seems to be either an absence of or intolerance for imagination or speculation. Thought is devalued and sacrificed for the physical act, in which there seems to be more compulsion than pleasure. Because of this, the impulsive person seems to be lacking in his ability to have meaningful and empathic relationships with others. Other people are viewed in terms of their use or compliance in some immediate action at hand. The impulsive person's inability to take distance from himself assures that reflectiveness and revision are not a part of his style. Individuals with impulsive disorders may become sociopaths, alcoholics, and drug addicts because of their perceptual and cognitive styles that lead to indiscriminatory behavior, dependency on objects outside of themselves, and need for immediate gratification. When confronted by physical difficulties, perceptual and cognitive styles may be exaggerated in the face of rising anxiety and frustration. The physician cognizant of the predilection of his patient to such actions may allay some untoward precipitous and catastrophic behavior by attempting to anticipate the anxiety. This may be done easily by simple formulations of what the difficulty is, how it will be investigated and treated, and what the prognosis is. The physician may be able to prevent acting out by matter-of-fact limit setting in terms of his own or the hospital's authority. Longer term care may require frequent brief reinforcement of the terms of the initial contract between patient and physician.

Depressive

A case may be made for a basic depressive life or neurotic style. It is characterized by reacting to internal or external events less with anxiety than with depression and less with an active response than with one of withdrawal. It is a style marked by passivity and one that is easily and readily vulnerable to environmental manipulation. Although it contains characteristics to be found in the hysterical and impulsive styles, it is less ritualized, less structured, and in many ways more primitive. Although individuals may, in the face of insurmountable catastrophes, react with a giving-up-given-up state, the depressive is always so predisposed. The precipitating stimulus is frequently mild and sometimes merely imagined. A psychological and physical withdrawal immediately ensues. The psychological stance includes ideations of inadequacy and emptiness, sometimes proceeding to more aggressive self-condemnation. Expression is more often given to fears of being left, abandoned, or ignored and to attitudes of helplessness or hopelessness. These individuals are inordinately dependent on external supplies coming from others in the environment and seem to have an omnipresent fear that these will be denied them for one reason or another, usually because they feel undeserving. Their whole life style seems to be one of depending on external supplies, and their behavior is a manipulative attempt to achieve this. Their behavior is marked by a passive aggression that defies the environment to deny them of their just but undeserved due. Because they are always fearful that external resources will be withdrawn and that they will come face to face with their own emptiness, much of the cognitive style is aimed at achieving involved and symbiotic relationships with others. When there are not others around with whom to make these involvements, attempts at refuge from the internal feelings of displeasure may lead to dependence on drugs or alcohol. When there is a sense of total abandonment, the characteristic posture is one of helplessness. When this is not effective in securing the attention and needs of others, hopelessness that defies help may ensue. The passivity of this state is not without aggressive manipulation, which is directed at both the self and others. The individual entrapped in this state is both vulnerable to his own destructive acts and prey to those who would take advantage of him for their own purposes. It is more than likely that this state itself has correlative and analogous biological aspects that make the individual more vulnerable to the environment. At times of physical illness, the patient with this predilection gives up and becomes entirely dependent on the environment. He may do this even while maintaining the semblance of independence through defiance. This calls for a reassuring, sympathetic, nurturing attitude on the part of the physician and nursing staff, who may also have to decide to what extent regression is to be allowed. The description presented here should not suggest that these individuals lack perception or even great capability at times when they are not faced with or experience the threat of diminished external supplies.

Infantile

The infantile personality described by Ruesch[4] is mentioned here because it contains characteristics that have been mentioned for the preceding five personality styles. In this way, this style is more amorphous and has resulted in less rigid, formalized, and consistent patterns of cognition and behavior. Ruesch identified an infantile personality as the core problem in psychosomatic medicine identifying: (1) arrested or faulty social learning, (2) impaired self-expression channeled through either direct physical action or organ expression, (3) persistence of childhood patterns of thinking and ideation, (4) dependency and passivity, (5) rigid and punitive conscience, (6) overextended ideals, and (7) absence of ability to integrate experience. Ruesch, less concerned with specificity factors, did not offer an explanation of why one organ system rather than another was chosen for the expression of conflict. Rather, he outlined a therapeutic approach, rare in the history of psychosomatic medicine, for physicians working with patients having infantile or immature personalities which included: (1) reeducation through benevolent firmness; (2) instructing the patient as to the manipulative and implicit content of his complaint; (3) the reduction of long verbal productions to single words or sentences concerning problems; (4) the externalization of feelings and emotions as objectifications in their own right, rather than via organ expressions and complaints; (5) the acceptance of the patient himself as a psychological and biological entity distinct from others; and (6) the model of the physician as a consistent, accepting, available, and self-expressive person. Marty and De'Uzan have used the term *la pensée* opératoire to identify the thought activities of individuals they observed who were similar to these.[5] More recently, John Nemiah and Peter Sifneos have used the word *alexithymia* to idenfity the difficulty of patients similar to these groups have in describing their feelings.[6] To a large extent, these seem to describe a number of characteristics common to infantile and immature stages of development. Similarly, Kahana and Bibring[7] have described immature patterns of regressed behavior among medical patients. The terminology used, e.g., the angry, demanding patient, although possibly descriptive, serves a questionable purpose in relating to the patient as a person.

Psychotherapeutic Note

In addition to the brief discussion of the measures suggested above that the physician assume in response to patients with specific characteristics, pharmacological agents may often serve as useful adjuncts in helping the individual adjust to the present emotional or physical problems for which he seeks assistance. The use of psychopharmacological agents in individuals with the various styles described above should be directed at the prevailing affect and associated somatic correlations. When anxiety seems to be the motivating force, the transient use of short- to intermediate-acting barbiturates in nonaddictive individuals or such minor tranquilizers as the benzodiazepines is suggested. When depression seems to be the predominant affect, the use of the tricyclic or imipramine-derivative antidepressants may modulate the experience of the patient to the extent that psychotherapeutic intervention becomes more feasible. Some patients with both anxiety and depression will benefit from a combination of an antianxiety drug and an antidepressant medication.

References

1. Engel, G. L.: *Psychological Development in Health and Disease*, p. 392. Philadelphia, W. B. Saunders, 1962.
2. Shapiro, D.: *Neurotic Styles*. New York, Basic Books, 1965.
3. Fairbairn, W. B.: *Psychoanalytic Studies of the Personality*. London, Tavistock Publications, 1952.
4. Ruesch, J.: The infantile personality. Psychosom. Med. *10*: 134, 1948.
5. Marty, P., and De'Uzan, M.: La "pensée opératoire." Rev. Franc. Psychoanal. *27*: suppl. 1345, 1963.
6. Nemiah, J. C., and Sifneos, P. E.: Affect and fantasy in patients with psychosomatic disorders. In *Modern Trends in Psychosomatic Medicine, II*, O. W. Hill, editor, chapter 2. New York, Appleton-Century-Crofts, 1970.
7. Kahana, R. J., and Bibring, G. L.: Personality types in medical management. In *Psychiatry and Medical Practice in a General Hospital*, N. E. Zinberg, editor, pp. 108–123. New York, International Universities Press, 1964.

CHAPTER 5

On Growth and Development

Another way of thinking about ourselves, our patients, and who we are is in terms of growth and development and the phase of life we are within. We have little difficulty with the tripartite divisions of childhood, adulthood, old age. These are quite separate and distinct in our minds. Immediately, visions appear before us: the happy days of summer; commitment to jobs, child-rearing, spouses; sage white heads nodding by the fire. These are the idyllic images, not those of tragedy and pathology: the child with the broken toy or home; the separation of spouses; the disabilities and decadence of age. This tripartite division has been further divided into more minute phases: infancy, early childhood, later childhood, adolescence, young adulthood, middle aging, mature adulthood, early aging (senior citizens), senescence. Erikson speaks of the eight ages of man.[1] A set of 14th-century tapestries in the Lehman Wing of the Metropolitan Museum of Art identifies 12 ages. Schwab et al.[2] talk of the "tired housewife" syndrome, Hertz[3] of the "executive child," Levinson[4] of the "turning point" or "second- (perhaps third or fourth) chance" phenomenon of middle aging. Specific ages—such as 30, 39, 65, 73—have come to have symbolic meaning in contemporary society, similar to the ages of 13 and 21 in previous generations. These are seen as transition points from one status to another within society. It is as though one suddenly awakens to find a further transformation of oneself, especially as he or she is viewed from without. The expectation is frequently unrequited. In contemporary society, it seems as though the transition points are constantly altered, frequently lowered, as if we were in a rush to get along with the things of life, to raise its members up sooner to engage in a producer-consumer-oriented economy. This suggests that growth (and aging) is in part a process from without, similar to the trophic effect of sunlight on green plants. Such incentives toward growth and differentiation are societal imperatives, a process of recruitment to fill the ranks of those ahead who are themselves moving into the next time-limited phase of growth, development, differentiation, and aging. It seems to me that two social imperatives of aging are the emergence of one's children into adolescence and the effect of inflation on the older adult.

THE TASKS OF LIFE

Implicit in the concept of life phases is that of *tasks* and duties (see Table 5.1). Society, largely composed of those who precede us, provides the challenge and incentives—the trophic stimuli, promises of greater rewards, autonomy, challenges, carrots on the end of the string. Each of these is contingent on a set of rules specific for the responsibilities to be absorbed. There are tasks, expected forms of behavior, ways of the younger acting in respect to the older. A Japanese tea ceremony comes to mind. It is far from a pretty little ritual in a tea house in a garden as viewed by the tourist. In its older form, it was a ceremony of obeisance of younger, less wealthy and powerful lords and merchants to a greater one. Each aspect of the ceremony emphasized this mutual commitment: bending double to enter the small tea house of fidelity, the excruciating kneeling, the preparations of the tea as ritually as a chemical experiment or a communion service, the offering of the cup (whether it is turned twice to the right or once to the left), the acceptance of the cup, the spoken words that go with each, and the offering and taking of the symbolic sweets (wafers). These, with their variations from merchant to merchant or war lord to war lord, contain their own specific pledges in terms of what is promised and what is expected in return. Implicit in this are the duties and responsibilities of the older toward the young that they tend and bring up. To a large extent, these tasks are life phase dependent and, in our time, almost decade specific. They are also specific in terms of the individual relationships. This is not only between generations but also within generations in terms of how potential or real same-age competitors relate. These are rules of the game. There have even developed rules of avoiding, dropping out, or otherwise sidestepping the game, but this is another story.

THE NEEDS OF LIFE

The tasks of early development have been made quite specific according to several traditions. Each of these help us to think about our

Table 5.1*
Temporal Correspondence of Several Neurological, Psychological, and Ethical Developmental Sequences

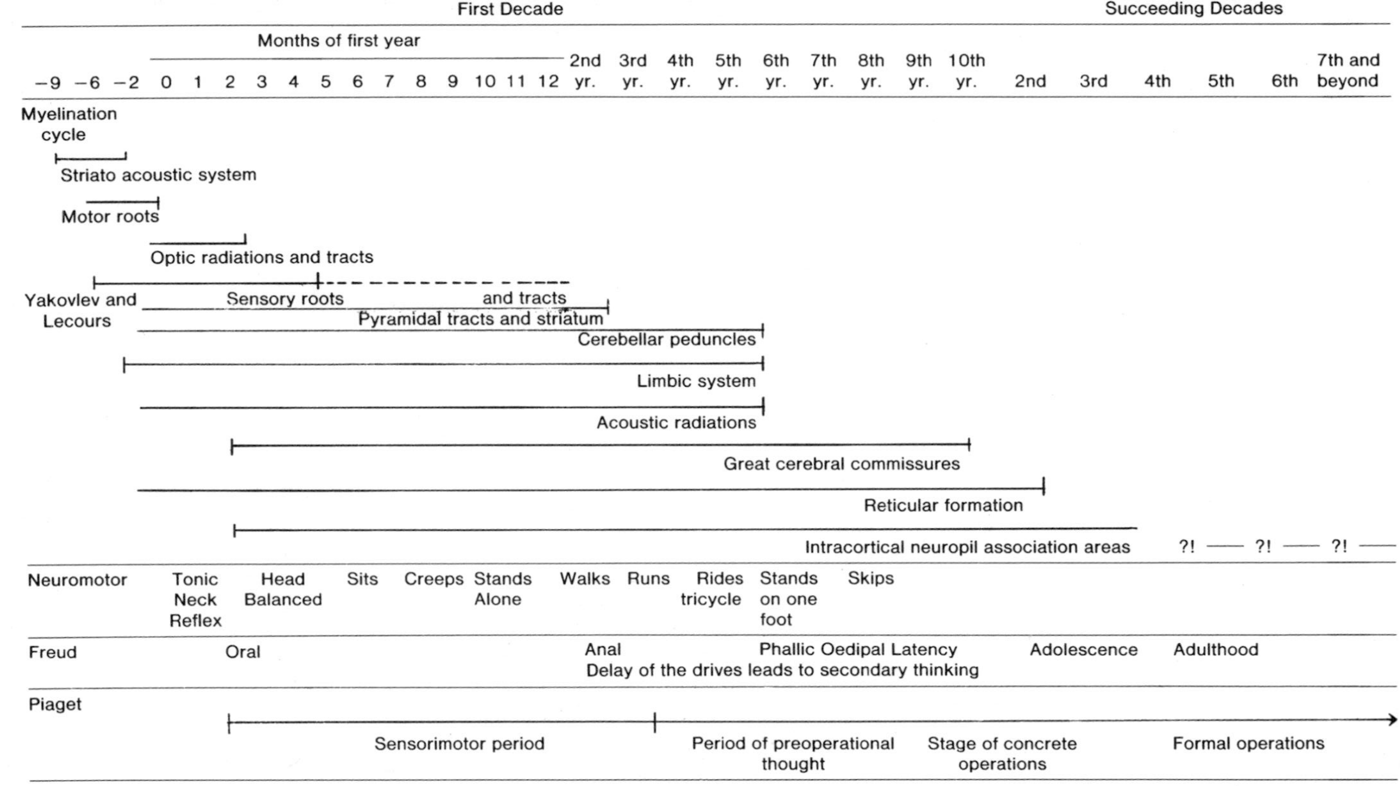

Table 5.1—*Continued*

First Decade — Months of first year: −9 −6 −2 0 1 2 3 4 5 6 7 8 9 10 11 12; 2nd yr. 3rd yr. 4th yr. 5th yr. 6th yr. 7th yr. 8th yr. 9th yr. 10th yr.

Succeeding Decades: 2nd 3rd 4th 5th 6th 7th and beyond

Spitz	Infant maternal dialogue →	
	Primal cavity preobject	
	Object specificity	
	Smiling response (1st organizer of the psyche)	
	Stranger anxiety (2nd organizer of the psyche)	
	"No" response (3rd organizer of the psyche)	
Mahler	Separation-individuation process →	
	Autistic phase hatching period →	
	Practicing	
	Rapprochement (refueling)	
	Object constancy (libidinal)	
	Omnipotence: Separation	Resolution of omnipotence →
Erikson	Oral-respiratory sensory stage (sucking)	Incorporative mode (biting)
	Muscular-anal	
	Locomotor-genital	
	Latency	
	Puberty and adolescence	
	Young adulthood	True genitality
	Adulthood maturity Postmaturity	

Trust vs. mistrust → Autonomy vs. shame and doubt Initiative vs. guilt Industry vs. inferiority ——— Identity vs. role confusion

Intimacy vs. isolation

Generativity vs. stagnation

Ego integrity vs. despair

Kohlberg†	Early childhood	Adulthood
	1st stage—orientation to punishment and reward and to physical and material power	
	2nd stage—hedonistic orientation instrumental view of human relations	
	3rd stage—"good boy" orientation, seeking to maintain expectations, win approval	
	4th stage—orientation to authority, law and duty, seeking to maintain a fixed social or religious order	
	5th stage—social-contract orientation emphasis on equality and mutual obligation within a democratically established order	
	6th stage—morality of individual principles of conscience that have logical comprehensiveness and universality	

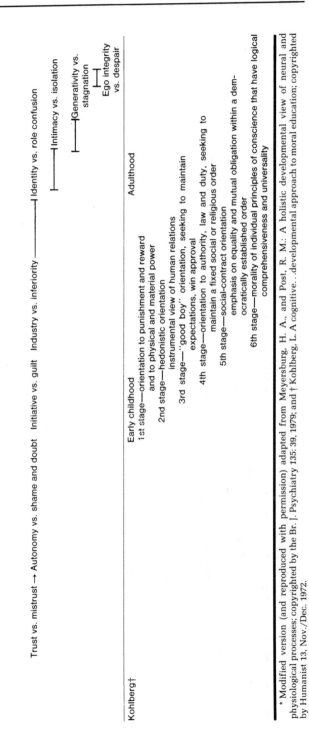

* Modified version (and reproduced with permission) adapted from Meyersburg, H. A., and Post, R. M.: A holistic developmental view of neural and physiological processes; copyrighted by the Br. J. Psychiatry *135*: 39, 1979; and † Kohlberg, L. A cognitive. . .developmental approach to moral education; copyrighted by Humanist 13, Nov./Dec. 1972.

patient as the person she or he is at that phase. Sigmund Freud focused largely on the development of emotions and defenses vis-à-vis the relationship between mother, child, and father across the first 4 or 5 years of life.[5] He saw these first as a function of biological developmental processes—the drives toward the satisfaction of life *needs*.

Oral Phase

The earliest need is air, and a primary postuterine experience is that of obtaining oxygen, necessitating immediately learning the alternating process of sucking and swallowing with that of breathing, an experience regulated at the mother's breast. This complex, initial maneuver is dependent on a host of other factors: the maturity and intactness of the newborn; his state of alertness; the experience and preparation of the mother; her state of alertness; the physical intactness of the mother, including the condition of her nipples, her production of milk, and her anxiety, exuberance, or sadness; the supporting figures, mothers, mothers-in-law, ladies and men in-waiting, nurses, midwives, physicians, spouses. This *oral* phase of development characterizes the first year of life, a constant exchange of giving and receiving, a basic pattern of interaction that takes on nuances of complexities and sophistication as the process is repeated and extended.

Mother and Child. The oral phase may be viewed as a primal stage of *regulation* and *homeostasis*, based on feedback between mother and child. Many things contribute to its unique characteristics in the specific mother-child dyad, the smells of each, how the child is held, the usual circumstances of nursing, what other things the infant sees, feels, hears, and tastes while nursing. Pleasure and gratification are experienced in this dyad. René Spitz studied the first year of life in a number of different cultural and social settings, suggesting that it is fundamental to the setting of attitudes, both positive and negative.[6, 7] Daniel G. Freedman,[8] in cross-cultural studies, determined that the newborns of different cultures frequently show different levels of reactivity at birth that can be demonstrated on neurological examination, suggesting that maturation is greater or lesser at the time of birth in different races and cultures. Thus, the initial level of mother-child interaction will be differently tuned. Dependent upon neurological development, it will occur at a slower or greater pace.

The oral phase can be differentiated into a number of subphases indicating degrees of maturation and evolution toward separation and autonomy. Margaret Mahler suggests that the child in the first year of life passes through several stages.[9] The first is autistic, lasting about 1 month. The child essentially experiences the world as himself. A second stage, commencing after 1 month and continuing for most of the remainder of the first year, she views as a symbiotic one between child and mother in which each experiences one another as an obligatory extension of the other. This is followed by a separation-individuation stage lasting through the third year, during which the child develops an emerging identity distinct and separate from the mother. René Spitz observed that around the age of 6 months, the infant no longer smiles at any adult, but demonstrates "anxiety" when a stranger, as opposed to the mother, appears. How the child comes to identify this experience as anxiety and to master it may be crucial to subsequent development; it will depend upon cognitive (language), as well as emotional, cues from the mother and others. The child's experience of this may serve as the basic mechanism of alert (signal anxiety) to new experiences and potential danger throughout his life. Within the first year of life, with the differentiation of strangers from mother, there develops an early abstractive process during which the infant adopts a transitional object—a blanket, a teddy bear—that is identified with the mother by its feel, smell, taste, and color.[10] Renata Gaddini has noted that transitional objects are less likely to develop in cultures where mothers or their surrogates are constantly present during the first 4 years of life.[11] It is assumed that the need for an internalized abstractive object to take the place of the real external one (mother), who is always present, is not necessary. Robert Levine, in his transcultural studies, suggests that the traditional Western thought sequence of cause and effect develops differently in cultures where parent-child separation occurs at later ages. Juxtaposition of cause and effect is related to concrete events occurring in close temporal relationship. The explanation relating these rarely goes beyond the concrete observation. When necessary, explanations rely upon traditional tales or the supernatural.[12]

Anal Phase

In the second year of life, emotional and cognitive development comes to be focused around function and *control* of other processes than breathing and sucking-swallowing, especially those of the gastrointestinal tract. The focus on anal sphincter control varies from culture to culture and from time to time within cultures, apparently dependent upon social and familial attitudes. Whenever it occurs, it emphasizes another delegation of control from the mother to the developing child, whose task it becomes to accept a measure of self-control. Whether he can or not will depend on many factors, the first of which is biological readiness. The extent to which a culture recognizes this as symbolic of this phase of development will influence the parent-child relationship over this issue. Obviously, control is only symbolically manifested around anal sphincter mastery. It relates to control of other biological processes such as breathing (breath holding), eating (demands), verbal development and usage (yes and no), and early locomotion (moving toward, away, not moving). Not the least of these are the verbal and nonverbal learning of yes and no, the development of a sense of will and willingness in the emerging self. Anger and rage and their control seem to be emotions relating to this stage of development.

Phallic Phase

Freudian developmental psychology also identifies a phallic phase of development, during which the infant takes cognizance of *himself* or *herself* around bodily parts, especially the genitals. This includes a greater self-awareness and self-absorption than has taken place earlier and may be related to other self-stimulatory (pleasurable) activity such as thumb sucking. The difference is one of more consciously taking parts of the body as objects, especially objects of self-exploration and stimulation. It is also partly a process of the increasing differentiation of self from another. In the anal phase, the differentiation comes around the discovery and *identification* of *will*, i.e., "I am able to make a difference in what happens; I can determine; I can affect others; and I am aware of it." The phallic phase is one of increased differentiation from others by the awareness that "I am not only different, but I can give to or find pleasure in myself." The formation of self becomes increasingly concretized around this sense of autonomy and involvement with self. It is an early phase of knowing oneself. At the same time, it allows for futher separation from others (especially mothers), individuals of the opposite sex and some identification with individuals of the same sex. Cognitively, it identifies the evolution of the abstractive process, the extrapolation and grouping of individual differences with classes. It is during this phase of development that dreams and the capacity for fantasy may be discovered and, with these, the opportunity for further self-stimulation.[13] With these comes the sense of a self-world and one of *privacy*. It is suggested that the sense of shame develops during this phase, a kind of self-censoring that contracts the sense of self.[14] This is at least partly learned. It seems to me that a New England childhood is frequently one of learning through shaming, as common language suggests, "I would be ashamed to look at myself in the mirror, hear myself talk, show my face." For the Japanese, shame is to lose face and self (*jibun ga nia*), as when one is dismissed from a group.[15]

In Western society, much attention is addressed to this phase of ego development in terms of its derivatives in later life, specifically in the continuing differentiation of the self from others, in terms of self-satisfaction and self-absorption. When this separation from others is highly skewed and leads to a solipsism markedly apart from interactions with others, we speak of narcissism.

Oedipal Phase

The oedipal phase is obviously dependent upon the prior ones, especially combining the developing senses of autonomy (anal) and self (phallic) and exerting these on significant others, the parents and, to a lesser extent, siblings. The obligatory transactions are seen with the parent of the opposite sex on the one hand and the parent of the same sex on the other. Whatever and however the need in the individual is perceived, this would seem to be decidedly molded by trophic need of and stimulation from the parents. There seems to be a heightened impetus on the part of the parents during this phase to emphasize sex-based behavioral differences for boys and girls. The respective roles are emphasized, and incentives are provided to identify with the parent of the same sex. Within the same sex, however, the role of the child and adult are carefully distinguished. In this internal segregation is the implicit promise of things to come, once full growth and learning of roles have been completed. Based upon the parental relationship a model of interaction with individuals of the opposite sex is developed on a conscious level. This is a phase of development that also demands and especially engenders conflict in the individual. It is a challenge and a demand to give up or reshape earlier ways, to *learn* roles rather than just be roles. Willfulness and self-absorption and even the residue of infantile activity are brought together, consolidated, and molded under the self's increasing sense of autonomy to follow a sex-identified pattern. Important in this process is the further development in abstractive processes, especially relating to the concept of future, especially a future that is dependent on consequences of present acts. It does make a difference. Further regulation of one's actions can now be learned.

Latency

At one time, considerable lack of attention was directed at that phase of development from ages 6 to 12 known as the latency period. It was as if development had gone into suspension while cognitive learning took place. The conflicts or tensions of earlier stages of development occurring at the behest of parents was suspended or partially taken over by part-time surrogate parents, i.e., teachers, who emphasized group conformity and learning. To some extent, it represented the parent's lesser attention (partial withdrawal), secondary to the lesser developmental and physical needs of the child. School and associated activity facilitated through reinforcement the regulation of motor, emotional, and cognitive processes that had previously evolved. The family sustains this separation with emotional support (approval, incentive), appropriate clothing, housing and, especially, food, and further extensions into culture-specific institutions (especially religion). Less attention was addressed to the internal processes occurring within the individual. It is as if, with the oedipal phase of self, development was temporarily completed, and the further evolution of the satisfaction of earlier needs was suspended and went underground. Certainly, it is in part supplanted by the increasing social (external) demands of the culture. Parent and child withdraw a bit from the internal world. Through fantasy (fairy tales), there commenced a cultural binding of the internal private world of the individual, allowing it to become public. Whatever conflicts that occur are addressed when there is a change in *external* behavior, such as prolonged enuresis, thumb sucking, school phobias, tics, tantrums, hair pulling, and too-obvious retention of transitional objects.

There are other ways of looking at latency. Rather than as a relatively inert phase, it may be that the self-identity has become such that it has evolved an internal need (one of self-regulation). Certainly this seems to be a time of increased stabilization of autonomic nervous system and organ function. This need may be also viewed as one for privacy, perhaps in part absorbed from the observation of the parents' need for privacy, apart from the child. The child's need for privacy requires acknowledgment, permission, and opportunity. Externally, these are manifested by secrets between peers, private jokes, whispered communications, secret societies, and private explorations of genital similarities and differences.

Increasing attention has been given to the blurring and overlap of the phases of development. Various explanations are offered, including the effect of communication processes, especially television, which allow us to look in on different phases of development, past and future, than our own. Perhaps this influences our behavior, if not our action and our speech. We become increasingly sensitive to and aware of these other phases. Thus, the latency-age individual adopts and tries on behavior of the adolescent. In reality, this is imitative behavior, mimicry. The behavior does not have the same symbolic significance as it does in the adolescent. Viewed in this light of imitation, this behavior is age specific rather than age discordant. Such a view is of practical importance for parents and counselors, inasmuch as the same behavior occurring at different ages requires different remedial and/or reinforcing approaches. Phases of development are only partially age dependent, depending on biological maturation and cultural and family organization. They are also less discrete than charts suggest. They do overlap with one another, and there is much backward and forward movement in behavior across identified chronological divides. Individuals may regress or progress to specific behavioral levels characteristic of another phase. Such regressions and progressions occur at times of illness and social demands, respectively. Significant in latency as it occurs across cultures is the emergence of a more adult-like concept of death, which may influence attitudes about adolescent or adult life.[16]

Adolescence

There are many ways to think and feel about adolescence. Similar to childhood phases, these are described largely from the viewpoint of those outside, less often from those within. Most important to the adolescent is that it is *his* or *her* adolescence, not that as seen by the viewer nor that of any other adolescent. He or she does not want to be told what it is, what it is like. It is also not the adolescence that the parent knows it is. The defiant defense of the adolescent, saying and affirming it is "mine," is perhaps the essential core of what adolescence is. It is a rapidly increased process of self-dedifferentiation, even if it progresses under the cloud or subterfuge of identification. Peter Blos courageously and helpfully wrote about his work with individuals in the adolescent years.[17, 18] He saw this developmental phase as a very individual one. He viewed it as a second-chance phenomenon, an opportunity to reformulate, perhaps restructure, the products and residues of earlier developmental phases. In his terms, adolescence can be seen as an ontological recapitulation of phylogeny, in this case of the earlier psychosexual developmental phases. And, indeed, with the benefit of some distance, the adult can identify, through various stages of adolescence, regressed behavior that reflects oral, anal, phallic, and oedipal conflicts and preoccupations. These are identified by such characteristics as passivity-dependency-withdrawal, demandingness-defiance-willfulness, self-absorption-introversion-narcissism, and sexual identification in attraction-differentiation, correlating with their respective stages. As an opportunity for regrouping, repair, and reformulation, adolescence is a time to review the conscious past (roots), explore feelings, review and reshape defensive patterns, renegotiate relations with significant others of the past in the present (parents), and experiment in new relationships with members of the same and opposite sex.

Another way of viewing adolescence is as a way of trying on different styles of adulthood, not unlike that which occurs during the oedipal stage. In adolescence, the identification with the parent of the same sex may be obscured, extended, and/or transferred over to a surrogate parent, such as a teacher, an uncle or aunt, or an admired and available individual selected because of his or her professional (vocational) interest. This frequently results in painful conflicts between parent and adolescent as comparisons with surrogates are made or as values disparate from those of parents are assumed. In turn, these rapid changeovers, driven by the adolescent's quest and need for identity, provoke and surface unresolved old conflicts of the earlier stages of development. Again, many of these have to do with parents and the recasting of the relationship of the adolescent with these. The smoothness of this remarkably unsmooth phase is dramatically influenced by external events, including physical health, available friends and surrogate persons, presence and health of parents, siblings, and other environmental influences and occurrences. Because this is an age of increased experimentation, adolescence as adulthood cannot be mentioned without reference and concern about sexual orientations and activities, birth control, pregnancy, abortion, drugs, and dropouts. But neither can one think about adolescence without thoughts of maturation, growth, determination, differentiation, individuation, expectation, anticipation, commitment, purpose, satisfaction, and hope.

Adulthood

More recently, mankind has had the luxury of recognizing more discrete phases of development within the broader age categories. Adulthood can be divided into 4 or 5 decades. These are variable stages, greatly dependent upon cultural and vocational influences. For the relatively small number of individuals in the world who go on through college, the fulfillments and tasks of adolescence extend well into the twenties. For many professional students, adolescence remains expanded, stunted, incomplete, and/or unresolved well into the thirties. The tasks, so eloquently identified by Blos, of establishing patterns of adult sexuality and partnership, resolving relationships with parents (including leaving home), and identifying a career path, remain largely in limbo. The student selecting a professional path such as medicine is far from his or her identity as a surgeon or ophthalmologist when he or she enters medical school. Much uncertainty and differentiation remains. He or she may change his or her mind several times in the course of the 4 years of the medical curriculum or even once residency education has begun. While this process of "What am I going to do; Who am I going to be?" is taking place, other patterns of adulthood also remain in the process of formation. This is so in terms of stable relationships with other adults, including professional associates, as well as social and family relationships. This is so, whether or not financial independence from parents has been achieved or a marriage has been consummated. The individual is seen and sees himself or herself in a student role, a special status involving privilege on one hand and dependency on the other. The privilege is associated with the luxury of extending one's education far beyond that usually granted to members of a society. In doing so, society both allows and enforces the continuation of dependency in many areas on itself. Most often these are momentary, but they are also in other areas of control: the rules and regulations of the institution; the hierarchy of student and professor; the mere designation of "student" or "doctor in training" by society at large. Full status has not been attained. Parents, whether financially supporting or not, are intimately vested in the support of this endeavor.

Such intrusions by other adults, parents, professors, sometimes only a few years older, are gradually relinquished during the residency and fellowship years. Some lingering traces will remain for those individuals remaining in the sometimes protective framework of institutions, firms, and junior partnerships. The variations of managing these in limbo transitions of prolonged education are many. The problems resulting from these are also many. They demand further investigation and analysis.

The Social Imperative

As we have observed in the foregoing, it is difficult to discuss Freudian developmental psychology without resorting to its relationship with development viewed from other perspectives. Erikson found that he could not do this without emphasizing the greater social milieu in which emotional development occurred. He especially emphasized the tasks and obligations and sanctions that the mother-child dyad and subsequently the mother-child-father triad were subject to by the greater society. From his transcultural work, he was able to observe both similarities and dissimilarities in arriving at a framework of development that extended well beyond the formative years of early childhood through middle life and old age. His view of age-specific needs and tasks and the mutual fit or mis-fit of these between generations contributed a more complex as well as an extended model for thinking about human behavior. Specifically, it reemphasized the effect of the greater environment not only on early development but on reshaping early patterns of behavior at later stages. Early patterns, once recognized as uneconomical for the individual, could be redressed at various phases in the life cycle. The idea of a "second-chance phenomenon" came to be extended to a "third"- or even "fourth"-chance phenomenon in later decades. Presently, in parts of Western society a major "turning point" or perhaps a second "breaking away" phase is seen in the latter fourth and early fifth decades. It is as if for many not only do adolescent tasks remain incomplete and unresolved over decades, but that there is within present society a flexibility, perhaps related to an economic luxury, that allows for this process to continue. It does not go unnoted in passing that this "delayed adolescence" precipitates around the time of the adolescence of one's own first-born progeny.

Old Age

As a greater number of individuals—the survivors—live longer while there is a declining birth rate, secondary to later marriages and limited procreation, there has occurred in Western societies a change in the ratio of old to young. This change in and of itself has both broad and social etiologies and consequences. Some of these are readily acknowledgeable; others remain subtle and require further research before full understanding and explanation can be achieved and, hence, attempts at remediation can be made. Serious attention to the aging has recently increased as specific and new problems have been identified. Notable have been those that suggest a biology of aging significantly different from that of the middle aging adult.[19] These biological changes affect metabolic processes of all organ systems, including the central nervous system and its related cognitive functions. The social aspects of aging are all too obvious for many of us. They include economics, housing, diminished activity, increased illness, enforced dependency, forced institutionalization, and malnutrition. The list is of legion proportions.[20] The behavioral and psychological problems are intimately related to the social and biological.[21] The three perspectives do not always adequately identify discrete social, psychological, and biological factors; many are intimately intertwined. Both discrete and global approaches are often necessary. Commonplace to aging, all too often, seem to be isolation, abandonment, loneliness resulting in apathy, anomie, and eccentricity. Ill physical health; diminished mental ability; depression; inadequate finances; poor housing; lack of transportation; distant, absent, and unavailable relatives and friends are inevitably components of the social ills of aging.

The bulk of patients in state mental hospitals, chronic disease hospitals, veterans' hospitals, and nursing homes are elderly patients, many with central nervous and other organ system diseases. Some of these diseases are related to chronic substance abuse, especially alcoholism. Others are degenerative, for as yet unidentified or unexplained reasons. The clinics of general hospitals are the railroad stations of the poor elderly. Frequently, they are the only port of refuge. The elderly come carrying the baggage of chronic symptoms, some relating to disease, many relating to depression, and others resulting from social deprivation and isolation.

Largely because we are ignorant of precise factors relating to aging, these problems cannot be approached objectively or economically. There is a need for research at every level and from a number of perspectives, not the least of which is an ethical one. For students of medicine, it is an overwhelming and difficult area to approach. Yet, for all but pediatricians and obstetricians, the touch of the sick elderly remains and constitutes the bulk of patients presenting to clinics, hospitals, and offices.

ADDITIONAL CONCEPTUAL MODELS OF BEHAVIOR

Cognitive Development

There are other ways of thinking about development, some more complete than others, many in the process of continuing formulations. Piaget has emphasized cognitive development as a way of conceptualizing behavior.[22] This also would seem to be intimately associated with maturational physical processes, including anatomical development of the central nervous system. Piaget speaks about increasingly complex levels of mental operations, beginning with relatively simple one-dimensional processes and extending to three-dimensional processes over time. The dimensions refer to the number of operations involved in solving problems. These operations can be identified for relatively specific ages and are dependent on such complex and still somewhat poorly understood phenomena as memory, learning, and abstraction and their interactions. Obviously, cognitive development does not take place independent of emotional development. The two are not necessarily separate processes but merely different ways of addressing development, each addressing or emphasizing a specific aspect of it. Omissions or failures, for whatever reason, in one system of conceptualization are often accounted for in a relating stage in another system. Most often, the various developmental theories are best viewed as complementary rather than antagonistic.

Learning Theory

Learning and learning theory, while necessarily closely related to cognitive development, are based along a continuum of stimulus-reinforcement-response in which the factors can be interchanged and/or contingent on one another.[23] A simpler model in some ways, it lends itself to experimental designs for more discrete analysis, observation, and formulation. Its methods allow for measurements in psychological and physiological systems which allow for replication. Although much of behavioral learning was at one time addressed to the so-called voluntary neuromuscular system, more recently Leon DiCara and Neal Miller, on the basis of ingenious experiments, have raised the question whether the same principles are not applicable to the autonomic sympathetic and parasympathetic nervous systems.[24]

Among the so-called structuralists, Konrad Lorenz has identified imprinting as a phenomenon basic to behavior.[25] This is the classic experiment in which he observed that, at a critical period of development, ducklings would follow the first leader observed (in this experiment, Konrad himself) rather than only the mother duck. Presumably the story of the ugly duckling and the swan is based upon an older observation of this phenomenon. What is unique in this observation is the identification of *critical periods* for behavior to be learned. The same experiment done several days earlier or later would not achieve this result. Several animal experimenters utilize this principle in their experimental designs. Myron Hofer has identified the development of gastric ulcers in rat pups separated from their mothers at a specific time when subjected to a stressful stimulus at a later stage of development. Pups separated prior to or after this critical period did not develop gastric ulcers when subjected to the stressful stimulus.[26] James Henry and co-workers found similar associations in the greater susceptibility of female mice raised in isolation to breast carcinoma in a crowded and complex living environment than mice not so reared.[27]

It is obvious that a number of developmental formulations and schemes have been identified which augment our understanding of behavior and add to our frustration in identifying a single conceptual approach. These formulations have been derived on the basis of different scientific methodologies and a priori conceptual orientations. A task before behavioral scientists is to identify the extent to which the different languages used to think about behavior overlap or are identical in describing the same phenomenon. Frequently, the empirical observation (data) is distorted or blurred because of the conceptual orientation of the observer, leading to a tautological problem. Conceptual orientations need not be mutually exclusive and are perhaps best considered as temporary and crude tools for interpreting data while we await more refined ones. In an attempt to construct an integrated approach to behavior, presently it seems sufficient to interpret our data within the context of multiple formulations, utilizing those that best explain the data at that point in time (see Table 5.1). Although it is possible to postulate that there are implicit ethical overtones in most developmental theories, Kohlberg would have us consider a developmental scheme in the evolution of an individual's ethics.[28] Wilson takes us further back in phylogeny to think about a sociobiological ethical imperative intrinsic in nature, or at least in the animal kingdom.[29] Specifically, he cites the cooperative efforts of dolphins in assisting a maimed member of a group of dolphins.

Apart from the above, there are other philosophical or religious traditions and orientations which influence and modify behavior, awareness of which is important to us as physicians working with patients. A common example is the refusal of many members of the Jehovah's Witness sect to accept blood transfusions. Even more common are dietary and fasting traditions of many religions that occasionally may compromise good health care or mandatory medical attention. Many individuals, some seeing themselves as existentialists, deemphasize, even ignore, the influence of the past as a determinant of behavior and events in the present. Such an orientation may sometimes severely compromise a patient's acceptance of optimal health practices and medical treatment or of the physician's emphasis in communicating them.

Although one or more of the above approaches may be essential for analyzing, formulating, and conceptualizing a specific problem in a patient, obviously it is impractical to submit every situation to an analysis by each of these orientations. Nor is it possible for each physician to be equally knowledgeble and facilitative in utilizing every approach. However, what is common to most of these approaches is a developmental attitude: that the identification of biological, social, and psychological antecedents or predicates is crucial to understanding the present problem. There will be times when one or another approach will be more useful in understanding and caring for the patient.

References

1. Erikson, E.: *Childhood and Society*, ed. 2. New York, W. W. Norton, 1963.
2. Schwab, J. J., Bialow, M., Brown, J. M., and Holzer, C. E.: Diagnosing depression in medical inpatients. Ann. Intern. Med. 67: 695, 1967.
3. Hertz, D. G.: Culture-, age-, and sex-related attitudes: Conflict areas in teaching and practice of psychological medicine. In *The Teaching of Psychosomatic Medicine and Consultation-Liaison Psychiatry*, C. P. Kimball and A. J. Krakowski, editors, Bibliotheca Psychiatrica, No. 159. Basel, S. Karger, 1979.
4. Levinson, D.: *The Seasons of a Man's Life*. New York, Alfred A. Knopf, 1978.
5. Freud, S.: Introductory lectures on psycho-analysis, part III. In *Standard Edition of the Complete Psychological Works of Sigmund Freud*, J. Strachey, editor, vol 16. Hogarth Press, London, 1963.
6. Spitz, R.: *First Year of Life*. New York, International Universities Press, 1965.
7. Spitz, R.: *No and Yes: On the Genesis of Human Communication*. New York, International Universities Press, 1966.
8. Freedman, D. G.: *Human Infancy: An Evolutionary Perspective*. Hillsdale, N. J., Lawrence Erlbaum Associates, 1974.

9. Mahler, M.: *Human Symbiosis and the Vicissitudes of Individuation*, vol. I. New York, International Universities Press, 1968.
10. Winnicott, D. W.: *The Family and Individual Development*. London, Tavistock Publications, 1965.
11. Gaddini, R.: Transitional objects and the process of individuation: A study in three different social groups. J. Am. Acad. Child Psychiatry, *9:* 347, 1970.
12. Levine, R. A.: *Culture, Behavior and Personality*. Chicago, Aldine Publishing Company, 1973.
13. Bettelheim, B.: *The Uses of Enchantment: The Meaning and Importance of Fairy Tales*. New York, Alfred A. Knopf, 1976.
14. Piers, G., and Singer, M. B.: *Shame and Guilt*. New York, W. W. Norton, 1973.
15. Doi, T.: *The Anatomy of Dependency*. Tokyo, Kodanshi International, 1973.
16. Nagy, M. H.: The child's view of death. J. Genet. Psychol. *73:* 3, 1948.
17. Blos, P.: *On Adolescence: A Psychoanalytic Interpretation*. New York, Free Press, 1960.
18. Blos, P.: *The Adolescent Passage*. New York, International Universities Press, 1979.
19. Hayflick, L.: The cell biology of human aging. Sci. Am. *242:* 58, 1980.
20. Neugarten, B., editor: *Middle Age and Aging: A Reader in Social Psychology*. Chicago, University of Chicago Press, 1968.
21. Kahn, R. L.: Brief objective measures for the determination of mental status in the aged. Am. J. Psychiatry *117:* 326, 1960.
22. Piaget, J.: *The Development of Thought: Equilibrium of Cognitive Structure*. New York, Viking Press, 1977.
23. Goldiamond, I.: Behavioral approaches and liaison psychiatry. In *Symposium on Liaison Psychiatry*, C. P. Kimball, editor, Psychiatric Clinics of North America, vol. 2, no. 2, Philadelphia, W. B. Saunders, 1979.
24. DiCara, L. V., and Miller, N. E.: Instrumental learning of systolic blood pressure responses by curarized rats: Dissociation of cardiac and vascular changes. Psychosom. Med. *30:* 489, 1968.
25. Lorenz, C.: *King Solomon's Ring*. New York, T. Y. Crowell, 1952.
26. Hofer, M.: Studies on how early maternal separation produces behavioral change in young rats. Physiol. Behav. *15:* 245, 1975.
27. Henry, J., Meehan, J. P., and Stephans, P. M.: The use of psychosocial stimuli to induce prolonged hypertension in mice. Psychosom. Med. *29:* 408, 1967.
28. Kohlberg, L.: A cognitive-developmental approach to moral education. Humanist. 13, Nov./Dec. 1972.
29. Wilson, E.: *Sociobiology: The New Synthesis*. Cambridge, Harvard University Press, 1975.

CHAPTER 6

On Life Phases

Although an acquaintance with developmental concepts of growth and differentiation is absorbing, enriching, and facilitative in our approach to the patient, a more phenomenological approach is frequently more easily accepted, more utilitarian, and less complex. Retreating for a moment to an old formula, let us consider the idea of *needs* of the individual as requiring satisfaction from the outside by others. The satisfaction of these needs (or demands) becomes the obligation of others: mothers, fathers, teachers, suppliers. In each phase of life there are specific needs demanding satisfaction through the specific tasks (obligations) of others, who are themselves in another phase of development.

The Experience of Illness

When our middle aging mother of four comes to us with a "lump" in her breast, it does not take much imagination on our part to have some idea of both her needs and obligations. Based on our experiences with our own mothers, the mothers of others, aunts, wives, perhaps grandmothers, other patients, we readily have an initial sense (gestalt) of what her life patterns, responsibilities, concerns, and tasks may be. We may even have a pretty good idea of some of her needs. We will expect her first preoccupation to be with the meaning of the mass. Both her concern and ours will center around the possibility of malignancy, cancer. Her way of manifesting this concern may depend on her customary way of handling problems, anxiety, other feelings that she may have. In addition, her response will be modified by her previous experience: with others who had a similar problem, knowledge, previous illness, general reflections, and philosophy of life. One woman may react with great alarm, as if the feared diagnosis was certain, another in a matter-of-fact way, a third as if nothing happened. Each of these may be handling alarm or (signal) anxiety in a different way: the first, giving full, if not counterphobic, expression to it; the second, in a measured rational and intellectual way; the third, with almost complete denial, as far as the masking of anxiety is concerned. A physician concerned with his or her patient's emotional processes will need to learn how to get at, set the stage, for determining what the underlying concern (anxiety) is, how the patient is handling it (with what defenses), and how adaptive these defenses are at the particular stage of illness. In other words, the physician will want to find out what the consequences are for the patient and for others of this way of handling her feelings. Does denial lead to lack of acceptance of the possibility of illness and then failure to pursue medical investigation and treatment? Does denial help keep the woman together until such time as she can come to terms with the possibilities? Does her acute reaction help to get everything out on the table, clear the emotional field (so to speak) in order to approach the problem more rationally? Does the "cool, matter-of-fact approach" conceal a cauldron of emotions that in some way will operate to shape her behavior adaptively or maladaptively? In the course of her diagnosis and treatment, the physician will need to effect through the relationship an opening into these processes of reaction, always with the question in mind of their adaptiveness or maladaptiveness at that particular time for the patient and her family.

The woman with the "lump" in her breast comes with other baggage than her personality, her characteristic way of behaving. Until recently, her concerns and preoccupations were about other things. These things remain, although they may for the moment take second and third place to her present concern. Most probably her concern has been with the orchestration of a busy spouse and four children, each going forth in a different direction. She may have an aging parent or in-law toward whom much of her energies have been expended. No doubt she will have more than one or two reflections: about her relationships with her spouse, her satisfaction or dissatisfaction with one or more of her children, her annoyance with the complexity or seeming stagnation of her present state of existence, her preoccupation with one or more of the community activities with which she is involved, certainly a concern about finances, innumerable worries about her relationships with significant other persons, and plans for the future. The above and others can all be more or less expected for the life phase of this individual. In addition, because of her specific life situation, there will be infinite variations. She may be menopausal, premenopausal, or postmenopausal, and that may affect how she sees herself or how others see her. She may be widowed, separated, divorced, and/or in the middle of an affair. She may be at a point of turning or breaking away. She may be on the verge of establishing "her own identity" outside of the home and family in a vocational sphere of her own; or she may be getting ready to return to the home and to "her own interests" after many years as being one of the wage earners of the family.

The "lump in the breast" will cast at least a momentary shadow across her life. With concern and anxiety, there may develop sadness and anger, which may be associated with either withdrawal and isolation or the obverse, increased outer-directed activity with others. No doubt on some level or another, there will be a summing up, however transient, an accounting of where she is, how she got here, where she *was* going. But, foremost will be the concern of how to get through this, how to get this thing organized. This will depend on others: family, physician, friends. The specifics of her other activities, concerns, and preoccupations may need to be identified and sometimes explored. However, we already may have a pretty good sense of her multiple roles, tasks, and obligations in satisfying the needs of others and herself. The important quantifiable sets are her sex, age, marital status, number of children, and illness symptom or sign. An idea, gestalt, or designation of her personality style or life style will help in getting a relationship with her and us going. The identification of ethnic and racial background and religious orientation will tell us something more. A knowledge of her obligations to others in the home, with relatives, friends, and social and business associates outside of the home adds dimension. We will have an idea of a pattern that has suddenly been challenged, interfered with, and broken unexpectedly in a moment's time. It is followed by more than a moment of uncertainty: What now?[1]

Although common reactions dependent upon the nature of the illness and the patient's personality may occur across the life-span or during several life phases, the moulding of these reactions is to a large extent dependent on the specific life phase and the responsibilities, obligations, needs, and tasks thereof. Much of the reaction to the signs and symptoms of illness will depend on the bonding attachments to other individuals, institutions, and also things (vocation). Again, for the middle years, and to a lesser extent for the later years, the preoccupations with life will usually be tantamount to those of death and even the process of dying. For most, there has developed a commitment to life identifiable as commitment to specific tasks of life, specific relationships with other individuals, and specific identification with a vocation or profession and within it to one or more special interests. With illness, the concern of the individual may focus on these very *special* and *specific* commitments. Much of the reactions to and negotiations with illness will focus around the commitment to specific persons and groups. This may become one of intensification or loosening. It is within these special bondings and attachments that the self is found, manifested, and extended. It is around the times of confronting illness or the threat of illness that the concept of self may be intensified in terms of its meaning based on these relationships. These occur at other times in life, frequently at times of transition from one life phase to another. It is as if at each transition from one phase to another, in the enlarging view of self, there is a simultaneous closure and an opening. There is an exchange of one's old self for a new one. Childhood is given up for the turmoil of adolescence, adolescence for the reluctant limitations and fantasied independence of adulthood, early adulthood for the deepening experiences of middle aging, and the latter for an increasingly indeterminate phase of reflection and resolution.

Of Earlier Development

Moving backward, let us briefly consider the needs and tasks of early childhood with those responsibilities and obligations of early parenthood. There develops a bonding between the infant and mother, based upon the biological needs of both mother and child, resulting in the phenomenon of *attachment*.[2] The mother is driven to nurture, symbolically by the pressure of milk coming into her breast. The child "is driven" to cry and suck. There results a pattern of mutual demand and supply. Involved in this process are all of the senses of both individuals: taste, smell, visual, auditory, and tactile, the tentacles through which the world comes to be felt, experienced, and in time, known. These memories, encapsulated in chemical signatures, will shape feelings and behavior for the rest of the individuals' lives. But there is a double-edged sword contained within these as later development emphasizes, in the obligation to separate, the phenomenon of *separation*.[3] The latter begins with increased mobility, a timed process that is culture dependent. The nature of future attachments and separations will be shaped by this primordial one, not only with other individuals, but also in terms of the object world. This earliest stage of development is obviously dependent on the supplies of nurturance. Such supplies are supported and guaranteed by significant others: spouses, parents, and other family members.

Later childhood takes place in an increasingly social context, experienced in separation from mothers and families for increasing periods of time. The individual is immersed in a peer culture which emphasizes similarities and differences, based on ages to a large degree and on sex, race, and ethnic backgrounds to a considerable degree. Separation involves exposures to a larger world of biological and social experiences, including those to infectious disease and patterns of behavior deviant from one's own background. These exposures in the social milieu begin to shape both biological and social development. Biologically, a whole set of processes, some obvious, others subtle, will be set in motion and shaped. Processes of assertiveness, containment of aggression, discharging anxiety, and control will add to and modify earlier programmed autonomic mechanisms. Socially, basic patterns of bonding and attachment will be shifted away from the nurturing generation to that of the peer group. Difficulties with the process of detachment and identification with the peer group may be observed in deviant social and biological processes. Likewise, the occurrence of social events (such as the death of a parent)[4] or disease (such as rheumatic fever) will affect development in both spheres.[5]

Adolescence

Adolescence, which seems increasingly to blur with later childhood on one end and early adulthood on the other, involves processes of both increased attachment, in terms of identification (some increased modeling after the parent of the same sex), and increased separation from both parents, with the beginning of some accommodation or rapproachment. Around these processes are the specific tasks of increased differentiation of the individual in terms of: (1) sexuality and relationship with significant others, (2) career or vocational orientation, and (3) separation from parents. The special obligation and task of parents during this phase, in addition to that of maintaining their own relationship, is that of maintaining an optimal amount of tension between "holding on and letting go." Although this is fraught with seeming constant conflict, it in reality is often executed with a sense of serious playfulness by both parties. Although increasing shaping of adult identifications takes place during this time, definitive molding of these roles will continue throughout the rest of life.

Early Adulthood

Early adulthood sees for some an embarkment into life based upon the above identifications; for others, it is an extended phase of trial and error, often similar to an extended adolescence, but with an adult hunting license. These are culture bound, to some extent based upon the class of origin. They are also temporally bound, based upon the phase of the greater culture. Perhaps they are also family bound, based on a generational evolution in which successive generations of a family evolve as if according to an inherent differentiating principle specific for that family, with an imperative to move in a specific path building upon what has gone before. The needs and obligations of the young adult diverge, depending upon the paths of commitment chosen. Those entering into a committed relationship with another person, resulting in the establishment of a family and beginning on a vocational path, will have assumed tasks and obligations sooner and different from those who focus on and attend to further individual development in terms of advanced education, continued dependency on parents or others for financial and emotional support, and fewer commitments to significant others.

On Maturing

In the late twenties and early thirties, the emerging middle years, the tasks and obligations of the identified paths of individuals will seem increasingly similar. Both will be in the process of assuming greater responsibilities in the roles of family and vocation and commitments to a limited number of other individuals and activities. During this phase, there is a deepening of patterns, a stabilization, and a constancy. These may not occur without major life crises incurring major revolution or evolution. Nevertheless, the end point for the individual is that of a further differentiation, based upon the less definite differentiation of the past, which will characterize much of the remaining years. These are years of deepening. They are also years of bearing increasing demands of emerging adolescents on one hand and aging parents on the other. The bearing of these does not go untouched by those unresolved adolescent processes that remain within us or by the outlook that we have developed toward the years of recession that loom before us and is mirrored by the now aging grandparental generation. For many, these may be best characterized as the circus years, three ring ones, with the center holding forth. These are also years of coping with real problems and assuming the responsibility for them. There is the involvement with one's children and younger colleagues, for which considerable time and responsibility are assumed, on one hand and the sense of obligation and duty to the biological and social problems of aging sustained by the aging generation on the other. Both of these bring into varying degrees of focus or refocus one's own developmental processes and raise the question of alternatives at a time when there are still, albeit increasingly limited degrees of professional, social, and individual freedom.

This is also a time when both acute and chronic illness escalates.

Many of the disease processes that will shape future development and life occur at this time: hypertension, coronary artery disease, adult-onset diabetes, rheumatoid arthritis, gastrointestinal diseases, cancer, accidents, alcoholism. In attending to these, for optimal care of the patient, the physician will need to get a sense or grasp of the harried executive with chest pain, the tired housewife with colitis, the over-the-hill teacher with diminishing resources, the widowed mother with hypertension and five children, the salesman of the year with "indigestion" and alcoholism. A simple question—such as "How's the family?" or "What's going on at the office?"—may open a floodgate of response that will be an intrinsic therapeutic part of the doctor-patient relationship and set the stage for treating the myocardial infarction, peptic ulcer, and/or alcoholism.

Settling or Settling In

The maturity of middle aging relates to settling in, a consolidation of psychological defenses manifested by fairly regular patterns of social interactions with other individuals and institutions. Accommodations have been made, and roles attained or assumed are followed easily, despite pressures and demands from generations below and above. This is despite assaults of others and of illness upon the integrity of the self. This phase of maturation is thwarted by vocational and social threats as well as by compromising illnesses. The extent to which these are borne, resisted, and accommodated depends upon the previous experiences and the personality structure of the individual and the intactness of the social matrix within which the individual and her or his family resides. The maturing concept of death during this phase results in its acceptance, as opposed to the denial or ignoring manifest in earlier phases of development. The acceptance is of the reality of death, rather than a resignation. With this acceptance, increased emphasis is placed on living and the work of living. Making some kind of mark on and in life becomes increasingly important for the individual, whether it is in terms of one's own profession, an effect upon her children's development and achievements, and/or a cohesiveness of one's self-concept. The tasks and obligation of this phase are present and directed on many sides and in many spheres. There is the essential pressure from the young in the several phases of development below: children, students, junior colleagues. There are the demands from the several phases above: parents, grandparents, aunts-uncles, and more senior colleagues. There is the entrustment and commitment to maintaining and nurturing the institutions of society, of which the individual becomes more and more an integral part. For the healthy (one is tempted to say of body, mind, and spirit), these years in a Western society have an increasing viability in years, lasting beyond the age of 70, waning gradually and sometimes imperceptibly during the sixties.

At varying ages above 70, depending on biological and social factors, there is a gradual to abrupt decline in the activities of the previous phase.[6, 7] Biological factors seem especially to relate to a decline in mental functioning, resulting in cognitive deficits that interfere with concentration, recent memory, sometimes judgment, and abstractive processes. These may independently or co-dependently relate with social factors that result in especially high incidences of depression.[8] Associated with these changes and depression are medicines given for one or more diseases, such as hypnotic sedatives and narcotics, and dependency on alcohol and other addicting drugs. The withdrawal into chronic illness and increasing dependence is fostered by social isolation of the individual from the nuclear family, decreased in size and proximity, and an inadequate social support system. There is a detachment, alienation, and anomie that occurs in many which relates to an increasing incidence of suicide. In an economic sense, there are just too many older people to care for. Many are crowded into state hospitals of one kind or another; many move into proprietary nursing homes with varying levels of attention and stimulation.

Despite this, there are tasks and obligations of the aging generation toward others. Their lives and experiences can prove especially valuable to younger generations, especially those once or twice removed. Their experience and knowledge of history tend to modulate the instant fads of the present and to place them in perspective. Their reflective processes can serve society well in integrating and synthesizing the experiences of society across the boundaries of several generations. Those who survive intact become the *elders* of a society, who serve directly as well as symbolically as integrators and synthesizers of that society. Through them, neither the treasures of the past nor the hopes of the future are entirely lost.

A seemingly major problem at the present time is that of the communication gap across generations. It is difficult to estimate how widespread and general this is or how different it is from previous times. The loss of the extended family through separate domiciles, greater geographic distances, social escalation, or downward mobility can be cited as contributing to the social isolation of generations from one another in an increasingly technological culture which is more peer-oriented than intergenerationally oriented. A fuller analysis of this 20th-century change and its significance requires a greater historical distance.

The nature of medicine's work is attending to individuals in all phases of life and development. In working with patients we find that thinking about their duties, tasks, obligations, and needs on the basis of their life phase assists us in relating to them and in anticipating their reactions to illness and disability.

References

1. Holland, J.: Psychological aspects of cancer. In *Cancer Medicine*, J. F. Holland and E. Frei, III, editors. Philadelphia, Lea & Febiger, 1974.
2. Bowlby, J.: *Attachment and Loss*. Vol. I: *Attachment*. New York, Basic Books, 1969.
3. Bowlby, J.: Separation anxiety. Int. J. Psychoanal. *41:* 89, 1960.
4. Brown, F.: Childhood bereavement and subsequent psychiatric disorder. Br. J. Psychiatry *112:* 1035, 1966.
5. Lynn, D. B., Glaser, H. H., and Harrison, G. S.: Comprehensive medical care for handicapped children. III. Concepts of illness in children with rheumatic fever. Am. J. Dis. Child. *103:* 120, 1962.
6. Busse, E. W.: Biologic and sociologic changes affecting adaptation in mid and late life. Ann. Intern. Med. *75:* 115, 1971.
7. Neugarten, B. L., editor: *Middle Age and Aging: A Reader in Social Psychology*. Chicago, University of Chicago Press, 1968.
8. Kahn, R. L., Zarit, S. H., Hilbert, N. M., and Niederehe, G.: Memory complaint and impairment in the aged: The effect of depression and altered brain function. Arch. Gen. Psychiatry *32:* 1569, 1975.

PART 2

PHASES OF ILLNESS; REACTIONS TO ILLNESS; IMPRESSIONS OF ENVIRONMENTS AND SITUATIONS; TASKS OF PATIENTS AND DOCTORS

CHAPTER 7

The Illness Onset Situation

Recently, increased attention has been directed toward the illness onset situation, looking at the relationship between what has been going on in the life of the patient proximal to the experience of illness. Specifically, researchers have become concerned with the idea of stress and specific stress factors that may correlate with disease onset. This is not a new idea, but an old one packaged in new terms. Physicians have always sought causes for the occurrence of disease. More ancient cultures have sought external factors, some as high as the heavens above in terms of the wrath of an offended god. Others, such as the later Greeks, sought explanations in terms of the humors and various colored biles within the body as accounting for both physical illness and psychological indisposition.

More recently, the eminence of epidemiological thinking in the latter 19th and earlier 20th centuries directed our attention to more precise relationships of environmental factors to illness. A thinking that began with the specific relationships of microorganism to pathophysiological and pathoanatomical alterations in the body placed renewed emphasis on the external environment, albeit a more proximal one than that of the gods above or the devil below. Later thinking in this tradition required the interposition of other factors in the equation of microorganisms and diseases. The idea of vectors, intermediate hosts, and carriers was often necessary to flush out the equation. Because each of these also relied upon an environment for its existence, other organic and nonorganic factors were sought as requisite ones for the exploration of the previous microorganism → disease relationships. Attention was turned both outward to the milieu externa and inward to Claude

Bernard's *milieu interna*.[1] Both of these environments seemed cluttered with factors that facilitated or altered the completion of the disease cycle from primal initiator to consumate end. Epidemiologists continued to explore the environments of microbes, vectors, hosts, and carriers and identified such factors as climate, host and vector life cycles, crowding, famine, and war and peace as relating to the waxing and waning that is still with us despite immunizations, vector eradication, and antibiotics. A good example of this is tuberculosis, whose waxing and waning seems to have continued relentlessly over thousands of years regardless of therapeutic interventions.

Immunologists addressed the internal depths and processes of the organisms that lent susceptibility or resistance to infestation and infection, resulting in altered states of health and disease. What are the factors that lend protection from these external agents in one individual and susceptibility in another? How do they develop? At what level(s) are they best described and identified? How do the description, the identification, and the explanation lead to effective intervention by the physician?

The idea of stress as relating to the development of illness has become a major concern of modern medicine. Popular as well as academic periodicals are full of stress-related articles, frequently by the same authors writing in different styles. Fundamental questions—such as "What is stress?" and "What is illness?"—are sometimes elusively addressed and frequently self-defined; e.g., stress is defined as relating to anything that is stressful; or stress is something that results in a strain, where strain is presumably measurable in terms of a reaction. We are left with the problem of whether strain should be seen as illness when it is protective or only when it is maladaptive. The idea has led to many questions and much debate. It is an important idea if we can narrow it down to identifiable particulates. Hans Selye saw stress as an external factor eliciting a response in a specific hormonal axis, namely that of the adrenal cortical-pituitary axis, which was a first line of defense of the organism. He called this the stress adaptational syndrome.[2] Stress here is defined in terms of the reaction it provoked (strain). Later, he identified a group of pathophysiological and, subsequently, pathoanatomical states that he called diseases of adaptation. It was as though these were processes that failed to turn off after the provoking factor (stress) was no longer present. The defensive measures continued and resulted in organ system change in their own right. Perhaps there was an internal failure of a feedback mechanism, perhaps something like a motor running over time. Others, sticking with a physiological model of stress, have suggested that what is stressful or what results in stress is an ineffective or overeffective response in the organism, i.e., one in which there is not enough response to curtail the offending agent or one in which the response is more than enough, either one resulting in compromised function of the organism.[3] A physiological orientation has taken us forward in identifying finer mechanisms of atunement and adjustment at the micromolecular levels. Perhaps in time these will have correlations with more gross behavioral observations of coping and adaptation.

Many of the aggravations and provocations assaulting the human organism, the individual, are environmental in a sense other than microorganisms and climatic factors. Human adversaries are increasingly of macro proportions, created by other human beings and, sometimes, ourselves. This has led to our preoccupation with the possible relationship of disturbing interpersonal and social events and the onset of illness. When we look at the various lists of major life events compiled by Holmes and Rahe,[4] Rahe et al.,[5] Masuda and Holmes,[6] Coddington,[7] Dohrenwend and Dohrenwend,[8] Uhlenhuth and Paykel,[9] Paykel,[10] and others, we are struck with how frequently these crises involve a sense of loss in real, imminent, or fantasied terms. Loss is easy to feel and understand. We can easily identify our vexations when we lost a penny or a favorite toy in childhood or a girlfriend or boyfriend in adolescence, the death of a parent in middle age, and our own loss of health in advancing years. We can see how the loss of a job with resulting unemployment leads to a whole series of losses, including those of self-esteem and a diminished sense of self, as well as money. It is somewhat harder to consider such things as promotion, marriage, or moving to San Francisco as life crises and even more difficult to think of these as losses. Here we need to do a somersault, identifying that such passages and transitions are not without their losses as well as gains: losses of routine, rituals, relationships, and familiarity.

What then do these changes, transitions, and losses (and gains) have to do with illness? Some are not difficult to understand; for instance, when one moves from one part of the country to another, there may be different climates, water supplies, and environmental pathogens, each of which may stress the unaccustomed and unprotected individual.

A little harder to contemplate is the relationship of loss to illness. Certainly the loss of a job may alter one's life style (a newer term for a way of life or a standard of living), resulting in less food, inadequate housing, boredom, despair, and a sense of ennui.

How about the death of a spouse, child, or parent? What profound havoc does this play with our feelings—not only our thoughts but those feelings derived from, expressed, and identified in terms of physiological alterations, such as tears, cardiovascular changes, and gastrointestinal functional changes, that occur with feelings of grief, despair, sadness, pathos, emptiness, anger, and anxiety? Indeed is grief itself more than dis-ease, but rather verging on disease?[11] Does prolonged grief contribute to fixed physiological and anatomical alterations? A more difficult question might be, What occurs in the absence of grieving, i.e., grieving that is repressed, denied, neither felt nor expressed? Is the above model of grief a physiological process attempting to defend and eventually to shed the provoker and facilitators of loss, leaving the survivor to go his own way? When it is incomplete, unexpressed, and unfelt does it result in delayed processes of a more chronic and perhaps insidious nature that result in fixed alterations of physiological and anatomical processes and structures? The nature of these relationships is interesting. They constitute much of the preoccupation of psychosomatic medicine, which investigates the relationship of mind and body. Over the years, as in the rest of science, there has been an attempt to get away from the global and sometimes speculative nature of these relationships and move toward the specific, particulate, discrete factors that lend themselves to isolation in the laboratory under the stricter controls of the scientific method. There have been attempts to elaborate these factors using animal models, where organisms of the same genetic stock are subjected to various early life experiences and later stressful life experiences to see the effect of these on specific physiological systems. For example, James Henry and colleagues showed that male mice subjected to increasing crowding in a complex cage will develop hypertension and its sequelae concurrent with increasing combative behavior.[12] Female mice in the same environment will develop mammary carcinoma or cancer.[13] The hypertension of the former can be remitted by castration and reinstituted by the administration of testosterone. The incidence of mammary carcinoma in the latter can reach almost 100 per cent when the subjects are reared in isolation after early separation from mothers, until in adulthood they are placed in the complex cage where they develop carcinoma. Another example is Myron Hofer's work with rat pups separated from their mothers at a critical time period after birth.[14] These rats, when subjected to an environmental stress at a later phase of development, are subject to a higher incidence of gastric ulcers than control animals. In these experimental designs, environmental variables and biological processes are related. Partial explanation of the mechanism for the development of the latter has been possible.

So work in these areas based on clinical examination is getting more specific and scientific, using animal models. The latter help us in our thinking about human diseases. Herb Weiner has emphasized the unique combination of factors deriving from biological and psychological predisposition and combining at a single point in time with an environmental situation, resulting in illness onset and the precipitation of disease.[15] Using the model of peptic ulcer disease, he has suggested and demonstrated that a biological marker, elevated pepsinogen 1, is related to the development of ulcers in young enlisted men subjected to the duress of bootcamp. Those with high pepsinogen levels most at risk for peptic ulcer were those who on psychological testing and psychiatric evaluation demonstrated higher dependency and passivity scores and ratings.

The work goes on with a continual procession of new, intriguing findings. Hofer has recently found that the offspring of female rats subjected to early maternal separation and sustaining gastric erosions upon separation, but not so subjected themselves, had a higher incidence of gastric ulceration than controls.[16]

What is the significance of these studies to work with human beings, the men, women, and children fixed in some phase of life, living in one environment, one kind of family or another, each one specifically at risk for one kind of process or another on the basis of genetic endowment and earlier life experience? Of what significance is this to our task of finding out what is going on in the present? After all, we have the immediacy of identifying and interceding with the acute bleeding ulcer, the asthmatic attack, or the hypertensive crisis. What do we need to know about the present and accumulated life crises, the early life deprivations and separations? Of what practical importance are these in the here and now?

The answer is, not a great deal. In this situation, our task is one of reaction and action. First, we need to diagnose the acute process and stabilize the patient's condition. There will be time enough, hopefully, for the reflective work of asking questions, investigating, looking at relationships—the longer term work of the clinician-investigator. Now, we must act, replace lost fluids and blood, bring down the pressure, dilate the constricted bronchioles.

But, not infrequently, often during the midst of the extending infarct in our 45-year-old white man who is arguing about admission to the coronary care unit, we find him more concerned about his recent separation from his wife, his loss of job, the defection of a son. For him at this moment, the heart attack is of secondary importance, if acknowledged at all. His preoccupation is with the loss. He cares little about anything else, perhaps nothing. Even after he is admitted, under protest, and hooked up to monitors, intravenous fluids, and catheters, his concerns, worries, and demands are about the state of his personal affairs, children, wife, or business. He is inconsolable unless you can take a moment—while you are examining, listening to tell-tale murmurs, monitoring for arrhythmias, and estimating medication dosages—in the midst of all this to listen long enough to his anxiety, anger, and remorse that your resulting comment will be reassuring, supportive, attentive, and tuned into where he is at.

This may indeed be the emergency attention required, if only to persuade him to accept admission, to accept diagnostic and therapeutic procedures. Later, there will be time enough for more extended investigation, counseling, even referral to others. At the moment, we cannot avoid tuning in and rendering care to all aspects of the human condition. And as we detonate the urgency of the moment, our own and the patient's, we can begin the second task of the physician: to reflect upon the significance of these relationships, a man's heart attack and his life. It may lead us toward adjusting and tuning our relationship with the patient or, perhaps, toward identifying a longer term and specific therapeutic course. It may even bring us to further clinical evaluations of other patients who come to us with their myocardial infarctions. For a few, the constant and recurring observations of these relationships between illness and life events will lead toward the laboratory of experimental design where they can be tested in more imaginative and definitive detail.

References

1. Bernard, C.: *Introduction to the Study of Experimental Medicine.* New York, Dover Press, 1957.
2. Selye, H.: *Stress in Health and Disease.* Boston, Butterworths, 1976.
3. Ursin, H., Boade, E., and Levine, S.: *Psychobiology of Stress: A Study of Coping Man.* New York, Academic Press, 1978.
4. Holmes, T. H., and Rahe, R. H.: The social readjustment rating scale. J. Psychosom. Res. *11:* 213, 1967.
5. Rahe, R. H., et al.: A model for life changes and illness research. J. Psychosom. Res. *8:* 35, 1964.
6. Masuda, M., and Holmes, T. H.: Magnitude estimations of social readjustments. J. Psychosom. Res. *11:* 219, 1967.
7. Coddington, R. D.: The significance of life events as etiologic factors in the diseases of children. I. J. Psychosom. Res. *16:* 7, 1972.
8. Dohrenwend, B. S., and Dohrenwend, B. P.: *Stressful Life Events: Their Nature and Effects.* New York, John Wiley, 1974.
9. Uhlenhuth, E. H., and Paykel, E. S.: Symptom intensity and life events. Arch. Gen. Psychiatry *28:* 473, 1973.
10. Paykel, E. S.: Life stress and psychiatric disorder. In *Stressful Life Events: Their Nature and Effects,* B. S. Dohrenwend, and B. P. Dohrenwend, editors, pp. 135–150. New York, John Wiley, 1974.
11. Engel, G. L.: Is grief a disease? A challenge for medical research. Psychosom. Med. *23:* 18, 1961.
12. Henry, J. P., Meehan, J. P., and Stephens, P. M.: The use of psychosocial stimuli to induce prolonged hypertension in mice. Psychosom. Med. *29:* 408, 1967.
13. Henry, J. P., Stephens, P. M., and Watson, F. M. C.: Force breeding, social disorder and mammary tumor formation in CBA/USC mouse colonies: A pilot study. Psychosom. Med. *37:* 277, 1975.

14. Hofer, M.: Studies on how early maternal separation produces behavioral change in young rats. Psychosom. Med. *37:* 245, 1975.
15. Weiner, H.: *Psychobiology and Human Disease.* New York, Elsevier North-Holland, 1977.
16. Skolnick, N., Ackerman, S., Hofer, M., and Weiner, H.: The vertical transmission of acquired ulcer susceptibility in the rat. Science *208:* 1161, 1980.

CHAPTER 8

Environments of Illness: The Emergency Room

ON GETTING SICK AND GETTING TREATED

Following the onset of the symptoms and signs of illness, after varying intervals of time, the patient seeks the assistance of others. Sometimes this is from or at the behest of a close relative, spouse, parent, or child; at other times, it is from a colleague, the woman upstairs, a registered nurse who lives down the block, or the corner druggist. In time, with the recurrence or persistence of the symptom, the sufferer moves perceptibly closer to the state of illness, giving further acknowledgment to his altered state of feeling by seeking an appointment with his physician or with one who has been recommended to him. Depending on the severity of the symptom and the anxiety and fantasies it arouses in him, considerable delay may have resulted while he has tried one thing after another in his fervent desire to rid himself of the distress. For most individuals, to seek professional assistance means the acknowledgment of illness and the assumption of an altered social role in terms of relationships with significant others, that is, the physician, nurse, or other professional consultant. The step from health into illness is not an easy one. It demands of the individual an ability to overcome his natural psychological defenses against human frailty, vulnerability, and mortality. It also demands that the individual acknowledge and trust the beneficence and nonmaleficence of a helping other individual. One does not easily lie down for another individual, allowing the touching, palpation, probing, and percussion of the physician. Nor does one easily submit to the interrogations of another, especially the physician whose queries are apt to invade every aspect of the individual's life, an intrusion that is every much as real as that of the physical examination into every orifice of the body. To corroborate this, we merely need to hook our patient up to monitors recording blood pressure, galvanic skin resistance, cardiac rate, and other physiological processes to observe the marked fluctuations that appear in these as the patient undergoes an examination, whether it be the interview or the physical, or ourselves.

Thus, one does not move easily into illness and even less into the physician's office or the emergency room, where he is increasingly likely to go after hours. How he gets there, with whom, and whom he sees there will all affect his reactions to this early phase of illness. There is another side to the equation which is society and its agents, including the physician. Society allows, gives permission, to the individual to become ill, in the process extracting from him a prescribed behavior and granting him a temporary or permanent reprieve from his other societal tasks and obligations. The patient and the physician are expected to act in certain ways, to conform to more or less stereotyped roles of patient and doctor.[1] To the extent that both do this, society affirms and supports. Families of ill patients also have duties and obligations. Indeed, some have suggested that illness in the individual is also illness in the family.[2] There are disruptions of schedules; accommodations are made, there are shifts in the internal family dynamics and the relationships of individuals. These are not done without the emergence or repression of emotions and affects of irritation, frustration, anxiety, anger, sadness, and sometimes, perversely, pleasure. The family role frequently begins wih mother and the proverbial chicken soup, the permission to stay home, to remain in bed, to be succored with comics or television serials, to be ministered to, to have every wish granted. Siblings are expected to conceal or give up their ambivalences and to practice kindness and solicitations, and fathers are expected to step down from their proverbial business-as-usual role to offer sympathy and bear gifts. The solicitations of grandparents, aunts, and uncles bring up an encore in those communities where extended families still live proximal to one another. Likewise, the school or office is obligated to suppress its annoyance at the break in routine and the place to be filled and to remain solicitous and at least sympathetic, if not empathetic, to the absence of one of its participants.

The official sanctifier of illness is the physician, who, through her examinations, gives authenticity to the symptoms, supporting them with the identification of physical signs, and offers a name or diagnosis conforming to the legitimate medical nomenclature of the culture. At this point, or even before, the tasks of patient, doctor, and significant others are defined. The doctor's task is to investigate, inquire, examine, diagnose, and begin the process of instituting effective measures of intervention. The patient's task is to submit to extensive inquiry, examination, and extended laboratory procedures and eventually to take his medicine as recommended by the doctor. This does not happen in a vacuum. All around in the giant amphitheatre are family, friends, colleagues, other doctors, nurses, aides, students, chaplains, and social workers, all with sanctioned and significant roles in the arena of illness. These roles and their interactions with the patient are part and parcel of what illness is all about. From the times of antiquity to the present in different cultures, although extended manifoldly, the process of becoming ill, being attended, and getting well is remarkably the same, despite the uniqueness of some diagnostic and therapeutic procedures. For instance, the Japanese model of Morita therapy is an excellent example.[3] The ill patient is moved to a quiet and darkened room, confined to a tamarac of clean cool bedding with soft pillows. He is allowed only clear fluids, few visitors, and an abundance of quiet. Mother and sisters and/or nurses tip-toe in with the fluids, whisper in soft voices, and leave. The physician, with his wisdom and sanctity, examines wordlessly then gives some encouraging words and leaves. Time elapses. Fasting continues for a week or more. The patient moves from the pad to a chair, sitting up for increasing periods of time; teas of different blends are brought; soft food is added. The physician examines, nods wisely, says a few more words, withdraws. The room becomes lighter; the door to the garden is opened; birds sing; the chords of a zither are heard from without. The physician returns and asks the patient to walk with him in the garden, a few steps at a time. They walk in silence, speaking occasionally of the flowers, the tinkling waterfall, the uniformity of nature, life, death, and illness. Time heals. The food is stronger, traditional country. The patient begins to take baths, sometimes with the physician. They talk a bit more, about the world outside, about going back to the family, the home, work, society. The family comes to stay, moves in with the patient. They live the traditional life; they cook, take baths, walk in the garden. Now 4 weeks have passed, and the threads of life are picked up. The fever is cured, wholeness is restored; it is time to get back among the well. The privileges of the sick are relinquished and removed. One is reinstated into society and accepts again the responsibilities of the well.

The emergency room of the hopital is perhaps a harsher introduction to the emerging sick role of the patient and his family. It begins sometimes with the anxiety-provoking siren of the ambulance, which brings the patient into a sea of lights and a marketplace of illness brimming with other patients. The inquisition more often than not begins with routine data collection, including who is going to pay. The patient gets triaged, i.e., someone (often a student) asks a few questions, takes vital signs, temperature, blood pressure, pulse, respirations; decides on the immediacy of the problem; moves the patient into "Hold" or past "Go," into the inner sanctum of the boys and girls in white, green walls, and machines. This is a fast-action room. Chests and abdomens are laid bare; airways, intravenous lines and catheters are inserted; stethoscopes are raised; bodies are palpated and percussed; blood is taken and ordered; x-rays are taken; wards and intensive care units, if not surgeries, are alerted. The patient is "in and out" of what is going on. With what feelings? Relatives wait in the anterooms. The patient has become a patient. He is in his first environment of illness. It is, to say the least, a moving one. He will move from here to others; he will exchange these doctors for others. He begins a long parade through other environments of illness, other rooms, and other voices.

What of these, their effect on the patient's experience and behavior and the behavior of those of us who in the white light of night and the artificial light of day live our lives in these environments? What have we to learn of our patients and ourselves?

References

1. Parsons, T., and Fox, R.: Illness, therapy and the modern urban American family. J. Soc. Issues *8*: 31, 1952.
2. Anthony, E. J.: The impact of mental and physical illness on family life. Am. J. Psychiatry *127*: 138, 1970.
3. Reynolds, D. K.: *Morita Psychotherapy*. Berkeley, University of California Press, 1976.

CHAPTER 9

Environments of Illness: The Intensive Care Phase

Over the last several decades, following a rush toward private and semi-"private" rooms, the modern hospital has retreated toward the larger open wards of former times for the care of the acute patient needing special attention. The need for these became increasingly obvious. Highly knowledgeable and skilled personnel are at a premium, as is the elaborate and expensive equipment required to extend life support systems, such as respirators, cardiac monitors, defibrillators, and hypothermia units. The surveillance of such equipment and patients requires teams of individuals comprised of various expertise, working together over a 24-hour period.

These environments are not without their own iatrogenic hazards. By some they have been designated as "Enormous Rooms"[1] in which feelings of isolation, alienation, disenfranchisement and anomie develop, succored by, and in turn succoring, anxiety, despair, sadness, and disorientation. Similar to the emergency unit, they, their staffs, and patients are segregated off from the rest of the hospital units, with their slower and less episodic pace. The nurses and workers within are "high-energy types", eager and programmed to keep busy and involved, going at a rapid pace under pressure. The demands of patient care, attention to the equipment, recording, responding to slight and major alterations that occur, and keeping in constant and emergent contact with physicians and others is omnipresent. Abram[2] and Kornfeld[3] have described the toll this takes on nursing and other personnel. It is not unlike battle fatigue and stress response syndromes for some,[4] and they have suggested that periodic holidays for rest and rehabilitation be instituted for these special forces of health. Some hospitals have experimented with personnel rotations of limited duration on these units alternating with general nursing care on less intense units. An analysis of these environments and the recommendations based on them suggests the stresses and strains experienced by personnel on these units. They are constantly under pressure, almost always working at peak capacity, always faced by imminent disaster, working with equally harassed physicians and distraught relatives. It is a place of uncertainty where death is frequent and imminent, pain and discomfort are ubiquitous, and passions run high, albeit tightly controlled.

Into this, from the emergency room, from the home, from the office, from the street, the acutely and severely ill patient, the patient with chest pain, the severely injured, the tragically burned, the patient with acute renal failure, the patient with respiratory failure, the comatose, and others are rushed, frequently bypassing the emergency room. In no time, they are stripped, bared, bedded down, hooked up to monitors, catheterized, attached to life support systems. Most have never experienced such an environment. The environment is foreign, unknown. The patients are unknowing. Few sights are familiar. There are few if any windows. Lights blaze night and day. There is constant activity. Machines are more animated than the people with their gurgling, beeping, suctioning, and rasping sounds. The patients are almost all in altered states of consciousness,[5, 6] varying from the comatose to fluctuating levels of mild delirium, occasioned by their underlying illness and/or its treatment, including sedatives, analgesics, tranquilizers. Together with heightened arousal or depressed states resulting from anxiety, sadness, anger, fear generated by the illness, the experience, the treatment, and the environment, there is every reason to suspect that the patient is at risk for untoward emotional and behavioral consequences of considerable magnitude. And he is. These untoward states have been called the "intensive care unit syndrome" and have been further identified as a new dis-ease of medical progress.[7, 8] Obviously, its causes and correlates are varied, but aspects of it seem to be related not only to the patient's illness and its treatment, but also to the effect of this strange and confusing environment. There is no question that anxiety and a sense of urgency and emergence hang heavy in the air for patient and staff alike, also affecting close family members who enter and exit for 5 minutes at the bedside.

The intensive care unit syndrome may be characterized along a spectrum of severity which includes: mild to severe alterations of consciousness (i.e., from mild confusion to deep coma); specific *cognitive* deficits in the areas of attention, orientation, memory, and judgmental and abstractive ability; agitated or depressed *motor* (conative) activity often relating to the presence of delusions and/or hallucinations; and *affective* states, primarily of anxiety and depression. The identification of these before their full-blossomed states is frequently overlooked or ignored. More careful observation and testing suggest that few if any patients fail to experience at least mild alterations in these functions in the intensive care unit. Some individuals seem more at risk than others: those with previous histories of altered states, for whatever reason; those experiencing toxic and withdrawal states from alcohol and drugs; those with previous insult to the brain either from trauma or metabolic abnormalities. Medications used in treatment—analgesics, sedatives, and the hypnotic minor tranquilizers—are frequently incriminated as at least adjuvants in predisposing an individual to such states. In addition to what happens in these environments, the physical environment itself seems to play an important part in the emergency of these states. It is, as we have said, a strange one; in the words of patients, "Like nothing I had ever experienced before, like the moon, nothing familiar, weird sounds, strange machines, garbed and sometimes masked doctors and nurses, no day—no night, nothing orienting, a sense of timelessness, yet always a disaster—patients coming in, sometimes leaving dead. You begin to wonder whether it's you or them. You begin to think and then you lose yourself. You wake up and it's all strange, like when you were a child and moved to a new house. But when it's gone; you're caught in the present, and you wonder how you got here, whether you'll get out, and where you'll go."

These are not only environments of care. Frequently they are also environments of intensive research of patient care. Cassem and Hackett[9] have identified rather characteristic phases for patients' experiences during this period in coronary care units (CCU). The initial phase of 2 days is one of heightened anxiety, which correlates directly with pain and is associated with denial and impulsive acting out. Peaking around the second CCU day, the anxiety phase is followed by an increasing sense of sadness, associated with regressed characterological traits that include passivity, dependency, and plaintiveness. For some patients, this diminishes after the fourth day; for others, it is frequently a prolonged phase which extends into the convalescent phase or even after.

The intensive study of such special care environments is obviously useful in the identification of behavioral and emotional states which can be anticipated and intercepted for other patients. These studies have led to changes in the structure of these environments; the medications used; the facilitation of orienting processes (the inclusion of windows, turning off bright lights at night, the presence of clocks and calendars); and attention to stresses and strains on nurses, physicians, and families.[10] Kornfeld's work led to the direct remediation of a number of conditions. Leigh et al. suggested a CCU in which patients could benefit from both an open and enclosed environment through the use of moving partitions around the patient's bed.[11] The identification and further investigation of specific behavioral states may assist us in understanding and sorting out physiochemical correlates, thereby contributing to a larger population. For instance, the study of specific postoperative states (such as hypervigilance or catastrophic reactions) in some patients undergoing cardiac surgery may identify models for investigation at a more particulate level (see Chapter 19).

Only very general extrapolations may be made from one intensive care area to another. Each unit requires study in terms of its own uniqueness and the specificity of the multitude of factors operating therein. Respiratory care units are different from cardiac units, and the latter are different from burn units or the isolation units of intensive and aggressive cancer chemotherapy. The specificity of these environments needs identification, analysis, and further study at increasingly microscopic levels. They are excellent laboratories for the study of human behavior, where the variety of coping and adaptive processes in the face of stress and tragedy offers the behavioral scientist a richness unavailable elsewhere.[12]

Before leaving the intensive care units and our patients, we must consider the transfer phenomenon identified by Robert Klein and coworkers which appears coincident with patients' proposed transfer to the convalescent unit.[13] This is a phase marked by heightened activity associated with self-reported, observed, and physiochemical markers of anxiety in patients prior to discharge from coronary care units. Perhaps ironically, patients frequently have mixed feelings about leaving the intense and acute environment. Some patients give verbal expression to these feelings such as: "It's like being thrown out of the nest; you either fly or.... I'll be on my own out there, the nurses will be way down the corridor, the doctors will be too busy to see me." Anxiety in some patients is so high as to be associated with the occurrence of arrhythmias and, consequently, the delay in transfer. Efforts to smooth the anxiety around transfer have included preparing the patient in advance, acquainting the patient with members of the staff or the unit to which he is to be transferred, and having a nurse accompany the patient to the new unit and remain there for a limited time. Families are not dissimilar from patients in the state of their emotions throughout the hospital period, and they also need preparation and support through times of transition.

References

1. Cummings, E. E.: *The Enormous Room*. New York, Boni & Liverright, 1922.
2. Abram, H. S.: The psychiatrist, the treatment of chronic renal failure and the prolongation of life. I. Am. J. Psychiatry *124:* 1351, 1968.
3. Kornfeld, D. S.: Psychiatric problems of an intensive care unit. Med. Clin. North Am. *55:* 1353, 1971.
4. Horowitz, M. J.: *Stress Response Syndromes*. New York, Jason Aronson, 1976.
5. Engel, G. L., and Romano, J.: Delirium, a syndrome of cerebral insufficiency. J. Chronic Dis. *9:* 260, 1959.
6. Ludwig, A.: Altered states of consciousness. Arch. Gen. Psychiatry *15:* 225, 1966.
7. McKegney, F. P.: The intensive care syndrome: the definition, treatment and prevention of a new "Disease of Medical Progress." Conn. Med. *3:* 633, 1966.
8. Nahum, L. H.: Madness in the recovery room from open heart surgery or "They kept waking me up." Conn. Med. *29:* 771, 1966.
9. Cassem, N. H., and Hackett, T. P.: Psychiatric consultation in a coronary care unit. Ann. Intern. Med. *75:* 9, 1971.
10. Kornfeld, D. S., Zimberg, S., and Malm, J. R.: Psychiatric complications of open heart surgery. N. Engl. J. Med. *273:* 287, 1965.
11. Leigh, H., Hofer, M., Cooper, J., and Reiser, M. F.: A psychological comparison of patients in "open" and "closed" coronary care units. J. Psychosom. Res. *16:* 449, 1972.
12. Moos, R. H., editor: *Coping with Physical Illness*. New York, Plenum Press, 1977.
13. Klein, R. F., Kliner, V. A., Zipes, D. P., et al.: Transfer from a coronary care unit. Arch. Intern. Med. *122:* 104, 1968.

CHAPTER 10

Environments of Illness: The Convalescent Phase

In many institutions hospitalization has become a series of graduating changes or musical chairs from arenas of intensive and emergency care through those of convalescence and rehabilitation. As we have begun to observe and are still in the process of learning, these environments with their special apparatuses of diagnosis and therapy and their highly skilled personnel are ones that frequently pose additional dilemmas and burdens on the patient, who is already compromised by an acute and sometimes chronic change in health.[1] They are alien environments and as such are threatening and disorienting. In each, the tasks of patienthood are specific for that stage of illness, whether implicit to the sick role or explicitly stated in terms of the nature of the illness and the therapeutic processes. Likewise, the roles of the professional members of the health team change both perceptibly and imperceptibly in each of these environments, as the therapeutic modalities and phases of illness demand. The environments themselves reflect these tasks and develop an ambience and aura of their own like different parts of a city or even different cities. The pace changes and with it the order and routine. As we move from one to the other, we are reminded how often function dictates structure as opposed to the reverse, even though contending with the rigidity of structure frequently confronts and sometimes thwarts optimal function in these facilities.

In moving patients and staff from one of these arenas to another, we are talking essentially about *change*. We need to be mindful of both the exciting and anxiety-provoking aspects of change for us, in both our healthy and our illness states. Change suggests the unknown and the unexpected. The simple question for all of us is, "What's next? What will it be like? How will it be different from this?" These and similar questions are useful and appropriate. When spoken and answered, they serve as an orientation to the future, a way of getting a hold on it, attempting to gain some control of it, if only in one's mind. This is a positive approach, especially for the ill, if only because it indicates a future, a continuation of life, and a will to live. So the sense of imminence is not felt nor confronted without ambivalence, the hopes and fears of the unknown. Robert Klein et al. have portrayed this well in their study of the transfer phenomenon in patients about to be transferred from the coronary care unit to a convalescent unit.[2] But we shall see a similar heightened response at the time of all exits and entrances. Anticipation and preparation for these changes may be positive and forward looking when we have a clear idea of what lies ahead. It is only by a study of these successive environments—the patient and staff inhabitants and the special processes that take place within—that we can facilitate smoother transfers. Our preparation for understanding and studying these come from our own experiences of exits and entrances, our own transfers in time and space and transitions from one phase of life and experience to another. With some efforts, we may recall the first day of school, or the first week of high school, the first year of college, the first 2 years of medical school, and the early waking nightmares of internship.

The specific phenomenon of musical chairs or beds for our patients is relatively new and increasingly rapid. The need can be explained on the basis of technology and the reduction in the number of days of treatment, which relates perhaps more to the monetary basis of a technological culture than the needs of the patient. Even before, and certainly shortly after, admission to a unit, the anticipation of removal to a new unit is in the air. Thus, the patient and staff are confronted immediately with two tasks—adjustment to the present environment of care and simultaneously preparing for the next. In terms of coronary care units, many hospitals now have graduated changes from one coronary care unit to another and then to another in 1-day or 2-day stages. With adverse or optimal change, there is the possibility of moving back one step or advancing two. Again, change equals uncertainty, which may be specific for the patient. What is the meaning of the change? Objectively? What does the patient feel and think the change means? How do we communicate what we think about the change—cognitively, affectively? With change, there is always uncertainty, sometimes optimism, and sometimes despair.

The environments of illness following the acute phase of illness are of several kinds, implying different tasks. Some are relatively rapid transition zones of stabilization leading to discharge. Others are more uncertain points along a continuum of chronic illness and debilitation. For many, the convalescent phase is itself a transitional one between the acute illness and a longer rehabilitative phase. To a large extent, the convalescent phase may be seen for many patients as a pivotal one. Much of what evolves here will set the stage and patterns for future adjustment. What does not occur or evolve here may constitute the seeds of chronic maladaptation. Thus, this somewhat neglected period, occurring when much of the Sturm und Drang of immediacy is over, requires focus and emphasis in its own right.

We have already addressed the less intense, lower keyed atmosphere of convalescent units in comparison with the charged and sometimes raucous nature of acute care units. Things, at least for the hospital, are indeed more sedate, calmer. There is a suggestion that recuperation, involving stabilization, gradual resolution, and the initial steps of recovery, is the major order of business. For many patients, having made it through the battles of acute illness, convalescence is used, if not seen, as a refuge for rest and relaxation. They can let down a bit, recover from the ravages experienced in the war zone. For one thing, most express fatigue caused by the stresses and lack of sleep that inevitably occur in the intensive care unit. These patients enter a withdrawal phase, a turning away from the congratulating relatives, the satisfied physician or surgeon, and the smiling nurse. They wish to be left alone to lick their wounds, nurse their bruises, and sleep. The nurses, doctors, and relatives in the environment have other plans. A conflict ensues; misunderstanding occurs. Labels are tossed about. Consultants are called. Occult processes are suspected and investigated. More tests and more examinations are ordered. The patient is seen as lethargic, depressed, ungrateful, or all three. This is one pattern. It seems useful to use George Engel's term of conservation-withdrawal, a state which presumably is truly restorative, including psychological, physiological, and social variables.[3] It needs further identification and investigation. This stage is transitory and self-limiting.

Another group of patients is more bright eyed and bushy tailed. Invariably, they have breezed through the intensive care period with little or no untoward difficulty. They arrive on the new unit victorious and ready to pursue such a course. They are a source of inspiration to the staff, relatives, themselves, and others. Some falter. In retrospect, it would seem that some have not accepted their illness and perhaps are repressing feelings which are not consciously acknowledged. If so, the question becomes, why? Why do they need to? This is an interesting state, not frequently commented on, that requires further analysis and investigation. Those who falter commonly have such peculiar phenomena as fever of undetermined origin, gastric hemorrhages, or other symptoms or signs that defy the identification of specific etiologies. Sometimes depression ensues (see Chapter 19).

Still another group seems to be set for a long convalescence and possible chronicity. This group, in retrospect, seems to be comprised of those who have been more dependent on others. Sometimes they give a history of early and chronic illness. Relationships have been established largely around these illnesses. The most recent illness is one more factor in cementing such a relationship. In the uncertainty of the present illness and the surfacing anxiety precipitated by change, dependency and plaintiveness, not necessarily without an ingratiating quality, dominate the interaction with staff members. There are new complaints and an incessant string of little needs, which suggests a major need for reassurance and especially reassurance that the previous status quo will be regained.[4]

A fourth group can truly be likened to the victims of war, specifically of shell shock. The term "catastrophic" seems appropriate. To some extent, they fit Grinker and Speigel's[4] descriptions of amnestic reactions in soldiers under fire and some of Mardi Horowitz's stress response syndromes.[5] This process begins in the intensive care unit and may persist well into the convalescent period. Its onset is precipitous, most often occurring with the onset of illness, operation, or sometimes a few days later. The patient lies motionless, moving only his eyes. Still, he seems alert, tracking with his eyes the source of every sound. He answers direct questions monosyllabically without change in facial expression. He submits to physical examination and processes passively and without behavioral manifestations of any kind. There is sparce interaction with others, nurses, physicians, relatives. Obviously, it is disturbing for all. Repeated neurological and psychiatric examinations are performed, invariably nonspecific in their findings. Recovery otherwise seems uneventful. One morning, the physician walks in, the patient is sitting up, taking nourishment, engaging as if nothing happened. But these patients are amnesic for what has happened. They do well through discharge. Thereafter, some manifest anxiety, others show depression, and a few have symptoms best explained later as conversion. In therapy, at a critical juncture, the veil of amnesia suddenly lifts, and memory of detailed content for every event during the period of catastrophe pours forth. There is an abreaction, with hyperventilation and its sequelae. A patient recalls, "I was afraid to move, for fear I'd wake up and find myself dead."

A fifth group of patients comes and goes as if indeed nothing happened. They seem to have lived low-keyed, even hypoactive, lives without flair, routinized existences of dedicated plodding, noncomplaining, making their way, and keeping to themselves, minding their own business, and largely unminding of others. We know even less about this group. Their anonymity seems to shield them from further description and from follow-up and investigation. We wonder whether, with this further assault of life by illness, they follow a course of silent depression and further withdrawal and join the comparatively large number of people who do not make it back to active involvement in the home, work, and community.

We are considerably preoccupied with the sixth group of patients. They cannot and do not go unnoticed. Meyer Friedman and Ray Rosenman are constantly reminding us of them.[6] These include those with the hard-driving, conscientious, competitive, and aggressive behavior pattern type A. They are not without internalized anger and a timewatch agenda. Much of their behavior is a variant of obsessive and compulsive traits. Many have been successful in the business world. They continue to strive. Statistics demonstrate a high correlation with coronary artery disease and subsequent myocardial infarction. Yet to be determined is the sequence of this profile. Does the behavior pattern lead to a life style that spawns elevated cholesterol and triglyceride levels, or are these coincidental associates? What part do early development and social environment play in the evolution of these patterns and their biological correlates? Regardless of these speculations and research, we note several distinct patterns of reaction in the aftermath of the "coronary event."[7]

The first pattern is congruent with the pre-illness pattern of behavior. Characteristically, the individual pursues his illness as relentlessly as he pursued his life style. Not infrequently, he walks into the doctor's office or even to the emergency room. He minimizes his distress, lingering up to 14 hours in seeking medical attention, in the meantime explaining it away in terms of indigestion, pleurisy (an antiquated term belonging to the 19th century), or pneumonia. Belatedly he comes, even then telling the doctor, "It's not much, just some indigestion," an example of the psychological process of minimalization. Reluctantly, he allows himself to be examined, to be interviewed, to have an electrocardiogram, some blood work, perhaps a chest x-ray, all the while saying it is not much, he should be on his way, he is in a hurry, he has much to do. When asked to take it easy, slow down, give the doctor a chance, he becomes easily irritated, indeed angry, and reacts: "How would you like to be here? It isn't as though this is the only thing I have to do. Just fix me up and let me get the hell out of here." In the event of admission to the coronary care or surveillance unit, this person is frequently defiant, protesting. Once there, he challenges—"You'll see. I'll be all right. I'll be out of here tomorrow." He will be demanding, wanting to know what is being done, when it is being done, why something is not being done. He continues to minimize and deny that "anything is really wrong with me." He means the denial; he believes it, even after he is told that he has suffered a heart attack, a myocardial infarct, a coronary occlusion. He acts as if nothing has happened. If and when he does accept it, it is with minimalization: "Just a bit of heart strain, huh doc?" He demands a telephone. He has to get hold of his wife, needs to find out what's going on in his business, or about a business deal. He demands of the staff: "What's going on? When am I going to get out of here? When will this or that procedure be done? When the hell is the doc going to come back and let me go?" He is a bit of a problem for everyone. When his family comes in, there is a long list of instructions, he becomes irritated, anxious, demanding. He refuses to become ill, to accept his illness. He defies it and those who would treat it. He cannot and does not relax. Sedation paradoxically seems to aggravate him. It blurs his orientation, makes his mind "fuzzy," causes him to believe "someone is doping" him, he does not like it. He is restless, increasingly suspicious, and demanding. What do we do? How do we manage him? Confront him? Help him? It is not easy. It taxes the entire staff. Concerted and continued efforts are needed by all. As he does progress, however defiantly, he slowly accepts that he has had a heart attack, perhaps a "slight one." He adjusts in his way: "I'm not going to let a little thing like that slow me down.""I'm going to lick it, get on top of it, do it right, take off some weight, relax a bit." As he moves into the convalescent areas, he is the first to be up and about, clean shaven, abreast of the morning news, out of the room addressing the nurses, conversant with other patients and their problems, telling them how to face them, handle them, do something about them. He begins racing to get out, get back in the harness. He is a good and a bad patient. He follows orders and medication schedules well. But he is always a step ahead, always a little bit ahead of schedule, running, running, running. Some of us are cautious about whether or not jogging is for him

But there is another path for this kind of patient, perhaps a more frightening one. There is a flip-flop pattern. The same kind of man, the same angry man with clenched fist and a timewatch strapped to his wrist running against time sometimes stops, falters, and does not pick up. It is as though he gives up. What in retrospect might have been seen as underlying traits of dependency and passivity emerge, breaking through the layered defenses and patterns of aggressivity, reactivity, and anger. And this side of the man does give up, withdraw, give in, and retreat. And he usually does not come back. When he does, it is to the same pattern but in a different course. He will change, change jobs, wives, life style. But he will pursue the new ones with the same relentlessness. This is an exception and a different pattern of denial. The course for this second pattern, the given-up pattern, rapidly becomes permanent. The individual becomes housebound, often exchanging roles with his spouse. He is the subject of frequent anginal attacks, brought on by the least exertion, the slightest vexation or aggravation, the slightest pressure. His most frequent port of call is to the physician's office, from which he leaves with yet new prescriptions—for pain, anxiety, sleep, indigestion, or this or that. He is inconsolable for himself, his grief, his fear, his life. He always has a new symptom or set of symptoms: hyperventilation, with its rapid, sometimes deep, respirations or chronic sighing utterances, its light headedness, weakness, and tingling in the extremities and occasional spasms in the muscles of the hands and feet secondary to changes in CO_2 and its related effects on calcium concentrations in the serum. This man does not seem to launch a counterattack, to come back, to assert old claims, to reassert old authority. To what extent this pattern contributes to the staggering rolls of chronic morbidity in postmyocardial infarction patients, we do not know. It is an area for further study.[8]

There are, no doubt, other patterns of reactivity and response, for there are many people and many variants. Not everyone with coronary artery disease can be described as behavior pattern type A, and not every individual with this behavior pattern is a potential victim of coronary artery disease. We have yet to identify and isolate the more particulate factors and mechanisms in these relationships. Nevertheless, these identifications provide a point of orientation for the clinician and the beginning investigator. They lead us to seek out in greater detail the illness onset situation, what has been going on, and they help us in identifying something about this individual—what makes him tick, run (if you would). It also leads us to wonder and observe how these will affect his illness, his behavior during illness, and his readjustment afterwards. These observations become handles by which we try to get hold of the patient, get a grasp of what is before us in our ministrations to his needs and recuperation.

In the convalescent period, then, the patterns of behavior and personality of the patient emerge more clearly, can be identified and even measured, in order to assess to what they affect both convalescence and subsequent rehabilitation. Such identification and objectification is the task of the staff, the doctor, nurse, social worker, and chaplain and their respective students. There is both time and room to do it in these less acute although similarly busy and intense environments. When these are made and optimally conveyed to the individual and his family, the stage is set for the cooperative tasks of convalescence and rehabilitation.

Grieving

There are other tasks for staff, patient, and family during the convalescent period. After the "settling down" period, with its infrequent initial phase of conservation and withdrawal, much of the rest of convalescence may be seen as a period of grieving and, through it, of coming to terms with what has occurred. As such, convalescence, with its grieving process, is a bridge from the past into the future, from what has been to what may be. Grieving is such an important task of illness that many of us offer the hypothesis that, "He who does not grieve is doomed to experience prolonged suffering and perhaps further illness and disease." Grieving has specific stages that follow one another. When this sequence is delayed or aborted, we identify aberrant grieving processes that over the years have received specific labels. These have their own behavioral, psychological, biological and social correlates.

Acute grieving may be viewed as a normal course of convalescence. Although it begins during the acute phase of illness, the major part of grieving usually takes place during convalescence. As such, the convalescence is to a large extent synonymous with a grieving state. Grieving has biological, social, and psychological components that interrelate with one another. These can be broken down into four discrete stages, although each overlaps with the preceding and following ones. Central to the concept of grieving is its ebb and flow nature. Like the ocean it comes in waves, torrential and overwhelming, engulfing and nearly drowning its victim, receding, pulling away, leaving its subject exhausted and empty, only to return in full force, retreating once again, and, like the ocean in the storm, slowly relinquishing its fury, in this case over a period of weeks and months. Beyond these generalizations, grieving is a very private and individual process, for it relates to a specific lost object whose meaning is always intimately tied up with the very self of the individual. Grieving is always a process that relates to self-loss. It is as if big hunks of the ego have been gorged out. The repair work, while immediate for survival, is also lengthy in terms of full or near restitution.

As we think about the grief process in the ensuing discussion, we will begin to identify its similarity with the psychotherapeutic process. Indeed, there are some who would say that it is synonymous with brief psychotherapy and that it is essential if the individual is to go on to make the adjustments demanded by full rehabilitation and restoration.

The first phase of grieving begins in the acute care units and facilities. As we have seen, this first phase is frequently manifested by denial of illness, anxiety provoked by illness, or consequences of illness. In this setting, under the duress of a progressing process, the amount of anxiety correlates directly with the intensity of discomfort, most usually pain.[9] Components of primal anxiety (death) are no doubt mixed with those of anxiety more specifically relating to cognitive awareness of the illness. The defenses available to the individual with overwhelming anxiety are frequently those which we view as the more primitive ones, denial and sometimes introjection. Denial serves a number of purposes. It tends to keep overwhelming and annihilating anxiety at bay. When successful, it is possible, that it may to some extent dampen autonomic arousal, a frequent correlate of anxiety, although this requires further investigation. Such denial also has negative consequences, especially when it leads to a patient's refusal to admit that he is ill, delays his seeking medical attention,[10] causes him to refuse treatment for illness, and/or causes him to refuse to acknowledge illness or its consequences, despite his presence in the intensive care unit. Such manifestations of denial are obviously threatening to the care of the patient and disruptive to the routines of nurses, physicians, and other patients in the environment. This is even more so when denial involves such physical behavior as walking out of the unit, struggling with the medical staff when they attempt to administer medications, and other demonstrable and sometimes vociferous protests. Obviously, this approaches a near emergency and demands as immediate a resolution as possible. Realizing that the generating force of this behavior and denial is *anxiety* leads us to relate to the patient on this basis, even in the absence of his own acknowledgement. Obviously, this begins with attempts at *reassurance*, that things will be all right, that he will be taken care of. It will also include a straightforward simple *explanation* of what has happened and what is and will be done. When this can be delegated to one person, who will stay close to the patient and repeat this frequently, the behavior identified above is soon detonated. Instructions may need to be delivered firmly and very specific limits set in terms of what behavior will not be tolerated. By giving structure, such an approach brings with it reassurance and gains the patient's more rational acceptance of care. This process dispels uncertainty by identifying a course that takes both patient and caretaker into the future, however far. Later, in the care of the patient, we will need to reassess and reapproach his anxiety.

For the survivor, and not all individuals in these acute care units survive, anxiety reaches a peak by the second or third day and diminishes relatively rapidly over the ensuing intensive care unit course. It is followed by a period of sadness, which is usually a quiescent state in comparison to the hyperalert arousal state of anxiety. Sadness is defended against and manifested by the emergence of defenses characteristic of the individual's personality. In this stage, these may include passivity, dependency, plaintiveness, withdrawal, or attempts to overcome these by manifestations of independence, verbal assertiveness, and hyperactivity. Whatever defenses are used, the underlying feeling state is one of sadness. Many patients express this as "lying low, waiting to see what will happen, less fearful, not fighting so hard, but still apprehensive of the future, and beginning to be preoccupied about what changes the future will bring." Such expressions of feelings can be brought out relatively easily at this stage. When it is done, patients indicate that it is beneficial. However, the intensive care unit environment is seldom conducive to this activity, and most of this intervention is carried out, if at all, in the convalescent units.

Following admission to the convalescent unit and the transitional periods of transference anxiety and "conservation-withdrawal," the somewhat abortive grief processes identified above that occur in intensive care units are often spontaneously reopened. When they are not, it behooves the staff to become engaged in this task. This is not a task taken lightly. Few are emotionally able to engage in this kind of work. Furthermore, it is a task that takes time and is usually not admissible on time charts of nurses or the professional billing of physicians. It is also not a procedure done once over lightly but a process that requires continuity throughout the convalescent period. Most of all, the overt continuation of the grieving process requires the permission of the nursing and physician staff. When this is not done, grieving is likely to be ignored or outwardly suppressed by the professional staff, thus making patients unable and/or guilty about acknowldging to others or themselves the very intense feelings they have about being ill. During this time, a major function of the attending staff, aides, students, nurses, social workers, chaplain, and physicians is to provide an ambience that permits the patient to grieve.

The *initial stage of this grieving process* is one of helping the patient overcome the primitive defenses used against the intense feelings that the conscious fact of illness and the less than conscious feelings of annihilation have necessitated. Allowing the patient, by giving him permission, to express those feelings, frequently negative, about his illness and himself is the first step. Anger, anxiety, sadness, and shame are the basic ones. Once out, once expressed several times over, the patient, working in short periods with one who will permit and listen, is able to move on, slowly, to trying out other more sophisticated defensive stances or postures. This recapitulation of ontological feeling and defense states that are occasioned by illness assists the individual in a psychological restoration concurrent with a physical recovery.

These psychological processes occur hand in hand with physiological processes and are not independent of the interactions occurring with staff, family, and other patients in the marketplace of convalescence, the unit. Physiological factors will necessarily have to be taken into account in assisting the patient in reworking his self-view in the face of changed health status. The belief that the patient is in no condition to come to terms with these emotions and their physiological counterparts is relatively common, but it is generally not well founded. However, when marked physiological events are concurrent with the expression of intense emotions, it is prudent to proceed in this therapeutic process more slowly than one otherwise might. It is more likely, although equally difficult to demonstrate, that giving the patient an opportunity to work out these feelings verbally will prevent them from affecting untoward physiological processes through more subtle means. Unfortunately, there is not black and white, either-or, conclusive evidence one way or the other. Perhaps more important is the clinical experience that patients sometimes spontaneously carry through the stages of grief during this period without untoward event. They are more likely to do so in those environments that permit and encourage such a process. It is important to emphasize that this is self-work. Too often, the patient's anxieties and preoccupation may be directed at current and preexisting home and work problems, thereby effectively averting coming to terms with the more immediate near or partial loss of self. Some of the former problems may have to be addressed with suitable members of the staff, if the patient is to get on with the *self*-grieving process that convalescence demands and is. The former problems have been discussed in our considerations of the illness onset situation and stress and illness. The latter, except to the extent they are critical to the patient's convalescence, need to be delayed for consideration and resolution until the convalescent period is over. To this extent, the convalescent period represents a time of protection from the rigors of the external environments of life: home, work, the marketplace of social commerce. These will need to be addressed in the coping and adaptive processes of rehabilitation.

Not until emotions have been precipitated several times over in each of our work sessions can we begin to enter into an alliance with the patient, addressing the various defenses used to come to terms with the latent conflicts generated and the real problems occasioned by his illness. This *second stage of grieving* and therapy may be seen as one of reviewing with the patient the appropriateness and adaptiveness of different defensive stages. In another way, we might view this state as one of progressing from more primitive to more sophisticated defenses. This assumes that illness and the circumstances under which diagnosis, treatment, and care are given usually are associated with a regression in defensive patterns from the more sophisticated to the more primitive.

As we have discussed, this regression is adaptive and is encouraged by most systems of medical care. It is seen as a regression in the service of the ego,[11] thereby allowing the individual to submit to care. The convalescent stage is a retreat from a stage of submission to one of ascending autonomy. As such, the individual moves up the slippery slopes of psychological sophistication and social reinstatement, not without some faltering and slipping. To a large extent, the hierarchy of defenses will be seen very much in the patterns described by Anna Freud in *The Ego and Mechanisms of Defense*.[12] The more primitive defenses of introjection and denial will give way to those of projection reversal, and displacement of affect; rationalization and intellectualization; and, in some cases, sublimation, which is most frequently attained, when it is, during the rehabilitative phase of illness. Closer to reality at this stage is the resumption of those defensive postures characteristic of the individual's premorbid personality (see Chapter 4). Ascension to more sophisticated defensive patterns than previously attained is more likely to occur during the rehabilitative phase, when more learning and growth are likely to occur. But for the present, the defensive stage of grieving is a cooperative one by a physician, nurse, or other counselor of reviewing the adaptiveness and appropriateness of the patient's defenses in light of his or her daily activities, adjustment, and progress. Central to this view of ascension and striving is its sense of future. These are not done without the real and often subtle processes of persuasion that are intrinsic to all healing processes.[13] This *third grieving phase* can be easily facilitated with patients by inquiries into sleep patterns and dreams. Although these vary from individual to individual and from patient to patient, at least among cardiovascular patients there frequently occur what we see as "recovery dreams." Women frequently dream of having a baby; men dream of sexual intercourse. In other instances, when anxiety and depression are prominent, dreams of deaths or funerals are common.

The *fourth phase of grieving*, although initiated during the convalescent period, takes place largely during the rehabilitative phase occurring in other institutional environments, the hospital, the home, the office, and the social marketplace. Preparation for some of the latter environments does occur during the convalescent phase, including group and social processes that occur during this time.

As we have seen above, the stages of grief described as occurring during the convalescent stage are dependent upon the nursing and medical staffs for facilitation. These persons need to be attentive and attuned to the patient's emotion, available and ready to listen and give permission to the patient to talk and ventilate feelings, especially those of unpleasure. This is never easy. All too often we jump in with soothing comments and our own rationalizations, which essentially shut off the patient's expression. In these situations, our task is to keep quiet except for a gentle facilitation, usually an expression of attentiveness, sometimes a word or two, such as "Go on"; "Tell me more"; "That is tough." As this process is repeated, it is then possible to move into an examination of the patient's defenses, sorting out those that are appropriate from those that are not in the patient's attempted accommodation to his illness. This alliance between a staff member and the patient frequently lasts beyond the hospital and the convalescent period. Patients and sometimes their families, who are also in a state of grieving, continue to relate to members of the convalescent team who have worked with them during the grief process.[14] Although these contacts are often spontaneous, unscheduled, and minimally structured, they frequently evolve into genuine brief therapy sessions that address aspects of coping and adaptation.

A major function of the convalescent period is just that, convalescence. Over the years, partly because of improved diagnostic and therapeutic processes, this phase of illness has been diminished in duration. As a consequence, considerably less of the psychosocial aspects of convalescence occurs during this official period. Therefore, some of the tasks of convalescence remain incomplete, resulting in either abortive convalescence or a delayed convalescence, which either needs to be reopened or continued during subsequent phases of recovery and restitution. Grieving continues beyond the average 5 to 7 days of inpatient convalescence.

Group Therapy Processes

Measures other than the individual brief psychotherapeutic processes identified above have been suggested and instituted to facilitate some of the tasks of convalescence that cannot be completed in individual relationships because of limited time and personnel. Usually, these extension processes have been developed for patients recovering from similar illnesses. Group experiences for postmyocardial infarction patients and their spouses are now quite common.[15] These programs are organized by psychiatric nurses, social workers, chaplains, and psychiatrists. Patients and their spouses are brought together in a large room. The discussion is opened by the leader, who is usually assisted by a cotherapist. Problems are solicited from patients and spouses. The elicitation of these problems is facilitated by the therapists' knowledge of the common problems experienced by this group of patients. Available to the leaders are dietitians, vocational counselors, physicians, psychiatrists, social workers, chaplains, nurses, psychologists, physiotherapists, and others who can come to a session for didactic explanations regarding diet, return to work, medication, anxiety and depression, social resources, community and pastoral counseling, home nursing procedures, specific evaluation and testing measures, and rehabilitative exercises. Through this combination of specific didactic instruction and an opportunity to bring up common anxieties, fears, concerns, and reactions in a group situation, a bonding occurs that allows individuals to become members of a group. Such a group identification gives the patient and his family conviction that they are not in it alone and that they can identify and benefit from this identification with others.

Again, the timing and the content of these group sessions will depend upon the patient group and its specific problems, as well as available resources, especially time and personnel. Some may begin earlier in the course of treatment than others. Each will need to identify and experiment with ways of approaching specific problems. Many will combine a group approach with individual psychotherapy. Some will be more didactic and instructional than others. All may require the development of evaluation processes to measure costs and benefits.

Perhaps above all, the effectiveness of such group sessions serves to prepare the patient and his family for the next transitions to home and work. These, as we shall see, are not easy transitions and like all transitions are periods of uncertainty that engender anxiety, fear, and sadness, not unlike all comings and goings, entrances and exits.

References

1. Solzhenitsyn, A.: *The Cancer Ward.* Baltimore, Penguin Books, 1972.
2. Klein, R. F., Kliner, V. A., Zipes, D. P., et al.: Transfer from a coronary care unit. Arch. Intern. Med. *122:* 104, 1968.
3. Engel, G. L.: *Psychological Development in Health and Disease.* Philadelphia, W. B. Saunders, 1962.
4. Grinker, R., and Speigel, J.: *Men under Stress.* New York, Irvington Press, 1978.
5. Horowitz, M. J.: *Stress Response Syndromes.* New York, Jason Aronson, 1976.
6. Friedman, M., and Rosenman, R. H.: Overt behavior pattern in coronary disease: Detection of overt behavior pattern A in patients with coronary disease by a new psychophysiological procedure. J. A. M. A. *173:* 1320, 1960.
7. Halberstam, M., and Lesher, S.: *A Coronary Event.* New York, Popular Library, 1978.
8. Croog, S. H., and Levine, S.: Social status and subjective perceptions of 250 men after myocardial infarction. Public Health Rep. *84:* 989, 1969.
9. Cassem, N. H., and Hackett, T. P.: Psychiatric consultation in a coronary care unit. Ann. Intern. Med. *75:* 9, 1971.
10. Olin, H. S., and Hackett, T. P.: The denial of chest pain in 32 patients with acute myocardial infarction. J. A. M. A. *190:* 977, 1964.
11. Gill, M., and Brennan, M.: *Hypnosis and Related States.* New York, International Universities Press, 1959.
12. Freud, A.: The ego and mechanisms of defense. In *The Writings of Anna Freud,* revised edition, vol. 2, New York, International Universities Press, 1966.

13. Frank, J. D.: *Persuasion and Healing*. Baltimore, Johns Hopkins University Press, 1973.
14. Friedman, S. B., Mason, J. W., and Hamburg, D. A.: Urinary 17-hydroxycorticosteroid levels in parents of children with neoplastic disease: A study of chronic psychological stress. Psychosom. Med. *25:* 364, 1963.
15. Bilodeau, C. B., and Hackett, T. P.: Issues raised in a group setting by patients recovering from myocardial infarction. Am. J. Psychiatry *128:* 105, 1971.

CHAPTER 11

Environments of Illness: The Rehabilitation Phase

The rehabilitative phase of illness occurs after the phase of convalescence. To some extent, the terminal and incompleted tasks of convalescence become the initial ones of rehabilitation. Similar to the initial phases of the other environments of illness is a transitional period in which the anticipation and attendant emotions of impending change are transformed into the unanticipated facts of reality in the new environment.

The environments of rehabilitation are considerably different from those of the acute and convalescent units of the general hospital. They have a different ethos. They differ in appearance, ambience, pace, smell, and physical structure. The personnel are different. Perhaps they walk less softly and strut with greater vigor and certainty. There is less of a sense of urgency and emergency and more one of schedules, routines, and structured and deliberate activity. The units are separate and segregated from the central marketplace of medicine. Their organization is different, and the inhabitants wear different costumes and come from different therapeutic traditions and orientations. Most often, the predominant sense is that of purposeful, structured, vigorous, organized activity. Of course, within the genre of rehabilitation centers and facilities, there are differences, depending upon the therapeutic services rendered. Those primarily oriented toward orthopaedic problems are considerably different from those attending chronic respiratory problems, and the latter are different from the reconstructive and plastic orientations of the later stages of burn treatment. However, in contrast to the special and the convalescent units, there is usually a greater staff mix. The traditional doctor-nurse team is greatly augmented to include physical and occupational therapists, vocational and rehabilitation counselors, social workers, chaplains, and frequently volunteer lay persons who assist in the activity programs. More often than not, these are extended care units providing an interlude sometimes of considerable length, between acute hospitalization and home. Hence, they become a kind of retreat and even temporary home for some. Even after discharge, many will return as outpatients to continue specific rehabilitative treatment or therapy. So there is also a bit of a sense of chronicity that prevails, which is in contrast to the sense of directed activity that is manifested. The appearances of these places are also different. There is a new assortment of gadgets, machines, instruments. There are great stainless steel tubs for soaking and whirlpool baths, electric machines for thermal therapy, ultrasound machines for shaking loose painful and frozen joints. There are parallel bars, jump ropes, obstacle courses, and other gymnastic equipment, so they are partly gyms. But they are also largely schoolrooms for learning and relearning gross and fine motor skills. Arts and crafts are prominent. There are specially designed bathrooms, kitchens, and other rooms to help the disabled individual develop negotiable skills in altered environments accommodative to specific impairments. There may be laboratories for behavioral procedures: biofeedback and other kinds of modification for patients with cardiac arrhythmias, essential hypertension, obesity. There are rooms for didactic instruction, group therapy, psychodrama, Alcoholics Anonymous meetings, and Weight Watchers meetings and special audiovisual centers for learning and therapy. Some institutes have simulated factory and office environments in which to instruct patient rehabilitation. We speak of these environments as ones of rehabilitation, where the major tasks are coping and adaptation. The questions are raised: Coping with what? Adaptation to what? What are these general terms? What do they mean? How general, how specific are they? What are the processes involved? Where do they begin? Where do they end?

The transition from the convalescent unit of the acute and general hospital to the rehabilitation hospital is abrupt and, in many ways, discontinuous. The more passive physical care of convalescence becomes exhortative, active, vigorous care of rehabilitation. It is time to get on with the show. The past has occurred; the future is at hand; it is time to move. The orientation is largely directed at the concrete, rather than the abstract. This is translated into and measured by changes in behavior through learning, accomplishment, attainment, progress. For the most part, these represent motor behavior: walking, talking, using hands and fingers, getting in and out of bed, bathing, using bathroom facilities, using prostheses of one kind or another, hearing, feeling, eating, telephoning. To assist in the accomplishment of these objectives are trained individuals with specific skills, whose orientation is specifically goal directed, measured on graphs and charts. To a large extent, they are purposeful, oriented to single objectives, a step at a time, with another step to follow until attainment of that objective is maximum. Then, it is on to the next. Oftentimes, the patient is scooped up and carried on this wave of purposefulness, vigor, and direction. At other times, it can be overwhelming, even defeating. The tempo may have to be modulated, scaled back, objectives reduced or extended over a longer time period.

During all this, there is still the business of unfinished grieving. Added to it are the lesser, although real, losses associated with the previous environment and the uncertainty of the present one. The change of pace, however vigorous, is disconcerting. There are few corners to which one can retreat. The family and friends are carried along in the tide of optimism, bathed in the belief that all is being done, hoping against hope that total rehabilitation will occur. The patient—once again dislodged, displaced, under the bright lights and stainless steel of rehabilitation—has mixed sentiments, ambivalence, uncertainty, and lack of clarity. The tasks of grieving remain incomplete, even while active and assertive coping becomes the order of the day. The message is of the future, not the past. This is hardly an environment for grieving. Those who would assist and extend this grieving work have part-time positions. Their work is also action directed. They are called to assist with specific problems phrased in such terms as lack of motivation, loss of will power, uncooperative, inability to concentrate, doesn't seem to care, has no interest, unable to learn, is withdrawn, doesn't participate, doesn't seem to understand, can't get a grasp of it, seems to have just given up, has no spirit, is negative, gets into conflict with the staff, always wants to do something else. This is in contrast to the "good guys," who are less often seen and studied, with whom the former are compared. The former are unlike these "good" patients who can't wait to get started; are always ahead of the game; are cheerful and energetic; are difficult to keep up with; are going too fast; have only one objective; are constantly busy, engaged, involved, and highly competitive; are natural leaders brimming over with energy; are never ornery or out of sorts; learn well; and make fine progress.

What are the differences? How can we sort these out? Get at the particulate? The specific variable underlying them? Needless to say, some relate to the degree of disability, but that is not enough. Next, we explain it on the basis of personality, and that helps. But then, we note that frequently there is a flip-flop, either way. In some, it is as though the soft underbelly of assertive, vigorous coping comes bottoms up, exposing almost unlimited dependency and passivity. In others, the reverse occurs, and they suddenly and miraculously do better in the face of adversity. In the one case, the end, there is nothing left, it is all too much; in the other, now there is something, suddenly some kind of meaning has been grasped, a challenge, a focus, something to conquer. Still, the specific factors elude us. Personality and behavior patterns, even with their potential for flip-flop, does not seem specific enough. We turn toward environments. What are the stimuli from without? The environments? Who are the significant others? Where are they? What do they represent? What has this got to do with the capacity for attachment and reciprocity? What other social resources, supports? Where, who are the friends, associates, families? What of material factors, beginning with money, employment, insurance, collateral? These are important, perhaps an ingredient, but not all. We grasp; we grasp for words: "faith," "hope." These are also important, but are they enough? Determination, willfulness, motivation, and performance are the ideographic factors identified by Ursin et al. in their study of paratroopers.[1] They are certainly something. How are they measured? How are they explained? How do they relate to anger, meanness? What? But we have all heard these expressions used: "too mean to die," "those who fight survive longer." We are reminded of Robert Ader's animals, handled before weaning, demonstrating greater susceptibility to disease than nonmanipulated ones.[2] Is there something in baring the teeth, rather than turning the other cheek? But this is not quite it, not quite the vital difference. We grope in the murky past, go back to ancestors, survivors, explorers, pioneers. Are there familial traits, adaptive genes, epigenetically transmitted factors, or a combination? Do they relate to a peculiar combination of childhood experiences, adverse as well as growth facilitating challenges and provocations for differential growth? What of environmental influences and their timing? How do these fit into the formula? How do they explain? How do we get at the specific factors within each? We return to the present. We settle for less, littler pieces, those that move us millimeters rather than kilometers. We note different patterns of responses, responsivity, arousal, and alertness. We explore the bases of these patterns. With what are they correlated—biological factors, biological traits, personality again; specific psychological mechanisms, the environment? Some can be investigated, some correlated, some used in explanation. Even more important, those isolated can be tested in experimental design.

So these environments of rehabilitation become laboratories of study, observation, and analysis for the development of carefully worded hypotheses that are further explored through deliberately constructed experiments, leading to observations which support or fail to support the hypotheses. Then we begin again, go on to the next link and the next, retreat, develop a new tack, pursue. What are the discrete variables that make a difference? If all patients are equally ill, why do some seem more so than others? Why do some get better and some worsen? We go back to Cluff et al.'s study of Johns Hopkins patients psychologically tested and physically and immunologically examined prior to an impending Asian flu endemic.[3] Were those with the more positive psychopathological test scores more vulnerable, less able to handle the symptoms and signs of the viral infection than those who did not show susceptibility or did not demonstrate the same pattern of illness behavior, even with evidence of infection? What of the social variables? We are on the surface of our investigations in this area of coping and adaptation. Our terms need more precise definition. We need to study specific environments, disease processes, and individuals in and for specific detail. These are environments still on the frontier, awaiting explorers and pioneers who will work at all levels of analysis from the macro to the micro.

Grieving processes continue. They take place among other patients with similar and dissimilar dysfunctions and losses. In these environments of rehabilitation, the losses are brought out, laid bare, examined, measured, and objectified, not only for the individual but before the group, the therapists, the teachers of rehabilitation. There is no coverup. Confrontation is the name of the game: these are the facts, this is what can be done, this is what cannot be done. Let us get on with it. Where one is in the process of grieving will affect how one gets on with rehabilitation. Wounds still have to be licked, cultivated, and perhaps used to obtain attention, position, or advantage. Denial of disability both emotionally and factually may lead to failure to participate and cooperate as actively as one could or should. In this situation, more active grieving may be the physician's order. Let us go back, review the event, open it up, recount the losses, indulge in the feelings about these losses, cry, get angry, feel it all all over again. Once a day, three times a day, once every week. Feel it! Express! Now, let us take a look at how well you are doing. Look, when you set your mind, grind your teeth, really tell yourself that you are going to do it, you will. Not yet? Well, let us do the first part of it; that's good. Now the next. Remember, how you learned to ride a bike—one step at a time, a few falls, perhaps a cry, and then suddenly you were off down the block, and it was not too much longer before "no hands."

Grieving processes demand frequent backing up if they are to continue to move forward. There is a need for many to return to the scene of the crime to review, to recount. Sometimes help and reminders are in order. With greater repression and denial, a good detective is needed, someone who can help move the patient back, rediscover the scene, the facts, the recovery feelings, and bring them out in the open for expression and examination. How successful was the coverup anyway? What is the need for it now? What were its consequences? What are the consequences of it now? Moving to and fro—the past, the present. Now, for the future. It is time for new approaches. With all that expression, the old defenses are not all that necessary. Perhaps they are useful once in a while, when in the doldrums, but not now. What is the problem now? Is it the failure to see any change or gain? Is this fact or feeling? Let us look at it. Is the feeling preventing the fact or vice versa? Maybe we are all pushing too hard and need to slow down and take one step at a time, smaller steps. That will get us further. Remember, we are working together. Other memories, too, keep crowding in and getting in the way. What if? That is so, but . . . .

Grieving also involves looking at the future, perhaps transiently feeling a void, certainly an expansiveness of uncertainty, occasionally a surrealistic landscape. The future looms eternal. Grieving begins to fill that up, first sparsely, frequently not very attractively, oftentimes with the relics of the past and sometimes with mere, but foreboding, shadows. Let us look again. This *is* looking forward, anticipation, expectation, the projection of one into a future. Grieving is providing a bridge from here to there, not without a few defensive barricades along the way, hurdles that may block or be jumped. Grieving begins to fill up that future with symbols of light as well as dark. Throughout this is the concrete pain and despair of rehabilitation. It moves so slow. It takes so long. It gets in the way of other things. It is monotonous. It is isolating. It requires so much perseverance, stamina, belief, commitment. The path is not always clear. What will be the end point? With what degree of satisfaction? How will we know? Will we have to keep this up forever?

Grieving involves learning. In a sense, it is a learning to cope with loss and feelings about loss. Coping involves learning, learning of new things, especially about the self and feelings about the self, a growing in self-awareness, and a discovery of other aspects of the self. Grieving involves growing. Coping leads to a new level of adaptation to life, physically, emotionally and socially. It is hard—grieving, learning, growing, feeling, adaptation.[4, 5]

References

1. Ursin, H., Boade, E., and Levine, S.: *Psychobiology of Stress: A Study of Coping Man.* New York, Academic Press, 1978.
2. Ader, R.: The effects of early life experiences on developmental processes and susceptibility to disease in animals. In *Minnesota Symposium on Child Psychology*, J. P. Hill, editor. Minneapolis, University of Minnesota Press, 1970.

3. Cluff, L. E., Canter, A., and Imboden, J. B.: Asian influenza. Arch. Intern. Med. *117*: 159, 1966
4. Moos, R. editor: *Human Adaptation: Coping with Life Stress.* New York, Lexington Books, 1976
5. Coehlo, G. V., Hamburg, D. A., and Adams, J. E.: *Coping and Adaptation.* New York, Basic Books, 1974

CHAPTER 12

On the Use of Drugs

Since antiquity, the use of drugs has constituted an integral part of medicine and the priest-doctor-patient relationship, the tangible embodiment of giving. Perhaps derivative and at least similar to the communion service, there is, in the giving of a pill, the tangible expression of giving help and assistance. The pill is a gift. It is life supporting and health giving. It is a promise, one cementing the relationship and the expectation of its continuation in the future, one of availability, caring, and expectation. In the latter sense, gifts do not come without attachments, again expectations. The giver expects specific behavior of the given. He will take the pill as prescribed. If he does so, if he follows the doctor's orders, if he obeys, there is the promise that he will get better, feel good, be returned to health and function. So the exchange of the pill is a complex business. It is an exchange of something much larger than the size of a pea. It comes with its own larger pod or aura, rooted in the traditions of the past and serving as a bridge to the future. The exchange is sanctimonious and solemn. There is a ritual: a physician seated at her desk; the prescription pad bearing her name open; the patient sitting nearby; the doctor saying that she is going to give him something that will help; that it is important that he follow instructions carefully; that the pill is for something very specific and must be taken regularly; that if he has any question, do not hesitate to call; that the pill will need to be taken so long; that there will then be time for reevaluation; that there may be some risk, however slight or infrequent; that if he should experience this or that not to hesitate to call. All of this implies and imposes a heavy burden of expectation and duty on the part of the patient. In turn, if the patient obeys, follows the rules, the physician's expectations of recovery and good health will be fulfilled. In a sense, this formal presentation of a prescription has some of the aspects of a Japanese tea ceremony, originally symbolizing the obeisance of business associates to a mighty merchant or lord through the gift of tea and tokens of ginger or cakes binding the participants together, one protecting, the other supporting and following.

There are many elements in this exchange. Those already noted—of promise and expectation, of giving and receiving, of instructing, of following, of caring and accepting care—and others are outside the essential active ingredients of the pharmacopeia. They are implicit in the exchange. How the exchange is made will affect the success of the transaction. And there are many variations in such transactions: Maybe this will be of some help. Perhaps we had better try something else. Some of my patients do well on this. If you do as I say, you will feel better. It is important that you follow these orders exactly. If this does not help (or do any good), I want to know. With this, you should be over this (better) in short order. I think you will find this helpful. Maybe this will help. I want you to take this. I am giving you this because I expect it do this on the basis of its action on that; and, if this works, then you will be feeling better. Well, that is all there is to it. Take this, what I have written down, and get on your way. This will make you feel better; if it does not work, let me know. You will be all right; just take this. I do not know if this will help, but let us give it a try. If this does not work in a day or two, give me a call.

There are common elements in these exchanges, but there are many variations. All indicate a relationship. All obviously include an exchange and an expectation. Some are solemnly presented. Others are casually tossed out. Some are given with great assurance, practically a guarantee, and others with a sense that, if not completely satisfied, return the unused portion for a refund. Some are presented with nonchalance, others cavalierly, if not this, then that. Today, many patients are solemnly presented with a long list of sobering contraindications and warnings of side effects: "I have to tell you this, although it is unlikely to happen. You may get very depressed, develop a rash, experience light headedness, have some difficulty with your thinking. These are infrequent, but they do happen. Maybe you should talk this over with your husband." So there occurs a tailoring of the prescribing process that is an interfunction of both the physician's and patient's personalities. On the one hand, the physician's sense of role will structure his prescribing habits; on the other hand, his sense of his patient may modify this form. For the patient, the acceptance will depend on such basic things as trust, perhaps a capacity for belief and hope, buttressed by his sense of the physician's expectation and belief that the gift is appropriate and powerful. These will all affect the effectiveness of the gift.

Of course, for specific patients, the physician's style may be adjusted or altered to accommodate the patient's style in order to assure the success of the transaction. The strings of the transaction extend into the future. Whether or not the pill proves effective, although it depends in part on the prescribing process, also depends upon what the patient expects that the physician wants to hear. Many patients do not want to displease the physician by telling him that they do not feel any better. They do not want to hurt his feelings or experience his displeasure or irritation. Some others, of course, may take pleasure in presenting such a disappointment, oftentimes with a grin: "You see, it did not help any more than anything else you or any other doctor has given; I guess there just is no hope for me." So the doctor will have to look for more objective evidence in order to evaluate effectiveness or noneffectiveness.

Finally, we get down to the pill itself, much smaller than the trappings suggested above. Of course, pills have colors and shapes, all guaranteed to have certain, although nonspecific, effect upon the swallower. They also have taste and sometimes flavors, artificial or natural. Some are purposefully made bitter, as if to be more effective. Others are sweet, as if to reflect the nature of the transaction. Still others are as tasteless as possible, the very word suggesting out of flavor. In the old days, physicians were wont to ask what color pill a patient desired and sometimes what shape. Others were convinced, as were their patients, that if a pill were bitter or sour, it was guaranteed to drive away the evil spirit. On the other hand, a sugar pill conveyed love and something that was good for you, like mothers and chicken soup. Pills that are hard to swallow because of shape or size tend to emphasize "taking one's medicine like a soldier." Alcohol and or other "stimulant" bases frequently assured that the medicine would be taken, if not for one purpose then for another. There is, it would seem, a kind of imprinting that takes place in the effectiveness of a medicine, something like "just like Mother or old doctor so and so used to give me," that more or less recalls some of the other aspects of being sick and being cared for. So in many ways the pill is a memory capsule; big things come in small packages. And these are all fundamental to persuasion and healing.[1]

Drugs also have purposefully active ingredients, guaranteed to affect at least one organ system and frequently several. For beginners, we can think of drugs as stimulants or depressants. They can be so either directly in terms of their effect on the central nervous system or indirectly and secondarily through their effects on other organ systems.

Whether or not they are thought to affect specific receptor binding sites in one organ system, invariably there will be some receptor sites in other organ systems that will be affected, therefore resulting in "side effects." Side effects are perhaps defined as unwanted, sometimes undesirable, effects of the drug as opposed to the desired effects of the drug. Few drugs are without unwanted effects. It is the latter that greatly interfere with our prescribing habits, because while we are telling the patient what we want the drug to do for him, we are also telling him what we do not want the drug to do but what it might do. There is at least a bit of a double bind in this.

Presently, perhaps, a majority of the drugs we prescribe have primary or secondary effects upon the central nervous system and are incriminated in alterations of cognitive functions in terms of attention, orientation, memory, and judgmental and abstractive functions. These also affect mood and frequently motor behavior. Again they can be separated into those that effect an increase or a decrease in all or selected functions. Inasmuch as many drugs that we use are directed at the sympathetic and parasympathetic nervous system affecting internal organ systems, we are aware of their direct or indirect effects on bodily feelings composing and affecting feeling states and moods. They may do this directly or indirectly through the alteration of physical function that affects emotional states because of the unwanted side effects, e.g., muscular incoordination, tremors, urinary retention. Drugs may upset balances, as in the case of some antibiotics that not only act directly or indirectly against pathogens but may alter normal and symbiotic microorganisms that serve vital functions in homeostasis.

So in a very real sense, the symbolic bittersweet pills of older times are still with us. It leads some of us involved in patient care to hold any medication suspect until proven otherwise, to look for possible adverse relationships secondary to drugs in any situation which we cannot readily understand. Indeed, one might offer the suggestion that the *Physician's Desk Reference*[2] listing most of the prescription drugs is as valuable to the physician as the dictionary is to lexicographers or the Bible to theologians.

So drugs are an important part of medicine for their real as well as their symbolic effects. They need to be used with knowledge and humility. They do not always act in the same way in different individuals for all kinds of reasons, beginning with the prescribing situation and its expectations and extending through different genetic substrates that affect receptor sites, binding, and metabolic deficiencies. There is no single way of giving or of receiving. We are all different in these interactions, physicians and patients. As physicians, we give drugs to help patients, to alleviate their dis-ease. That is why our patients come to us. The giving and the receiving are mutual, based on trust, expectation, and hope. The smoothness of such transactions is marred by mismatched communicants—physicians and patients—unwanted intrusions participant in this process (including regulatory agencies), and undesirable side effects (expected and unexpected). These factors and others affect the patient's ability to follow, or in present-day terminology to comply with, instructions. Attention, education, and judicious forthrightness are necessary. Drug advertisements need to be taken with the salt of wisdom gained by a physician's experience.

References

1. Frank, J. D.: *Persuasion and Healing*. Baltimore, Johns Hopkins University Press, 1973.
2. *Physicians Desk Reference*. Oradell, N. J., Medical Economics Co., 1980.

CHAPTER

13

On Placebos and Their Use

Placebos are another thing. All of what we have said about the giving and receiving of drugs holds for placebos, except, of course, if we tell a patient that we are presenting him with a placebo, a tablet with an inert ingredient. This would, I suppose, puzzle him. He might even wonder whether there was some catch in it. At times, we do just this. But this is in a controlled experiment in which we have the patient's consent. He knows that he may be getting the "real thing," that is, the drug with the active ingredient, or a placebo with the inert one. Even then, in order to make the two a bit more equivalent, it is not unusual to add a bit of atropine or some small amount of a substance with tastes and effects of its own, albeit different from the test drug.

Controversies over the use of placebos have always been with us and are likely to continue. Perhaps, we can quickly get over the more obnoxious ones. There is something deceptive about the use of placebos, something unfair. This deception and unfairness obviously is squarely on the shoulders of the giver, the deceiver. And first we must turn our attention to what effect this practice has upon him. Just what effect does it have on him? Is it possible that it might undermine his trust in himself, his trust in other aspects of his practice? To what extent does it relate to his concept of lying? If it is so easy to be deceptive here, "although this is different," does it contaminate his sense of self, his sense of integrity, his veracity in other circumstances? Suppose he is successful, i.e., he gets away with it, he uses the placebo and "proves" that the patient's complaint goes away just as fast, perhaps even faster than with the active ingredient? What has he proved? Suppose he is even right in his assumption that the patient's complaint was not totally based upon a measureable pathophysiological and pathoanatomical event? Does that in and of itself negate the complaint? Suppose he gives the patient an injection of sterile saline, rather than a "pain killer" or a tranquilizer, and the pain or anxiety goes away? Really, what has he accomplished, what proof? Yet, these are daily occurrences. Frequently, the triumph is applauded. News of it runs up and down the corridors from nurse to nurse, from aide to aide, physician to physician. The patient is labeled in terms not worth repeating, all suggesting that there is nothing wrong with her. Her complaint is nothing; it is nonexistent. She becomes a malingerer. She is not to be trusted. Somehow, she has failed to keep an implicit contract by responding to something that was nothing. Her complaints are no longer heard. If they are, the syringe of saline is close at hand. Relatives find out, perhaps friends, business associates. The patient and his complaints are no longer real. The question here is who has been deceived? Whose faith, trust, belief has been most undermined? Since, in these circumstances, in the environs of the hospital or office few secrets are kept, even from patients, the deception becomes well known, sometimes even triumphantly announced to the patient: "Look, see you don't really have anything. We tested it out with saline; you're okay." That's at least a benign statement in comparison with the sense of hurt, anger, and frustration that is sometimes presented. But who is the loser? The patient, the physician, the nurse participant, the family, the hospital, the medical profession?

Let us go back a step. Have we really proven what we set out to do? Is this a scientifically controlled experiment? Is it set up so that, with enough random trials under the same situation, we can get a significant difference between response to the active versus the inert substance? Are these given by the same person in the same way? Is the patient told the same thing each time? Is the patient's complaint for which she is getting the placebo identical each time? Are variables or significant bystanders present at one time but not present at another? Would we accept this design, if we were not so set in our attempts to prove the patient a malingerer, deluded, upset, anxious, dependent?

This is all before we get to thinking in bona fide ethical terms and concepts. These are just plain everyday medical terms. We shall rest the case for the moment with the questions: What have we done to our own integrity? How will this affect our behavior with other patients? How will it affect our commitment to the scientific method, our commitment to believing the sincerity of our patient?

The case is well stated and argued in ethical terms. Sissela Bok has taken the lead in these discussions.[1] She comes up on one side. Others consider an alternative position, as is the wont of those involved in the dilemmas of ethics. It makes us stop to think, not only about the problem at hand, but about other related problems. When it all becomes too much, we fall back on established patterns and positions. The question is a simple one: Is it ever right to lie? Or is it so simple? Did you ever lie? When? Why? Oh! Not so simple. The question leads us up and down all kinds of alleys and into all kinds of situations. It is a good and worthwhile game. It sharpens our awareness of the issue, of others, and, finally, of ourselves. But let us get back to the question with our patient. Are there other issues to consider first?

What about informed consent? Why that? Well, is this not some kind of test, an experiment? Are you not asking a question, trying to find a way of getting an answer? Yes? and are you not using the patient as your guinea pig? Well, not quite, but in a way, yes? Okay, does the patient not need to know what is planned and why it is planned in order to agree or refuse to be a participant? Yes, but that would spoil the experiment? Really? Suppose you outlined the experiment, explained why (complex, huh?), got permission, then what? Not the same—how? Perhaps not statistical enough? Do you need unbiased observers, not knowing what has been given? If this is a "real" experiment, do you need controls? The patient as his own control is okay? What about the human subject experimentation review committee? The patient's informed consent? And the purpose of all of this is to prove that the patient does not have a real pain.

So, we have scrambled up a number of issues here. We have gotten into how scientific medicine really is; what good scientific methodology is; and what relationship these have to medical practice. Is the scientific method itself an intrinsic ethic of medicine? How is that for starters? That will take us a ways from our patient and our problem in a hurry. But, you see, this comes way before the question of whether it is ever right to lie. It comes considerably after the question, "What is it going to do to the physician, the giver, the perpetrator in this instance?"

The question gets knottier as we go along. We have looked at the placebo issue first in terms of how and perhaps why drugs are given in the first place. What is the meaning of the drug in the doctor-patient relationship? How is it given? With what intent? With what expectation? In this process, we have suggested that the patient is a mutual participant with the physician. There is a mutual expectancy rooted in trust and belief, expectation and hope,[2] so any drug, pill, placebo, or injection carries with it more than its active ingredient, more than even its inert ingredient.

Then we have the whole question of an intrinsic ethic, not only intrinsic to the physician but to the field of medicine itself, the adherence to a scientific method. And we have superimposed on this the ethics of informed consent.[3] This is not simple. Nor is it simple to carry out. But that is not all. We have the ethic of confidentiality,[4] privacy, and privilege. Who knows? What do they do with it? Whose property is this knowledge? We can go on. We can raise questions of nonmaleficence,[5] primum, non nocere of beneficence or of its possible opposite, primum, do something.[6] Now we can begin to add to this at a startling rate. We can address the issue in terms of patients' rights,[7] patients' obligations or duties, positive or negative results (consequences), and others.

In considering all of this, we have not yet mentioned that the administration of placebos often does correlate with measurable physiological changes the same way placebos sometimes correlate with the diminution of symptoms. Does this make a difference in your thinking? Does this spare the patient from becoming an addict to the narcotic that the patient would otherwise have gotten? Does this justify the practice, its scientific and ethical delivery?

The matter of placebos is not easily put to rest. Between the beginnings—i.e., the idea—and its initiation and the practice, much needs to be sorted out, examined, put in order, reviewed, tested, rereviewed by one (the physician) and all (ourselves).

References

1. Bok, S.: Placebos. In *Lying: Moral Choice in Public and Private Life*, p. 61. New York, Pantheon Books, 1978.
2. Bok, S.: *Lying: Moral Choice in Public and Private Life*. New York, Pantheon Books, 1978.
3. Donagan, A.: Informed consent in therapy and experimentation. Med. Philos. August, 1977.
4. Kimball, C. P.: The issue of confidentiality in the consultation-liaison process. In *The Teaching of Psychosomatic Medicine and Consultation-Liaison Psychiatry*, C. P. Kimball and A. J. Krakowski, editors, Bibliotheca Psychiatrica, No. 159. Bassel, S. Karger, 1979.
5. Beauchamp, T. L., and Childress, J. F.: *Principles of Biomedical Ethics*, Chapter 4, p. 97. New York, Oxford University Press, 1979.
6. Holland, J. F.: Ethics for a clinical investigator: Non primum non nocere. Am. J. Med., *66:* 554, 1979.
7. Curran, W. J.: The patient's bill of rights becomes law. N. Engl. J. Med., *290:* 32, 1974.

CHAPTER 14

The Homecoming

In thinking about the homecoming, a number of associations come to mind. First is the film, "The Diary of a Mad Housewife," in which a woman returns from the hospital after months of treatment for an emotional disorder. A great homecoming party is thrown at her by her large Italian family. As she comes into the seemingly quiet house, there is an eruption that rivals Mount Vesuvius in brilliance and noise. Children and relatives tumble up and down the stairs, chairs turn over, a spread of food for thousands appears, in every corner and doorway are people talking, eating, pushing, kissing, and making merry. It is a welcome back to sanity and the sanctity of husband and children. Through the housewife's eyes, the scene blurs, fades away, returns; she focuses momentarily on one seemingly distorted aspect after another—her husband with the woman who cared for her children while she was gone; the child who blames her for being gone; the party that does not seem to be for her, but for everyone else. She is ready to go back to the hospital. Pinter, the playwright, wrote *The Homecoming*, sparser in detail, essentially stressing the pain and barrenness of homecomings, perhaps following Thomas Wolfe's novel, *You Can't Go Home Again*.

All of this is to emphasize the pain of returning, the pain coming so closely on the heels of the anticipation and expectation of returning. Expectations rarely match reality. Change has taken place; it has taken place in the absence of the returnee. Things have changed. A different routine has been established. Furniture has been moved. Old rules have been violated. Things have not been kept up. Another person has been in the kitchen. The children have been allowed to run wild. Things seem to have gone along despite the absence of the person. There is so much that needs to be done. Order needs to be restored. It is a bittersweet time. It is good to be back. But, how can I get everything back to normal? It is good to be needed. There is so much to do. The place needs a good cleaning. Order has to be reestablished and the children gotten in hand.

There is inevitable conflict. Those who have waited at home in anticipation look for praise. They have survived despite the deprivation. The spouse has managed everything from the financial books to the cleaning, shopping, meals, wash, and garbage. The kids have not been easy, always one problem or another, frequently out of hand, even defiant. The cost has been great. Plans had to be changed. Things will have to be different. Instead of praise, even faint praise, criticism is heard. There is disappointment. Suppressed feelings—anger, anxiety, fear, sadness—erupt in different ways: silence, going out, defiant acts, arguments.

So, the homecoming is not an easy thing. There is still grief work to be done before reparation can occur. At some point, the grief work will be just this precipitation of feelings by the family members as well as the patient. A general catharsis is needed. If it does not occur spontaneously and/or if it is not monitored well when it does happen, with humor and engagement, the process of mutual reparations for real and fantasied omissions and commissions is less likely to occur, and the poorly covered wounds will remain as weak scar tissue.

Out of the catastrophe of illness can occur change which is growth for each individual involved. It will take time to realize this, to become aware that spouse and children have learned new tasks which have given them a greater sense of themselves and of their responsibility. When these are integrated with those of the returning person, he or she will find a greater cohesiveness, rather than a lesser one, with the family who stayed behind.

Here we have spoken of the emotional things in the homecoming. These can be prepared for, anticipated, to a limited extent during the end stages of the convalescent and/or rehabilitative phases of illness. But homecoming is an inevitable event. Supports are needed. These are likely to come from the outside, from friends who have experienced similar things, illnesses, homecomings; from fellow patients who have been in the hospital at the same time; from others.

But there are physical things also that affect adjustment at these times. There are the specific disabilities that require alterations in structure and function. These affect both identified patient and family.[1] To a considerable extent, they are badges of infirmity and symbols of change and uncertainty. The prostheses, the special routines, the medication, the reduced activity are all daily reminders of change. All family members need to get used to these, to understand them and to come to know their feelings about them. For the child, who experiences the first serious illness of a parent, it is a major shock, one not easily gotten used to. Children react to these processes differently, depending on multiple factors: previous relationship, past personal experience, age, other supports, family communication processes. For the adolescent boy who sees his father for the first time laid out with feet up in a hospital bed, it may be as a giant or king fallen. The outward reaction may be of defiance, leaving home, transfer of allegiance outside of the home, taking over. For the adolescent girl, who may be expected to take over for her mother, this may not only place upon her great burden and responsibility, taking her away from her friends and school activities, but may greatly interfere in the reworking of the oedipal relationships that are the psychological tasks of this period of growth and development.[2] The younger child will react to his sense of loss relative to his age at its occurrence. Outward manifestations are frequently withdrawal and/or uncustomary tantrums or the development of somatic symptoms that are not readily explainable on a physical basis. Some of these may occur at a time some distance from the actual family catastrophe. When they occur, a heavy sense of guilt is laid on the parent, who feels the illness was his fault. At these times, through mechanisms of projection and blame, fault is piled upon fault, compounded and exchanged between all parties in the verbage: "If it had not been for that, then this would not have happened."

These processes can be facilitated, attended, and objectified by the more dispassionate neutral outsider, who certainly can be the family physician and/or a good family friend. When considered as part of a grief process, the model of therapeutic intervention is the familiar one of assisting, oftentimes in a family group, opening the subject of the patient's illness for discussion—the effect it has had on each member of the family and the feelings associated with these effects, followed by a limited exploration of the psychological defenses and behaviors that the members have used or demonstrated in attempts to handle the repressed or suppressed feelings. All of this information is right there in the package of the family, ready to be brought out in bits and pieces, made into real objects each to be examined, picked up, turned over, moved around, examined for its constructiveness and destructiveness, altered, changed, discarded, upgraded in its usefulness. These topics are all right there. Everyone knows it. They have just been brought out, made real objects for talking about.

These processes sometimes may need to be extended over a longer period, especially when illness is chronic and the extent of alterations to be made is great. They may have to be attuned to the specific disabilities and experiences and their effects and consequences upon the identified patient and his family. Obviously, they will also depend on the psychological health of the family members. They will also depend heavily on the availability outside of the family of social supports, near relatives, friends, colleagues, work and social institutions. Formal group processes, including formal psychotherapy and informal self-help groups for individuals with similar problems or disabilities, have been useful.[3]

In a sense, homecoming is a big scene. It becomes a field day for the precipitation, however presented, of internal feeling. This lasts and, depending on how it is processed, will directly affect the emotional and physical health of all members of the family. An illness in the family puts all members of that family at risk for uncertainty and change. This sometimes leads to growth in some, to decompensation and illness in others. It is a time when more, not less, support and attention by medicine may be needed. Thus illness lasts long after its onset and the acute, convalescent, and even rehabilitative phases. It is not over until the patient, with the allowance of the family, the employer, and other social forces, gives up the sick role and returns to equal status within the greater society. The homecoming is also a phase of the illness experience that has not been well studied in terms of the specific coping techniques that augment for maximum adaptation, adjustment, and rehabilitation.

References

1. Anthony, E. J.: The impact of mental and physical illness of family life. Am. J. Psychiatry *127:* 138, 1970.
2. Blos, P.: *The Adolescent Passage.* New York, International Universities Press, 1978.
3. Videka, L. M.: Psychosocial adaptation in a medical self-help group. In *Self-help Groups for Coping with Crisis,* M. A. Lieberman and L. D. Borman, editors. San Francisco, Jossey-Bass, 1979.

CHAPTER 15

On Dying and Death

For some reason, present-day society acts as if it has suddenly rediscovered death. Whether this is a delayed reaction after a war-ravaged world or a manifestation of anticipatory fear of potential nuclear confrontation, is uncertain, although it is possible. The issue of death is not the important one. Since the Garden of Eden, it has always been known, and succeeding cultures have developed elaborate forms to contend with it. It is woven into all of the artifacts of culture. Life, in a sense, derives much from this phenomenon. Death, after all, is a phenomenon for those left behind to deal with. So far as we know, it is of little importance to the departed. For the living, it is of major importance. It is something to be dealt with. It rips out of the individual a piece of real self which has to be replaced by symbols through the process of grieving.

Dying is another matter. From the outset, it is important to emphasize that our patients are more concerned about dying than death. After all, the concept of death has evolved through every age of the individual, beginning in early childhood. It has always been with us, changing with each stage of development (see Chapter 22). Even in dying, if that is what we are going to call it, the patient is less concerned with the abstract connotation of death than the actual process of dying, the pain of dying. Despite the current fiction by the War-Lords of dying and the bargains they would proffer, our patient is more concerned about the pain of living. There is neither space nor time for the luxury of contemplating death. The anxiety witnessed is less one about death and dying and more one of painful living. Our patient does not have time nor space to contemplate the abstractions of death. That is for the relatively healthy. Our patient is more concerned about getting another breath, seeking relief from pain, getting some sleep, and not being bothered by yet another procedure or series of interviews. The latter are all right when he is better.

The fact is that the intransitive verb *dying* is neither an end state nor an irreversible one. Most individuals have had brushes with death several times in their lives. These have been significant influences and have, no doubt, contributed to their evolving an abstractive sense of death. More important, perhaps, is the fact that they did not die and the effect of that on the present phase of life we identify as dying. Almost everything about them, up to a point, is focused on the fact of living, whether these be heroic life-sustaining efforts or merely ameliorating supports of living without pain or other discomfort. After all, it takes a relatively comfortable patient to engage in the luxury of addressing the abstractions of death. This is most obvious in the acute care units of treatment. In these arenas, the patients are more concerned about the pain and discomfort of living. Their complaints are of these. They do not have time or patience for entertaining ideas about the hereafter. Although they may express elements of hopelessness, that it is no use, that they cannot go on, that they might as well give up or be given up and allowed to die, they are addressing the real pain of living and are seeking relief through human intervention, whether that be the administration of drugs or a process of ventilating their concerns to another individual. Once we begin to focus on these environments, the patient and attendants therein, we begin to identify a number of factors that begin to change our preconceived notions of dying and letting die. In the first place, these environments, rather than being final way stations on the path of death, are temples of hope and symbols of man's determination to help and restore, the basic elements of medicine and nursing. Our patients and their families come with great expectations and hope, with prayer and a belief in miracles. The despair—sometimes manifested by patients, more often by burdened relatives, and occasionally by fatigued physicians and nurses—says more about the specific orientations of these individuals, rather than being based on objective fact and rational decision. It is sometimes the projection of the relatively well person onto the relatively sick person, who, for whatever reason, believes that he would not want to be in the same boat. Of course he would not. But what if he were and it was the only boat there was. Would his tune change? It often does.

Our studies suggest that—because of the underlying illness; its treatment; the emotions of anxiety, fear, sadness, and anger; and the strangeness of these environments—the majority of patients in these environments have major compromises in their mental status (see Chapter 19).[1]

That is, they are confused and sometimes disoriented as to who they are or where they are or what time of day or what day or month or year it is. They may have deficits in memory, usually more recent as compared with past. Their attention span is limited. Their concentration is poor. Their judgment is often impaired and their abstractive abilities absent. This is hardly the time to discuss concepts of death in any rational way. The patients are more intense in their identification of pain, their discomfort over their confused state. They are more concerned about losing their marbles than their life. They are worried about their dreams and nightmares, about not sleeping and about what is going on at home rather than the next world or the one after that. These patients are trying to hold onto themselves, their environment, and the family that comes and goes. They need relatively constant reorienting to their environment and those within it, with what is going on with them and theirs, with people from the outside world from which they have come and to which they have some anticipation of returning, the only world they know. They need, at various levels of sophistication, a knowledge of what is going on and other elements of certainty in an arena where nothing is certain. It is not always the time to speak of the certainties or uncertainties of death, unless this is what is on the patient's mind.

At the time of life crisis, where the finality of life is more certain than not, there are more important things for the rational person to be concerned with than coming to terms with his maker. At these times, his best confidant may be his lawyer, who will assist him in ordering his affairs and willing, for a variable period of time, how those who mean most to him will be protected and cared for. Such planning and concrete action restore a sense of self, direction, determination, control. This process is reintegrating, a way of reasserting the self and the impact of this self on others.[2] In former times, it is said that a "lingering death" was to be desired over an instant one so that the ill might have time to go through the elaborate arrangements of putting an estate measured in land, property, and contracts in order.

I suppose that it is only human to put distance between the healthy and the ill, the living and the dying. It is pragmatic. As a human process, it is frequently facilitative. It is a distance that allows for objectivity. It also allows for the healthy to grant a state to the ill in which they can be relieved of obligations while they permit designated ones among the well to render care to them. This is done in trust and the expectation of help. Traditionally, this has put illness in the light of being bad and, hence, the enemy, as opposed to the healthy and the good, the saviors. A war is declared against disease and illness. The latter shall be overcome. In the days of scourges and plagues, the ill and their diseases were viewed as enemies. As disease came to be separated from the ill, the war was raged increasingly against disease, although the battlefield is most often within the patient who is subjected to an array of chemotherapies. The technique of medicine has been one of the physician gaining an alliance with the individual, his healthy parts against his bad, unhealthy parts. The physician and patient ally together to fight the evil disease within the latter. In a sense, of course, the patient is put in a position of fighting against parts of himself, a parasite, bacteria, or virus taking up residence therein or a malignant cell, somehow transformed from his own being. There may be a paradox here that medicine is only beginning to face.[3] For the present, however, the foundation of medicine is established, similar to religion, on the concept of health and illness, the healthy and the ill, a fight against disease and the return to health and the sustenance of life. It has not been as much the idea of a medicine to counsel the dying as to counsel the living. To do the former, especially prematurely, may be to counsel loss and defeat.

The formulations here do not relate to methods of care, to ideas regarding the moment of death dependent on the absence of one wriggle on an electroencephalogram. They do not relate to decisions of when to sustain or not sustain machine-related life support systems. These are technical factors that are made on the basis of sound medical decisions, addressing the reality of end points and consequences. They are another matter, for consideration elsewhere. Here, we have been concerned with counseling the living, attending to the processes endured by the living. We know less about the dying, only that they do not all die.

References

1. Davies, R., Quinlan, D., McKegney, F. P., and Kimball, C. P.: Organic factors and psychological adjustment in advanced cancer patients. Psychosom. Med. *35:* 464–471, 1973.
2. Bowers, M. K., Jackson, E. N., Knight, J. A., and LeShan, L.: *Counseling the Dying.* New York: Thomas Nelson & Sons, 1964.
3. Sontag, S.: *Illness as Metaphor.* New York, Farrar, Straus and Giroux, 1978.

PART 3

SELECTIVE STUDIES OF ILLNESS: ON RELATIONSHIPS

CHAPTER 16

The Evolution of the Biopsychosocial Approach

OVERVIEW

The term psychosomatic medicine has undergone theoretical shifts during the last 30 years. Following Cannon's initial observations of specific physiological changes accompanying specific emotions, Dunbar emphasized the relation of specific diseases to personality and life styles. Alexander introduced the ideas of illness onset situation in terms of conflict specificity and organ vulnerability. Wolff elaborated a sophisticated experimental design to investigate the relations of environment, psychological stress, and bodily reaction. Mason and others used new techniques of hormonal research to study end organ reaction to provoked stress. Others are focusing on intracerebral processes by which endocrine function is triggered. Miller has shown that autonomic responsivity can be conditioned. Engel and the Rochester school have emphasized illness onset in terms of loss and the development of the giving-up—given-up state, with affects of displeasure, helplessness, and hopelessness that, through endocrine mechanisms, may put the individual at risk for somatic dysfunction. Psychosomatic medicine has come to embrace all illnesses rather than "Alexander's Holy Seven." Its preoccupation has shifted from concern with intrapsychic events and disease to include the environments in which illness occurs. A linear model of causality has given way to a cyclical model in which illness is viewed as behavior representing the final common pathway resulting

---

Modified version (and reproduced with permission) of article from Annals of Internal Medicine 73: 307–316, 1970; copyrighted by the American College of Physicians.

from interrelated factors within the frameworks of psychology, physiology, and environment for each individual, resulting in the biopsychosocial approach.[1]

Psychosomatic medicine is the designation used by those physicians who, through formal research investigations and observations on the basis of clinical work, have come to believe and to practice that human illness cannot be conceptualized or treated by a single factor-single disease approach but that all illness depends on a multiplicity of factors involving the somatic and psychological processes of the individual in relationship to the environment. An understanding of the development of this concept is essential both for diagnosis and therapy and may be best gained by a brief review of psychosomatic medicine as it has developed during the last half century, especially in the United States.

Ideas regarding illness as a reaction to emotional conflict are as old as recorded history[2] and are observed today among ancient cultures that have retained their traditions. An example of this is the Navajo Indian concept of illness,[3] which views any maladjustment or dysfunction of the individual as representing a total disharmony in the life of the sufferer. This disharmony is identified as occurring in the three spheres: spiritual, somatic, and social. It is of interest that they have devised a system of "specialization" in which there is a hierarchy of practitioners treating each of these respectively. In Western civilization especially, the 17th-century Cartesian[4] philosophical distinction of the body and the mind as separate entities gave impetus to a similar dichotomy in 18th- and 19th-century medicine. This attitude was bolstered by the remarkable advances made during this period in the identification and understanding of specific factors that were of major etiological significance in enhancing specific somatic processes. As science and medicine became more defined during this period in specifying a single cause-single effect basis for all observable phenomena, those processes that did not lend themselves to such formulations were defined as functional illnesses. Until the present, those disorders of behavior, emotion, and thinking have fallen under this label, although many investigators of mental illness have always felt that eventually underlying or associated organic features would be discovered.[5]

With the dramatic and rapid formulations of Freud and his colleagues in the late 19th century, especially as they related to hysteria and conversion reactions,[6] a peculiar paradox was introduced into medical thinking. Biologically oriented physicians discussed the physiology of obvious somatic and behavioral processes in psychological terms—that is, terms that did not always have apparent substance in biochemical or physiological measurements. The psychological measurements could not be easily measured and could be only vaguely seen or felt and even more vaguely approximated in semantic formulations. These formulations seemed so idiosyncratic and specific to the individual that Freud and Breuer found it difficult to use them as models capable of generalized application. Yet the biologically trained analysts remained adamant in following the 19th-century model of specific cause and specific effect in approaching illness states. Several of the early analysts turned their attentions uncritically to the interaction of psychological states and somatic conditions other than simple conversion. Groddeck[7] and Deutsch et al.[8] had similar beliefs that all organic disease was an expression of unconscious conflict or represented conversions, respectively.

PHYSIOLOGICAL BEGINNINGS

Serious endeavors at inspecting the mechanism by which psychological expressions or conflicts are translated into somatic processes were not acknowledged formally until 1939, when the American Psychosomatic Society was founded. The founding of this Society represented an attempt to correlate biological processes with psychological concepts formulated to a large extent in the terms of psychoanalysis. Impetus for these attempts was stimulated by Cannon's[9] work on the physiological accompaniments of fear and rage. On the basis of detailed laboratory experiments, Cannon hypothesized that an organism responds to emergency situations with adaptive changes in the total physiological economy and that emotional states activate physiological functions that prepare the organism for the situation these emotions signify. He suggested that the organism responds to fear and rage as though preparing for fight or flight by the inhibition of anabolic and storing functions of the body and the activation of catabolic ones that would release energy for the organism's response. Cannon observed that the latter process was largely mediated through the autonomic nervous system, with the catabolic sequence precipitated by epinephrine while the anabolic processes were stopped via parasympathetic inhibition. Later, Funkenstein, King, and Drolette[10] were able to demonstrate a correlation of the differential reactions of induced anger and anxiety in experimental subjects with the selective elaboration of norepinephrine or epinephrine, respectively. Whether the anger was directed inward (repressed) or outward (expressed) correlated with or determined whether the individual would physiologically respond with an epinephrine or norepinephrine response.

The relationship of emotion to physiological processes was now clearly established. This has remained one of the most productive approaches within the psychosomatic tradition and has been extended to an investigation of the responses of all hormonal systems to stresses and the associated emotion.[11-13] The hope of these workers is to arrive at a basic physiology and biochemistry of the emotions and defenses whereby illnesses characterized by organ responses mediated by these hormones may be understood. These workers observe specific responses secondary to specific environmental stresses. They feel, after Selye,[14] that the response, although it may be adaptive for the organism in handling the stress, may also lead to disease (diseases of adaptation) by upsetting the internal balance of the body. In one way or another, an organ system reaction once sensitized to respond to a stressful event may continue to do so with stereotyped and overused responses to similar or even to different stress processes. Gellhorn[15] has continued to consider disturbance in behavior and somatic processes as largely mediated through the autonomic nervous system and essentially as alternating sympathetic and parasympathetic responses in relation to the emotions. The resulting behavior of the individual depends on the effect of the interaction of parasympathetic and sympathetic processes on any level—peripheral or central, external or internal—to the central nervous system. This complex approach appreciates the cyclical or feedback processes of the body whereby a process once induced may in itself give rise to feelings or behavior that in turn give rise to further dysfunction. Benedek and Rubenstein,[16] in one of the classic psychosomatic investigations, demonstrated by the psychoanalytic study of women during their menstrual cycle, using vaginal smears as an indication of the phase, that: (1) an active, extroverted, heterosexual tendency motivated behavior that paralleled estrogen production; and (2) while parallel to the progestin phase, psychosexual energy is directed inward as a passive-receptive, retentive tendency. Thus, in the hormonal cycle, a specific and correlatable emotional and behavioral cycle exists. Steroid receptor sites[17] have been identified in the forebrain, rhinencephalon, and hypothalamus, suggesting how the peripheral elaboration of hormones may affect behavior. Alternatively, it has been proposed that the forebrain may in some way inhibit the feedback action of gonadal hormones controlling pituitary function and hence influence sexual behavior. Internal clocks have been hypothesized in response to environmental stimuli that in turn regulate the growth and development of organisms.[18] The synthesis of biogenic amines in abnormal amounts or of a defective nature within the central nervous system and the effect of these on man's emotional state have concerned investigators such as Schildkraut and Kety[19] and form the basis on which psychosomatic concepts may be extended to the brain—that is, brain function may be a product as well as an initiator of psychic processes. Again, the cyclical nature of a process remains for consideration, that is, that either the emotion may give rise to a biological change or the biological change may give rise to the emotion: the "biopsycho" part of the relationship.

CLINICAL SOMATOPSYCHIC CORRELATIONS

This phenomenon is of particular interest in looking at specific somatic processes that have been correlated with more or less classical emotional states.[20] Among these are suicidal behavior with frontal lobe meningioma, depression (often labile) with carcinoma of the pancreas, delusions with temporal lobe astrocytoma, psychotic episodes secondary to hypoglycemia associated with adenomas of the pancreas, agitated depression with hyperthyroidism, anxiety with pheochromocytoma, depression and apathy with pernicious anemia, behavioral aberrations with Wilson's disease, tension and fatigue with Addison's disease, euphoria and depression with Cushing's disease, and depression and paranoid delusions with parathyroid adenomas. These emotional aberrations, far from being specific, are probably more properly viewed as resulting from delirium,[21] in which the behavior and emotions observed are as likely to be dependent on the individual's psychology as on the specific metabolic derangement caused by the underlying pathological process. In some cases, however, perhaps dependent on the specific location of chemoreceptors within the central nervous system, one emotion rather than another is more likely to be stimulated. The relationship of the brain ribonucleic acids and memory retention[22] and the correlation of ribonuclease activity and age[23] touch on yet another aspect of brain, behavior, and emotion interrelationships.

PERSONALITY-ILLNESS SPECIFICITY

At the same time that Cannon was investigating the physiology of the emotions, a group of investigators was studying and systematizing their observations that many individuals with specific diseases also had similar personality characteristics and traits. Dunbar[24] reviewed the literature and collected psychosocial data on more than 1,600 patients to identify a personality profile for what she considered eight illness states in which psychosomatic relationships could be established: fracture, coronary occlusion, hypertensive cardiovascular disease, anginal syndrome, rheumatic heart disease, cardiac arrhythmias, rheumatic fever and rheumatoid arthritis, and diabetes. She was able to establish specific characteristics for each of these groups in the categories of family history, personal data, health record, injuries, general adjustment, characteristic behavior pattern, neurotic traits, addictions and interests, life situation immediately before onset, reaction to illness, and areas of focal conflict and characteristic reaction. In broad strokes she was able to establish an outline that has served subsequent investigators as a preliminary model for looking more closely at each of the multiple factors associated with the natural history and manifestation of a disease. On the basis of these observations, Dunbar formulated the "personality specificity theory of disease." For example, patients with hypertension were observed as having a need to keep peace, resolving conflicts over seeking satisfaction within themselves, and devoting themselves to the achievement of external long-range goals. Obsessive and compulsive traits with perfectionistic inclinations were also noted. Conflicts between aggressivity and passivity were seen as erupting in occasional outbursts of rage. Patients with rheumatoid arthritis were identified as quiet, sensitive individuals who combined posing as a good sport with ingratiating appeal for sympathy, beneath which much hostility was present. These patients had many neurotic traits that were viewed as defenses against guilt and depression related to sexual conflicts. Trends toward perfectionism, cleanliness, orderliness, and punctuality were also noted.

Ruesch[25] termed an "infantile personality" as the core problem in psychosomatic medicine, identifying: (1) arrested or faulty social learning, (2) impaired self-expression channeled through either direct physical action or organ expression, (3) persistence of childhood patterns of thinking and ideation, (4) dependency and passivity, (5) rigid and punitive conscience, (6) overextended ideals, and (7) absence of ability to integrate experience. Ruesch, less concerned with specificity factors, did not explain why one organ system rather than another was chosen for the expression of conflict. Rather, he outlined a therapeutic approach, rare in the history of psychosomatic medicine, for physicians working with patients having infantile or immature personalities. This approach included: (1) reeducation through benevolent firmness; (2) instruction as to the manipulative and implicit content of his complaint; (3) reduction of long verbal productions to single words or sentences concerning problems; (4) externalization of feelings and emotions as objectifications in their own right, rather than via organ expressions and complaints; (5) acceptance by the patient of himself as a psychological and biological entity distinct from others; and (6) the model of the physician as a consistent, accepting, available, and self-expressive person.

Personality studies of patients with various diseases are still very much a part of psychosomatic medicine. Subsequently, Marty and De'Uzan[26] and Nemiah and Sifneos[27] have suggested similar, but not necessarily identical "personalities," *la pensée operatoire* and alexithymia, respectively. Friedman and Rosenman,[28] on the basis of both retrospective and prospective studies, have identified a type A behavior pattern that correlates with heart disease. Men identified as having type A characteristics seem to be "doers" capable of accomplishing their particular functions, although chronically harassed by their various commitments, ambitions, and drives. They are competitive, with an eagerness to win and demonstrate superiority in all their endeavors. Predominant is a sense of time urgency. Subjects demonstrating these characteristics exhibit significantly greater average serum cholesterol, triglyceride, and beta to alpha lipoprotein ratio. In a prospective study by these investigators, three factors (abnormalities in lipoprotein pattern, hypertension, exhibition of type A behavior pattern) were of prognostic significance in identifying coronary-prone individuals. The exhibition of the behavior pattern alone served as the most important single prognostic factor.

THE CONFLICT ONSET SITUATION

Alexander and French[29] and their colleagues were most influential in fusing psychoanalytic concepts with organic dysfunction during the 1950's. Studying the "holy seven" diseases—hyperthyroidism, neurodermatitis, peptic ulcer, rheumatoid arthritis, essential hypertension, bronchial asthma, and ulcerative colitis—Alexander and his group moved away from a personality specificity concept toward one of conflict specificity. Although not denying the importance of an individual's personality traits in predisposing the individual to particular types of conflict, Alexander turned the attention of his followers to the immediate situation of the individual at the time he developed his illness, the onset situation. For peptic ulcer disease, Alexander described three vectors: (1) the wish to incorporate, receive, take in; (2) the wish to eliminate, give, expend energy; and (3) the wish to accumulate or retain. When there was conflict among these, gastrointestinal disturbance resulted. When frustrated by external events the vulnerable individual, through repression, will channel this frustration via the vulnerable organ system that ultimately will manifest disease, in this case duodenal ulcer. Other psychological constellations or vectors were hypothesized for patients with other psychosomatic illnesses. In addition to the emphasis on the immediate conflictful situation experienced by the personality-predisposed individual, Alexander gave emphasis to the concept of organ vulnerability, presumed to be on the basis of genetic heritance or early developmental factors. The illness conflict situation is viewed as arousing latent unresolved conflicts occurring in early stages of psychosexual development that sensitized the organ system under development and tuning at that stage for patterns of response at later times of similar conflictful situations.

Nemiah and Sifneos,[30] by studying patients afflicted with two psychosomatic diseases, such as peptic ulcer and asthma occurring at different times, combined Ruesch's[25] concept of the infantile personality (personality specificity) with Alexander and French's[29] concept of situation onset (conflict specificity) in an attempt to arrive at a unified etiological concept for psychosomatic processes.

Weiner and co-workers,[31] in perhaps the most classical investigation in psychosomatic medicine, studied the interrelationship of constitution, psychological predisposition, and environment in the precipitation of duodenal ulcer. Mirsky[32] studied the response of enlisted men to 16 weeks' exposure to basic military training. On the basis of pepsinogen levels determined before the experience, groups of hypersecretors and hyposecretors were selected. These men were then subjected to gastrointestinal roentgenological examinations, psychoanalytically oriented anamnestic interviews, and psychological tests. Subsequent roentgenological examinations from the eighth to sixteenth week of training showed the development of ulcers in five of the hypersecretors who previously had demonstrated normal gastrointestinal function. Of the 63 hypersecretors, nine developed or had had duodenal ulcers. None of the hyposecretors demonstrated deranged gastrointestinal activity.

Mirsky's consideration of the constitutional factors associated with the development of duodenal ulcer—namely the high familial prevalence, hypersecretion of pepsinogen, and blood group O in those patients with or developing this condition—led him to suggest the term "somato-psycho-somatic" to replace the former term psychosomatic illness.

THE CORNELL SCHOOL

Wolff[33] subjected individuals with somatic processes such as ulcers, asthma, and urticaria to multiple stress situations including interviews in which conflict-laden anamnestic material previously obtained from the subject was reintroduced and further probed. They demonstrated how conflictual situations (expressed in modified psychoanalytic concepts), learned or conditioned responses (explained in Pavlovian terms), and environmental stress were interrelated in precipitating a response of an organ system. Using sophisticated experimental designs to record physiological measurements, their contribution to psychosomatic medicine was both one of method and of incorporating behavioral concepts. Their explanation of why an organ system was vulnerable to physiological dysfunction was expressed in terms of both bodily and psychological defense. The organ system used was that which was most appropriate to the organism in fending off a hostile environmental stress, whether an actual physical assault or something symbolic of such a threat. Wolff's disciples in time scattered to a number of major teaching centers, each carrying on his own phase of psychosomatic investigation.

Grace and Graham and co-workers[34, 35] studied the attitudes of patients to symptoms, correlating these for many somatic processes. By attitude they meant a clear and unambiguous statement of what was happening to the patient and what he wanted to do about it at the time of the occurrence of the symptom. For instance, a patient experiencing urticaria simultaneously saw himself as being mistreated or being victimized in a difficult life situation—"I was taking a beating." Patients experiencing diarrhea were found to be in life situations that they expressed as "I want to get rid of it." On the basis of this they suggested that emotion be defined as "an attitude and the associated bodily changes."

Hinkle and Wolf[36] extended the methods of the Cornell group from the traditional psychosomatic diseases to investigation of patients with diabetes mellitus. Noting that diabetes mellitus is a notoriously labile and unpredictable syndrome, they explored the relationship of life stress to fluctuations in the patient's symptoms and physiology so far as the diabetic condition was concerned. Using the interview method previously described and following blood glucose, ketones, and fluid balance, they followed patients in long-term studies. They concluded:

1. Life experiences may play an important role in determining the onset and possibly constitute a factor in the cause of diabetes mellitus.
2. There was a specificity and uniformity to the stressful situation precipitating ketosis—namely, conflicts that threatened the real or symbolic dependency of the individual, usually on a parent or parent surrogate, and in which there was an inability to express anger or hostility for fear of further disrupting this relationship.
3. Conflictful situations in which the individual was able to express his hostility did not result in ketosis.
4. When the individual avoided situations in which his dependent relationships might be threatened, during which situations anxiety prevailed, hypoglycemia developed.

Thus, it was not only the situation but also the way in which the individual coped with the situation that determined his physiological response.

INDIVIDUAL SPECIFICITY (BIOLOGICAL DETERMINANTS)

Individual variations of autonomic reactivity in response to stimuli have been studied by Sontag and Wallace[37] and by Bridger and Reiser,[38] among others. Sontag and Wallace measured changes in heart rate and other factors of fetuses in response to stimulation of the mother and noted that differences existed between fetuses and between different periods in the life of the individual fetus in response to different stimuli. For example, acceleration of fetal cardiac rate in response to activity of the mother or to vibration in one fetus might not occur in response to smoking, whereas the reverse might hold for another fetus. Bridger, Birns, and Blank[39] noted that neonates differed as to the level at which a stimulus starts to produce a response, the type of response produced, and the degree of response. They also demonstrated that a response pattern remained constant to the same stimulus on subsequent testing. These studies suggest the individual variation of the organism early in life and support Alexander's constitutional factor as the basis for organ system specificity and possible vulnerability in response to environmental situations.

THE ILLNESS ONSET SITUATION

Turning their attention increasingly to the external environment of the individual, disciples of Wolff such as Holmes and Rahe[40–42] viewed the social situation preceding the onset of any type of illnesses in individuals. They amassed an amazing array of data for different populations on the basis of retrospective and prospective studies, indicating that there was general agreement among populations as to what constituted a "life stress" and the degree of seriousness of this factor. Subsequently, they demonstrated that there was up to a 0.8 correlation between events rated as necessitating major readjustment and the onset of illness in subjects over a 2-year period. Preliminary findings also suggested that there is a correlation between the severity of illness and the number of life crisis units accumulated during a 2-year period. At this time the Holmes group has not offered explanations of (1) how these crises are translated into specific pathophysiological mechanisms within the individual or (2) the nature of the processes that protected the 20 per cent of those studied who accumulated high life crisis scores from succumbing to illness. Nevertheless, an 80 per cent correlation is impressive and emphasizes the importance of the physician's focusing on the recent events and life situation of his patient during his initial interview, if only to be aware of what problems may still be relating to the illness.

Specific pathophysiological correlations have been made to life situations, behavior, attitudes, and emotions by other of Wolff's workers, such as Schottstaedt et al.,[43] who studied the excretion of fluids and electrolytes in patients subjected to a variety of stresses that caused psychological discomfort.

GENERAL SYSTEMS THEORY

Grinker and Robbins[44] have investigated psychosomatic relationships for many years. On the basis of their experience, they have come to emphasize a "field theory," in which they suggest that no one conceptual approach is ever appropriate for the entire explanation of a particular process but specific aspects of a number of theories would help the physician ascertain and formulate what was going on with a particular individual at a particular time. In other words, Grinker stressed fitting theory to the patient and his individual life situation and proceeding from there, rather than fitting patient to theory. His attention has turned much more to the adaptive processes of the individual in response to emotions induced by stresses of various kinds. Adaptive processes have been correlated with adrenal cortical activity by his group as well as by Cleghorn and Graham,[11] Hamburg and Adams,[12] Mason,[13] and others.

OBJECT LOSS, AFFECT STATE, AND ILLNESS

Greene,[45-50] working with the Rochester Group during the early 1950's, shifted attention from personality and intrapsychic processes as single determinants relating to psychosomatic disease and pioneered the development of looking at what was happening in the object world of the individual in terms of interpersonal and other object relationships. Also shifting his emphasis from the acceptable psychosomatic diseases of that era, he turned his attention to the improbable area of reticuloendothelial diseases. Studying patients with lymphomas, leukemias, and Hodgkin's disease, he demonstrated not only similarity in premorbid personality factors in patients afflicted with these processes but also the proximity of object loss to the onset of disease. Studying patients over the course of their illness, he was able to correlate the onset with a real, threatened, or imminent loss; exacerabtions with disruptions in crucial object relationships, notably intrafamilial and physician-patient ones; accelerations at periods of major life change, such as the menopause and separations; and death with ultimate object loss, such as the marriage of a child.

Schmale[51] extended Greene's observations by investigating the relationship of separation and depression to the onset of any illness. He found that a majority of hospitalized patients reported experiencing object loss (real, threatened, or imagined) and feelings of helplessness and hopelessness immediately preceding the onset of symptoms of illness. With Adamson[52] he also investigated psychiatrically hospitalized patients, demonstrating the recent loss of a highly valued source of gratification and the emotional reaction of defeat or "giving up."

Engel and co-workers,[53–64] studying the phenomena of disease and illness from the perspectives of physiological medicine, psychoanalysis, and behavior, suggested that organisms react to unpleasant stimuli and situations with responses of either anxiety or depression-withdrawal (also called conservation-withdrawal). These identify opposite physiological mechanisms that he has demonstrated in experimental work. The conservation-withdrawal response is invoked when ego mechanisms fail and the ultimate "given-up" state ensues. This is a physiologically hypoactive state, in contrast to the "flight-fight" hyperactive response, and occurs either when the latter is depleted or when the response to an external stimuli is one of "freezing" or "standing still in one's tracks." Each of these systems, when inappropriately used or overused, may lead to Selye's "diseases of adaptation."[14]

On the basis of their research over the past 25 years, the Rochester group has conceptualized a giving-up—given-up state[65, 66] that it regards as a frequent and nonspecific condition for the onset and exacerbation of both psychiatric and somatic disease and which includes the following characteristics:

1. An unpleasant affective quality is verbalized as "It's too much, I can't take it anymore." These affective expressions may be polarized toward hopelessness, in which one both refuses help and is unable to help himself, and helplessness, in which the individual, although not refusing help, is nevertheless unable to help himself.
2. The patient views himself as less intact, less competent, less in control, less gratified, and less capable of functioning in a relatively autonomous fashion.
3. Relationships with objects are less secure, and the patient may feel himself "given up" by these.
4. The present environment is perceived as no longer supplying the same guidelines for the behavior of the individual as formerly.
5. There is a gap or break in the continuity between a sense of past and of future.
6. Memories and feelings of a former time and of similar quality are reawakened and become part of the present. They suggest that the "giving-up" phase occurs when there is a failure of usual defenses and coping devices of the individual in handling the stresses of life, with a resulting awareness of the loss of or inability to achieve gratification. The "given-up" phase marks the identification that all attempts to continue to struggle or to expect external supplies for assistance have ceased. Although regarding this stage as "neither necessary nor sufficient for, but only as contributory to, the emergence of somatic disease, and then only if the necessary predisposing factors are also present,"

the group noted a high correlation between the presence of this state historically and the onset of illness in extensive retrospective and prospective studies currently in progress. Specific psychiatric and somatic vulnerabilities are conceptualized as having their basis in the genetic and epigenetic heritage of the organism. The specific biological component of this state is viewed as one in which systems concerned with defense against injury and with obtaining or conserving supplies are activated or in some way disrupted. It is hypothesized that the giving-up—given-up state is one basically associated with a biological one of physiological hyporeactivity, as suggested by Engel and Reichman's[54] studies of Monica, the infant with the gastric fistula.

Engel has gone further in his consideration of psychic and somatic interrelationships in his theoretical formulations about conversion reactions.[67] Rejecting the Freudian and Alexanderian identification of conversion as being a physical phenomenon representing or symbolic of an unconscious psychic conflict mediated through the voluntary or somatic neuromuscular system, Engel (similar to F. Deutsch[8]) proposes that the autonomic nervous system may also mediate the external expression of unconscious conflicts. Engel draws on his experiences with patients with such diverse processes as those involved in pain[68] and ulcerative colitis. Citing the antidromic activity of afferent fibers carrying nocioceptive impulses as a feedback mechanism resulting in the elaboration of tissue-toxic chemical substances (neurokinins, substance P, histamine) at the nerve receptor site, he suggested a mechanism whereby the physiological dysfunction of vulnerable organ systems can similarly be mediated in response to unconscious psychic conflicts. In other words, the characteristic defense process of an individual unconsciously fearing injury mediated or expressed through a vulnerable or conditioned organ system might be exacerbated or stimulated to defend against the "injury," causing tissue reactions in the relevant organ system axis which, if chronic, lead to permanent morphological and physiological dysfunction (diseases of adaptation). The disease state induced by such a process represents not the conversion itself but a complication of it. For example, the vulnerable individual who has reached an impasse in a domestic, professional, or social situation may unconsciously feel like "getting rid of" or "tossing up" the whole business. This verbalized formulation of his reaction to the process may be defended by many factors, including both reality and conscience (superego), and therefore gains little further objectification. Through bodily processes, however, the psychologically and physically vulnerable individual might give symbolic expression to this desire by channeling it through the autonomic nervous system, resulting in a gastrointestinal disorder such as diarrhea or vomiting, which could secondarily result in colitis or peptic ulcer due to tissue reactions to the elicitation of local noxious factors.

ADAPTATION

Many investigators have recently turned their attention from etiological relationships of psychic and somatic processes to a study of individual's adaptation[69] to illness and disease in the anticipation that more fruitful and pragmatic considerations for the treatment of the illness may be forthcoming. The adaptational studies have also cited behavioral and physiological correlates of coping and have attempted to discern between those processes that were beneficial and those that were maladaptive for the protection of the organism. Schwab and colleagues[70] have identified "somatopsychic" relationships occurring in patients with somatic disease and have described four patterns or responses: (1) grief and depression, (2) anxiety and denial, (3) changed self-percept, and (4) disturbed interpersonal relations. Others have noted that the way in which an individual copes with a disease process or a potentially life-threatening procedure correlates with and has predictive value as to the outcome of that procedure. They have studied patients: (1) with specific illnesses associated with such disease entities as hemophilia[71] or diabetes[35]; (2) undergoing procedures such as hemodialysis[72–74] or cardiac surgery[75–80]; (3) dying of cancer[81, 82] or chronic disease[83]; and (4) with permanent physical impairment such as paraplegia[84] in an attempt to find factors that might influence both the course and therapy of these conditions.

Endocrinological investigations, such as those of Hamburg and Adams[12] and Greene and co-workers,[85] have attempted to identify physiological and biological correlates of behavioral and emotional response by correlating the latter with adrenal corticoid, growth hormone, insulin, glucose, free fatty acids, and other chemical levels. Such efforts at correlation may prove helpful in our understanding of the physiology of protection, recovery, and adaptation and of the relation of these factors to the individual's psychological response to catastrophic disease and trauma.

The importance of recognizing that any individual experiencing a change in his health is confronted with a catastrophic disruption in his usual homeostatic adjustment to his environment is central to the thesis of those who study the adaptation of humans to stress. This upheaval extends beyond the individual and affects the domestic and social situations in which the individual negotiates and necessitates adjustments within them. The ill individual invariably experiences the shock of his own vulnerability, which in essence is a suggestion or recognition of his proximate mortality.[86] This real vulnerability and threatened mortality invoke a grieving process[87–89] that includes disbelief, shock, intellectual acceptance, anger, guilt, repudiation, denial, withdrawal, and various attempts directed at self-restitution. This seems to be an appropriate reaction for both the individual and his family, but the patient and his family may need the encouragement and the permission of the physician to acknowledge and express their grief. In a sense, the individual who, in association with his disease, can pursue the work of the grieving process will resolve many of the ambivalences and conflicts occasioned by his disability and be able to make the realistic decisions that are imperative for his adaptation to his and society's changed percept of him. On the other hand, the individual who is unable to work through his grief by expression of his feelings and thoughts with his physician and other supporting individuals may be less likely to meet the psychological and physical adjustments necessary for survival. Catastrophic illness may itself precipitate a depressive reaction or a conservation-withdrawal state that seriously interferes with the patient's ability to fight his disease.

THE BIOPSYCHOSOCIAL APPROACH

In summary, a survey of the literature of the last 50 years demonstrates a decreasing preoccupation with single factors, either psychological or somatic, in the cause of disease and increasing attention to the multiple factors associated with illness, which has caused many investigators to study the environmental field of the individual who becomes ill. Thus, at this time, the term "psychosomatic medicine" applies not to a discrete set of diseases but rather to an approach to illness that studies the interrelationships of the biological, the psychological, and the social—the biopsychosocial approach. On the basis of these researches, the following formulations may presently be made:

1. All illnesses have psychosocial aspects that influence their cause, precipitation, manifestation, course, and outcome.
2. Cause-and-effect relationships between psychic and somatic processes are of lesser significance than establishing the interrelatedness of psychological, social, and biological processes and their effect on one another in the ill patient.
3. The study of how an individual adapts to stresses biologically and psychologically and on what underlying factors these responses depend has become a major area of psychosomatic research.
4. There is no fundamental difference between mental and physical illness, but all illnesses have psychological and somatic components.

5. There is no special treatment of psychosomatic diseases as opposed to any other diseases, but in the treatment of all illnesses there are therapeutic procedures that are required for the psyche as well as for the body.

6. The approach to the individual suffering from a specific illness is specific depending on the idiosyncracy of the patient's life situation, which includes, in addition to attending to the disease process, attending to the psychological and social correlates.

7. These interrelationships and correlations can be made by the physician only if he pursues an interview method that will allow the patient to make these associations.[62]

8. Patients confronted with particular procedures and illness situations may experience them in similar ways. The physician identifying this common experience will be able to help his patient anticipate and adjust to the experience.

9. Anxiety, grieving, and depression are parts of the illness experience of all patients. Attention to these factors on the part of the physician by permitting and encouraging his patient to express his feelings will facilitate adjustment.

10. A recognition of the patient's personality characteristics will assist the physician in structuring his relationship with the patient in a manner that will be most therapeutic.[90]

References

1. Engel, G. L.: The need for a new medical model: a challenge for biomedicine. Science *196:* 129, 1977.
2. Alexander, F. G., and Selesnick, S. T.: The psychosomatic approach in medicine. In *The History of Psychiatry*, pp. 388–401. New York, Harper and Row, 1966.
3. Kluckhohn, C., and Leighton, D.: *The Navaho*, p. 192. Garden City, N. Y., Doubleday, 1962.
4. Descartes, R.: *The Discourse on Method and Metaphysical Mediations of René Descartes*, pp. 125–141. London, Walter Scott, 1967.
5. Freud, S.: *Collected Papers*, J. Strachey, editor, p. 268. New York, Basic Books, 1959.
6. Breuer, J., and Freud, S.: The psychic mechanisms of hysterical phenomena. In *Studies in Hysteria*, Nervous and Mental Disease Monograph Series #61. New York, Nervous and Mental Disease Publishing Company, 1937.
7. Groddeck, G.: *The Book of the It*. New York, The New American Library, 1961.
8. Deutsch, F., Thompson, D., Pinderhughes, C., et al.: *Body, Mind and the Sensory Gateways*. Basle, S. Karger, 1962.
9. Cannon, W. B.: *Bodily Changes in Pain, Hunger, Fear and Rage*. New York, Appleton & Co., 1920.
10. Funkenstein, D. H., King, S. H., and Drolette, M.: *Mastery of Stress*. Cambridge, Mass., Harvard University Press, 1957.
11. Cleghorn, R. A., and Graham, B. F.: Studies of adrenal cortical activity in psychoneurotic subjects. Am. J. Psychiatry *106:* 668, 1950.
12. Hamburg, D. A., and Adams, J. E.: A perspective on coping behavior. Arch. Gen. Psychiatry *17:* 277, 1967.

13. Mason, J. W.: The scope of psychoendocrine research. Psychosom. Med. *30:* 5, 565, 1968.
14. Selye, H.: *The Physiology and Pathology of Exposure to Stress.* Montreal, Acta, 1950.
15. Gellhorn, E.: The tuning of the nervous system: Physiological foundations and implications for behavior. Perspect. Biol. Med. *10:* 559, 1967.
16. Benedek, T., and Rubenstein, B. R.: *The Sexual Cycle in Women: The Relation between Ovarian Function and Psychodynamic Processes,* Psychosomatic Medicine Monographs, Vol. 3, Nos. 1 and 2. Washington, D. C., National Research Council, 1942.
17. Sawyer, C. H.: Some endocrine aspects of forebrain inhibition. Brain Res. *6:* 48, 1947.
18. Adkisson, P. L.: Internal clocks and insect diapause. Science *154:* 234, 1966.
19. Schildkraut, J. J., and Kety, S. S.: Biogenic amines and emotion. Science *156:* 21, 1967.
20. Steinhilber, R. M., Peterson, H. W., Jr., and Martin, M. J.: Emotional states caused by organic diseases. Postgrad. Med. *39:* 621, 1966.
21. Engel, G. L., and Romano, J.: Delirium, a syndrome of cerebral insufficiency. J. Chronic Dis. *9:* 260, 1959.
22. Booth, D. A.: Vertebrate brain ribonucleic acids and memory retention. Psychol. Bull. *68:* 149, 1967.
23. Sved, S., Kral, V. A., Enesco, H. E., et al.: Memory and serum ribonuclease activity in the aged. J. Am. Geriat. Soc. *15:* 629, 1967.
24. Dunbar, H. F.: *Emotions and Bodily Changes: A Survey of Literature on Psychosomatic Interrelationships.* New York, Columbia University Press, 1954.
25. Ruesch, J.: The infantile personality. Psychosom. Med. *10:* 134, 1948.
26. Marty, P., and De'Uzan, M.: La "pensée operatoire." Rev. Franc. Psychoanal. *27:* Suppl. 1345, 1963.
27. Nemiah, J. C., and Sifneos, P. E.: Affect and fantasy in patients with psychosomatic disorders. In *Modern Trends in Psychosomatic Medicine,* O. W. Hill, editor, Chapter 2. New York, Appleton-Century Crofts, 1970.
28. Friedman, M., and Rosenman, R. H.: Association of specific overt behavior pattern with blood and cardiovascular findings. J.A.M.A. *169:* 1286, 1959.
29. Alexander, F., and French, T. M.: *Studies in Psychosomatic Medicine.* New York, Ronald Press, 1948.
30. Nemiah, J. C., and Sifneos, P. E.: A study of the specificity of current psychological factors involved in the production of psychosomatic disease in patients, each suffering from two psychosomatic illnesses (abstract). Psychosom. Med. *30:* 553, 1968.
31. Weiner, H., Thaler, M., Reiser, M. F., et al.: Etiology of duodenal ulcer. Am. J. Dig. Dis. *3:* 285, 1958.
32. Mirsky, I. A.: Physiologic, psychologic and social determinants in the etiology of duodenal ulcer. Am. J. Dig. Dis. *3:* 285, 1958.
33. Wolff, H. G.: *Stress and Disease.* Springfield, Ill., Charles C Thomas, 1953.
34. Grace, W. J., and Graham, D. T.: Relationship of specific attitudes and emotions to certain bodily diseases. Psychosom. Med. *14:* 243, 1962.
35. Graham, D. T., Lundy, R. M., Benjamin, L. S., et al.: Specific attitudes in initial interviews with patients having different "psychosomatic" diseases. Psychosom. Med. *24:* 257, 1952.
36. Hinkle, L. E., and Wolf, S.: A summary of experimental evidence relating life stress to diabetes mellitus. J. Mt. Sinai Hosp. *19:* 537, 1952.
37. Sontag, L. W., and Wallace, R. F.: Preliminary report of the Fels Funds. Study of fetal activity. Am. J. Dis. Child *48:* 1050, 1934.
38. Bridger, W. H., and Reiser, M. F.: Psychophysiologic studies of the neonate: An approach toward the methodological and theoretical problems involved. Psychosom. Med. *21:* 265, 1959.

39. Bridger, W. H., Birns, B. M., and Blank, M.: A comparison of behavioral ratings and heart rate measurements in human neonates. Psychosom. Med. *27:* 123, 1965.
40. Holmes, T. H., and Rahe, R. H.: The social readjustment rating scale. J. Psychosom. Res. *11:* 213, 1967.
41. Rahe, R. H.: Life crisis and health change. In *Psychotropic Drug Responses: Advances in Prediction*, P. R. A. May and R. Wittenborn, editors, pp. 92–125. Springfield, Ill., Charles C Thomas, 1969.
42. Rahe, R. H.: Life change measurement clarification (editorial). Psychosom. Med. *40:* 95, 1978.
43. Schottsteadt, W. W., Grace, W. J., and Wolff, H. G.: Life situations, behavior, attitudes, emotions, and renal excretion of fluid and electrolytes. IV. Situations associated with retention of water, sodium, and potassium. J. Psychosom. Res. *1:* 287, 1956.
44. Grinker, R. R., and Robbins, F. P.: *Psychosomatic Case Book*, pp. 31–38. New York, Blakiston, 1954.
45. Greene, W. A., Jr.: Psychological factors and reticuloendothelial disease. I. Preliminary observations on a group of males with lymphomas and leukemias. Psychosom. Med. *16:* 220, 1954.
46. Greene, W. A., Jr., Young, L. E., and Swisher, S. N.: Psychological factors and reticuloendothelial disease. II. Observations on a group of women with lymphomas and leukemias. Psychosom. Med. *18:* 284, 1956.
47. Greene, W. A., Jr.: Some perspectives for observing and interpreting biopsychologic relations and doctor-patient relations. Perspect. Biol. Med. *2:* 453, 1959.
48. Greene, W. A., Jr., and Miller, G.: Psychological factors and reticuloendothelial disease. IV. Observations on a group of children and adolescents with leukemia. An interpretation of diseases development in terms of the mother-child unit. Psychosom. Med. *20:* 124, 1958.
49. Greene, W. A., Jr.: Role of a vicarious object in the adaptation to object loss. I. Use of a vicarious object as a means of adjustment to separation from a significant person. Psychosom. Med. *20:* 344, 1958.
50. Greene, W. A., Jr.: Role of a vicarious object in the adaptation to object loss. II. Vicissitudes in the role of the vicarious object. Psychosom. Med. *21:* 438, 1959.
51. Schmale, A. H., Jr.: Relationship of separation and depression to disease. I. A report on a hospitalized medical population. Psychosom. Med. *20:* 259, 1958.
52. Adamson, J. D., and Schmale, A. H.: Object loss, giving up, and the onset of psychiatric disease. Psychosom. Med. *27:* 557, 1965.
53. Engel, G. L.: *Psychological Development in Health and Disease*, p. 387. Philadelphia, W. B. Saunders, 1962.
54. Engel, G. L., and Reichsman, F.: Spontaneous and experimentally induced depressions in an infant with gastric fistula. J. Am. Psychoanal. Assoc. *4:* 428, 1956.
55. Engel, G. L.: Studies of ulcerative colitis. I. Clinical data bearing on the nature of the somatic process. Psychosom. Med. *16:* 496, 1954.
56. Engel, G. L.: Studies of ulcerative colitis. II. The nature of the somatic process and the adequacy of psychosomatic hypotheses. Am. J. Med. *16:* 416, 1954.
57. Engel, G. L.: Studies of ulcerative colitis. III. The nature of the psychologic processes. Am. J. Med. *19:* 231, 1955.
58. Engel, G. L.: Studies of ulcerative colitis. IV. The significance of headaches. Psychosom. Med. *18:* 334, 1956.
59. Engel, G. L.: Anxiety and depression-withdrawal: The primary affects of unpleasure. Int. J. Psychoanal. *43:* 89, 1962.
60. Engel, G. L.: *Fainting*. Springfield, Ill., Charles C Thomas, 1962.

61. Engel, G. L.: Guilt, pain and success facilitated by the pain of glomus tumor and peptic ulcer. Psychosom. Med. *24:* 37, 1962.
62. Morgan, W. L., and Engel, G. L.: *The Clinical Approach to the Patient.* Philadelphia, W. B. Saunders, 1969.
63. Engel, G. L., Greene, W. L., Jr., Reichsman, F., et al.: A graduate and undergraduate teaching program on the psychological aspects of medicine. J. Med. Educ. *32:* 859, 1957.
64. Engel, G. L.: A unified concept of health and disease. Perspect. Biol. Med. *3:* 459, 1960.
65. Engel, G. L., and Schmale, A. H., Jr.: Psychoanalytic theory of somatic disorder: Conversion, specificity and the disease onset situation. J. Am. Psychoanal. Assoc. *15:* 344, 1967.
66. Engel, G. L.: A life setting conducive to illness. The giving-up-given-up complex. Bull. Menninger Clin. *32:* 355, 1967.
67. Engel, G. L.: A reconsideration of the role of conversion in somatic disease. Compr. Psychiatry *9:* 316, 1968.
68. Engel, G. L.: "Psychogenic pain" and the pain-prone patient. Am. J. Med. *26:* 899, 1959.
69. Romano, J., editor: *Adaptation.* Ithaca, N. Y., Cornell University Press, 1949.
70. Schwab, J. J., Bialow, M., Brown, J. M., et al.: Diagnosing depression in medical inpatients. Ann. Intern. Med. *67:* 695, 1967.
71. Agle, D. P.: Patients with hemophilia and related states. Arch. Intern. Med. *114:* 76, 1964.
72. Kempf, J. P.: Renal failure, artificial kidney and kidney transplant. Am. J. Psychiatry *122:* 1270, 1966.
73. McKegney, F. P., and Lange, P.: The decision to no longer live on chronic hemodialysis. Am. J. Psychiatry *128:* 267, 1971.
74. Friedman, E. A., Goodwin, N. J., and Chaudhrey, L.: Psychosocial adjustment to maintenance hemodialysis. N. Y. J. Med. *70:* 629, 1970.
75. Meyer, B. C., Blacher, R. S., and Brown, F.: A clinical study of psychiatric and psychological aspects of mitral surgery. Psychosom. Med. *23:* 194, 1961.
76. Abram, H. S.: Adaptation to open heart surgery: A psychiatric study of response to the threat of death. Am. J. Psychiatry *122:* 659, 1965.
77. Kornfeld, D. S., Zimberg, S., and Malm, J. R.: Psychiatric complications of open heart surgery. N. Engl. J. Med. *273:* 287, 1965.
78. Kennedy, J. A., and Bakst, H.: The influence of emotions on the outcome of cardiac surgery: A predictive study. Bull. N. Y. Acad. Med. *42:* 811, 1966.
79. Kimball, C. P.: Psychological response to the experience of open heart surgery. Am. J. Psychiatry *126:* 348, 1969.
80. Kimball, C. P.: A predictive study of adjustment to cardiac surgery. J. Thorac. Cardiovasc. Surg. *58:* 891, 1969.
81. Norton, J.: Treatment of a dying patient. Psychoanal. Stud. Child *18:* 541, 1963.
82. Davies, R., Quinlan, D. M., McKegney, F. P., and Kimball, C. P.: Organic factors and psychological adjustment in advanced cancer patients. Psychosom. Med. *35:* 464, 1973.
83. Friedman, S. B., Chodoff, P., Mason, J. W., et al.: Behavioral observations on parents anticipating the death of a child. Pediatrics *32:* 610, 1963.
84. Hohmann, G. W.: Some effects of spinal cord lesions in experienced emotional feelings. Psychophysiology *3:* 143, 1966.
85. Greene, W. A., Conron, G., Schalch, D. S., et al.: Psychological correlates of growth hormone and adrenal secretory responses in patients undergoing cardiac catheterization (abstract). Psychosom. Med. *31:* 450, 1969.
86. Kimball, C. P.: Death and dying: A chronological discussion. J. Thanatol. *1:* 42, 1971.
87. Lindemann, E.: Symptomatology and management of acute grief. Am. J. Psychiatry *101:* 141, 1944.

88. Janis, I. L.: *Psychological Stress: Psychoanalytic and Behavioral Studies of Surgical Patients*. New York, John Wiley, 1958.
89. Engel, G. L.: Is grief a disease? A challenge for medical research. Psychosom. Med. *23:* 18, 1961.
90. Shapiro, D.: *Neurotic Styles*, Chapters 2–5. New York, Basic Books, 1965.

CHAPTER 17

Psychosocial Aspects of Cardiac Disease in Children and Adolescents

SYMPTOMS AND SIGNS

The symptom or complaint of the child (or parent) is a verbal symbol indicating a disturbed state of the organism. The verbal symbol is never exact, only approximate, never specific for a given process (whatever its framework of reference), but always subjective. As such, symbols always imply an infinite number of associations—past and present, conscious and unconscious, intended and unintended—which may or may not have greater or lesser significance to the physician-interpreter.

The job of the physician is to interpret the symptom into the languages of medicine, which today in our expanded view of the field includes not only the physioanatomical, but the social (environmental) and the psychological. Until the symptom is considered within each of these realms of logic, it remains confined to the inscrutable and subjective field of the patient, inaccessible to the physician's objective approach. Hence, the physician's first role is that of verbally elaborating the symptom as presented by the child and parent, the facts upon which his subsequent analysis is based.

The elaboration, clarification, and objectification of the symptom take place within the interview (see Chapter 2), its crucial success depending upon the initial relationship that is established between patient and physician. The interview process may be augmented by the physician seeing that his patient is at maximum physical and emotional ease and

---

Modified version (and reproduced with permission) of article from Heart and Lung 2: 394–399, 1973; copyrighted by the C. V. Mosby Company.

giving the individual ample time to express his discomfort, including his anxieties, fears, sadness, and anger. As the child and his parent become more at ease through expressing their feelings to a patient and empathic listener, they become more able to collaborate with the physician in the detective-like manner of diagnosis. What is the symptom like? Where was the child? With whom was he? How was it responded to? In this manner, the physician is most likely to obtain the answer to his ultimate question: Why now, at this time? These questions and their answers, elaborated in the context of an open-ended manner, rarely directly, allow the physician to accumulate the data with which he can construct his interpretation and diagnosis.

Herein is contained the first criterion for accumulating the data upon which the psychosocial consideration of the symptom may be determined. Herein also rest the foundations of therapy by allowing the patient to talk and helping him clarify what is going on in the expectation that relief will be forthcoming. All patients and their physicians have apocryphal ideations and fantasies about symptoms that, in the course of rational approaches, may be exposed. Through the process of exposure these become diminished. If they do not, the physician should suspect delusions or hypochondriasis, which will need further elaboration and analysis, possibly by a psychiatrist. We all have emotional reactions around symptoms, which include anxiety, depression, and anger and the defenses that we develop to contain these feelings. In elaborating the symptom, some of these feelings, through expression, are simultaneously relieved. Symptoms also have symbolic aspects idiosyncratic for the individual. Frequently they suggest vulnerability and sometimes the possibility of death. With symptoms that become identified with cardiac disease, these symbolic aspects become exaggerated because, quite realistically, the heart is equated with life itself. In these instances, the symbolic identifications themselves give rise to emotions and defenses against these that may lead to complicating behavioral reactions interfering with further diagnosis and therapy. Before the latter may proceed, it is necessary to identify and give reassurance regarding these symbolic aspects.

In the patient suspected of having cardiac disease, a number of other processes may interfere with the elaboration of symptoms by the physician. Organic brain syndromes[1] are frequently observed in instances where congestive heart failure has led to hypoxia and the ensuing compromise of cognitive functions. These deficits may be elaborated during the interview by identifying confusion on the part of the individual regarding his whereabouts and the sequence of events leading up to the present, a diminished ability to pay attention, and an impairment of rational processes, most readily assessed by examining the patient's abstractive ability. Inasmuch as these impairments of brain function in cardiac patients are usually acute and transient, attention to the metabolic aspects will frequently lead to rapid amelioration.

Symptoms suggestive of cardiac disease frequently occur during times of life stress,[2] especially when losses have taken or are about to take place. In addition to suggesting cardiac pathology, these symptoms may reflect symbolic reactions to these environmental insults and suggest physiological processes of noncardiac origin involving muscular tension and/or more subtle psychophysiological processes, such as conversion. In addition to the temporal proximity of these symptoms to a major environmental event—real, threatened, or imagined—the atypicalness or bizarreness of its description, the similarity of the symptom to that of a key person in the individual's environment, the presence of exaggerated or bland affect inappropriate to the complaint, and the uses made of the symptom by the patient will increase the physician's suspicion of a conversion process.[3] It is well to remember that children may have conversion processes superimposed upon cardiac disease that may mimic the symptoms of that illness. Frequently, these occur in individuals and their families who have been unable to cope with their anxieties and depressions occasioned by heart disease and become preoccupied with somatic processes, developing an oversensitivity and awareness of their bodily state bordering on the delusional. Such individuals require not only careful and continual assessment by their physicians, but they also need therapists who have almost infinite patience and empathy. Scheduling these children and their parents relatively frequently for a limited and structured time period of 15 to 20 minutes helps diminish the need for episodic and dramatic medical attention.

The common syndrome of hyperventilation,[4] frequently associated with aerophagia, may present with symptoms that first suggest a cardiac basis. These symptoms include choking, shortness of breath, rapid respirations, generalized weakness, dizziness, palpitations, numbness of extremities, and headaches. Although hyperventilation and its symptoms may be related to other causes, most frequently they are reactions to anxiety. Both electroencephalogram (EEG) and electrocardiogram (ECG) changes have been correlated with anxiety hyperventilation states.

Similarly, symptoms and signs such as anxiety, phobias, palpitations, overbreathing, headache, nervousness, and fatigability may initially be identified as relating to cardiac disease. However, on more definitive examination, they may lead to the identification of depression or, less frequently, an incipient schizophrenic process.[4]

The signs of cardiac disease, although more objective than symptoms, may also give rise to affects and the defenses against these for realistic or unrealistic reasons. On the basis of medical folklore, signs may be misperceived and misinterpreted, leading to unnecessary emotional discomfort. Signs may also become the constant reminder and badge of the sufferer's infirmities. The manner and degree to which he can accept and adapt to these physicial signs and their limitations will help the physician gauge his psychological adjustment.

ATTITUDES OF CHILD AND FAMILY

The attitude of the child toward his cardiac disease depends on his life stage and the attitudes and reactions of his family, teachers, and peers. The extent to which his illness remains unclear or is misperceived by any of these people will severely compromise the child's potential for maximum acceptance and adjustment. Overreaction to illness by parent, physician, or teacher, leading to unnecessary restrictions and overprotection, interferes with the child's progress through life stages, leading to failures to complete certain age-specific tasks.[5] The time at which the disease is experienced and identified in the life of the child and the procedures and reactions to the illness may influence the child's maturational development conceptualized in psychosocial terms.[6,7] Physiological maturation may also be influenced by the direct effect of the disease on physical development and, secondarily, by the indirect effect on brain function by the delayed learning of motor skills occasioned by physical limitations.[8]

The child who experiences prolonged separation from his family, who necessarily undergoes painful and complicated procedures, whose range of activities is severely compromised by his illness relative to those of his peers, and who experiences frequent absences from school becomes isolated from both family and the usual peer social units that are the essential matrix of growth and development in a culture. Initial isolation and eventual alienation, a feeling of differentness, and an ultimate sense of anomie are possible, although fortunately infrequent, sequelae. In some senses, the child with either congenital cardiac disease or that acquired in early childhood is a disadvantaged child.[9] Especially in the first 3 years of life, the child is likely to exhibit intellectual deficiencies relative to those of his peers. Later he is likely to be unduly influenced by the exaggerated responses of his parents, incorporating their own feelings of inadequacy, guilt, frustration, and irritation at having either produced or nurtured a defective child.[10] To assuage these tendencies, physicians concerned with the care of families with handicapped children from before birth through adolescence need to explore the healthy and unhealthy reactions to the child's illness. When this is accomplished and when it is possible to treat the child with a minimum of restrictions and procedural investigations and corrections, psychosocial growth and development are most likely to proceed unimpeded.

Frequently, the child goes through phases of manifesting guilt and, in his attempts to ascribe casuality to his illness, attributes it to his own carelessness and neglect of his health, exposure to infection, and poor eating habits.[11] He expresses anxiety about infections, medications, hospitalizations, and surgery. Most often he associates illness with pain, physical restrictions, social handicaps, heart disease, crippling, and death. Some children with congenital heart disease depict themselves graphically smaller than normal children.[12] It is inferred that they have a constricted view of their body, possibly because of the restrictions imposed on them. Some express the belief that something is missing and that in a sense the world needs to make up for this omission. Others attempt to place blame on their parents for their illness.

Mothers of children with congenital heart disease frequently show apprehension regarding the behavior of newborns, uncertainty about diagnosis, and fears of death for their child.[13] The excitement of giving birth becomes burdened with a sense of doom, disappointment, and frustration. The response is to become overprotective. These mothers are frequently frustrated in their attempts to provide their child with a normal active life because of repeated assessments, hospitalizations, cardiac catheterizations, and the possibility of surgery. Their frustration is increased by the development and discipline of behavior problems related to unsatisfactory adjustment.

ROLE OF THE HEALTH TEAM

The role of the physician and his team in the psychological adjustment of the child and his family to cardiac disease is crucial. To the extent that he takes time to listen to the anxieties of the parents and the fantasies of the child, he will be able to combat irrational beliefs emanating from misconceptions and folklore. To the extent that his explanations are simple, direct, and clear, he will fulfill his role as teacher, dispelling many of the fallacies that are popularly held regarding heart disease. To the degree that he is rigid, authoritarian, overly cautious, and conservative in his approach and management, he will transmit this to parents, who in turn will be rigid, overprotective, and domineering.[14]

The perceptive physician frequently discovers that his role with adolescents with chronic illness and their parents is one of mediation in which he attempts to seek acceptable compromises for the youth straining against the restrictions of parents and society, which include those additional taboos occasioned by the illness. Failure on the part of the physician to fulfill this role may lead to the abandonment by the adolescent of his treatment routine, thereby simultaneously courting disaster and incurring the displeasure of parent, physician, and other authoritative persons. Continuity of management by a physician and his staff who are familiar with the patient, family, and community remains the keystone of ideal care.

SOCIAL AND PEER ATTITUDES

Much education of the public still is required in informing them about heart disease in order to allay anxieties and fears based upon prevalent misconceptions. This is especially true as it relates to congenital and acquired cardiac problems experienced by many children. Although requiring periodic evaluation and occasional intervention, the limitations imposed seldom are such as to unduly hamper the normal growth and development of the child.[15] When this message is successfully conveyed to parents, teachers, and other individuals involved with children, much of the dread of childhood cardiac disease, which is based on superstition and unfounded beliefs, may be overcome. When parents and teachers are able to take an objective approach, this will affect the attitudes of the afflicted child's peers, who are quick to exploit the differences and imperfections in one another. This differentness is exaggerated by unnecessary concern and restrictions.

In those instances of severe cardiac disease which has impaired both physical and subsequent social maturation, the child may indeed suffer many of the handicaps attributed to the so-called disadvantaged child. His intellectual and motor development may be impaired, leading to a discrepancy between chronological age and level of achievement. Superimposed on this may be additional handicaps occasioned by overprotective parents and the ensuing dependency that such relationships cultivate. A child so burdened adopts "sick role"[16] behavior and attitudes that will pursue him throughout his life. This is characterized by dependency, passivity, manipulative behavior, using the illness to achieve social sympathy and gain, making excuses for one's behavior and performance on the basis of cardiac disease, and the consequent emotions of frustration, fear, and hostility.

HOSPITALIZATION

The strange world of the hospital, taken for granted by the accustomed staff, is one of fear and anxiety for child and parent alike. This sanctuary of truth and potential cure for the health worker is more frequently viewed as one of pain and death by the uninitiated. Few enter these halls without feeling their mortality on one level or another. Added to these given fears are those occasioned by the specific procedure, catheterization, or surgery, in which pain is not unknown.

The reactions of the child to the hospital frequently reflect those of the parent. The degree to which the parent has been able to feel empathetic distance and objectivity, while maintaining simple, direct, honest communication regarding the nature of the illness and its evaluation, determines in large measure the objectivity and cooperative participation of the child. Most children show some observable reaction to the experience of hospitalization and treatment as distant from the effect of the illness itself.[17] Some will exhibit reactions that require special and, at times, strenuous modes of adaptation, usually self-limited but sometimes lasting for weeks or months after hospitalization. These reactions are greater in preschool children who, in addition, need to cope with separation from parents, and in children with previous limited capacities for adaptation. Studies suggest that such prophylactic measures as increased visiting hours for parents and psychological preparation of child and parent for hospitalization do much to reduce the incidence and severity of reactions.

It is suggested that a child views any kind of surgical intervention through the perspective of the developmental level he has attained or from a regressed level.[18] Anxiety induces regression, whose effects will be observed in terms of changes in feeding, sleeping, and toilet behavior. Aggressivity, irritability, restlessness, and the development of somatic preoccupations all may be exhibited by a child whose usual coping defenses are inadequate to handle the demands and insults of hospitalization. Underlying such behavior may be the presence of an organic brain syndrome and/or pain.[19] The astute physician should always keep these possibilities in mind, for they are open to diagnostic and therapeutic intervention.

Observations by the author of adolescents undergoing cardiac surgery have noted the use of a spectrum of defenses, varying from a painful denial to relatively sophisticated mechanisms of identification and sublimation, in which the patient becomes absorbed with the activities of nurses and physicians and projects for himself career interests fashioned after them. Displacement has been observed in terms of the adolescent's concern with disfigurement and the operative scar. The more anxious adolescent may seem unusually withdrawn with constricted affect, engaging only limitedly with peers or surrogates alike. Some will project their unspoken fears onto parents, occasionally with expressions of blame and hostility. Such reactions are most frequently observed in adolescents from families where there has been little discussion and preparation for impending surgery.

The threat of death of a child undergoing surgery is always present and experienced by the family. Parents react in a unique manner depending on each one's personality structure, past experience, and the individualized meaning and specific circumstances associated with the threatened loss.[20] Recognition of these factors assists the hospital staff in coping with parents. Initially, parents are unable to incorporate detailed information regarding the disease and its clinical course. They require careful guidance and may need repeated explanation. In committing the child to the hands of the cardiologist or surgeon, they are wary of being isolated from the treatment in which they need to be participants. Parents of children undergoing repeated or prolonged procedures may be considered as sustaining chronic grieving reactions requiring understanding and support by the staff.

ORGANIC BRAIN SYNDROMES

Because organic brain syndromes have been so frequently ignored or overlooked as factors in contributing to abnormal behavior in patients with cardiac disease and undergoing surgery, these conditions cannot be emphasized often enough. A chronic organic brain syndrome is considered to be irreversible and implies morphological or structural damage to the central nervous system, frequently associated with focal neurological dysfunction. Workers have been particularly concerned with the effect of cardiac conditions on the intellectual development of the child, noting the greatest impairment when the occurrence of the disease has been early and the severity great.[21] However, much of the intellectual impairment noted seems to be secondary to the physical restrictions occasioned by the cardiac disease regarding motor development. After the age of 3, there is less correlation between physical incapacity and intellectual functioning as measured by intelligence tests. Children with cyanotic heart disease scored significantly below those with acyanotic disease and well children. When structural damage has occurred there may be a significantly poorer capacity for auditory-visual integration than that of normal children, which may be viewed as the "product of the aberrant development of intrasensory liaison."[22] Others have failed to correlate an intelligence quotient (IQ) difference in children with congenital heart disease, suggesting that those that have been observed may be explained on the basis of anxiety and neuroses secondary to the illness. Physicians may be aware of current controversy regarding sex differences in IQ's of children undergoing cardiac surgery.[23] Surprisingly, the verbal IQ's of girls were less than their own performance IQ's and the verbal IQ scores of boys.

The behavioral disturbances associated with organic brain syndromes include emotional lability, short attention span, social incompetence, vacillating work habits, and meddlesomeness. When chronic brain syndromes are present, their effect on the child depends to a great extent upon the way in which he and his parents perceive his limitation. Greater insight, more optimistic personalities, better economic circumstances, and excellent professional guidance have been found to facilitate rehabilitation and diminish the deficits based on brain damage.

Acute organic brain syndromes are reversible and more likely to arise from disturbances in function secondary to metabolic and circulatory disorders. Medications, perhaps, are most frequently implicated in these conditions. These include analgesics, sedatives, and anesthetics, as well as drugs that alter circulatory mechanisms leading to hypoxia. When impairment of cognitive functions in the areas of orientation, memory, concentration, and abstraction is observed in the patient with cardiac disease, careful evaluation and attention to possible underlying factors are imperative.

In summary, the effects of cardiac disease and its procedures of evaluation, treatment, and correction on the psychosocial development of the child and adolescent depend on many factors. These include: the specific disease[24, 25]; the age at which it develops; the extent to which it interferes with the acquisition of age-specific developmental tasks[26]; the associated secondary effects it has on brain function; and the attitudes of parents, physicians, other adults, and peers. The extent to which the appropriate individuals are able to assist the afflicted child to cope adequately and to adapt to the handicaps invoked by the illness will determine the degree to which the child experiences integration of himself with the society in which he lives. Failure to achieve this ideal will lead to the adoption of sick role behavior, which will insure that the child will bear the scars of his affliction in terms of dependent and immature behavior.

References

1. Engel, G. L., and Romano, J.: Delirium, a syndrome of cerebral insufficiency. J. Chronic Dis. *9:* 260, 1959.
2. Mutter, A. Z., and Schleifer, M. J.: The role of psychological and social factors in the onset of somatic illness in children. Psychosom. Med. *28:* 333, 1966.
3. Engel, G. L.: "Psychogenic pain" and the pain-prone patient. Am. J. Med. *26:* 899, 1959.
4. Senn, M. J. E., and Solnit, A. J.: *Problems in Child Behavior and Development,* pp. 116–117, 129. Philadelphia, Lea & Febiger, 1968.
5. Erikson, E.: *Childhood and Society,* pp. 247–274. New York, W. W. Norton, 1963.
6. Carey, W. B.: Psychologic sequelae of early infant health care. Clin. Pediatr. *8:* 459, 1969.

7. Lourie, R. S.: The first three years of life: An overview of a new frontier of psychiatry. Am. J. Psychiatry *127:* 33, 1971.
8. Chazon, M., Harris, T., O'Neill, D., et al: The intellectual and emotional development of children with congenital heart disease. Guy's Hosp. Rep. *100:* 331, 1951.
9. Richmond, J. B.: Disadvantaged children and what they have compelled us to learn. Yale J. Biol. Med. *43:* 127, 1970.
10. Glaser, H. H., Harrison, G. S., and Lynn, D. B.: Emotional implications of congenital heart disease in children. Pediatrics *33:* 364, 1964.
11. Lynn, D. B., Glaser, H. H., and Harrison, G. S.: Comprehensive medical care for handicapped children. III. Concepts of illness in children with rheumatic fever. Am. J. Dis. Child. *103:* 120, 1962.
12. Green, M., and Levitt, E. E.: Constriction of body image in children with congenital heart disease. Pediatrics *29:* 438, 1962.
13. Glaser, H. H., Lynn, D. B., and Harrison, G. S.: Comprehensive medical care for handicapped children. I. Patterns of anxiety in mothers of children with rheumatic fever. Am. J. Dis. Child. *102:* 90, 1961.
14. Glaser, H. H., Lynn, D. B., and Harrison, G. S.: Studies of comprehensive medical care for handicapped children. II. Relationships of doctors-in-training with pediatric outpatients. J. Med. Educ. *36:* 1283, 1961.
15. Adams, F. H., and Moss, A. J.: Physical activity of children with congenital heart disease. Am. J. Cardiol. *24:* 605, 1969.
16. Kasl, S. V., and Cobb, S.: Health behavior, illness behavior, and sick role behavior. I. Arch. Environ. Health *12:* 246, 1966.
17. Prugh, D. G., Staub, E. M., Sands, H. H., et al.: A study of the emotional reactions of children and families to hospitalization and illness. Am. J. Orthopsychiatry *23:* 70, 1953.
18. Freud, A.: The role of bodily illness in the mental life of children. Psychoanal. Study Child *7:* 69, 1952.
19. Webb, C.: Tactics to reduce a child's fear of pain. Am. J. Nurs. *66:* 2698, 1966.
20. Friedman, S. B., Mason, J., and Hamburg, P. A.: Behavioral observations in parents anticipating the death of a child. Pediatrics *32:* 610, 1963.
21. Rasof, B., Linde, L., and Dunn, O.: Intellectual development in children with congenital heart disease. Child Dev. *38:* 1043, 1967.
22. Birch, H. G., and Belmont, L.: Auditory-visual integration in brain-damaged and normal children. Dev. Med. Child. Neurol. *7:* 135, 1965.
23. Honzik, M. P., Collart, D. S., Robinson, S. J., et al: Sex differences in verbal and performance IQ's of children undergoing open-heart surgery. Science *164:* 445, 1969.
24. Aver, E. T., Senturia, A. G., Shopper, M., et al.: Congenital heart disease and childhood adjustment. Psychol. Med. *2:* 23, 1971.
25. Kennedy, J. A., and Bakst, H.: The influences of emotions on the outcome of cardiac surgery. Bull. N. Y. Acad. Med. *62:* 811, 1966.
26. Wrightstone, J. W., Justman, J., and Moskowitz, S.: *Studies of Children with Physical Handicaps. I. The Child with Cardiac Limitations.* Bureau of Educational Research, Publication No. 32. New York, Board of Education of the City of New York, 1953.

CHAPTER 18

Emotional and Psychosocial Aspects of Diabetes Mellitus

INTRODUCTION

The psychosocial aspects of diabetes mellitus may be considered from several facets, all of which have relevance to the understanding and treatment of the patient with this condition. These include: (1) the role of psychological factors in the cause of diabetes, (2) the psychosocial environment in which exacerbation or worsening of the diabetic condition occurs, (3) the reaction and psychosocial adjustment of the individual suffering with diabetes, and (4) the physical and psychological sequelae of this condition.

ETIOLOGICAL FACTORS

Since the times of antiquity, observations have been recorded associating the onset or precipitation of diabetes mellitus with emotional shocks or upsets. This notion has remained, although the nature of the relationship has undergone a number of variations and refinements as our understanding of the disease has become more complex.[1] Clinicians[2] are frequently aware of the sudden precipitation of diabetes mellitus accompanying a catastrophic environmental occurrence in the life of the individual. This correlation, however, is far from the rule and has not held up in statistical epidemiological surveys. Such surveys have attempted to correlate the onset of diabetes mellitus with emotional

---

Modified version (and reproduced with permission) of article from Medical Clinics of North America 55: 1007–1018, 1971; copyrighted by W. B. Saunders Company.

reaction to catastrophes such as war. Hence, although these correlations may occur, they are not of sufficient prevalence to identify the cause of diabetes on emotional grounds; nor has research uncovered an entirely satisfactory mechanism for such a relationship. At the same time, in individual terms, it behooves the clinician attending the patient with a recent onset of diabetes to look for whatever correlating events may exist in the individual's psychosocial field.

A number of investigators have focused their attention on the personality traits of patients with diabetes, attempting, when possible, a retrospective or premorbid assessment.[3] Their conclusions have identified such factors as passivity, dependency, immaturity, sexual maladjustment, insecurity, indecisiveness, and masochism. It has been noted that these personality traits are similar to those of individuals with other chronic illnesses. Some investigators have questioned whether there might not be a core personality[4] for patients with chronic illness and whether this might represent: (1) the fixation of personality development at the time of illness, (2) a regression to an earlier personality constellation with the onset of illness,[5] or (3) a common genetic constitutional basis for both the psychological structure and the physiological process. The latter hypothesis would suggest that both personality and physiological traits are genetically determined and are inherited together.

Other investigators refute the association of any specific personality factors with diabetes mellitus and would explain that those studies where such correlations have been made were based on the reaction of the individual to the diabetic condition, suggesting that, because there are limited responses to the catastrophe of illness, a number of similar reactions would be likely to appear.

For the clinician caring for patients with chronic illness, diabetes mellitus in particular, attention to the individual's personality may be a key to helping the patient adjust to his illness. Recognition of dependency, immaturity, and passivity in a patient with diabetes may help the physician to direct his therapeutic efforts toward a modification of these traits. Awareness of the emotional lability that frequently exists in patients with diabetes mellitus will alert the physician to the need of bringing the individual's ambivalence, hostility, anger, sadness, and anxiety into the open through ventilation and clarification—important ingredients of the therapeutic process.

Hinkle, Evans, and Wolf,[6] on the basis of intensive studies of patients with diabetes under experimentally structured situations, have stressed the unique and idiosyncratic physiological response of the individual to environmental events. Whereas some patients may react to a common situation with a shift in the direction of ketoacidosis, others may respond with a decrease in blood sugar, and still others may even sustain an insulin reaction. Their explanation for this variance has considered the effect of the environmental stress on the emotions of the individual and his specific reaction in terms of defenses to that event.[7] Depending on the speed and sophistication of the defense, the more "intact" or "mature" individual may be less likely to show major fluctuation in the physiological processes governing glucose metabolism, whereas the more vulnerable individual, with fewer or less sophisticated psychological defenses, may be more likely to show major alteration. Whether these are in the direction of ketoacidosis or hypoglycemia depends upon the basic response pattern of the individual perceiving the stress.

When psychological defenses are not sufficient to maintain homeostasis, reaction to the stress may be in the direction of "conservation-withdrawal"[8] or in the direction of a "fight-or-flight"[9] reaction. Either of these presumably have specific physiological counterparts.

The significance of these observations and their theoretical explanations for the clinician addressing his attention to the patient is their emphasis on the individuality of response to stress and the fact that this is dependent on the psychohistory of the individual. The physician assisting the patient in his management of diabetes over the course of time could come to predict how the patient would react to a particular crisis at a particular time in terms of his total behavior, psychological and physiological.

Rather than focusing on specific conflict situations in the precipitation of diabetes mellitus, investigators such as Rahe[10] and Slawson et al.[11] have turned their attention to the broader environmental field preceding the onset of the syndrome. Impressed by the significant correlations between life crises and illness onset, they and their co-workers have worked out a scale assigning life crisis units to various catastrophes, based on ratings given to these by various population groups.

Through prospective and retrospective studies of individuals becoming ill in a given period of time, they have correlated both onset and severity of illness with various life crisis units. In their reports, they have emphasized that life crisis units acquired cumulatively over a given period are as likely to correlate with illness onset as are major single events. Hence, the repeated bombardment of the individual with crises batters down his defensive reactions and diminishes his ability for readjustment, adaptation, and homeostasis. When he no longer has the capacity for this readjustment, he has, in the terms of the Rochester group, entered a giving-up—given-up state[12] characterized by helplessness or hopelessness, the inability to project a future, a self-concept of diminished coping ability and adequacy, a turning away from previous interaction with the object world, and an attempted recathexis of the past.

This behavioral and psychological state is presumed to have physiological counterparts. Current investigations are directed toward eliciting these counterdynamics by an examination of hormonal levels attending this state. In preliminary work, currently under reexamination, Mueller et al.[13] suggested that chronic illness in general and depression specifically are associated with decreased insulin assays and glucose utilization curves. They also suggested that treatment of some of these states with antidepressant medication, such as amitriptyline, has remedial effect on glucose utilization curves.

Although many of these works are still preliminary, their present value for the clinician is to direct his attention to the specific psychological state of his patient. When this state is characterized in traditional psychiatric nomenclature of anxiety, depression, or both, the physician may find help for his patient in directing his therapeutic skills toward the amelioration of these affective states. The severity of the affective disturbance and the experience of the clinician will usually determine whether or not he will utilize psychiatric consultation for his patient. In instituting treatment, he will find that antidepressants and antianxiety agents are merely adjuncts, albeit sometimes powerful ones, to his overall psychotherapeutic skills of listening to his patient.

Bruch[14] and Rosen and Lidz,[15] in their several studies with severe diabetics, have suggested that, although there is no single characterological description fitting all individuals with this syndrome, those who are management problems are more likely to show greater and more severe psychopathology, reflected in their greater inability to adhere to medical routines. In these situations, they suggest that it is equally important to attend to the specific psychopathology, which in more severe situations is best effected through psychiatric referral. Mirsky,[16] who has studied diabetics from both endocrinological and psychoanalytical perspectives, conceptualizes diabetes mellitus as a syndrome with both genetic and epigenetic determinants that affect and are affected by physiological and psychological dysfunctions in an environmental field. Hence, he feels that in the approach to the patient with the syndrome of diabetes mellitus, each of these interlocking fields needs to be considered.

PSYCHOLOGICAL FACTORS IN THE EXACERBATION OF DIABETES

In the preceding section, we have identified a number of factors associated with the onset of diabetes that are of value to the clinician in attending to his patient. Many of these factors are frequently identified for the patient who goes out of control or suddenly experiences a rapid deterioration in a previously stable condition. As we learn more about physiological processes, we are beginning to be aware that, similar to the more gross behavior of organisms, physiological processes are also subject to conditioning. These findings, based largely on the work of Miller[17] and DiCara and Miller[18] at Rockefeller University, suggest that physiological dysfunctions that are subject to control in part or wholly by the autonomic nervous system may be aggravated or exacerbated by the same or similar stimuli that have precipitated previous occurrences of dysfunction. These stimuli may include environmental factors or the exacerbation of renewed psychological conflicts.

While the Miller group and others are presently directing their attention toward conditioning physiological processes with a therapeutic objective, the clinician may achieve some help for his patient by tuning in or and noting the similarities of circumstances attending the fluctuations in his patient with diabetes. By so doing, he may be able to direct his patient's attention to this; together they may form a therapeutic alliance in attempting to forestall or prevent a future constellation of circumstances predisposing to decompensation in the homeostatic diabetic state.

EFFECT OF THE DIABETIC SYNDROME ON THE INDIVIDUAL

Although the physiology of diabetes is still largely unknown, there is no question that this is a syndrome whose effects have diverse implications on the total functioning of the organism. It would seem that no organ, no system, and no process is spared from the ravages of this disease, which in modern times has been compared to the Great Imitator (syphilis) and the White Plague (tuberculosis) of previous ages. These repeated assaults on organ systems and their functions have both direct and indirect effects that at every turn challenge the adaptive and homeostatic mechanisms of the individual. The individual is aware of what may best be called autonomic lability,[19] marked by fluctuations in these processes and specifically in blood glucose levels which have direct effect on both the perceptual processes and the cognitive functions of the mental apparatus. These in turn have a direct influence on the individual's capacity to care for himself during these disruptions. Not only do they interfere directly with his hour to hour functioning, but they have indirect and more far-reaching effects on his total life style and adaptation.

Many of the concepts that we have considered in the preceding sections are of consequence in the understanding and approach to the patient with diabetes. The physician's major concern in the effective management of illness, however, is the reaction of the individual to his illness. Whatever the illness, there comes a time in the life of the organism when he is struck down with disease and disablement. This comes as a shock—the shock of recognition of one's vulnerability and destructibility and the inevitability of one's mortality. In the normal course of development of the individual, this concept is derived through a gradual metamorphosis in his exposure to the experiences of others, of history, and of the world so that to a limited extent one has an intellectual and even an intuitive awareness of vulnerability.

When one is confronted with illness in middle age, the shock has to some extent been prepared for, and the individual, however reluctantly, is already partially conditioned. Such is not the case for the individual struck by disease earlier in life. Concepts of vulnerability, destructibility, and mortality, although present and sometimes vivid, are ego alien, and the individual places much distance between himself and his fantasy.

When reality forcefully intervenes with both the acuteness and constancy of a condition such as diabetes mellitus, the whole subsequent development of this concept is altered. Vulnerability and inevitability of mortality become part of the individual before he has reached the stage in his life at which he has derived a mature intellectual concept of them. Together with the subsequent influence of his illness on his relationship with others and his physical development, the onset of disease seriously disrupts the execution and completion of the psychological tasks set for him in his particular life stage. The severity and consequence of the disruption will depend upon which stage he is in at the time of onset and his ability and the ability of others to adapt to this interference so as to minimize its impact.

Children and Adolescents

In the best of situations, however, the physician may observe and can hypothesize this interruption. For the child, who is gradually edging his way toward independence from parents, catastrophic illness and its subsequent management mean at best a slowing and at worst a retrogression in this process. The parent and the parent surrogate, the physician, loom large in their superego roles of taking over, regaining the control so difficultly won by the individual over himself. Should illness strike during a stage during which the drive toward independence is particularly rapid, as in adolescence, the illness and its management may loom large and become the focal issue around which the skirmishes and sometimes battles of adolescent rebellion are waged. When this occurs, the chances that the individual will ever be able to approach the management of his illness objectively are diminished, for he will always have difficulty separating it from the other issues involved in separation of child from parent and generation from generation.

Thus, when diabetes occurs in an early stage of development, the ties to parents may be reinforced, limiting the usual exploration away from parents and leading instead to greater dependence and frequently passive acceptance of this situation. Illness occurring at a later stage is more likely to precipitate a stormier pattern in the parent-child ambivalence over issues of separation and control. Illness requiring the dietary, health, habit, and medication control that diabetes does obviously enters into the midst of this maelstrom.

The illness that complicates the separation of the man-child from his parents almost always results in isolation and alienation from his peers. In the case of diabetes, this differentness imposed by the disease situation is more difficult to objectify, both for the individual and his peers. He is different, has to eat and drink differently, needs to have injections, and never can do what the rest of the kids do. If he tries to break this routine, he is likely to have his mother and doctor "hollering" at him. He has all kinds of restrictions that contaminate the field of his peers, pressing for the abandonment of parental jurisdiction in their peculiar dietary preferences, their blatant disregard for hygienic mores, and their overt sexuality.

Coupled with the usual delay in physical development and maturation endured by individuals with chronic illness in general and diabetes in particular, the alienation, isolation, and subsequent sense of anomie of the adolescent are intensified. These burdens impede the completion of progressive life styles. The demands of adolescence—progressing toward independence from family while maintaining amicable relations, separating aggressive drives from sexual impulses to combine with competitive vocational drives, and moving from primary to complex secondary processes reflected in a maturing of personality—are all likely to be retarded and impaired. It will remain for the next phase to accomplish that work that has remained undone and to repair as much as possible the defects of residual trauma.

In addition to recognizing the direct implications of diabetes and its management on the life of the child and adolescent, the physician assisting the patient and his family in this would do well to acquaint himself with Erikson's life stage chart.[20] A knowledge of these developmental stages will help the physician make the appropriate decisions as to how his patient's illness is managed. Depending on the life stage, it is imperative that as much of the responsibility as possible for managing the illness be given to the patient. Parents and physicians should be seen as consultants in this management rather than as imposers of the routine.

Physicians, as well as other counselors, should be available to hear the subject's and his parents' feelings and attitudes about his illness and its effect on his life. The other counselors may include nurses, social workers, psychologists, or clergymen. Probing may not only be ineffective but invasive of the individual's privacy. Several medical centers have established special adolescent diabetic clinics where physicians and others interact with the patient as counselors and consultants, rather than as authoritarian figures. Summer camps for diabetic children and adolescents have been established where many of the principles mentioned here are established in a group setting. In these clinics and camps, didactic instruction is available, although not forced upon the subjects. Efforts are made to reinforce and condition positive habits developed by the patient while refining unsatisfactory ones. At all times, the responsibility of the individual to manage his own illness is emphasized.

The physician who sets up a routine schedule for reevaluation and counseling establishes a program that attends not simply to serum levels, urine tests, and insulin dosages. Diabetes in such settings is approached less as a disease and more as a syndrome which, in Mirsky's[16] terms, has both psychological and physiological manifestations and conceptualizations.

Much of the work of the physician or his staff frequently needs to be directed toward the parents of the diabetic. Overt or covert guilt on the part of one or both parents is invariably present. They blame themselves for passing on a genetic endowment as well as being participants in the environment where phenotypic expression has occurred. Their need to handle this guilt may be expressed in attempts at rigid control over the behavior and care of their children. The resulting dependency will only engender resistance, resentment, and hostility—actions and affects almost certain to reinforce parental guilt. Both the guilt and the well-meaning response to it are best shared by one of the medical staff, who may be able to disarm and dilute the potential for familial disharmony.

Parents themselves may be victims of this genetic endowment and may see this mark on their child as a cause for closer identification or rejection. They may project onto the offspring their resentment, anxieties, and depressions toward their own affliction, or they may hasten to embalm this chosen one in a symbiotic entanglement in which management patterns and other aspects of the illness are compared and imitated, destroying the emerging individuality of the child. Predilection for positions of special status and a penchant for manipulation may then become the outgrowth and hallmark of the diabetic. The parent who himself has had a parent with diabetes may attempt to project the identity of that parent onto the child, who then is predilected if not doomed to follow in the parent's footsteps.

Adult Onset

For the individual who is subject to chronic disease processes later in life, such as the patient with adult-onset diabetes, the picture may be somewhat different. By the late twenties, personality configurations are pretty much set, and the experiences of the individual are more likely to exaggerate particular traits than to alter them markedly.

In the case of the individual whose previous health history and psychological development have been relatively smooth, confrontation with a process such as diabetes may come as a stunning shock. This shock may be catastrophic for such an individual and symbolize much more than a complex derangement of body chemistry. It may come as the first note sounding the death knell of the individual's fantasy of immortality.

Such a shock may at first be met with denial, which only subsequently may metamorphose through increasingly sophisticated and more adaptive defenses. The initial denial may be manifest by the refusal or inability of the individual to accept treatment. Hence the physician's first job may be that of empathetic patience while his patient works through to a second stage, which might be called the dawn of recognition.

When the disease process is not a malignant one, the physician may well adopt a policy of quiet watchfulness. In more rampant processes, however, he may need to adopt a more forceful approach, which will necessitate achieving a therapeutic alliance with the patient against the disease earlier in its course. In any event, the second stage is frequently one in which, with the physician's permission, the patient may ventilate his anxieties, depression, anger, and guilt about his disease.

Once the physician has precipitated this stage by getting the patient to express his feelings, he will become aware of his patient's feelings and conflicts about the disease. This process may need to be repeated periodically throughout the ongoing management of a diabetic. As the patient experiences relief in this ventilatory process, he will reach a third stage in this reactive self-grieving process in which he will be more able to handle his illness objectively. During this stage, the patient is receptive to the educational and didactic instructions for the management of his disease that the physician, nurse, or other health professional may provide.

In the fourth stage, the afflicted person is ready to begin the slow process of reintegration and resolution by which he attempts to make the modifications and refinements in his life style required by the disease process. The extent to which he can do this determines the homeostasis that he will achieve and depends to a large extent on the maturity and flexibility of his premorbid personality.

For the physician guiding a patient through such a program, it is necessary to recognize that these stages frequently overlap and that a particular stage may be revisited with a new assault or exacerbation of the underlying disease process. With each exacerbation or further deterioration, recognition and handling of the affect and defenses identified in the second stage (anxiety, depression, anger, and guilt) are of the utmost importance. Until these are explored, the patient does not easily respond to platitudes of encouragement or forgiveness. The guilt that one has as it relates to his disease may be projected outward onto the physician, close relatives, and associates or directed to the self. In the latter case, depression may become of such magnitude that specific and independent treatment by a psychiatrist may be advisable.

With the development of major infirmities in the relentless course of this disease, there will be times of increased emotional distress and psychic disturbance that may require special consultation and assistance. These occur at times of strokes, impotency, neurological dysfunctions, amputation, coronary insufficiency, and other major complications associated with diabetes. Also, at such times the physician needs to be available to spouses and other close relatives for consultation. The ravages of the patient's disease have ramifications of sometimes even greater magnitude for the family. As with age, the repeated assaults of the disease process wear away at the most stalwart of individuals, eroding optimism and undermining defenses until the individual first gives in and subsequently gives up. To an extent, diabetes in some individuals may be seen as an acceleration of the aging process.

Much of the interaction between patient and physician centers around diet. Diet is a source of conflict for the patient as well as for the physician, and much of the patient's guilt frequently stems from his violation of the physician's edicts. Realizing that dietary problems evoke the sometimes nostalgic reminiscences of parent-child conflicts, the physician will be wary of precipitating a recrudescence of these factors. He may, in such circumstances, leave the instructions of diet to a matter-of-fact didactic presentation by himself, a nurse, or an office assistant. Accusations and confrontations will only increase the resistance of the patient, resulting in further dietary indiscretions, and precipitate the wrath of the physician in his indignation and impotency in maintaining control over others.

ORGANICITY

An aspect of the diabetic syndrome that is acknowledged but frequently not considered is the fluctuations and alternations in consciousness that occur. When these are acute, as they are in episodes of ketoacidosis and insulin reactions, they are, of course, immediately noted. However, the effect of these alternations on the individual is less often considered. What effect alternations in blood sugar may have on the mental apparatus is yet to be documented with absolute certainty, although it is supposed that severe derangement in the nervous system as occasioned by these fluctuations may result in cellular death. When these complications occur at a young age, their cumulative effect over a lifetime may result in obvious chronic organic changes, betrayed by irreversible deficits in the cognitive functions of orientation, concentration, memory, and abstraction. Such changes may also be associated with other consequences of the syndrome, which seems to accelerate the aging process presumably through its effects on the vascular system.

Even less attention has been given to the effect of acute alternations of levels of consciousness, which result in major cataclysmic disruption in the mental apparatus. These alternations may be considered as loosening of the ego control and censoring over unconscious processes, precipitating repressed conflicts onto the already chaotic scenes attending ketoacidosis or insulin coma. This loss of mental control increases the anxiety and emotional discomfort arising from the physiological dysfunction.

When this disruption is reflected in agitated behavior, interfering with treatment, prudent administration of phenothiazines or butyrophenones, in sufficient amounts to control symptoms, is indicated. Specifically, perphenazine or haloperidol, 2 mg at hourly intervals for three or four oral administrations, may control agitation without seriously compromising other treatment. Once anxiety is controlled, the cumulative amount of the medication, usually 4 to 8 mg, may be administered at 8-hour intervals, adjusted as indicated, for the remainder of the episode. The reason for this is that the hallucinations and delusions occasioned by the illness remain as memories for the individual and, depending upon their bizarreness, continue to have a potential for being disruptive to the individual's emotional status. These disruptions are occasionally so pronounced as to warrant more extensive consideration in psychiatric consultation.

OTHER CONSIDERATIONS IN MANAGEMENT AND THERAPY

Among the keys to therapy in the treatment of the diabetic are the use of techniques that are incorporated in the therapeutic interview (see Chapter 2). An initially open-ended, partially structured interview allows the clinician to find out what point the patient has reached at a given juncture in his life in his adjustment to the disease. It allows for the introduction by the patient of material that bears upon multiple aspects of the individual's life field, that may directly or indirectly relate to his diabetic status, and that frequently aids the physician in identifying and selecting the appropriate resources for remediation. Because a major part of the interview process allows an opportunity for the patient to give verbal objectivity to subjective feelings, therapy is frequently initiated in this simple process.

The extent to which the patient engages in this process depends upon the tacit permission he has from his physician to do so, and it will depend for its successful execution upon the relationship that is developed. In turn, the relationship depends upon how each of the parties to the therapeutic dyad identifies his or her roles and contract with the other. The physician who is identified by the patient as being interested in him rather than merely in his disease will obviously learn more about his patient than the results of urine tests, insulin units, and feelings of fatigue, faintness, and restlessness. He will identify domestic, social, and professional conflicts and aggravations that may be intimately related to the control of his patient's condition.

As a teacher, the physician will foresee the need for discussing with his patient plans for marriage, children, careers, and retirement, among other topics. As a counselor, he is frequently able to assist his client in clarifying and objectifying some of the conflicts that relate to the life and illness of his patient. Of necessity, because of the greater sophistication of his patient engendered by the attention of the press to diabetes and illness, the physician becomes the final arbiter in resolving conflicts over methods of control, diet, oral sulfonylureas, and insulin.

As a practitioner of prevention as well as of remediation, he will need to serve, if only by public designation, as prophet and oracle about the eventual progress and ravages of the disease process. In this role, he may utilize what he has learned regarding prophylaxis and care. Above all, the physician needs to disentangle himself, repeatedly and often painfully, from the patient-assigned role of parent, unless he would become the inheritor of the unresolved conflicts and ambivalences of that relationship. His paradoxical role is one of maintaining objectivity while simultaneously eliciting his patient's subjective feeling, of achieving empathy while preserving professional distance.

As if this relationship were not complicated enough, he may need to extend it to the immediate family, parent, or spouse. This will not be achieved within the context of a single interview or illness episode, but will be reflected over the long course of the patient's life. From time to time, specific social or psychological problems will necessitate referral to the specialist. At times of prolonged or agitated depression, related to or independent of the diabetes, psychiatric referral may be necessary.

In summary, the physician working with the diabetic may find the following points helpful:

1. The individual and the disease process are not separate entities but are intimately related with one another. The earlier the onset of the process, the more interrelated are the disease and the developing personality. Therefore, the physician treating the diabetic is treating the patient, not the disease.

2. Both onset and exacerbations of the disease are frequently related to events in the broad psychosocial environment. The management of the disease process will in part depend upon attention to these other factors occurring in the patient's life. Upon identifying these factors, the aid and assistance of other professionals may be necessary for effective remediation.

3. The effect of diabetes on the patient's life will depend on many factors, including age of onset, severity of disease process, personality of patient, and professional and social responsibilities of the individual. The emotional and psychological aspects of diabetes resulting from these factors will depend on the reactions of the patient to the illness; the physical, personal, and social conflicts that develop because of the illness; and whether other psychological conflicts or psychiatric illness develop independent of diabetes.

4. The psychological aspects of diabetes relate to the patient's adaptive capacity and resources, such as premorbid personality and social, economic, and family strengths. The adaptive capacities of the individual will in turn depend on the life stage of the individual and the severity of the disease process. For the individual with diabetes, continued readaptation is necessary.

5. At times of failure of adaptation, specific psychiatric illness may develop that will require treatment in its own right. Most frequently, this presents as reactive depression.

6. In the treatment of diabetics, attention needs to be focused on the effect of the diabetic process on the mental apparatus in terms of transient or chronic deficits in perceptual and cognitive processes.

References

1. Treuting, T. F.: The role of emotional factors in the etiology and course of diabetes mellitus: A review of the recent literature. Am. J. Med. Sci. *244:* 93, 1962.
2. Menninger, W. C.: Psychological factors in the etiology of diabetes. J. Nerv. Ment. Dis. *81:* 1, 1935.
3. Dunbar, H. F., Wolfe, T. P., and Rioch, J. McK.: Psychiatric aspects of medical problems: The psychic component of the disease process (including convalescence) in cardiac, diabetic and fracture patients. Am. J. Psychiatry *93:* 649, 1936.
4. Ruesch, J.: The infantile personality. Psychosom. Med. *10:* 134, 1948.

5. Grinker, R. R., and Robbins, F. P.: *Psychosomatic Case Book*. New York, Blakiston, 1954.
6. Hinkle, L. E., Evans, F. M., and Wolf, S.: Studies in diabetes mellitus. IV. Life history of three persons with relatively mild, stable diabetes, and relation of significant experiences in their lives to the onset and course of the disease. Psychosom. Med. *13:* 184, 1951.
7. Hinkle, L. E., and Wolf, S.: A summary of experimental evidence relating life stress to diabetes mellitus. J. Mt. Sinai Hosp. *19:* 537, 1952.
8. Engel, G. L.: *Psychological Development in Health and Disease*, p. 387. Philadelphia, W. B. Saunders, 1962.
9. Cannon, W. B.: *Bodily Changes in Pain, Hunger, Fear, and Rage*, pp. 66–79. Boston, Charles T. Branford, 1953.
10. Rahe, R. H.: Life crisis and health change. In *Psychotropic Drug Responses: Advances in Prediction*, P. R. A. May and R. Wittenborn, editors, pp. 92–125. Springfield, Ill., Charles C Thomas, 1969.
11. Slawson, P. F., Flynn, W. R., and Kollar, E. J.: Psychological factors associated with the onset of diabetes mellitus. J. A. M. A. *185:* 166, 1963.
12. Engel, G. L., and Schmale, A. H., Jr.: Psychoanalytic theory of somatic disorder: Conversion, specificity and the disease onset situation. J. Am. Psychoanal. Assoc. *15:* 344, 1967.
13. Mueller, P. S., Heninger, G. R., and McDonald, R. K.: Studies on glucose utilization and insulin sensitivity in affective disorders. In *Proceedings of NIMH Workshop on Recent Advances in the Psychobiology of the Depressive Illness*. T. A. Williams, M. M. Katz, and J. A. Schields, editors. pp. 225–248. Washington, D. C., United States Government Printing Office (DHEW 70-9053), 1970.
14. Bruch, H.: Physiologic and psychologic interrelationships in diabetes in children. Psychosom. Med. *11:* 200, 1949.
15. Rosen, H., and Lidz, T.: Emotional factors in the precipitation of recurrent diabetes acidosis. Psychosom. Med. *11:* 211, 1949.
16. Mirsky, I. A.: Emotional factors in the patient with diabetes mellitus. Bull. Menninger Clin. *12:* 187, 1948.
17. Miller, N. E.: Learning of visceral and glandular responses. Science *163:* 434, 1969.
18. DiCara, L. V., and Miller, N. E.: Instrumental learning of systolic blood pressure responses by curarized rats: Dissociation of cardiac and vascular changes. Psychosom. Med. *30:* 489, 1968.
19. Keen, H.: Diabetes and nervous activity. J. Psychosom. Res. *9:* 87, 1965.
20. Erikson, E. H.: Eight ages of Man. In *Childhood and Society*, pp. 247–274. New York, W. W. Norton, 1963.

CHAPTER

19

Psychological Responses to the Experience of Open Heart Surgery

OVERVIEW

In an effort to select criteria predictive of patient response to open heart surgery, 54 patients were interviewed preoperatively and followed postoperatively. They were separated into four groups on the basis of previous adjustment, anxiety regarding the operation, and orientation to the future. Postoperatively, the highest mortality occurred in group IV ("Depressed"). Morbidity was greatest in groups II ("Symbiotic") and III ("Denying Anxiety"), whereas most improvement, based on actual functioning in a role capacity, was noted in group I ("Adjusted"). Factors related to the care of these patients at the time of surgery are discussed.

Since heart surgery was first performed in the early 1950's, the incidence of postoperative emotional reactions and long-term readjustment problems has been noted to be greater and perhaps different in kind from responses to other types of surgery. This phenomenon has been the subject of several reviews,[1] and many authors have focused their attention on one aspect or another of the surgical experience in an attempt to delineate factors involved in these responses.

Untoward responses to surgery, not directly related to the technology of the procedure, have long been noted to occur with greater frequency after specific operations. Lindemann[2] and Hollender[3] have described high incidences of "rage" and depressive reactions in patients undergo-

---

Modified version (and reproduced with permission) of article from the American Journal of Psychiatry *126*: 348–359, 1969; copyrighted by the American Psychiatric Association.

ing hysterectomies. Weisman and Hackett[4] have discussed a specific "black-patch delirium" in patients after cataract removal. Other investigators[5, 6] have noted specific reactions to surgical orchidectomy and mastectomy. Janis[7] has considered preoperative anxiety as a factor determining postoperative response, whereas Knox[8] emphasized preoperative life styles as a guide to predicting long-term postoperative adjustment. Kornfeld et al.[9] stressed the postoperative environment as a determinant of psychological adjustment.

The present report, derived from a larger study,[10] is concerned with the observation and description of patients undergoing open heart surgery and their responses to this procedure up to 15 months later.

METHOD AND MATERIALS

Fifty-four adult patients consecutively admitted for open heart surgery in two periods (April to July 1966 and October 1966 to March 1967) were interviewed on the day prior to surgery. The investigator identified himself as a member of the cardiopulmonary team who was specifically interested in determining some of the experiences of patients undergoing surgery and in following them during their hospitalization and periodically thereafter. The investigator suggested that it was necessary to get to know the patient better and to find out what his life and disease course had been.

The interviews, lasting 45 to 90 minutes, were conducted in an open-ended, nondirective manner after a method developed by the medical-psychiatric liaison group at the University of Rochester.[11–15] The interview material was either written up as recalled by the interviewer (16 cases) or recorded on tape (38 cases). Subsequent to the interviews, the data were reviewed with the purpose of identifying the following:

(1) The presence or absence of anxiety, how it was manifested and handled, and whether it was expressed or denied.

(2) The "life style" of the individual, the adequacy of his ability to handle other "life crises," and the adequacy of his handling of the stresses of the imminent operation.

(3) The patient's orientation to the future, his expectation of surgery, and his anticipation of goals, future roles, and relationships.

On the basis of these items, it was possible to set up several groups that could subsequently be used to correlate with postoperative responses.

Postoperative observations and responses were made on a daily basis. These contacts, which lasted from 5 to 30 minutes, included unobtrusive observation of the patient as he was attended by the staff, an evaluation of his mental status, and an attempt to obtain a verbal description of how he was feeling. In addition to these primary data, notes and records were reviewed, the nursing and medical staffs were consulted, and relatives were often interviewed in an attempt to obtain a comprehensive perspective of the patient's reactions.

Prior to the patient's departure from the hospital, he was interviewed at greater length to learn how he felt about the experience in retrospect. Thereafter, most of the patients were followed at the time of checkup visits to the cardiac clinic at 1- to 3-month intervals up to 15 months. At these times, 20- to 30-minute interviews assessed the adjustment the patient was making, his physical status, and his general resolution of the operative and hospitalization experience.

Eight patients were observed in greater depth and over a longer period of time. Three were seen postoperatively in short-term intensive psychotherapy because of emotional problems that were intensified by the surgical experience. One patient was seen for many weeks before and after surgery for exploration of long-standing emotional problems. Four patients were seen for many weeks before and after hospitalization on the rehabilitation unit where they had been referred because of neurological complications. One patient was seen on the psychiatric unit after rehospitalization for treatment of a depression.

Initially, the study was conducted in two parts. A preliminary investigation of 16 patients was done in the spring of 1966. The data from these interviews were analyzed, and correlations were made between postoperative responses and preoperative assessments. At this time the work of other investigators was reviewed. In the fall of 1966, a second series of 38 patients was interviewed and followed along modified lines developed on the basis of a review of the methods originally used. These patients were grouped as indicated in the next section, prior to surgery. For the purposes of this report, the data from the two series are combined. Demographic and illness characteristics are recorded in Tables 19.1 and 19.2 and are discussed in another paper.[10]

RESULTS

Groups

On the basis of the preoperative interview, four groups were identified. Statistics relating to these groups are included in Table 19.3.

Group I ("Adjusted"). This group comprised patients whose general level of functioning in the past, in the immediatate period preceding the hospitalization, and at the time of surgery was assessed to be intact, purposeful, and realistic. In general, the patients had coped adequately or successfully with previous life stresses, including their cardiac disease. Business and domestic affairs had been successfully conducted.

Table 19.1
Demographic Characteristics (N = 54)

Characteristic	Number
Age (years)	
Range	18–72
Average	45
Median	46
Sex	
Female	33
Male	21
Race	
White American	38
First-generation American	13
Immigrant	2
Black southern-born American	1
Religion	
Protestant	36
Catholic	17
Jewish	1
Current marital status	
Married	42
Single	1
Divorced	8
Widowed	3
Social class	
Professional	4
Blue collar	6
Skilled	5
Semiskilled	22
Unskilled	17
Education	
Grade school or less	16
High school, 2 years or less	15
High school, graduate	15
College or technical school, 2 years or less	4
College graduate	3
Graduate professional school	1

Surgery was viewed as desirable, necessary, and potentially lifesaving. Usually these patients were able to express a moderate uneasiness, fear, or anxiety about the procedure, but their defenses to cope with these apprehensions seemed adequate and intact. They did not deny the possibility of their dying at the time of surgery. However, they expressed confidence that the surgery would not only be successful but would also enable them to pursue carefully identified objectives and plans in the future.

Table 19.2
Illness Characteristics of 54 Patients

Characteristic	Number
Valvular lesion	
Rheumatic	
Mitral	32
Aortic	13
Mitral/aortic	3
Mitral/tricuspid	2
Congenital	
Atrial septal defect	2
Aortic	2
Age at initial episode of rheumatic fever	
Under 12	24
Illness like rheumatic fever, under 12	6
12–22	6
Adult	2
Other	
Rheumatic fever not known or remembered	12
Nonrheumatic congenital lesions	4
Previous cardiac surgery	
1 closed commissurotomy	11
2 closed commissurotomies	2
1 open valvulotomy	2
1 closed commissurotomy, 1 open valvulotomy	4
Total	19
Other illneses	
None	31
Episodic	
Cholelithiasis	7
Hysterectomy	6
Appendectomy	3
Total	16
Chronic	
Schizophrenic	2
Conversion	2
Duodenal ulcer	1
Arthritis	1
Idiopathic thrombocytopenia	1
Total	7

These patients expressed many object relationships in their past and present life and looked forward to the fulfillment and continuation of them after surgery. These relationships included continuing and fulfilling role functions or jobs, carrying on meaningful relationships with spouses and/or children, plans for trips, and other forms of pleasure.

Table 19.3
Characteristics of Groups

Postoperative Period Characteristic	Group: Adjusted I (N = 13)	Symbiotic II (N = 15)	Denying Anxiety III (N = 12)	Depressed IV (N = 14)	(Total = 54)
Early					
Unremarkable	6	5	0	4	15
Catastrophic	2	3	6	2	13
Euphoric	1	4	1	1	7
Altered states of consciousness	3	3	2	1	9
Dead	1	0	3	6	10
Intermediate					
Phase I, anxiety	0	0	4	2	6
Phase II, general reaction	12	15	9	8	44
Phase II, complication	2	6	3	3	14
Dead	0	0	0	2	2
Posthospital (3- to 15-month follow-up)					
Improved	9	1	3	1	14
Unchanged	3	8	3	1	15
Worse	0	5	2	1	8
Dead	0	1	1	3	5
Total dead	1	1	4	11	17

While manifesting some apprehension, these patients seemed confident, controlled, and direct in expressing their feelings regarding the operation as well as in reviewing their life and disease histories.

Group II ("Symbiotic"). These patients had "adapted to" their illness state and were living in a "symbiotic" relationship to it on the basis of primary and secondary gains achieved, usually over a lifetime of illness. In their past life they had demonstrated considerable dependence on a parent that often had been transferred onto a spouse. There was a high incidence of failure to separate from a parent, as seen in the need of many of these patients for a continuing close relationship with a mother or father. Many demonstrated unresolved grief of many years' duration for a deceased parent. Cardiac decompensations and, where traceable, the onset of the initial episode of rheumatic fever could be correlated with major stressful life situations (e.g., loss of a parent, spouse, or child; marriage; change of life).

In this group, cardiac symptoms were experienced in situations in which the patient felt threatened. These patients looked to the operation as a means of maintaining a status quo that may have been recently threatened. They did not view the future as holding anything different for them than the present or the past. They stressed the need for a long recovery period during which they expected to be cared for by a family member. Otherwise, specific objects or goals for the future were not delineated.

As a group, these patients tended to deny apprehension about the operation and were varyingly successful in controlling expression of that emotion. However, by direct breakthrough during the interview, manifest behavior (e.g., increased motor activity), attempts at skirting discussion of the operation, dream material, or on the basis of interviews of relatives, anxiety could be recognized not only as being present but also as partially acknowledged and dealt with.

Group III ("Denying Anxiety"). This group comprised patients whose previous lives were characterized by a persistence and adequacy in coping with the stresses of life. To a large extent, symptoms and signs of the illness were minimized or denied, and the patients persisted in an active and productive life. At the time of surgery they showed a hope for relief and improvement of a deteriorating physical condition that they could scarcely deny any longer. At the same time, they manifested much uneasiness concerning the approaching procedure, which they were, for the most part, unable to verbalize. They tended to deny anxiety and used a variety of defenses in an attempt to control it, such as focusing on other events in their lives, displacement, and projection. These patients seemed rigid, hyperalert, at times suspicious, motorically hyperactive, sleepless, and without appetite. They sometimes had difficulty in relating to or talking with personnel except in very stilted, general terms that placed a distance between them and their illness. Their orientation to the future seemed appropriate. They looked forward to resuming former roles and relationships, but they had no other goals or objectives.

Group IV ("Depressed"). These patients presented a varying picture of previous coping ability with life stresses. Some had a lifelong saga of disappointments and hardships and had over a prolonged interval first "given in" to their disease state and ultimately "given up."[16] Others had had a relatively successful previous life but, in the face of a recent onset or exacerbation of their cardiac symptoms, had experienced a simultaneous worsening of their psychological adjustment. At the time of surgery, all of these patients seemed clinically depressed. For the most part, they denied having anxiety about the procedure, and there was no evidence to suggest that they were experiencing anxiety. Their motivation for surgery was characteristically verbalized as: "They (the doctors) thought I should have it." Their expectations of surgery varied from "It won't change anything" to "I won't survive." Their orientation to the future was poor. They were able to identify few object relationships that had held or would hold meaning for them in the future. The opportunity of jobs or role fulfillments were not identified. The future was poorly conceived and, if planned at all, was expressed in vague, unrealistic terms. For many patients the future seemed to be an abyss of hopelessness.

Responses

Postoperatively, periods characterized by specific kinds of responses were identified as follows:

1. The Early Period. This period included the immediate postoperative interval lasting 5 to 7 days and corresponded to the time spent in the intensive care unit (ICU). Four discrete responses characterized this period.

Unremarkable. After a transient delirium (as defined by Engel and Romano[17]) lasting up to 36 hours postoperatively, patients falling into this category were oriented in all dimensions. They were obviously uncomfortable and made no particular efforts to deny this. They were cooperative in accepting treatment and were observed struggling to help themselves.

Catastrophic. In the immediate postoperative period, these patients lay immobile. Their faces appeared as affectless masks. The eyes were usually closed but when open they seemed to be staring vacantly. They were passively cooperative and responsive to the ministrations of the nurses and physicians attending them. They were oriented in all dimensions and replied appropriately, although monosyllabically, to questions directed to them. There was no attempt at spontaneous conversation or elaboration.

Under close observation over a prolonged period, this state seemed to be one of hyperawareness and hyperalertness. In response to any sudden noise in the room, there was a direction of attention by the patient, manifested by a flicker of the eyelids and directed gaze or movement of an extremity. This state lasted 4 to 5 days and ceased abruptly. Thereafter, patients were amnesic for this interval. It was observed in several patients that, at a moment of overwhelming anxiety long after hospitalization, they recalled an episode known to have occurred during this period. Impressionistically, patients showing this "catastrophic" response seemed as if they were afraid to move for fear of waking up to find themselves dead or severely mutilated.

Euphoric. Patients demonstrating this reponse were bright, alert, and responsive within 24 hours after surgery. They greeted the staff enthusiastically as though the operation had been "nothing at all." They were radiant, confident, and demonstrated considerable bravado. In the immediate postoperative period, there were fewer complications in this group than in any of the others, i.e., fewer hematomas, pneumonias, pyrexias, arrhythmias, and electrolyte imbalances. This group tended to have their intravenous lines, catheters, and other monitoring attachments removed early and to return to the general nursing units on the third or fourth postoperative day, in contrast to the usual transfer after 5 to 7 days. They were fully oriented, and their behavior was otherwise appropriate.

Altered States of Consciousness. In general these states were characterized by a prolonged period of delirium observed in the immediate postoperative period and extending over several days to several weeks, with a gradual improvement in cognitive functioning during this interval. This was a classic delirium with diminished cognitive functioning and fluctuations in levels of awareness; it was associated with electroencephalogram slowing and diminished amplitude. It was sometimes difficult to delineate a specific underlying cause of delirium.

Patients who fell into this group were divided into two subcategories. Subcategory A included three patients with classic delirium, some of whom had hallucinations and paranoid ideation. These patients varied in their awareness of the alien nature of these phenomena. Historically, most of the patients observed in this subgroup reported episodes compatible with previous cerebral emboli. In subcategory B were six patients who were unresponsive or comatose for varying periods after the operation and who demonstrated neurological signs indicating a focal lesion. On their return to consciousness, many of these patients demonstrated a hemiparesis, which generally improved. Such residua lasted beyond the immediate postoperative period into later stages of the hospitalization and were accompanied by prolonged cognitive deficits.

Dead. Eight patients died at the time of surgery and two within 48 hours after surgery.

2. The Intermediate Period. This period included the remainder of the hospitalization and commenced with the transfer of the patient from the ICU to the general nusing unit. Descriptively, three different phases were identified that are roughly the same for all survivors, regardless of their earlier or later responses. On their return to the floor, many patients experienced considerable anxiety and demonstrated much apprehension. They expressed this in various terms, e.g., "It's like being pushed out of the nest. Now you're on your own. You have to fly or . . . "; or, "Up there (ICU) you are never alone. If anything goes wrong, there are doctors and nurses right there. Down here, you don't get any more attention than anyone else."

With most patients, this phase was short lived and readily resolved. It was often associated with physiological accompaniments of anxiety. In four cases, arrhythmias were observed for which specific organic etiological factors could not be delineated. Other patients during this phase expressed annoyance about the inconveniences imposed upon them in a four-bed room or the reduced attention from the nursing staff. The most rapid adjustment was made by those patients with a euphoric response, and the slowest adjustment was made by the catastrophic reactors.

The major portion of this part of the hospitalization was characterized by a second phase that clinically appeared as depression. The patients became increasingly withdrawn, were less interested in relating with the nurses and physicians, and ignored relatives and other visitors. Later during this phase, the patients had complaints about their physical condition and/or the environment. At some point, there was a sudden shift that often followed an interval of several days during which the patients did little more than sleep. Then there was a gradual recathexis of the environment that characterized the third phase of the intermediate period, in which the patient began to anticipate the posthospital period and make realistic plans.

During this phase, occasional untoward complications developed. Pulmonary emboli and cardiac arrhythmias were common. Those patients identified during the early period as "euphoric" demonstrated a number of complications, e.g., conversion reactions, gastrointestinal hemorrhages, and pyrexias of undetectable etiology.

The last phase of the intermediate period was one of considerable anxiety on the part of some patients. It was not unusual for some to feel that they needed more time in the hospital "to adjust," despite the fact that their physical course had progressed smoothly. The patient had many questions concerning what he or other members of his family expected of him on his return home. There was concern about medications, diets, work, and sexual activity. Some patients realized for the first time that they were going to have sodium warfarin (Coumadin) and that prothrombin times would be required at regular intervals. This sometimes came as a sudden realization to the patient that the operation had not "cured" or "rejuvenated" him. Sodium warfarin and prothrombin times for him became the badge of his infirmity. At this time of preparing for a "return to life," the patient began to contrast his preoperative fantasies with postoperative reality. His ability to resolve these issues set the stage for the posthospital period.

3. The Postoperative Period. For the purpose of this review, it included the period 3 to 15 months after surgery. This was a period of readjustment and, often, rehabilitation. It was a time of realization, of attempting to establish a continuity between the present and the past, which were separated by the sometimes "unreal" and always dramatic interlude of surgery. Evaluations during this time were made on the basis of whether the patient was functioning on an improved, same, or worse level as pertaining to his job, domestic life, and satisfaction with himself as contrasted to his presurgical adjustment.

Correlations

On the basis of results organized into the above groups and responses, it has been possible to obtain general correlations between specific groups and specific responses (Table 19.3).

Group I ("Adjusted") patients demonstrated an unremarkable course in the early postoperative period, a relatively benign intermediate period, and an over-all improvement in long-term response.

Patients in group II ("Symbiotic") tended to respond to surgery immediately with varying responses. A number of patients experienced altered states of consciousness with specific residual neurological manifestations. The intermediate period was often prolonged to 5 or 6 weeks. Long-term responses were unchanged or worse from the preoperative level of functioning.

Group III ("Denying Anxiety") patients reacted with a catastrophic response in the early period. One-quarter of these patients died at surgery. In the intermediate period there was a greater number of cardiac arrhythmias as compared with the other groups. An evaluation of long-term responses identified these patients as functioning at varying levels when contrasted with the preoperative level.

Group IV ("Depressed") patients did poorly. Mortality was higher in each postoperative period than in any of the other groups. The survivors in group IV showed either no improvement or a deterioration in their previous level of functioning.

DISCUSSION

Groupings

By focusing attention on an evaluation of several characteristics in the preoperative interview, namely the patient's (1) expression and handling of anxiety regarding the operation, (2) previous general level of adjustment, and (3) orientation to the future, patients may be divided into four groups which, when correlated with postsurgical results, are seen to have prognostic implications. The concept of grouping as a predictive instrument is similar to that devised by Kennedy and Bakst[18] but also incorporates some of the observations and thoughts of other authors, notably Knox,[8] Meyer et al.,[19] Abram,[20] and Kornfeld et al.[9]

We have found four groups adequate for the population under observation and less cumbersome to work with than the six suggested by Kennedy and Bakst. The latter, however, evaluated patients earlier in the course of their workup for cardiac surgery and included a population that did not go on to have surgery. Many of these nonsurgical patients had characteristics similar to candidates in group II ("Symbiotic"). Although our groups have general characteristics that overlap with those of Kennedy and Bakst, we feel that our description of and emphasis on one salient characteristic of each group makes them more easily identifiable.

Abram's grouping on the basis of how patients handle the anxiety generated by the imminence of surgery (based on Janis'[7] work) presumes that anxiety is present in all patients. This has not been our experience with patients falling into group IV ("Depressed"), although it would seem to apply to groups I ("Adjusted"), II ("Symbiotic"), and III ("Denying Anxiety"). It may be argued that the depression observed in patients in group IV ("Depressed") is a defense against an anxiety not consciously acknowledged. However, stressing anxiety or the denial of it for this group does not seem clinically helpful for the identification of patients, although it may be worthy of theoretic and therapeutic consideration at another time.

It is possible that in the group appearing clinically depressed, this phenomenon indicates an entirely different psychological and physiological adaptation of the organism to stress as suggested by Engel, Reichsman, and Segal[21] on the basis of their Monica studies and by Weisman and Hackett[22] in their concept developed in "Predilection to Death." When group IV is juxtaposed with group III ("Denying Anxiety"), the contrast in affect and the absence of at least manifest anxiety is inescapable. Group II ("Symbiotic") is reminiscent of the poor responders or "hysterics" identified by Knox[8] on the basis of looking at patients who had unfavorable, as opposed to favorable, adjustments to surgery. In this group, "hysterical" personality traits were more frequent than in the other groups. There was also a higher incidence of postoperative psychophysiological and neurological complications.

The prognostic value of these groupings is dramatically demonstrated when we consider mortality in group III ("Denying Anxiety") and group

IV ("Depressed"). Attempts to correlate these groups with severity based on the cardiologist's functional rating, duration of heart disease, or age of patients in each group failed to demonstrate significant differences. Patients in group IV ("Depressed") were characterized by a past, present, and projected future of weak or absent object relationships in terms of spouses, parents, children, and jobs. In contrast, in group II ("Symbiotic") such relationships were often ambivalent. In group I ("Adjusted"), these relationships, especially with spouses, appeared marked by distance. A study of the significance of object relationships as a single determinant in determining response to stresses has been suggested by Greene.[23, 24]

Personality characteristics of patients with valvular heart disease as they relate to grouping and responses have been a concern of another aspect of this study.[10] At this stage of our data analysis, it seems that although there are many personality traits common to individuals in all groups, certain ones are more characteristic of one group than another, e.g., dependency in group II.

Specific Postoperative Responses

1. The Early Postoperative Period. In discussing the various responses in this period, it is pertinent to refer to the observations of Kornfeld and associates regarding the ICU, particularly in regard to the genesis of the phenomenon identified as cardiac delirium or psychosis by Blachly and Starr.[25] Kornfeld's group noted the onset of this as commencing several days after surgery and often ceasing upon the removal of the patient from the ICU to a regular nursing floor. Their investigation delineated the peculiar nature of the ICU and considered the possible significances of this environment in the etiology of "cardiac psychosis."

As we have observed in our study, postsurgery delirium lasting up to 36 hours can be detected in some degree in all patients. It may vary from transient deficits and alterations in cognitive functions to gross impairment associated with hallucinations and paranoid ideation. The latter phenomenon was observed in our series most often in patients who had a history compatible with previous cerebral emboli or had neurological dysfunction, presumably on an embolic basis, after surgery. The content of the prolonged delirium was usually identified as ego alien by the patient. In those cases in which the patient actually believed and responded to the content of the delirium, a review of the previous personality style indicated a greater predilection to suggestion.

It is notable that none of our patients exhibited the blatant, prolonged, and classical picture of postcardiotomy psychosis described by Blachly and Kornfeld. We have observed classical examples of the phenomenon identified by these investigators in patients not included in this series at Strong Memorial Hospital and other medical centers, but we have not had the opportunity to study these patients in detail. The infrequency of psychosis in the present study may be related to the preparation of the patient for surgery and the general relationships that prevail between staff and patient at the Strong Memorial Hospital.

All evaluations for surgery are carried out by the cardiopulmonary unit, and most communications with the patient are directed through the chief of this unit. Traditionally, it has been the policy of the unit to observe patients over several months prior to surgery unless this is contraindicated by the severity of the disease. A lengthy medical history that includes pertinent social data is solicited. The patient is given considerable information about his disease and the methods of investigation to be used.

One week prior to surgery, the patient is admitted to the hospital and during the subsequent interval is seen daily by the cardiopulmonary and surgery team while various minor procedures are performed. Catheterization has usually been performed during a prior admission. This week-long interval serves as a period for adaptation and information gathering by the patient. A nurse from the ICU visits the patient to acquaint him with what the postoperative experience may be like and to answer any questions that he may have. The patient usually visits the ICU prior to surgery. After surgery, the same intensity of contact with the patients is maintained by the staff. The probable therapeutic significance of our interview for the patients in this study has caused us to become engaged in an examination of this hypothesis.

The catastrophic response seems to be a specific psychobiological reaction to the assault of surgery, similar to Cannon's[26] fright response in which, to a varying extent, the elements of catatonia are present. Perhaps this serves as a means of binding anxiety that persists into the postoperative period and that the patient has difficulty in resolving initially because of his cognitive defects. The hyperalertness identified in this stage might be explained on the basis of inability of the patient with delirium to screen and select environmental stimuli. These patients give the impression that they are afraid to move out of fear that something dreadful might happen.

Kurt Goldstein[27] has drawn attention to a catastrophic reaction in patients with chronic organic brain lesions that occurs when the individual is confronted with a novel task requiring abstraction. This phenomenon seems stimulus specific and irreversible in contrast to the acute state identified by Meyer, which has a remittent course and which does not seem to be initiated by confronting the patient with a task he is unable to do. Rather, it seems to be continuation of the anesthetic experience.

Rheingold[28] identified such a response as having its prototype in the early mother-child relationship, suggesting that this may be more characteristic of the individual's specific defense system against trauma. Abram explains this response as a psychological response to a fear of death and as the anlage of the more extended and distorted cardiac psychosis of Blachly. Meyer and Blacher[29] saw this state as one of great vulnerability in which the susceptible patient is exposed to the unfamiliar stimuli of the ICU while still partially paralyzed from antiacetylcholine inhibitors. In our series, the catastrophic response does not seem to serve the patient adversely in the early postoperative period, but it may portend his subsequent difficulty to master anxiety during the intermediate period.

The euphoric response has not been previously identified in the literature. It is a dramatic one and seems to indicate a form of denial par excellence. It is matched by rapid physiological improvement. In the intermediate period, however, these patients experience psychological and physiological reactions, possibly suggesting a somatic expression of repressed conflicts and/or nonverbalized affect.

A higher incidence of embolic phenomena resulting in cerebrovascular accidents occurred in group II ("Symbiotic"). It can merely be observed that this occurrence enforces the dependent role previously enjoyed by the patient, and it may be speculated that predilection to increased clotting may be a correlate of predetermined psychobiological interaction.

The highest incidence of deaths among the depressed (group IV) during and immediately after surgery, although striking, is not unknown. Patients who seem helpless or hopeless frequently show signs of the "giving-up—given-up" state suggested by Engel and Schmale.[30] These individuals may be incapable of erecting the necessary physiological defenses to cope with the stress of surgery (Selye[31]).

It would be of interest to attempt a correlation of biological changes with the response patterns noted. On the basis of extensive observations of patients undergoing heart surgery, Blachly (personal communication) has hypothesized specific organic processes as a cause for the acute psychological disturbance he calls postcardiotomy delirium or psychosis. Correlating an array of intriguing data with postoperative behavioral aberrations, he suggests as the cause of these disturbances the production within the body of a specific catecholamine. This may be a commonly occurring amine that, when produced in excessive amounts, is "toxic" in its own right. Either of these is viewed as a hallucinogenic agent. Should such a substance be routinely found in patients exhibiting disturbed postoperative behavior, the question would remain whether the amine was an essential cause of a behavioral state or simply one of many aberrant factors to be demonstrated in a patient's failure psychologically to master stress.

We would suggest that all of these responses seem to be on the basis of a complicated interassociation of psychological and physiological events. In our study we have attempted to view the operation and its meaning for the patient in the context of his whole life experience, including the surgical and parasurgical events.

2. The Intermediate Postoperative Period. In considering this period, we are impressed by the frequency with which patients experience discomfort and anxiety on leaving the ICU to return to the general nursing units. This is in contrast to the experience of other investigators, notably Kornfeld. An explanation for this discrepancy may be in part related to the preparation of our patients for the ICU and the nature of the unit at Strong. It is important to emphasize that return to the general nursing unit from the ICU can be a time of stress and anxiety for the patient that may be overlooked by the staff. We have noted several episodes of arrhythmias occurring in patients expressing apprehension about their transfer from the ICU. Occasionally, an extra day or two in the ICU may convince the patient of his readiness to make the move.

The second phase of the intermediate period has been identified for all survivors as one of depression and withdrawal. A similarity between this and what Engel[11] has identified as "conservation-withdrawal" seems appropriate. This is a time at which the patient simultaneously experiences a "letdown" (which was expressed by one patient as, "I knew I was going to be all right now; I could give in to my fatigue") and attempts to withdraw, restoring his vitality generally by sleep. Such a response may be discouraging to the attending staff who, on observing improved physiological functioning, are confronted by a patient who seems depressed and withdrawn. This may be a necessary experience for the patient, a time for physiological and psychological adjustment and healing. The latter response may also symbolize a period of grieving for their suffering and what might have occurred—death.

As the patient emerges from the withdrawn aspects of this period, he may be preoccupied with conflicts identified in the preoperative interview that suggest his continued introspection and grief. In the last phase of the intermediate period, the patient prepares himself for the return home, and his need for reassurance regarding his fears is indicated by his many questions. Such apprehensions may need to be drawn out of the patient or the relatives by giving them time for expression.

3. The Posthospital Period. This need to express and confide persists long into the posthospital period. In the latter period, the physician may have to assist his patient in resolving the disappointments he may experience over the actual result of the operation. The unrealistic fantasies expressed by many patients in viewing the operation as one of rejuvenation, resolution of sexual maladjustments, or as a means of achieving long-fantasied success are perhaps present to some degree in all patients. The price of these, when unrealized, is a depression that may extend to the whole family and may result in the patient's failure to adjust to the demands of the family and environment and to his own internal demands.

CONCLUSION

In this report we have indicated how patients coming for open heart surgery may be grouped on the basis of factors identifiable in a preoperative interview and how, on the basis of the patient's postoperative response, correlations may be made between grouping and response. Patients manifesting considerable preoperative anxiety or depression have a greater risk of not surviving surgery or a greater morbidity after surgery than other patients. For others, the operation threatens to upset the balance that the disease has come to hold in their adjustment to life, and for this group there is a higher incidence of morbidity as well as a failure to realize an improvement in their life adjustment after surgery. Some of the factors operating in the intrapsychic and environmental fields of patients around the surgical period have been discussed in relationship to particular responses exhibited by patients. On the basis of this study, several questions have been raised that are currently under investigation:

1. Are there more objective ways than the interview in which individuals may be preoperatively evaluated for the presence of anxiety, depression, and poor coping responses?
2. Are there specific biological correlates that may be identified for the groups and responses cited in this paper?
3. Would those patients who were identified, due to psychological factors, as poor risks at the time of surgery benefit from limited psychotherapeutic intervention?
4. What are the possible models for such intervention?

References

1. Dubin, W. R., Field, H. L., and Gastfriend, D. R.: Post-cardiotomy delirium: A critical review. J. Thorac. Cardiovasc. Surg. *77*: 586, 1979.
2. Lindemann, E.: Observations on psychiatric sequelae to surgical operations in women. Am. J. Psychiatry *98*: 132, 1941.
3. Hollender, M. H.: A study of patients admitted to a psychiatric hospital after pelvic operations. Am. J. Obstet. Gynecol. *79*: 498, 1960.

4. Weisman, A. D., and Hackett, T. P.: Psychosis after eye surgery: Establishment of a specific doctor-patient relation in the prevention and treatment of "black-patch" delirium. N. Engl. J. Med. *258:* 1284, 1958.
5. Bowman, K. M., and Crook, G. H.: Emotional changes following castration. Psychiatr. Res. Rep. Am. Psychiatr. Assoc. *12:* 81, 1960.
6. Yamamoto, J., and Seeman, W.: A psychological study of castrated males. Psychiatr. Res. Rep. Am. Psychiatr. Assoc. *12:* 97, 1960.
7. Janis, I. L.: *Psychological Stress: Psychoanalytic and Behavioral Studies of Surgical Patients.* New York, John Wiley & Sons, 1958.
8. Knox, S. J.: Psychiatric aspects of mitral valvotomy. Br. J. Psychiatry *109:* 656, 1963.
9. Kornfeld, D. X., Zimberg, S., and Malm, J. R.: Psychiatric complications of open-heart surgery. N. Engl. J. Med. *273:* 287, 1965.
10. Kimball, C. P.: The experience of open-heart surgery. II. Determinants of post-operative behavior. Psychother. Psychosom. *18:* 259, 1970.
11. Engel, G. L.: *Psychological Development in Health and Disease.* Philadelphia, W. B. Saunders, 1962.
12. Engel, G. L., Greene, W. A., Reichsman, F., Schmale, A., and Ashenburg, N.: A graduate and undergraduate teaching program on the psychological aspects of medicine. J. Med. Educ. *32:* 859, 1957.
13. Kehoe, M.: The Rochester scheme. Lancet *2:* 145, 1961.
14. Romano, J.: Teaching of psychiatry to medical students. Lancet *2:* 93, 1961.
15. Schmale, A. H., Jr., Greene, W. A., Jr., Reichsman, F., Kehoe, M., and Engel, G. L.: An established program of graduate education in psychosomatic medicine. Adv. Psychosom. Med. *4:* 4, 1964.
16. Schmale, A. H., Jr.: Object loss, "giving up" and disease onset: An overview of research in progress. In *Symposium on Medical Aspects of Stress in the Military Climate,* pp. 433–443. Washington, D. C., Government Printing Office, 1965.
17. Engel, G. L., and Romano, J.: Delirium. A syndrome of cerebral insufficiency. J. Chronic Dis. *9:* 260, 1959.
18. Kennedy, J. A., and Bakst, H.: The influence of emotions on the outcome of cardiac surgery: A predictive study. Bull. N. Y. Acad. Med. *42:* 811, 1966.
19. Meyer, B. C., Blacher, R. S., and Brown, F.: A clinical study of psychiatric and psychological aspects of mitral surgery. Psychosom. Med. *23:* 194, 1961.
20. Abram, H. S.: Adaptation to open heart surgery: A psychiatric study of response to the threat of death. Am. J. Psychiatry *122:* 659, 1965.
21. Engel, G. L., Reichsman, F., and Segal, H. L.: A study of an infant with a gastric fistula. I. Behavior and the rate of total hydrochloric acid secretion. Psychosom. Med. *18:* 374, 1956.
22. Weisman, A. D., and Hackett, T. P.: Predilection to death. Psychosom. Med. *23:* 232, 1961.
23. Greene, W. A.: Role of a vicarious object in the adaptation to object loss. I. Psychosom. Med. *20:* 344, 1958.
24. Greene, W. A.: Role of a vicarious object in the adaptation to object loss. II. Psychosom. Med. *21:* 438, 1959.
25. Blachly, P. H., and Starr, A.: Post-cardiotomy delirium. Am. J. Psychiatry *121:* 371, 1964.
26. Cannon, W. B.: *Bodily Change in Pain, Hunger, Fear and Rage.* New York, Appleton and Company, 1915.
27. Goldstein, K.: On emotions: Consideration from the organismic point of view. J. Psychol. *31:* 37, 1951.

28. Rheingold, J. C.: *The Mother, Anxiety and Death: The Catastrophic Death Complex.* Boston, Little, Brown and Co., 1967.
29. Meyer, B. C., and Blacher, R. S.: A traumatic neurotic reaction induced by succinylcholine. N. Y. State J. Med. *61:* 1255, 1961.
30. Engel, G. L., and Schmale, A. H., Jr.: Psychoanalytic theory of somatic disorder: Conversion, specificity, and the disease onset situation. J. Am. Psychoanal. Assoc. *15:* 344, 1967.
31. Selye, H.: The concept of stress in experimental physiology. In *Stress and Psychiatric Disorder, The Proceedings of the Second Oxford Conference of the Mental Health Research Fund,* J. M. Tanner, editor, pp. 67–75. England, Blackwell Scientific Publications, 1960.

CHAPTER 20

The Biopsychosocial Approach and Chronic Illness

INTRODUCTION AND ORIENTATION

In an era when biochemical concepts have come to hold dominance as the ultimate explanation for behavior, liaison psychiatrists often occupy the last bastion in the academic arena where a developmental approach to illness remains. That an event happens to an individual along the course of life and that this individual suffers this event because of something peculiar and specific in his life at that time and reacts to this event both because of this and because of processes laid down from the moment of conception and may continue to react in this way is perhaps the hallmark of the psychosomaticist's mode of thinking. In this approach the individual is neither psyche nor soma alone nor both of these together, but also an integral part of a social milieu that potently and mutually interacts with him. In this synthetic, as opposed to analytic, approach to the individual *in* the social milieu, the psychosomaticist to a greater extent than most physicians needs to be versed in the theories and the application of the many different language systems that address themselves to behavior—essentially those embraced by the parent disciplines of biology, psychology, and social science. Even in writing this, I would prefer to use another term for "biology" so as to embrace physics and mathematics, because some of our thinking in psychosomatic medicine, I think, approaches more the relativism of physics than the taxonomic approaches of biology. Likewise, the term "psychology" has lost designatory meaning today and has been replaced by the more amorphous term "behavioral science."

Modified version (and reproduced with permission) of article in *Psychiatric Medicine*, G. Usdin, editor, 1977; copyrighted by Brunner/Mazel Company.

Thus, I use the former terms in a broad rather than a specific sense. Despite the theoretical complexities and ambiguities that have marked the historical development of psychosomatic medicine,[1, 2] the practitioner of this discipline is a pragmatic individual who in this day of technology might be most likened to a general systems analyst[3] who uses those theoretical approaches that fit best at a particular time in a particular place, leading to the most pragmatic approach to the specific problem at hand. In his hands, the approach is used that offers the best explanation at a given point in time. Indeed, with study, that approach in its idiosyncratic circumstance may contribute to studies that will amend and evolve theory. In the latter way, the psychosomaticist is similar to a naive anthropologist (i.e., unbiased observer) who branches out from his belief system in emphasizing as unbiased an observational approach as possible before resorting to theoretical concepts for explanation. He is first and foremost an observer who formulates his observations in terms of naive questions that would seek further data, utilizing whatever theoretical orientations that suggest where the most results will be forthcoming. The generalizations that he will eventually extrapolate from these individual forays into this situation at this time remain only in the broadest sense the approach to another situation at another time and place. In other words, the various kinds of specificity that have dominated psychosomatic thinking in the past are not formulations to be glibly applied to groups of individuals with similar disease processes but serve only as beacons to suggest a plausible approach for investigating this individual situation at this time. In this sense, a global synthetic approach toward understanding a situation necessitates an analytic approach utilizing several theoretical disciplines to explain naive observations. In our technological world we tend to observe from theoretical approaches rather than use these to explain the observation. Whereas all of this may seem obvious, inasmuch as it is essentially what we all think we do, it is an observational fact exactly what we do not do. We live in a society that conditions us, through payments, to look at objects from a specific theoretical approach, thereby compromising unbiased observation. In what follows, I shall discuss paradigms that are sometimes helpful in keeping our observational processes open, as opposed to closed, in our approach to situations along a spectrum of illness. At all times we will need to take our observations and formulate them in terms of environmental, psychological, and biological formulations. In doing this, we also need to be cautious in our natural predispositions to apply two-dimensional and linear relationships between different theoretical schemes in explaining our observations. As a last caution, if simplicity is what was desired, we individually and collectively would have stayed in the warmth of our original ideological cages which 19th-century science provided us. For idiosyncratic reasons known only to our individual selves have we ventured forth into this wild and spectacular land.

THE DEVELOPMENTALIST'S APPROACH

The graphic in Table 20.1 is a two-dimensional map to guide us to the three-dimensional individual existing in a four-dimensional world. We greet the central character alone, but in reality he exists and has existed at all times in a social milieu. He comes to us with a host of cohorts who in one way or another invade his space and affect his behavior, as he will tell us should we give him an opportunity. We greet this individual, as it were, at some predetermined way station between conception and death (or everlasting life). Something has happened. There has occurred a change in his and/or the environment's sense of himself as a functioning entity, which is called illness. He comes or is taken for help. His experience of illness is expressed in terms of social dysfunction, somatic discomfort, and emotional distress. Occasionally (when he is taken) these factors are denied by the individual, requiring either some other explanation of us and/or our attention toward those who have or would bring him to our attention. Then, our approach is first to the latter's discomfort in the anticipation that it will lead us into the system of the former. Immediately, as we begin our approach into the situation, we are led into the past system (determinants) of the identified patient, the present alteration of the individual and immediate environment (including family, friends, job), and the future expectations of the patient in the environmental milieu (prognostication, consequential). Thus, we have already evoked deterministic, evoluntionary, and consequential modes of how we shall think about this situation; these modes impose upon us and our observations specific biases inasmuch as we will look for causes, we expect change over time, and we anticipate consequences for all involved in this situation. Therefore we have, a priori, arranged our thinking and will look for a series of things that we shall attempt to string together in a connected (usually causative) way.

The Illness Onset Situation

Most immediately and usually, we focus on the question, "What has happened?" This is based on the premise that *something happened.*[4] We dress this up by calling it the "illness onset situation," and we look at it from the vantage point of the individual and significant others in the dimensions of place and of time. However, mathematically, we have a more complex set of relationships, inasmuch as we have three-dimen-

Table 20.1
The Stages of Illness

GENETIC	DEVELOPMENTAL	PRE-ILLNESS SITUATION	ILLNESS ONSET	ACUTE (ICU)	CONVALESCENT	REHABILITATIVE
Family Hx Aroused patterns (precursors of disease)	Personality Behavior patterns Illness	Life phase Life crises (immediate correlates)	Experience of symptoms Response to symptoms	Anxiety Sadness Delirium	Grief Restitutive	Adaptation and coping Altered organism
Pre-illness			Home/Work	Hospital		Hospital/Home

sional persons, who bring with them their pasts, present, and anticipated futures and who exist in a present spatial situation, and the interrelationships that these suggest. In order to get ourselves oriented, we seek out points of departure for our orientation in questions that suggest that something happened, something must have happened, to occasion change, and we suggest that this something must have occurred in some proximity to the change. This is based on data viewed in an empirical way. But it is dependent on how and whether we have developed psychologically[5] in a culture[6] which fosters an empirically based cause-and-effect mode of thinking. A correlate of this mode is the idea of *specificity*, i.e., that certain kinds of events or situations lead to specific reactions and frequently enough so for statistical validity (also intrinsic to this mode of thinking).

Most in vogue today is to view this "something" as stress,[7] conceptualized by Holmes and Rahe as an event that would occasion the most readjustment (in terms of getting used to, coping with, maintaining present stability, etc.) on the part of the individual sustaining that stress. On a statistical basis, a universal list of those events which would require the most readjustment in descending order has been established for adults (Table 20.2), others for children,[8] and still others for specific populations.[9] Common to these lists in terms of meaning of stress seems to be something that implies a symbol of object loss, which in Schmale's[10] terms may be real, threatened, or imaginary. Whereas the definition of stress and the computations attempting to demonstrate statistical relationship between stress and physiological dysfunction in terms of disease have become almost independent exercises in themselves, this relationship, whether causal or merely coincidental, is of importance to the clinician who would care for this patient with a knowledge of what other things have occurred in the patient's life in addition to this most recent somatic problem. Factors such as a business failure, a marital dispute, or an investigation by the Internal Revenue Service certainly may influence the patient's response in one way or another, e.g., compliance with medical regimen, desire to get well, or attention to the present problem.

As suggested above, there are difficulties with the present stress hypothesis when viewed as a causative relationship to somatically conceptualized illness. First is the problem of the universality of stress. Not all stresses are perceived as stresses of the same magnitude by different individuals. Second, psychological factors may intercede to alter the reaction to what might have been perceived as a stress initially, including such phenomenon as denial and learned coping behavior. Thus, a stress may not be perceived as a stress or reacted to as a stress or it might be perceived as a stress while at the same time both

Table 20.2
Social Readjustment Rating Scale*

Rank	Life Event	Mean Value
1	Death of spouse	100
2	Divorce	73
3	Marital separation	65
4	Jail term	63
5	Death of close family member	63
6	Personal injury or illness	53
7	Marriage	50
8	Fired at work	47
9	Marital reconciliation	45
10	Retirement	45
11	Change in health of family member	44
12	Pregnancy	40
13	Sex difficulties	39
14	Gain of new family member	39
15	Business readjustment	39
16	Change in financial state	38
17	Death of close friend	37
18	Change to different line of work	36
19	Change in number of arguments with spouse	35
20	Mortgage over $10,000	31
21	Foreclosure of mortgage or loan	30
22	Change in responsibilities at work	29
23	Son or daughter leaving home	29
24	Trouble with in-laws	29
25	Outstanding personal achievement	28
26	Wife begin or stop work	26
27	Begin or end school	26
28	Change in living conditions	25
29	Revision of personal habits	24
30	Trouble with boss	23
31	Change in work hours or conditions	20
32	Change in residence	20
33	Change in schools	20
34	Change in recreation	19
35	Change in church activities	19
36	Change in social activities	18
37	Mortgage or loan less than $10,000	17
38	Change in sleeping habits	16
39	Change in number of family get-togethers	15
40	Change in eating habits	15
41	Vacation	13
42	Christmas	12
43	Minor violations of the law	11

* From Holmes, T. H., and Rahe, R. H.: The social readjustment rating scale. J. Psychosom. Res. *11:* 213, 1967.

psychologically conceptualized and behaviorally conceptualized coping mechanisms intercede, thereby diluting or aborting a demonstrable somatic response to the stress. Another difficulty in stress research that looks only at physiological response is that response is frequently not looked for in other aspects of behavior, such as in the psychological or the social reference spheres. A further difficulty is our medical bias of looking for negative response patterns and pathology. Changed behavior that may at first be seen as pathological may be adaptive and protective in terms of the total organism.

Reaction to Stress

This area of investigation is in its infancy and is thwart with some of the same conceptual difficulties identified above. For a stress to be a stress, it may first have to be perceived as such on one level or another—that is, conscious or unconscious. On this basis, there are a relatively large number of different pathways that this reaction might take, depending on the sophistication of one's psychological, physiological, and social repertoires. Most basically, the percept on one level or another can be screened out as seems to be the situation in some patients with hypertension[11, 12] at one phase of the illness. The mechanism of this screening out might be seen as a psychologically conceptualized denial. In time, a physiological explanation may make this process clearer. In some situations it may depend simply on arousal threshold. With or without this screening out process may be sequential behaviors viewed as means of coping with the perceived stress, each with its biological, psychological, and socially observed correlates. The extent to which these are adaptive or maladaptive, I suggest, relates to a value system intrinsic to each of these disciplines and their subdisciplines, rather than being absolute in their own right. The only common denominator, perhaps, is that there is always a price to pay for experience, even if that experience contributes to growth, further development, and aging.

Rahe[13] has suggested that a stress is a stress to the organism when it results in a strain in the individual. Using this concept, it would seem that a strain is a measurable response in one system or another, recording the impact of that stress on that system. Again, this gives a wide array of systems and subsystems to evaluate. In terms of biological responses, we would look first at the entire organism for multiple organ system involvement and then more closely at specific organ system involvement. The idea of specificity is an old one and keeps turning up again in many forms. Alexander[14] proposed not only a psychological specificity but an equally important biological specificity to explain specific organ system involvement in disease. This was the concept of the vulnerable organ. Although he did not define this in detail, it seems as though he would resort to a genetic explanation for this vulnerability. Bridger[15] has observed that neonates respond to a specific stimulus with a physiological variation in a specific organ system that remains constant for that individual over time, although different neonates respond to the same stimulus with a different response in the same organ system or in a different organ system. To what extent this depends on genetic factors or in utero conditioning vis-à-vis maternal behavior remains unexplored. The idea of vulnerable organ specificity gained momentum with the Alexandrian- and Mirsky-inspired[16] work of Weiner et al.[17] They reported a prospective study of individuals presumed to be vulnerable for peptic ulcer disease by virtue of a biological marker, elevated serum pepsinogen levels, who were under the presumed to be stressful situation of boot camp. Not only did these investigators demonstrate the development of a significant percentage of peptic ulcers in this group as opposed to a contrast group of inductees who had low serum pepsinogen levels, but they also demonstrated that individuals with the more pathological scores on psychological tests and psychiatric interviews correlated with those hypersecreters who developed ulcers.

Biological vulnerability and specificity concepts are helpful in assisting the clinician in anticipating which systems are at risk in terms of the individual's most recent vulnerability, that is, the present illness. Knowing that an individual has a vulnerable cardiovascular system will alert the physician to the possibility of intercurrent changes in this as a response to illness, regardless of the present illness. In other words, the physician treating a patient who has multiple fractures as the result of an automobile accident would monitor the individual with a history of peptic ulcer disease or coronary artery insufficiency for those processes, respectively.

The concept of both psychological and physiological specificity continues to intrigue us. Friedman and Rosenman[18] have identified a correlation between behavior pattern type A (as distinct from a more amorphous behavior pattern type B) and coronary artery disease. Initially their observations included physiological and biochemical factors in the definitions of this pattern (i.e., elevated cholesterol and triglyceride levels, elevated blood pressure levels) as well as behavioral factors that Rosenman believes are best symbolized by a raised forearm with a clenched fist and a stopwatch strapped to the wrist. This description, with it emphasis on conscientiousness, industriousness, sense of urgency, competitiveness, and physical activity, obviously includes obsessive and compulsive characteristics and takes us back to some of

Dunbar's[19] earlier observations and suggestions that individuals with specific personalities are vulnerable to specific diseases. This hypothesis enjoyed brief popularity, partly because it was too global and did not identify specific enough characteristics subject to quantification. It also did not contribute to a medicine that was becoming increasingly preoccupied with the mechanisms by which these characteristics worked in effecting alterations in physiology. Ruesch's[20] observations, at the same time, led to the formulation of an infantile personality as the core personality for psychosomatic diseases—which were Alexander's "Holy Seven." Others have more recently introduced the idea of a similar personality for individuals reacting to stressful situations with primarily fixed pathophysiological processes (Nemiah and Sifneos' alexithymia[21]; Marty and De'Uzan's "la penseé opératoire"[22]). These core personalities seem too generalized and nonspecific for correlation with individuals with specific pathophysiological response patterns. Besides, they tend to belie clinical observations identifying different levels of sophistication in the cognitive, emotional, and social processes in individuals with different pathophysiological disturbances or the changes in these responses at different phases in the illness. As an example of the latter, Engel[23] has shown the presence of different emotional presentations and defensive patterns during the exacerbation, as opposed to the remission, phases of ulcerative colitis. The essential feature linking these various observations together may be more the fluidity and capacity for psychological regression and reconstitution in individuals particularly prone to experience stress via pathophysiological processes than a fixed personality concept. Some aspects of the alexithymic and infantile personalities are close to those of the borderline personality.[24, 25] A variety of, although not necessarily specific, pathophysiological reactions are seen in these individuals that correlate with fluctuations in psychologically conceptualized defensive systems.

Engel and Schmale[26] have proposed a specific response state to stress that puts the individual at risk for psychological and/or physiological dysfunction, depending upon that individual's specific vulnerability potential (Table 20.3). This state, the GU^2 (giving up-given up) is described as an initial response to a stressful situation. As such, it is an in limbo state. Much of their description is similar to those states identified as stress reactions (reactions to major civilian catastrophies, natural disasters, battlefield situations) by other investigators.[27] Individuals reacting in this way are characterized by an affect of helplessness or hopelessness, an expression of inadequacy, an inability to cope, a sense of futility, a diminished sense of and orientation to the future, and a preoccupation with the past—notably the misfortunes of the past. Some would see this as a reactive depression or as a grief reaction, but its

Table 20.3
The Giving-up—Given-up State

1. An unpleasant affect of helplessness or hopelessness
2. A sense of inadequacy; an inability to cope
3. A sense of diminished relationships with others
4. A diminished sense of future
5. A preoccupation with the past, especially the misfortunes of the past
6. A perception of the present environment as alien and of no longer providing guidelines for behavior

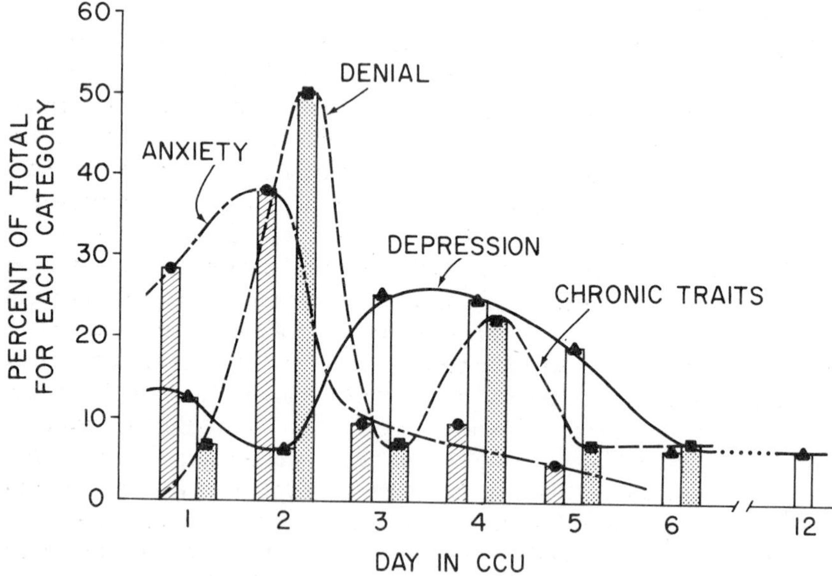

Figure 20.1. Psychological responses in a coronary care unit (CCU). (From Cassem, N. H., and Hackett, T. P.: Psychiatric consultation in a coronary care unti. Ann. Intern. Med. *75:* 9, 1971.)

essential component is, perhaps, its identification as a dynamic state. The individual may recoup at any point or may go on to some decompensation of behavior psychologically, physiologically, or socially. The importance of this concept in working with a patient already sustaining a major pathophysiological process is that this process in and of itself may lead to such a state.

Cassem and Hackett,[28] in their study of patients sustaining myocardial infarction, suggested that at least some of the early reactions of these patients suggest the GU^2 state (Fig. 20.1). They note that patients in the coronary unit first manifest behavior associated with anxiety. There is sometimes denial of illness, the emotions around illness, and/or the consequences of it. This may be associated with impulsive behavior and demands to sign out of the unit. Most directly, anxiety is related to the severity of the patient's condition and pain. Anxiety as the predominant experience peaks about the second day and is gradually replaced by depression, which in their study they identified as peaking on the fourth day. These studies, based on observations and patients' self-reports, depend on a number of factors—the backgrounds of the patients under study, the previous illness experience, personality characteristics, the orientations of patients toward physicians and nurses, and the hospital environment.

Kornfeld et al.[29] stressed the strangeness and oftentimes bizarreness of the intensive care unit environment as seen by the patient not previously familiar with hospitals (Table 20.4). They identified these environments as relatively small areas in which beds are crowded close together, through which large numbers of nurses, physicians, aides, students, and family members are constantly moving. There is frequently no differentiation between nighttime and daytime in these windowless environments, and the lights are usually on. Patients lie next to each other, each attached to intravenous feeding units, cardiac monitors, and automatic blood pressure recorders. In some intensive care units, such as those in which patients recover from open heart surgery, most patients are intubated, rendering speech impossible; some are placed on water-cooled mattresses in order to lower temperatures. In other units, such as burn units[30], patients may lie in isolation behind windows in special environments where they may be unclothed and in which they experience relative isolation from others. It is little wonder that in these environments, with the overstimulation of the senses on one hand and monotonous repetition on the other, that patients expe-

Table 20.4
The Intensive Care Unit Environment

1. An alien environment
2. Overstimulation in terms of sounds, number of individuals attending patient, other senses assaulted
3. Sensory monotony in terms of repetitiousness of sounds, sights, other sensations
4. Processes that interfere with communication
5. Absence of familiar individuals
6. Absence of usual day-night sequence
7. Physical discomfort of disease
8. Drugs interfering with cognitive processes
9. Crowding of beds, resulting in lack of privacy
10. Illness and death of other patients

Table 20.5
Altered States of Consciousness

1. Cognitive deficits: orientation, memory, concentration, abstraction (concreteness)
2. Emotional lability
3. Environment
4. Illness and injury: central nervous system, cardiovascular, gastrointestinal, respiratory, genitourinary, endocrine, hematologic, metastatic
5. Drugs: sedatives, analgesics, mild tranquilizers, steroids, specific drugs
6. Sleep
7. Withdrawal states: alcohol, narcotics
8. Previous episodes of altered states of consciousness

rience not only emotional reactions but oftentimes altered states of consciousness (Table 20.5) associated both with the environments and the underlying condition for which they are being treated. Specific factors that have been correlated with confusion, disorientation, impairment of memory and judgment, emotional lability, and inattention have been interference with sleep, narcotics, sedatives, minor tranquilizers, the absence of orienting stimuli (calendars or clocks), the cacophony of unfamiliar sounds, the frequent crises in the environment, the continual changes of staff, and the anxiety aroused by what is going on.

There are several important considerations regarding alteration of consciousness states.[31] Many psychiatrists, acting as consultants, misconceptualize these as acute psychotic states because of the delusions and hallucinations that are frequently associated with them, especially in their most severe forms. Although this characterization may be descriptively appropriate, it errs in failing to alert physicians to etiological factors that most often are multifactorial, not the least of which are such iatrogenic agents as analgesics and sedatives. Furthermore, a functional diagnosis adds an unnecessary burden on both the patient and his family. From a diagnostic point of view, there are a number of significant findings that separate these states from functional ones: (1) they are usually of brief duration, 3 to 7 days when untreated; (2) the delusions and hallucinations are more likely to be ego alien as opposed to ego syntonic; (3) they are responsive to relatively small amounts of butyrophenone; and they are responsive to relatively minor supportive forms of psychotherapy. From a theoretical view, these differences might be considered in terms of their relatively abrupt onset and limited duration, so that what is observed is an incipient stage of a process that bears a similarity to diseases considered functional in nature but that lacks some of the other factors usually associated with them.

These acute states[32] are potentially hazardous for the individual, the hospital staff, and other patients. In the acute phases, individuals may act upon the delusional and hallucinatory components, bringing harm to themselves and others. Experience has shown that these acute stages have prior stages preceding from hyperalertness and irritability through mild to moderate states of confusion (Fig. 20.2). These states usually go undetected, so that the acute agitated stage seems to develop suddenly rather than as a more severe sequence of the previous stage. Patients in acute stages of delirium should not be left alone (Table 20.6). The best attendant is usually a nurse's aide who can handle the patient in a matter-of-fact manner, simply reiterating orienting information concerning who the patient is, where he is, and what has occurred, while saying that everything will be all right in a little while. Meanwhile, it behooves the physician to seek out those factors that may be contributing to the delirium. Small amounts of a butyrophenone, repeated hourly three to four times, usually alleviate the agitation seen with these states and ameliorate the degree of confusion. Generally, when there

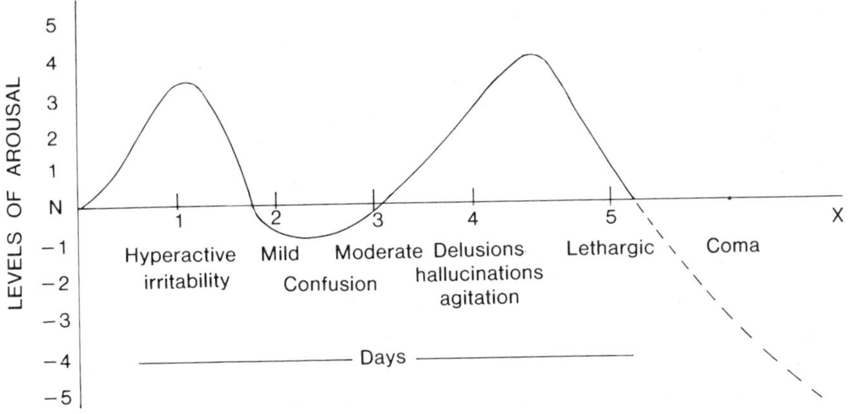

Figure 20.2. Stages of altered states of consciousness.

Table 20.6
Treatment of Altered States of Consciousness

1. Do not leave patient alone!
2. Nurse's aide
3. Direct, simple, repeated, orienting, reassuring remarks
4. Review medications, chemistries
5. Identify other possible causes
6. Reduce environmental confusion; change
7. Butyrophenones
8. Assess for further therapy

are no major contraindications, it is best to maintain the patient on the butyrophenone for 1 week to 10 days in order to give him some distance from the psychic upheaval he has experienced. A small number of individuals sustaining such states will require subsequent psychiatric counseling.

Impulsive behavior observed during the acute stage of illness is infrequent, but when it occurs it may be a matter for speedy resolution, especially when it involves a patient in the intensive care unit attempting to sign out against medical advice. Such individuals are usually not suffering from an altered state of consciousness, but rather are reacting characterologically to a state of heightened anxiety occasioned by an abrupt onset or exacerbated stage of illness. These individuals respond best to a benign authoritarianism, one that is straight forward, matter of fact, and definitive. Patients with obsessive traits will require elaborate explanation of what has occurred and of what to expect before demonstrating a willingness to comply with the medical regimen to perfection. Patients with hysterical traits may need permission to "carry on" in order to get through the denial and ventilate their anxiety. Thus, a knowledge of and a sensitivity for the defensive reactions of individuals with specific personality styles under stress[33] are essential for the clinician in his care for the patient at this stage in illness.

Knowledge of the patient's previous reactions to stressful experiences, including illness, is frequently helpful to the physician in anticipating reactions of patients to the present illness experience. Greene et al.[34] observed patients undergoing cardiac catheterization and defined four specific behavioral patterns with physiological and biochemical correlates that they believe may be indicative of the behavior to be anticipated during subsequent cardiac surgery. Some investigators[35] have correlated a history of a previous delirium with the postoperative delirium in cardiac patients. Klein,[36] studying patients in the coronary care unit, has correlated behavioral measurements with urinary catecholamine metabolites as potential indicators of adverse cardiac function. He has also noted that not only are patients vulnerable to intensive care units, but some patients are sensitive to the anticipation of being transferred from them,[37] expressing the feeling that they are being let loose and will no longer have the close attention that they have had. Anticipating this kind of response in some patients has led physicians and nurses working in this environment to prepare patients for transfer by listening for their expectations and hesitations. This is an increasingly important consideration in hospitals where patients may be transferred every few days through a gradation of lesser intensive care units, requiring a constant readjustment to changed environments, personnel, and regimen.

It is not infrequent to observe that patients who have had a relatively benign course in the intensive care unit situation sustain both psychological and physiological decompensation after or near the end of this phase of illness. This seems to be particularly true of individuals who use a denial of affect and sometimes of the severity of illness as the major defense during the initial phase. In postoperative situations, these patients may manifest acute anxiety attacks, fevers of undetermined origin, acute gastric hemorrhages, or pains of undetermined derivation (see Chapter 19). For the consulting psychiatrist, these occurrences may suggest a displacement of the patient's feelings through somatic processes. Dreams, which are particularly vivid at this time of convalescence, are useful in assessing the emotional status of these patients.

Convalescent Phase

The convalescent phase of illness commences with some stabilization in the patient's physiological course where less moment-to-moment monitoring is required. As suggested above, this transition point is greeted by patients in varying ways. Some patients may greet this with relief, as the end of an ordeal, others with enthusiasm and optimism, and still others with apprehension and trepidation. As the transition evolves, most patients settle into convalescence with a diminution of anxiety that is replaced by a sense of enforced confinement. To the observer, this may appear as depression,but perhaps the term conservation-withdrawal[38] is more apt. When feelings are verbalized, patients say they are relieved that they can let go a bit, settle back, rest, and put worries out of their mind for a bit. In this phase, they are less enthusiastic than their physicians, nurses, and family. They are more interested in turning to the wall, refusing visitors, and sleeping. They tend to fatigue easily, to show unsustained concentration, to pick at their food, and to demonstrate a sense of feebleness. In some, this phase is of limited duration and is followed, in postcoronary patients at least, by a period of exuberance that is expressed in terms of a sense of well-being, demonstrated by increased energy, and a regrasping of the business of living, catching up on the news, renewing business contacts, and getting reorganized. On the other hand, others may adopt a sick role that threatens to become chronic.[39] The liaison psychiatrist, in alerting the staff to these particular patterns in individuals, can assist them in trying to understand what is going on and in determining whether one or another kind of intervention is required.

This phase of illness, from a psychological viewpoint, lends itself to a grieving process model[40] (Table 20.7). Frequently, it is not until this time that the patient begins to accept, rather than just endure, the fact of illness. This acknowledgment of illness and of the real, threatened,

Table 20.7
The Grieving Process

	Day			
Intensive care unit	1	Shock:	Disbelief, denial, numbness	
	2	Ventilation:	Anxiety	regression
			Anger	introjection
	3			projection
			Sadness	identification
	4		Shame	undoing
				reversal
Convalescent	5	Defensive:		isolation
				reaction formation
	6		Guilt	rationalization
				intellectualization
	7			
	8			
	9			
Rehabilitative	10		Depression	(turning around on oneself)
	11			
	12			
	13			
	14		Hope	displacement
	↓			repression
	21			sublimation

and imagined impositions it places on life is the beginning of recognition and reckoning. In order to embark on these processes, emotions frozen or trapped during the acute phase may need to be released, especially those of anxiety, anger, and sadness. It is not until this phase that many patients come to an awareness of their vulnerability and of the possibility and probability of death at some point in the future. They may need to talk about this but find themselves in the midst of individuals who exalt life and deny death. Although discussions of, indeed preoccupation with, death and dying have joined the economic currents of our times for the well, these have less to do with the reality of anxieties about death for the ill. For those of us on the front lines, patients in acute situations seem eager to be cared for and have their pains ameliorated rather than preoccupied with seeking some promise of eternal life. During the convalescent stage of the acute illness, they often seem to gain greater relief after talking about their anxieties about death and grieving for what might have been and in turn knowing better than ever what will be, to regain control over their remaining life by getting things in order, including wills and arrangements for dependents and spouses.

Anger observed at this period is first directed at the self, manifesting as guilt over what the patient has done to bring this event on himself. Frequently, the anger is projected onto the physician, nurses,and family, which is always painful for these individuals. This may be an important transitional phase, and these recipients may need to be primed to endure it, while enabling the anger to become directed in more constructive ways. Similarly, sadness in the form of self-pitying is better shared with significant others than endured alone. The sadness may be viewed as for what might have been (death) as well as for what has been and will be. When this is ventilated, for which both permission and facilitation are required of the staff and family, the patient is freed to resort to his more characterological defensive patterns to cope with his changed state of being. During this phase of illness, patients may benefit from family conferences and group meetings with other patients and their spouses with similar disease processes. The value of these situations will depend on the individuals and families involved. Group processes have been found helpful in patients with tuberculosis,[41] myocardial infarction,[42] and chronic pulmonary disease,[43] in adolescents with diabetes, etc. These groups are frequently run by nurses, chaplains, dieticians, and physiotherapists under the guidance of a physician and a liaison psychiatrist. All of these professionals not only know their specific disciplines but have had long experience with the population under study. In these sessions, there is the recognition by the patient and his spouse (1) that he is not the only one in this situation and (2) that there are many common problems to be faced which may be ameliorated by being shared. In the course of these sessions, there is an opportunity for much didactic communication about the illness from the staff. Questions raised by patients and their spouses, frequently on the basis of anxiety, can lead to clarification as well as provide an opportunity for group ventilation. Reassurance, when appropriate, can be forthcoming. When controlled by experienced therapists, the use of confrontation can be utilized as part of the group process.[44]

Self-help groups—such as Mended Hearts, colostomy clubs, cancer groups, Weight Watchers, etc.—have proved helpful for some patients with chronic disease processes in their endeavors to live active and involved lives despite their disease. Obviously, although these seem helpful for some, they may be anxiety provoking for others, who may need a more intensive individual therapeutic experience with a personal counselor. When there are other problems in the family, a family therapist may be essential in order to help this already disturbed unit integrate yet another stress. Particularly vulnerable individuals are subject to more serious changes of behavior that require specific intervention by psychiatrists for further assessment, evaluation, and treatment. Some patients may experience depressive reactions; others develop chronic anxiety states; some express a wish no longer to live.[45] There has been increasing awareness of the psychological morbidity that is associated with chronic illness and that is related to the extent of the functional incapacity in the home and at work.[46] Some of these individuals develop functional symptoms similar to those associated with the underlying illness. For example, an individual with angina secondary to coronary artery disease may in stressful situations develop precordial pain in which there is no demonstrable evidence of coronary arterial insufficiency.[47] Postoperative cardiovascular patients may have episodes of hyperventilation which they relate to their underlying illness, but which are found to represent the repressed experience of breathing difficulty after surgery and anesthesia. Many of these reactions, which are at first reacted to as an emergency are best conceptualized as modified conversion reactions[48] and can be identified positively by obtaining a more precise description of the symptom, the situation in which it occurs, and the reaction of the individual and significant others to it (Table 20.8). The description is frequently atypical and differs from the somatically associated phenomenon; it is frequently presented with either exaggeration or indifference; it occurs in proximal relationship to a situation perceived as stressful, frequently one that threatens loss of support by a significant other; it may occur as a phenomenon masking depression or other psychiatric illness; and identifiable secondary gains may be easily ascertained.

In discussing the reactions to illness during the convalescent and rehabilitative phases, it is important to stress that objectified data of these processes are scanty. What has been mentioned above and what will be identified below are examples from relatively few intensive studies from which generalizations have been made. Each illness situation, as well as the environments in which it is handled, requires

Table 20.8
Conversion (Modified Concept)

1. Atypical presentation
2. Bizarre description
3. *La belle indifference*
   Exaggerated affect
4. Model
   - Self
   - Significant other
5. Stress (real, threatened, imagined, object loss)
6. Specific psychopathology—depression, obsessive disorder
7. Secondary gains

careful exploration and statistical analysis if we are to know enough to participate in these environments with maximum effectiveness. We need to use our eyes and ears as well as those of the individuals who consult us in order to develop hypotheses that further observations will help us sustain and amend in order to fill in the voids where experience and knowledge are presently lacking.

The Rehabilitative Phase

This phase of illness has only recently come under the increased scrutiny of researchers interested in coping and adaptation. Their vocabulary has been borrowed from all of the behavioral sciences. Among the patient groups studied have been (1) those with severe burns[49]; (2) those with poliomyelitis[50]; (3) parents of children with leukemia[51]; (4) patients undergoing surgery (see Chapter 19)[52]; and (5) patients undergoing chronic hemodialysis.[53] The tasks seen as necessary for coping and adaptation include[54]: (1) maintaining a sense of personal worth, (2) keeping distress within manageable limits, (3) maintaining or restoring relationships with significant people, (4) enhancing the prospects for recovering bodily functions, and (5) increasing the likelihood of working out a personally valued and socially acceptable life style after maximum physical recovery (Table 20.9). Essential psychological components for accomplishing these tasks depend on the individual's capacity for autonomy and mastery, adaptive ego mastery, and progressive differentiation in development. Indeed, the process of adapting to chronic illness and an altered sense of functioning is seen as a phase of individual development not unlike leaving home, marriage, and aging. Although the adaptive potential is partially related to the individual's past abilities in adjusting to stressful events, the current situation presents a challenge that offers new patterns for development. Adaptation is seen less in terms of compromise and conformity and more in terms of an individual's capacity for finding new and unique ways of

Table 20.9
Tasks of Coping and Adaptation

1. Maintaining a sense of personal worth
2. Keeping distress within manageable limits
3. Maintaining, restoring relationships with significant persons
4. Enhancing the prospects for recovering bodily functions (or alternatives)
5. Identifying the possibility and working toward an acceptable altered life style
6. Emphasizing an opportunity for growth, the development of new skills
7. Communication and demonstration of these capacities to others

Table 20.10
Specific Aids to Coping

1. Empathic, experienced helpers
2. Provision for helpers communication with each other with skilled professionals
3. Self-help groups: Mended Hearts, colostomy clubs, cancer groups
4. Availability of family counseling and therapy (remember the spouse!)
5. Models for identification
6. When possible, the resumption of former routines, functions, and relationships
7. Attention to the "cosmetic" deficits and changes
8. An opportunity to review and communicate past achievements
9. Medication: analgesics
10. Hope, determination, faith

meeting the demands of his infirmity. Essential to this new phase of growth (in addition to the patient's outlook) is the presence of others who begin to work with the patient from the earliest phases of his incapacity and who relate to him as a person, as opposed to a patient, an amputee, a burn patient, a cardiac, a chronic lunger, etc. On the other hand, through experience, these workers need to know at first hand the phenomena—biological, psychological, and social—specific for a specific disability (Table 20.10).

TACTICS FOR THE CONSULTANT DERIVED FROM SPECIFIC STUDIES OF COPING

There are several areas in which efforts to study individuals under the stress of physical illness have resulted in suggesting the unique and specific problems faced by these victims, the different kinds of coping strategies utilized, and potential therapeutic interventions. These include poliomyelitis—the scourge of the late 1940's and 1950's—burns, severe spinal cord injuries resulting in quadriplegia and paraplegia, hemodialysis and renal transplant, and cancer. The results and implications of these studies will be briefly reviewed not only because of the specific suggestions for management of patients with specific conditions, but also for those principles of management extrapolated from one group to another.

Hamburg and Adams[55] have identified 17 transition points, some inherent to the life cycle and others reflecting those intrinsic to urbanized, technologically complex societies. These are: (1) separation from parents in childhood, (2) displacement by siblings, (3) childhood experiences,[56] (4) illness and injuries of childhood, (5) illness and death of parents, (6) severe illness and injuries of adult years, (7) initial transitions from home to school, (8) puberty, (9) latter school transitions,[39] (10) competitive graduate education, (11) marriage, (12) pregnancy, (13) menopause, (14) periodic moves, (15) retirement, (16) rapid technological and social change, and (17) wars and threat of wars. Death of spouse, divorce, and job loss could be added at this time. The authors review two sources for what is presently known about coping: (1) severe injuries and (2) the parents of fatally ill children.

In their studies of severe injuries, they identify: (1) the resourcefulness of the individual, (2) the relatively large number of individual means of coping, (3) the spectrum of adjustment over time, and (4) the importance of group membership. Along the spectrum of adjustment, they suggest that victims (and probably their caretakers) initially exhibit efforts to minimize the impact of the disaster and its potential consequences. Individuals deny the nature of illness, its seriousness, and its probable consequences. These are viewed as avoidance defenses that prevent overwhelming catastrophic reactions and allow for a gradual acceptance of facts, preparing for the transition to the tasks ahead. As the individual begins to come face to face with his condition, he seeks information relevant to treatment and recovery. There begins the assessment of long-term limitations. At times during this phase painful reality becomes associated with episodes of depression. Gradually there is an increasing identification with groups. In a ward or unit situation where patients have identical or similar illnesses, there develops a firm sense of belonging. As the individual attempts to redefine his role vis-à-vis his altered physical state, there occurs the testing of significant others in terms of their support, interest, and attachment. These are first made with the caring staff, frequently with staff of the opposite sex. They then are made with spouses, fiancés, and other family members. Subsequently, they are made with work colleagues and supervisors.

In the studies of the parents of fatally-ill children,[57] workers again have identified a spectrum of reactions. During the initial shock phase after news of the physician's diagnosis of lymphoma, parents were only interested in the information that aided in handling the immediate situation and was helpful in making decisions about the immediate care of their child. Over time, often months, when the implications of the diagnosis had been assimilated, and during a second stage in which parents blamed themselves for not having paid attention to suggested earlier signs and symptoms, parents demonstrated information-seeking behavior from many sources. Knowing may be seen as a more active approach to coping in terms of preparing the individual for the future. At the same time, the searching for information carried with it a fervent hope that it would lead to discoveries. Over time, hope for a miracle in terms of a cure became attenuated to a hope for a remission or that the child would be well enough to go home for a weekend or for a birthday party. As prognosis for recovery diminished and death loomed closer, parents were observed to enter a phase of anticipatory grieving[58] during which they experienced preoccupation with many somatic symptoms: weakness, sighing, crying, insomnia, decreased libido, impotence, increased motor activity, and withdrawal from usual social and professional activities.

The success of coping in these situations, although different at different life phases, may be addressed in terms of (1) the effectiveness with which the task is accomplished, and (2) the cost to the individual of this effectiveness. It depends on the likelihood that the tasks can be accomplished according to standards tolerable to the individual and the group in which he lives. It includes seeking advanced information about the new situation, trying out new forms of behavior in anticipating new roles, and worrying about possible future difficulties. It is assisted by interpersonal closeness in which projected ideas, new patterns of behavior, and altered relationships are discussed openly. In these interpersonal situations—the ward, outside groups, and family—there is the opportunity for pooling of information, support, ventilating, trying out new ideas ,and testing out new models of role complementarity. This active effort supports the capacity for optimism and may overcome passivity and inactivity that may lead to pessimism. These tasks of coping for a specific individual may be formulated by four questions: (1) How can stress be relieved? (2) How can a sense of personal worth be maintained? (3) How can rewarding continuity of interpersonal relationships be maintained? (4) How can the requirements of the stressful task be met or opportunities utilized?

Kiely[59] views severe illness as a psychological stress depending upon its perception and cognitive appraisal and meaning attached to stress as modified by each other and the emotions aroused. The perceived stress is that of: (1) loss or threat of loss of psychic objects, which include body image, personal relationships, and body image; (2) injury or threat of injury to the body, including pain and mutilation; and (3) frustration of biological drive satisfaction, especially basic nurturement, libidinal needs, and avenues of aggressive discharge. Determinants of coping depend on: (1) personality, which may include stress-response patterns, reaction time, and vectors of response (approach-avoidance); (2) disease-related factors; (3) the life setting; and (4) the hospital environment. He suggests that cognitive coping styles include minimalization with selective inattention, ignoring, rationalization of the facts, and selective misinterpretation, sometimes leading to psychic delirium with hallucinations and distortional interpretations. Vigilant focusing in terms of obsessiveness and hypervigilance is another component of cognitive coping that leads to information about the environment during the first stages of incapacity. Concurrent with cognitive coping styles are affective coping responses, which include dysphoric affects in which women frequently focus concern over alteration of body image and men may be distraught over their physical helplessness and dependency on others. During this period, manifestations of fear and doubt are ubiquitous. Associated with affective coping responses are behavioral coping patterns suggested by Lipowski[60] which include active tackling with tasks imposed by illness or injury; capitulating, characterized by passivity, inactivity, and helpless dependency on others; and avoidance, an active effort to free oneself of the constraint implicit in the acceptance of illness or injury. A fourth component of coping identified by Kiely is that of the "courage to be," dependent upon the will of the individual and his capacity to change, characteristics that are probably rooted in very early development.

Poliomyelitis

Although poliomyelitis is no longer the threat that it was in the 1940's and 1950's, the studies by Visotsky et al.[50] and Davis[61] serve as an important key to our present approaches to patients with severe limitation of physical function in unfamiliar surroundings. During the early phases, the individual's concerns are: (1) the lack of information, (2) fear of worthlessness, (3) severe depressions, (4) restlessness, (5) boredom, (6) loneliness (7) fear of rejection by family, (8) helplessness, (9) fear of respirators and other mechanical equipment, and (10) concern over future prospects, physical and economic. Later during the rehabilitative phase, patient concerns are about: (1) financial, (2) future education, (3) occupational opportunities, (4) marital relationships, (5) permanent disfigurement, and (6) family and community relationships.

In approaching the patient with a chronic illness, the liaison psychiatrist needs to know: (1) the specific and common disability and burdens of the illness; (2) the preillness personality of the individual and the situational context in which the illness occurs; (3) that occasional individuals find paradoxical benefits in the illness, inasmuch as some aspects of it may mesh with preexisting personal needs; (4) the usual and specific psychosocial consequences of the disease. In the latter context, he needs to assess how the noxious impact of the illness is commonly detoxified, whether there are patterns of long-term learning processes that lead to increased resourcefulness, and what kinds of personal development result from such experiences.

Responses of patients during the acute phase are avoidance, minimalization, and concern over relationship with spouse, family, and specific aspects of the illness, including altered states of consciousness. Avoidance is again seen in later stages of the illness course at times of corrective surgery. This is more common in adolescents. Preoccupation with relationships with family also recurs during the chronic and rehabilitative phase. However, these are likely to be more specificly about the problems of carrying out role responsibilities in the family during hospitalization. Also during the convalescent period, concerns extend to those of economic security, maintaining a connectedness with the community, religion, and specific interactions with physicians and other treatment personnel. Depending upon the extent that the patient is able to feel an individualized relationship with a therapist, he will be able to project his concerns, express his anxieties, and try out various defenses and coping strategies for review. When this possibility does not exist, anxiety and depression frequently occur. The patient's determination to improve, although self-generated and probably related to early developmental factors, is significantly aided by family, staff, and the ward community. Most patients are slow to accept the fact that there will be permanent disability. In this regard, the patient is in a pivotal situation. Too rapid an acceptance of disability may lead to despair and despondency, which may lead to lack of maximum participation in the treatment program. On the other hand, expectations that are maximally discordant with reality may result in dashed hopes and total resignation at a future time, with failure to accept a limited recovery. The therapists working with these patients obviously walk the tightrope of portraying optimism while not promising more than what is realistically expectable. When this is achieved, the combination of a competent treatment program and a cooperative patient improves the chances of decreasing ultimate disability. When there is demonstrable physical progress, encouragement is given for further progress. Although that still biologically elusive phenomenon called hope is recognized as an essential component for rehabilitation in the face of adversity, when it is unrealistic it may lead to failure to accept disability and consequently to inappropriate behavior. Time, which includes patience, has an immunizing effect not only for patients but also for the caring staff and relatives. Perhaps of greatest importance is the interaction with other patients with similar disabilities and illnesses, which leads to overcoming the sense of isolation and loneliness and assists in the development of a sense of security. Open wards facilitate this kind of interaction. In these situations, it is important for the staff to be aware that this communal-like situation for the patient may lead to a sense of isolation and alienation for the spouse who is estranged from this enormous room while bearing the burdens of increased responsibility and worry, oftentimes alone. Attempts to involve the spouse in group activities with other spouses on the unit are sometimes helpful in overcoming this likelihood.

In the rehabilitative phases of chronic illness, Visotsky et al., in their study of respiratory centers, observed the patient's interaction with the staff, noting that after the initial contacts there was frequent testing of the staff that was often ignored. The testing was based upon positive and negative relationships in the previous treatment facility. This testing was a two-way process, for staff members were also quick to pidgeonhole patients, on the basis of early observations, into categories based on their experience with previous patients. Such early designations, without further specific objectification, frequently place a heavy and unnecessary burden on both patients and staff. These differential responses of patients to staff and staff to patients, who are likely to be together for a long time, include personality and cultural differences that may need to be addressed over time. This frequently falls to the consultant psychiatrist who comes from the outside and is at a bit of a distance from the day-to-day operations of the unit. The consultant may find himself in the role of confidant to both staff and patient; oftentimes when there is conflict, he becomes the mediator between the two. In this phase, the consultant's role is also to encourage the spirits and optimism of the staff burdened daily with heavy and emotion-laden problems, to identify dysphoric and emotionally restricted responses in patients, and to facilitate interactions of both patient and staff with each other and among themselves.

Interaction with family, friends, and professional associates is crucial to the future adjustment of the patient. These individuals are initially uncomfortable and fearful of their own health in hospital environments. Attention to these fears, through the matter-of-fact presentation of facts about the patient's illness, is important. As trust is gained, the staff can begin to listen to the specific concerns of family members and friends not only in regard to the patient but for themselves.

The interaction of patients with other patients may present a two-edged sword, inasmuch as a comparison of deficits and eventual competition are introduced that provide patients with a sense of mutuality while also emphasizing differences, setting up conditions for a recrudescence of repressed sibling rivalries. The extent to which these interactions are successful will depend on the individual's readiness for integration into a group and the presence of individuals competent in managing group processes. For the extremely handicapped, there may need to be protection by staff members until the group can begin to effect such support. There is the problem of in-groups and out-groups. There is above all the problem of limited knowledge about the interactions of groups, especially of those with chronic problems. It is likely that there are individual differences affecting the extent to which help may be forthcoming from a specific group, so that an individual's group experience may need to be titrated according to his needs.

Following discharge from active treatment units, patients experience an emotional letdown, including an increased awareness of limitations in physical recovery and sense of loss from the support of the ward. There is concern with the slowness of physical progress, unsureness about previous relationships, questions about one's own usefulness at home and in the community, and economic security. Through persistent effort, including self-care and the encourgement of medical help, the individual gradually develops new interests and comes to take a measure of pride in his perserverence, stoicism, and strength. Through a process of settling for short- and intermediate-term goals, the individual may continue to derive hope from more gradual progress.

Mastery in coping includes: (1) keeping distress within manageable limits, (2) generating encouragement and hope, (3) maintaining and developing a sense of personal worth, (4) maintaining or restoring relations with significant others, (5) enhancing prospects for physical recovery, and (6) enlarging prospects for favorable future situations.

Burns

Hamburg et al.[49] studied the responses of severely burned patients through the rehabilitative stage. Seen as a problem in adaptation was the struggle of each patient with his personal problem, related not only to the extent of the injury itself but also to the patient's interpretation of it. Also affecting adaptation were the life-threatening nature of the illness, pain, uncertainty about the course of illness, toxicity, sedation, analgesia, and the effects of these anxieties and therapies on the mental apparatus. Adaptation was further influenced by internal psychological processes, two-person relationships, and group processes.

Emotional problems during the acute phase were minimalization followed by a marked concern, which was addressed during the first several weeks to survival and subsequently to the extent of suffering. Concerns during this time frame are those of separation from home; doubt about future relationships with significant others; preoccupation with responsibility for the accident, which included both self-blame and blame on others; and adequacy of communication with the physician and hospital staff.

In the emergency situation there was frequently clouding of the sensorium (exacerbated by narcotics), emotional constriction with tight control over recognition and expression of emotions, a manifestation of a "blah" attitude, resignation, and the sense that "one must take what comes without complaining." Specific defensive mechanisms included: (1) repression and suppression: a conscious effort to avoid thinking of unpleasant experience, an automatic exclusion from consciousness of affect associated with the acknowledged and recalled traumatic experience; (2) denial: a rejection by the individual of some easily recognizable and consensually validated aspect of external reality so that the victim thought, spoke, or acted *as if* this aspect of reality did not in fact exist; (3) illusion, delusion, and hallucination: occurring gradually over time and related to both psychological processes and physical course; (4) regression: the presentation of demanding, complaining, attention-seeking behavior, markedly dependent relationships reminiscent of infantile dependence, and expressed need for frequently repeated reassurance from others; and (5) reworking: repetitive rumination over the traumatic experience in an effort to relieve residual tension. Less frequent and usually less severe defenses included withdrawal, religiosity, rationalization, and conversion.

Concerns during the later stages of treatment related to a more objective assessment of the severity of the injury, the extent of residual damage, disfigurement, change of life plans, and finances. In addition, concerns were expressed about residual problems prior to the accident; the inability to participate in important tension-relieving activities that had been satisfying, gratifying, and enhancing to self-esteem; the threat to the capacity to be loved by others; disfigurement; dependency on others; possible impairment of sexual function; and handling of aggression, hostility, and anger while in the dependent position.

Recovery mechanisms that facilitated recovery were (1) mobilization of hope, frequently derived by interaction with other patients with burns and members of the the staff who were capable of helping; and (2) the restoration of interpersonal relationships through personal assistance (patient and staff). Group processes facilitated a mutuality of experience in which intimacy was attained. In these processes, there was little attempt to mobilize sympathy. Humor was utilized as a basis for more communication, overcoming personal positions, and restoring self-esteem through positive interactions with others. There occurred the testing of key individuals in the environment, especially staff members of the opposite sex. Pride was taken in active participation in the recovery process.

Andreason et al.[62] also noted the presence of anxiety, depression, fear of deformity, and delirium in adult patients during the acute phases. These were accompanied by refusal to eat, removal of grafts, and hostility expressed toward relatives and staff. Such behavior was frequently exacerbated at times of surgical procedures. In several patients, they identified the loss of a will to live that led to a disengagement with staff and other patients and minimal compliance with the treatment regimen.

Seligman,[63] studying the emotional responses of children with burns, identified them as depending on preburn factors: (1) emotional stability; (2) the "accident" in which the burn occurred; and (3) the history, personality, and family situation of the child.

Positive factors in survival related to early denial and withdrawal. However, subsequent studies suggest that, although these responses may be adaptive in some children, they are not so in all, and behavior such as protest may be more advantageous in others, depending on timing, other losses, and parent and staff responses. Survival also related to the somatic responses (hypertension, ulcers, seizures, and infections), an interesting observaton that requires further attention. The authors emphasized the need for psychiatrists and social workers to work with family and the nursing staff attending burned children.

Quinby and Bernstein[64] addressed the difficulty of new nurses working in burn units, noting the difficult challenge to their personal and professional identity that was derived from the discrepancy between their idealized expectations, their conflict between these goals and reality, and their resolution of this conflict.

Quindlen and Abram[65] have noted the frequency of delirium in burned patients, identifying: (1) a disturbed metabolic equilibrium; (2) altered neurological function; (3) overstimulation by constant pain, surgical procedures, dressings, etc.; (4) lack of orienting stimuli—visual and auditory, aseptic isolation, and an inability to move; (5) emotional trauma due to disfigurement and disability; and (6) inability of the patient to handle previous emotional problems. In patients with neurological damage, they note the similarities between delirium of burns and Wernicke's encephalopathy in terms of the clinical symptoms and the pathological changes. In both there are cellular changes in the grey matter, especially in the hypothalamus.

Sophistication has rapidly developed in the treatment of burns. Special environments and new methods of handling patients with burns have led to an array of specific problems. One of these, much noted but still under study, is in the effect of the isolation of patients in order to prevent infections. In these units, patients are frequently unclothed, do not have direct communication with relatives, are often attended by masked and garbed staff, and are subject to a monotonous and unfamiliar environment. Burn centers are often distant from the patient's home, so that contact with family members is infrequent and sporadic. In these situations, it is important to develop an ancillary staff of workers who are able to stand in for the absent family and who are capable of writing letters, reading, chatting, and playing games. For the staff working in these special units and hospitals, support through group sessions led by psychiatrists and psychologists is helpful in bringing out the anxieties and despondencies that arise around patients and between staff persons.

Severe Spinal Cord Injuries

About 5,000 individuals per year are left quadriplegic or paraplegic secondary to cervical trauma, resulting in a total living population of such persons estimated at 150,000.[66] The average life expectancy of these individuals is 7 years, with 77 per cent of those under 25 and 55 per cent of those between 25 and 34 surviving more than 10 years. Life expectancy is first determined by the completeness of the lesion. Lesions to the first three cervical levels are rapidly fatal because of respiratory paralysis. C-4 lesions are marked by total dependency and a short life-span because of respiratory complications. C-5 lesions allow for neck motion, partial shoulder motion, and weak elbow flexion; there is better respiratory excursion, and life expectancy, therefore, is increased. C-6 lesions provide for full innervation of shoulder motion, elbow flexion, weak wrist extension, and poor grasp. C-7 lesions provide for elbow extension, which permits pushups from a wheelchair and other transfer maneuvers; there may be some digital extension.

The greatest cause of death in quadriplegics is renal failure secondary to urinary tract infection. Suicide, either as an overt action or as "physiological suicide," is common. In the latter situation, the patient neglects his personal and medical care, succumbing to decubiti, infections, or respiratory, cardiac, and renal failure. However, individual responses vary, resulting in different outcomes. A major national example is that of the new head of the Veterans Administration who suffered the amputation of both legs and his right arm by a grenade during the Vietnam War. He demonstrates an individual's response through perseverance and motivation to newer rehabilitation techniques. Many of these have been pioneered by Howard Rusk[67] at the New York University Rehabilitation Unit. Rusk believes that an optimistic attitude of the physician and others is all important. Rehabilitation should be started early and carried on dynamically to the highest possible level of self-sufficiency. The quadriplegic's existence consists of two phases, the bed and the wheelchair. Transfer from one to the other requires the help of an attendant. Constant problems include the potential for decubiti, blood pressure changes, proper nutrition, urine output, possible fractures and contractures, ankylosis, constipation, and renal infection. Frequent medical follow-ups and laboratory tests are necessary.

Despite severe impairment, with the assistance of special devices and through operant conditioning the patient can learn a number of skills that increase independence of function.[68] After discharge, comprehensive home care is needed. The best asset of the quadriplegic is a strong, unified, resourceful family. However, such a resource is frequently lacking, nursing homes are usually inadequate, and comprehensive specialized centers are few in number.

The acute phase of injury is manifested by spinal shock, the disappearance of all neural reflex below the transection. There is a flaccid paralysis, which later is followed by a spastic or hypertonic state of the skeletal muscles. Because spinal shock also affects the autonomic nervous system, there are marked variations in heart rate, respiration, regulation of blood pressure, control of temperature, and lack of bladder and bowel control. With return of reflex activity, the subacute phase is initiated. This is characterized by: (1) spasticity and contractures, both of which are influenced by emotional attitudes as well as physical factors; (2) management of elimination tracts; (3) decubiti; (4) blood pressure irregularities; (5) respiratory complications; (6) osteoporosis; (7) autonomic hyperreflexia; (8) phantom pains and sensations; and (9) impaired sexual function.

The predominant psychological aspect of quadriplegia is social atrophy,[69] the extent of which interrelates with personal motivation. Nagler[70] has identified seven distinct psychological reaction types to severe cord injury: (1) early anxiety and reactive depression with initial failure to adjust to situation with subsequent change; (2) psychotic reaction with paranoid features associated with premorbid personality; (3) hopeless indifference occurring most frequently in the less intelligent; (4) a psychopathic reaction characterized by hostility; (5) extreme dependency, emotional immaturity associated with subsequent addiction; (6) an emotionally explosive response with difficulty of channeling aggressive drives into productive accomplishments; and (7) an acceptance of disability, with good insight into limitations and potentialities. Shoutz[71] has classified negative, neutralizing, and positive reactions in individuals with quadriplegia, which are useful in viewing a patient's willingness to participate in rehabilitation. Negative reactions include gross confusion and uncertainty; panic or nonspecific anxiety; nightmares; fear of loss of sanity; fear of death or dying; fear of becoming a physical, emotional or financial burden; feeling different from others and shame on exposure; vulnerability to rejection or emotional or physical attack; feelings of self-punishment; suicidal thoughts and death wishes; uncontrollable hostility; rejection by friends, family, and society; feelings of being at the mercy of a cruel or unjust fate; feeling that the adult status is completely lost; and worry over the availability of physical assistance.

Neutralizing reactions are intellectual denial of illness; withdrawal from emotional reactivity through conversion of unpleasant affect; relief from responsibility of life; decentralizing the disability in relation to total personality; a feeling of having paid one's debts for past sins; and exploiting others. Positive reactions are fantasizing future success; thinking of the disability as a new opportunity to correct old errors; full appreciation of life by almost dying; faith and hope for a miracle cure; a feeling of interpersonal worth derived from the care of others; a feeling of being selected for spiritual trials of suffering; and developing good values from nonphysical aspects of existence. Masterman[72] identified the following characteristics that interfere with the rehabilitative process: academic underachievement, anxiety, dependency, depression, fantasy, guilt, hostility, hypochondriasis, interpersonal difficulties, inadequate emotional control, lack of self-confidence, lack of parental understanding, need for tender emotion, overprotection, projection of blame, psychosexual problems, reaction to standards, resentment of authority, reflection, social withdrawal, thinking insufficiency, and unrealistically high goals.

In reviewing these observations, it is important that the presence of any one of these characteristics is likely to be observed in an individual at one or another phase of the illness. It is not the occasional occurrence of any one of these reactions but rather a sustained response that bodes for good or maladjustment over the long haul. When certain characteristics interfere with therapy, attention is indicated. Although an individual's previous personality has been stressed as a major factor in his subsequent adjustment to traumatic injury, it is not uncommon to observe major alterations in an individual's personality, suggesting growth and maturational processes that accompany major stress and challenges.[73]

The typical reactions to quadriplegia can be identified by stages and the specific disabilities each individual faces. There is usually a withdrawal and isolation mechanism that minimizes the focus on self; a lack of spontaneity and initiative; a situational depression associated with disability and the future life role; a tendency toward ambivalence, indecision, and passive-submissive behavior; unrealistic thinking; and immature emotional expression.[74] There follows an attempt to compensate for loss of a sense of self, which includes the physical, sexual, and personal, and a resulting dependency on others. Low self-esteem relates both to these losses and the debilitating aspects of the illness, including shame, anxiety, and guilt over excretory functions. As in other illnesses, the first phase is one of anxiety, depression, denial, grief, and mourning, accompanied by passivity and passive aggression. Following this, there is an attempt to recrystallize the self, which may include the development of a new image based on acceptance and hope rather than hate. Aggression may be positively used in developing an active and constructive approach to the problems ahead.[75] Successful rehabilitation depends on: (1) realism and clarity of goals, (2) suitable value standards and behavior, (3) adequate tolerance for frustration, and (4) increasing degrees of autonomy.[76] The key factor underlying this is motivation focused on a positive reason for living. Motivation can be encouraged, if not instilled, through strong relationships and trusting ties among therapists, relatives, and the patient. All persons attending the patient need to exude realistic confidence, hope, and direction. Although only 10 per cent of all patients with quadriplegia reach viable vocational goals, those who are younger and have higher educational levels, good premorbid work histories, the ability to transport self, the ability to use special devices, and motivation have found work in clerical, sales, personnel, professional, technical, and managerial positions.[77] Presently, sheltered workshops offer the suitable environment for the severely disabled individual. With increased attention to the environmental needs of these individuals, opportunities in the open marketplace can be developed.

MacRae and Henderson[78] have stressed the need to teach patients with paraplegia and quadriplegia how to handle their sexual limitations. Such instructions include precise identification of neurophysiological alterations, including motor and sensory; the increased need for rest, comfort, and avoidance of pain; attention to the esthetically distressing aspects of bowel and bladder functions; and prolonged counseling relating to the psychosocial aspects of altered sexual functioning, including learning a variety of new techniques and unfamiliar performances. On the other hand, Hanson and Franklin[79] suggested that staff have tended to overemphasize the importance of sexual loss in men with spinal cord injuries as related to other functions. However, regardless of the extent of the individual's desire to become sexually reengaged, there remains the need for the staff working most intimately with the patient to assist him or her in giving expression to fears, anxiety, frustration, shame, fantasy, and wishes. More general sexual counseling may be given by informed individuals in group sessions with patients and spouses. The use of written and audiovisual materials may help in patient education and in drawing out emotional feelings around sexual problems.

Wing[80] has studied the later stages of rehabilitation in terms of vocational training for severely incapacitated individuals, finding: (1) initial lack of confidence in the ability to obtain and hold down a reasonable job, (2) improvement in confidence correlated with experiences on the unit and was accompanied by a decrease in self-rated anxiety and depression, and (3) increase in confidence correlated with sustained employment after discharge. Improvement depended on (1) an individual's ability to approach difficulties constructively, (2) a demonstration of the handicap's residual capacities, and (3) social influences, such as a community in which self-confidence in the face of severe difficulties was valued. Lack of improvement correlated with (1) passive or causal approaches to rehabilitation, (2) strong idiosyncratic and unconstructive drives, and (3) higher magnitudes of psychiatric disorder.

Concepts of functional behaviorism may be applied particularly in the area of rehabilitation. Goldiamond[81] described this approach as dealing with "the meaning or motivation of behavior in terms of its maintaining consequences." This pattern may be required for these consequences to occur. The behavior-consequence language deals directly with observable and potentially manipulatable events. The meaning of current behavior is assessed, e.g., it is determined to be attention getting, it is directed toward attaining a specific object, etc. On the basis of this, if the consequence is viewed as desirable, a program is developed that will alter the present methods by such techniques as negative reinforcement and encourage substitute patterns by such techniques as positive reinforcement. On the other hand, it may be necessary for patient and therapist to agree on an alternative goal. Once the goal has been mutually agreed upon, the therapist "develops a program which converts the current repertoire to the desired repertoire in a step-by-step manner." Programming includes programmed instruction, behavior modification, and biofeedback. Designing a program includes identifying the starting point; the present behavior pattern of the patient, i.e., his *current relevant repertoire*; and the steps required to reach the target. In turn, the *target-relevant repertoire* may become the current relevant one for the next target. A program requires a system of *response-contingent consequences* in which a "reward" is contained. Goldiamond has proposed a constructional approach, as opposed to a pathological one, by concentrating on the behavior to be established rather than on that to be eliminated.[82] In behavioral analysis, the focus is on goals rather than obstacles. Problem solving begins with the raising of questions based first on what the goal is and subsequently on what is presently available and what needs to be provided in order to attain that goal.

Other Neurological Disorders

To a varying extent, the reactions of individuals to other neurological disorders pattern themselves after those observed in patients with quadriplegia and paraplegia. In most of these disorders, at least initially, the extent of incapacitation is usually less catastrophic. On the other hand, the onset may be insidious and the course of the illness marked by remissions and exacerbations, each cycle leaving the individual further incapacitated. Consequently, individuals with progressive neurological disorders, such as amyotrophic lateral sclerosis and multiple sclerosis, live in constant awareness of further deterioration and incapacitation. There are also more or less specific characteristics related to different neurological diseases. In amyotrophic lateral sclerosis, for instance, the course may be marked by serious depression, sometimes of psychotic proportions, whereas in many individuals with multiple sclerosis, there is a peculiar *la belle indifference* that characterizes the process. The initial phases of the illness in these progressive kinds of disorders are marked by much anxiety over the still unknown basis of the early symptoms, their fluctuating presentations, the uncertainty of the diagnosis, and the elaborate examinations necessary for ascertaining the diagnosis.

Individuals experiencing subarachnoid hemorrhages and occlusive cerebrovascular disease have an intermediate course between the sudden cervical trauma in quadriplegia and the progressive diseases.[83] About 5,000 patients per year are admitted to hospitals with a diagnosis of subarachnoid hemorrhage. Fifty per cent of conservatively managed patients die during the initial hospitalization, frequently because of recurrent hemorrhage. Those surviving the initial episode have a 20 per cent risk of dying of recurrent hemorrhage within the next 6 months. Newer surgical techniques and active management during the acute phase have reduced these figures. Individuals with intracerebral hemorrhages are at greater risk when conservatively managed. Thrombotic strokes constitute the most common type of cerebrovascular accidents. When these events are secondary to extracranial occlusive cerebrovascular disease, surgical intervention is increasingly successful. Prognosis for return to previous function is better in those surviving subarachnoid hemorrhage than for those surviving thrombotic disease.[84] Ford et al.[85] reported that prognosis for survival can be made within the first few days after a stroke. Factors associated with early death are hemorrhage, advanced age, coma, signs of damage to extensive or critical areas of brain, and presence of cardiovascular disease. Functional recovery occurs most during the first month, with about half of the survivors regaining independence and up to 20 per cent requiring complete care. Over 5 years, mortality reaches 50 per cent.

Storey[83] followed 261 patients for 6 months to 6 years after subarachnoid hemorrhage. Forty-one per cent demonstrated personality impairment, whereas 5 per cent showed improvement, possibly because of a leucotomy effect. Impairment correlated with the amount of brain damage, central nervous system signs, and middle cerebral artery aneurysms. Most frequent changes were increases in anxiety and irritability with loss of vitality. Goldstein[86] noted the high percentage of catastrophic reactions in patients sustaining irreversible central nervous system damage. These reactions included marked emotional lability in patients with deficits in cognitive functions when confronted by a novel situation. Individuals with such disorders require careful attention and protection from overwhelming stimulation requiring quick and novel adjustment. Individuals attending such patients need to be succinct, direct, clear, calm, patient, and matter of fact in their relationship. The great lability of affect needs to be met with calmness and soothing reassurance rather than confrontation.

Feldman et al.[87] compared functionally oriented medical care and formal rehabilitation management of patients with hemiplegia due to cerebrovascular disease. They concluded that the great majority of hemiparetic stroke victims can be rehabilitated adequately without formal rehabilitation services if proper attention is given to ambulation and self-care activities.

Pain

Patients with pain for whatever reason require a complete and detailed psychosocial evaluation in order to assess the relative influences of organic, psychological, and environmental factors affecting it.[88] Pain has both a public and private meaning. The public meaning is that of scientific medicine that attempts to analyze it in terms of vectors: intensity, location, duration, radiation, quality, timing of onset, etc. These are then related to pains generally characteristic of organ system pathology. The private meaning of pain extends to all the painful experiences that the individual has ever had and the specific memories and interpretations which he relates to them. Generally, pain is seen as bad and frequently is associated with punishment, guilt, anger, sadness, and specific memories attending these kinds of feelings. It is also attended by the fantasy or expectation of obtaining relief not only through physical means but through the kinds of ministrations rendered by kind and empathetic parents. Whether or not there is a physical explanation for pain, the emotional sides need to be explored and suitably accommodated. When these aspects of pain have been attended to, the need for physical models of intervention are frequently of less magnitude.[89] Egbert et al.,[90] in a controlled evaluation of 97 surgical patients undergoing elective procedures, demonstrated that with encouragement and education about what to expect during the postoperative period, how to relax, how to take deep breaths, and how to move so as to remain comfortable after operation, the need for postoperative narcotics was reduced by one-half and discharge time was 2 to 10 days earlier than that of the nontreated group. Similar observations have been made for patients undergoing amputation and radical breast surgery. Zborowski[91] has addressed the cultural, sexual, and age differences in the expression of pain in a comparison of four ethnocultural groups—Jewish, Italian, Irish, and "Old American." Members of the former two groups are described as emotional in their responses to pain. Differences between these two suggested that, whereas individuals of Italian extraction were concerned with immediacy of the pain experience and were disturbed by the actual sensation which they experienced in a given situation, patients of Jewish origin focused on the symptomatic meaning of pain and upon the significance of pain in relation to their health, welfare, and eventually the welfare of their families. These attitudes relate to drug acceptance and pain relief. The Italian calls for pain relief, is concerned with its analgesic effects, and, on attaining relief, easily relinquishes his sufferings and manifests a happy and joyful disposition. The Jewish patient is reluctant to accept the drug and is fearful of the effect of the drug on his general health, its habit-forming potential, and the fact that the drug does not cure. When verified in the individual, such differences suggest that, in the first instance, it is important to relieve the actual pain by medication first, whereas, in the second, it is first indicated to relieve the anxieties with regard to the sources of pain. These two groups also tended to view physicians differently. The Italian group displayed a confident attitude, reinforced by the physician's administering a pain-relieving drug; the Jewish group maintained a skeptical attitude, feeling that the mere relief of pain by the doctor's drug did not testify to his skill to take care of the underlying illness.

"Old Americans," on the other hand, attempt to minimize pain and to avoid complaining and provoking pity, withdrawing when pain becomes too intense. In their relationships with the physician they tend to give matter-of-fact descriptions of the pain and assume the detached role of an unemotional observer. However, they are concerned about the sympathetic significance of the pain which correlates with a pronounced health consciousness. The "Old American" patient, in contrast to the Jewish one, is optimistic as opposed to pessimistic in his future orientation. The former's anxiety is greatly relieved when he feels something is being done in terms of specific activities and treatment. Irish patients, on the other hand, were depicted as stoic individuals capable of sustaining a great deal of pain. Intragroup variations were observed and were related to the degree of Americanization, socioeconomic background, education, and religiosity. The role of family in transmitting attitudes and emotional expression was also important in the reaction to pain by individuals. Hence, a knowledge of group attitudes toward pain is important to an understanding of an individual's reaction, a principle underscored by Hardy and his co-workers[92] in their early studies.

Cancer

Although cancer probably is not a unitary disease in terms of a single causative agent but depends on a host of perhaps different factors operating together over time, the phenomenon "cancer" as it is regarded by our present society is a more or less relentless and progressive disease ultimately resulting in prolonged suffering and death. The fear of and reaction to this phenomenon in Western society is perhaps greater than to any other illness. Although progress in terms of early diagnosis (carcinoma of the cervix) and various therapeutic approaches to other organ cancers has resulted in increased survival and 5-year cures, there remains a large number of cancers in which little progress in these dimensions has occurred. The absence of an identifiable single agent increases the anxiety that occurs when rational explanations are lacking and the unknown looms large. In a very real sense fear and anxiety in the minds of healer and patient alike are oftentimes synonymous with cancer.

Over the years, there have been attempts to identify specific personality characteristics of the individual vulnerable to developing cancer. LeShan and Worthington[93,94] identified precancerous traits that included a sense of despair and an inability to express hostile feelings and emotions in self-defense. Thomas and Greenstreet,[95] in their prospective study of health and illness in Johns Hopkins medical students, found no overt characteristics for individuals who subsequently developed cancer. Rather, intrigued by this being the only group for which they were unable to find a biological or psychological marker or predictor of subsequent illness, they attributed this finding to the individual's capacity for concealing feelings and their emotional expression. Later, Harrower et al.,[96] in a study of figure drawings by these students, identified a characteristic pose for those who subsequently developed cancer. This was a pose of "ambivalence," in which the figure had one arm extended outward and the other arm held in against the body. Kissen et al.[97] studied the personalities of individuals who smoke, suggesting that this behavior is utilized as a means of suppressing emotional expression. Goldfarb et al.[98] observed that patients with malignancies survive longer when they can decrease their anxiety by outward action. Koroljow[99] correlated the treatment of depression with temporary cessation of tumor growth in patients with cancer. Mueller and Watkin[100] correlated plasma free fatty acid with rate of growth of malignancy, similar to patterns in patients with fear, repressed anger, and depression.[101] These inconclusive and sporadic findings do not justify postulating emotions as an etiological factor in malignancy, but they suggest reactions commonly enough found among cancer patients to alert the clinician to consider therapy for them.

Several authors have noted the delay in seeking medical attention exhibited by patients with cancer. Henderson related a previous experience of cancer affecting members of family, friends, or acquaintances as a factor in delay, as well as personal anxiety. Relationship with a supportive physician and information were effective in bringing patients for diagnosis and treatment early. Hackett et al. found detection of cancer through routine examination ensured the least delay; worry about the condition reduced delay time more than pain, incapacity, or other factors; patients of higher social class sought help significantly sooner than the less privileged; and delay was less in patients who referred to their condition as cancer, tumor, or growth. Because early detection is considered the prime factor in the effective treatment of cancer, attention to the mechanisms of delay in patients with symptoms becomes the obligation of all physicians involved in the care of patients, including the psychiatrist.

Hinton[104] described patients "bearing cancer" as showing an initial preoccupation with physical symptoms, especially pain, disfigurement, concern over the future, loss of work, dependency, alienation, depression, anxiety, and aggression. Coping mechanisms included minimalization, vigilance, and the repressive ego defenses of repression, guilt, and projection. Suicidal attempts as messages of appeal, anger, and despair were relatively frequent. As opposed to rejection, some patients could accept cancer with a quiet courage or even a sense of bearing aloft. Milton[105] described several stages in the course of the patient with malignant disease. The first is the realization of a disease; the second begins with the diagnosis of the malignancy and the denial followed by the "why me?" reaction. There is then the preoccupation with the treatment of the disease and its effects, such as radical mastectomy, colostomy, and radical lymph node dissections. The third stage is that when incurability is realized. The fourth stage is that of the dying patient. The patient's fears include those of losing dignity and of becoming a thing. The initial defense of denial is followed by withdrawal and subsequently by accepting reality. Later, there may be rejection of consequences, false jocularity, and progressive feelings of rejection and rejection of others. Solzhenitsyn[106] has expressed the latter as "growing like a wall behind me, the patient on one side—friends, family on the other." For specific diseases, there are specific reactions such as the loss of a symbolic organ. Renneker and Cutler[107] reviewed the experiences of patients to the loss of a breast. This was frequently experienced as an end to productive motherhood and sexual attractiveness and activity. Although these feelings may be less expressed today, they are still present beneath the surface in many individuals and their spouses. Asken[108] cited the need for preoperative counseling and postoperative rehabilitation in patients undergoing mastectomy.

At different ages the management of cancer in the patient by the physician varies. Because, at least initially, many individuals equated the idea of having cancer with having a "terminal illness," the reactions of individuals are partly based upon their attitude toward death. The idea of death is different at different ages (see Chapter 22). Nagy[109] has written of the child's idea of death. At age 5 and under, death is perceived as like going to sleep. It is not permanent. The dead return. Close to the age of 10, death is seen as like going to another land after a short period, several days of stillness. The other land is described in heaven-like terms. The adolescent's concept of death is cognitively closer to the adult's, but affectively the adolescent has little relatedness with the concept. Even in the face of great illness, the idea of one's own vulnerability and ultimate destructibility is frequently held as absurd. Much of adolescence may be seen as death-defying acts of bravado both by the ill and the well. Only slowly during the early adult years does a more adult-like response to the inevitability of death occur. Marriage, the birth of children, and the ultimate death of parents give real testimony to the progression of generations and are documented by vows, buying of insurance policies, and the writing of wills. As the body of the individual or those of his friends begin to give way to the progressive and degenerative diseases of middle age, a more final acknowledgment of the death of the individual emerges and begins to shape the way in which the individual chooses to live his remaining life. This is true for both the ill and well. For the ill, the urgency to live as fully as possible, to complete those major tasks that have been undertaken, and to leave something behind are paramount. Such desire and activity may paradoxically interfere in the vital life relationships that the individual also wishes to leave behind, especially the personal legacy for one's children. For the older individual, the thought and subject of death, although omnipresent, are less the focus of interest. Death takes a distant second place to life, despite protests to the contrary. Illness and its potential threats to life may be more easily taken in stride, the individual bargaining to accept as much out of his remaining life as he can. Thus, the attitudes that one has toward death have much to do with the acknowledgement and acceptance of illness. This is further colored by the life phase the individual is in and the life tasks before him. What the physician tells the patient as well as how he does this will depend on where that individual is in his developmental course, what he can hear, what he can understand, what he can handle, and what he must handle to carry out his responsibilities to significant others and to himself in terms of the legacy he would leave behind. The physician takes his first cues from the patient, allowing open commun-cation and discussion. He can go no faster than the patient. The child's questions, which may sound the same as the adult's, are different. They demand different answers. The adolescent's dilemma is perhaps the most difficult for the physician, as are most adolescent dilemmas. Not only is it fraught with the physician's own countertransference in terms of his own adolescence, but he finds it difficult to accept the idea that the completion of adolescent tasks is as essential to the latter's life as the treatment of the disease. The management of these two courses frequently seems at opposite ends of a spectrum of life. In the adolescent much of the concern about death is manifested by the problems about living the life of the adolescent. Concern is displaced onto seemingly mundane preoccupations: Can one still wear a bikini? What about a wig? Death, like sex, is a very private and personal matter, one which is obvious and not obvious at the same time. The behavior of the individual will frequently seem to be contrary to the best interest of himself as patient. The resolution of this dichotomy is not always easy, nor is it with any problem of any adolescent.

In the adolescent,[110] personality integration has not been completed nor have adult defense mechanisms been fully evolved, thereby interfering with adult-like adjustment. Alterations in self-concept are frequent, resulting in a sense of being different and no longer belonging. Coping processes often reflect denial of illness, overcompensation, intellectualization, and anger. Dishonesty on the part of physicians, parents, or others is not tolerated. Periodic depressions occur but are brief. Alterations in body image relate to disfigurement incurred during the course of treatment: alopecia, radiation, dermatitis, and amputation. Interpersonal relations are compromised by fear of rejection, distrust, and overprotection by parents. Concerns over the future exist and, interestingly, are those about college, marriage, and children. Fears of sterility as well as sexual unattractiveness may lead to behavior resulting in out-of-wedlock pregnancy. Many of the problems observed are the results of failure by parents and other adults to view the adolescent as an individual in the stage of development with many of the preoccupations and aspirations of his peers. Death, even when acknowledged, is viewed differently than it is by an adult. Denial in this age group, when it does not lead to neglect of treatment, frequently seems to be a useful coping device. It is not unusual to observe the adolescent taking care of his parents while seeking his own courageous reachings out and relationships with peers similarly afflicted and often of the opposite sex.

In the adult patient, the physician's task is to support the life-appointed tasks that the patient has wittingly or unwittingly taken upon himself. These may be the ordering of business affairs, attention to present and future family affairs, and attempting to plan a course through a prolonged and progressive illness. He may need the assistance of experts other than the physician. A major task for mothers is the projection of her care of her children onto others for the future. These tasks are not easily or rapidly accomplished but are pursued deliberately and sometimes silently over many months. In the resolution of these problems, psychiatric counseling is frequently advisable. Norton's[111] account of her work with a dying mother of two is a graphic picture of one role that a physician can fulfill in the care of a patient. Stehlin and Beach[112] outlined four processes in the work of the physician with a patient with cancer. First is the assessment of the patient's attitude toward cancer. This depends upon an open discussion, which cannot be pursued until ventilation of affect has been facilitated. In this, the physician can use didactic knowledge, such as suggesting that the cancer did not begin yesterday; that the patient has already lived with it a long time; that, although there is much that is known, there is also much that is not; that the spread of cancer is related to many individual factors that include optimism, hope, and determination; that so long as life continues, one lives and can live as fully as possible. Second, he needs to clarify and explain the physical factors associated with the disease and the methods available for treatment. In doing this, he needs to stay with the patient, not going beyond what the patient is able to hear or understand. In doing this, he is communicating a sense of control. A third exploration involves an elicitation of the patient's attitudes toward life in general, his sense of self, of his will to live, and of his attempt to realize the full potential of this life by living as fully as possible at the present. The fourth dimension relates to the attitudes and personality of the physician; his ability to communicate that both he and the patient are in this world together and are potential victims of the same fate; that each of their lives are vital and directed, in this instance, allied against the disease in the patient; and that this, too, is part of living.

Davies et al.[113] have emphasized the organic factors affecting psychological adjustment in patients with cancer. Mild intellectual impairments are associated with better adjustment and longer survival. These are associated with less anxiety and despair. An apathetic, given-up attitude correlated with earlier death and greater illness. Many of the patients observed in this study were more concerned about their illness, pain and its relief, and getting home for a weekend than in talking about dying and death.

Schonfield[114] identified coping and return to work in patients successfully treated for cancer with lower scores on the morale loss scale and higher scores on the well-being scale of the Minnesota Multiphasic Personality Inventory (MMPI) than those in patients not returning to work. There were also lower scores on the measure of covert, although not overt, anxiety than in those not returning to work. The latter scored highest on situational fears. For many kinds of illness, seemingly successful management of the physical factors does not correspond with high levels of social readjustment, such as return to work. This has been documented in patients with mental illness and cardiac problems as well as others. Many of the factors influencing this factor are still in need of identification. Among the factors seemed to be those related to the anxieties and fears of the unafflicted and their efforts to put themselves at a distance from illness; the impetus for employers to maintain low company-paid health and death benefit plans; and the failure of private and public employers to make adequate accommodations for the handicapped. However, studies also suggest that much of the failure for coping relates to the altered sense of self in the individual. Repeatedly anxiety and depressed stages have been identified, although the extent and variations of these are often left undescribed. Identification and treatment of these stages seem unsystematic, oftentimes ignored, and unsuspected. After treatment procedures, medical facility staffs and physicians usually make only cursory examination as to social, business, and family readjustment. More recently, group therapy for patients with various illnesses has been proposed. Bilodeau and Hackett[115] have described group therapy for patients sustaining myocardial infarction and their spouses. Yalom[116] has recently reported on group therapy for cancer patients. In these situations, he emphasized that the psychiatrist must accept the anger of patients and both their own and their patients' sense of vulnerability and impatience in the face of the disease and death. Patients' irrational anger is frequently displaced. Patients expect physicians to meet unrealistic demands and to be all knowing, all protecting, and the ultimate rescuers. Rational anger was directed toward oncologists and surgeons who had left them uninformed and had excluded them from decisions affecting treatment. Patients felt that they had been abandoned at a time when support was most needed. The open group expression and confrontation was seen as allowing patients to move into a richer mode of experience. Yalom suggested that several months' experience as an apprentice is essential for most psychiatrists to participate in such group processes. More recently, Yalom and Lieberman have collaborated in a study of self-help groups—such as ileostomy clubs, Mended Heart societies, groups of individuals with hemophilia, ureterostomies, mastectomies, etc.—in an attempt to evaluate their roles in individual adjustment and coping.

Chronic Hemodialysis and Renal Transplant

Presently, there are about 7,000 individuals on hemodialysis. This level is expected to increase to a level between 15,000 and 30,000 individuals annually. The cost of maintaining this number of hemodialysis and a smaller subpopulation for one or more renal transplants each will compete for an increasing part of the health dollar. The ethical dimensions of this aspect of the problem have and will continue to concern all who are involved with it.[117] Since hemodialysis was first instituted, many physical and emotional problems have been observed in patients undergoing this procedure. Because of these two factors, scarce medical resources and difficulties in adapting and surviving in hemodialysis, attempts have been made to identify those factors which correlate with a good prognosis. Patient assessment is made on: (1) capacity for self care, based on previous emotional stability, stable behavior, wish to survive, and acceptance of authority; (2) capacity for rehabilitation, based on motivation, ability to adapt, firm identifications with family, friends, and occupation, and high self esteem; and (3) capacity to adapt to stress.[119] Successful adaptation correlates with: (1) high intelligence, (2) less defensive attitude, (3) less reliance on somatic defenses (hypochondriasis and hysteria), and (4) emotional support from family. Evaluation observes: (1) past and present level of functioning, especially in marriage and job: (2) ego resources for successful adaptation to increased demands; and (3) anticipated approaches to solving psychological problems occasioned by the treatment.

A number of observers have identified that adaptation occurs in a stepwise process.[118–120] The initial evaluation of suitability occurs in the first stage when the patient is in a severely toxic state, manifesting fatigue, apathy, drowsiness, inability to concentrate, depression, and emotional instability. This toxic state is directly related to the multiple metabolic imbalances that occur with decreased renal function and the resulting uremia. When the renal dysfunction has been prolonged, there may also be anemia which will contribute to the altered state of consciousness with its cognitive deficits in the areas of orientation, memory, concentration, and abstraction; emotional lability; and visual motor incoordination.

The second phase commences with the first hemodialysis and lasts 1 to 3 weeks during which the patient reaches physiological equilibrium—a decrease in blood urea nitrogen and improved electrolyte balance. This is accompanied by a decrease in apathy, an increased sense of well-being, and sometimes euphoria, sometimes identified as the honeymoon phase. It ends with the patient's awareness of his responsibility to assist in the program and progressively to take up his social and professional responsibilities. Associated with the dialysis experience, there may be transient episodes of anxiety and insomnia. A third phase, one of equilibrium, during which disenchantment and discouragement are present, occurs between the third week and the third month. During this time, the dialysand is physically weak, often anxious, sometimes depressed, demonstrates conflicts over dependency on the machine and the staff, and experiences headaches and episodes of vomiting related to the dialysis. Perhaps not enough attention has been paid to the relatively rapid and marked change in consciousness that occurs over the period of dialysis, with the individual reverting from a relatively lethargic state to one of hypervigilance and alertness after the electrolytic corrections. Electroencephalograms that have been taken throughout the dialysis correlate this physiologically.

Since the beginning of chronic dialysis, much has been written describing the neurological disorders that have been observed during treatment. Wakim[121] has described a dialysis disequilibrium syndrome as including headache, vomiting, muscular twitchings and tremors, disorientation, convulsive seizures, episodes of ventricular tachycardia, and other cardiac irregularities. He has correlated these symptoms and discusses their etiology in terms of cerebral edema caused by a reverse urea effect, hypoglycemia, alterations in carbon dioxide tension, changes in potassium and calcium levels, shifts in other electrolytes, and dehydration. Tyler[122] described neurological disorders occurring with infections and unusual central nervous systems tumors of possible reticuloendothelial origin, possibly related to immunosuppressant therapy in patients receiving renal transplants. Savoy et al.[123] and others have observed hyperparathyroidism in patients on chronic dialysis presenting with pruritus and emotional changes, including irritability, depression, and paranoid delusions. Raskin and Fishman[124] noted the occurrence of neurological disorders in renal failure as including subdural hematoma, Wernicke's encephalopathy, and mycotic and cytomegalovirus infections. Mahurkar et al.[125] described a syndrome they called "dialysis dementia" as a progressive mental deterioration with dyspraxia, facial grimacing, myoclonus, and general seizures. Alfrey[126] found evidence to suggest that the dialysis encephalopathy syndrome may relate to high central nervous system levels of aluminum as a result of the dialysate.

Thus, it would seem that it is difficult to separate specific metabolic factors from specific emotional ones in attempting to interpret the reactions of patients on dialysis during these two phases. Since the mid-1960's, investigators have been describing the psychological reactions of patients to dialysis.[127] Abram[128] discussed the stress of dialysis in terms of the emotional conflicts raised around dependency-independency, which frequently led to rebellion against the medical regimen. He stressed the need for criteria to be used in a process of selecting candidates. He identified the need of the psychiatrist to examine with the patient the meaning of prolongation of life for that patient while attempting a resolution of the conflict between dependency on the machine and staff with the inherent independence in maintaining a "normal" life. DeNour et al.[129] described uniform defenses of denial, displacement, isolation, reaction formation, and projection in nine patients undergoing dialysis over a year's time as being adaptive but leading to ego restriction that compromised interactions with others and adjustment to pre-illness life patterns. This study noted the dependency of patients on the machine and the difficulty in handling the aggression resulting from this dependency. Brain dysfunction was also identified as a compromising factor to successful adaptation. Beard[130] described the fear of imminent death as an immediate, initial, and recurring phenomenon at the time of diagnosis and throughout the spectrum of dialysis and transplantation. Discouragement, sadness, self-depreciation, hopelessness, resentment, and loneliness were accompaniments of the dialysis. On the other hand, fear of living related to a view of the less than satisfactory life, the sense of chronic debilitation, and the identification by self and others of the individual as handicapped. Successful coping related to an ability to share, enter into and maintain relationships with others, maturity, and a capacity for flexibility. Short and Wilson[131] described the unusual demands placed on the patient, family, and dialysis team, emphasizing the ubiquitous presence of denial and suggesting that, at least initially, it served as an effective mental mechanism that helped the various individuals cope with a continuing unsatisfactory situation. Although it may be appropriate for the individual and family at some stages, denial is inappropriate for the dialysis team both in terms of themselves and in terms of addressing noncompliance and other kinds of reactive behavior in patients and families. Halper,[132] in an excellent brief review article, noted the multiple difficulties encountered by patients in dialysis programs, including the fluctuation in cognitive functioning during dialysis that often leads to permanent deterioration. He identified denial, oftentimes seen as adaptive in the early stages of illness, as restricting during later stages, especially in the ventilation of the anger, pain, discomfort, and frustration that individuals on dialysis experience. He associated denial with suicidal behavior and the wish to no longer live, a phenomenon also identified by others. Abram et al.[133] correlated suicide with the death of a parent, divorce, and the relative threat of passivity and inactivity in the male. Goldstein and Reznikoff[134] noted its relationship to the lack of adherence to a treatment protocol as an attempt to reduce the anxiety resulting from the patient's recognition of his heavy responsibility in the program. McKegney and Lange[45] saw these patients as having had repeated losses, the most recent of which was renal failure, and who had essentially given up. They also identified the cognitive dissonance between patient and staff relative to objectives, goals, values, and the problems of life on dialysis. When such behavior and patients are identified, the option of ceasing dialysis by conscious decision needs to be addressed openly and individually with the patient. Glassman and Siegel,[135] using the California Personality Index and the Shipman Test, described the discordance between (1) test scores that revealed a high sense of well-being and low scores for anxiety and depression and (2) clinical observations of lethargy, depression, pruritus, peripheral neuropathy, and shunt infections. Massive denial, they felt, contributed to a delusional process that led to eating and drinking binges and decreased survival. DeNour and Czaczkes[136] correlated noncompliance with the medical regimen with low frustration tolerance and with primary and secondary gains from the sick role. Acting-out behavior, although present in both compliers and noncompliers, was greater in the latter.

A fourth phase of adjustment occurs between the third and sixth months for some, but not all, patients. In this phase, the problems encountered relate to living rather than dying. Patients have come to assume increasing responsibility for their care and have learned to be aware of imminent complications and the hazards of deviation from the prescribed regimen. There is also the recognition of the progressive deterioration and alterations that occur with chronic dialysis. Lindner and Curtis[137] described the accelerated atherosclerosis in these patients; Lim and Fang[138] reported the presence of gonadal dysfunction in uremic men; and Levy[139] found impotence and diminished orgasm as related to emotional factors. The conflicts around sexuality involve the symbolic significance of the urinary tract—their functional relationship to the urogenital system, urination, and genital activity. Viederman[140] viewed the whole process of hemodialysis as evoking conscious and unconscious fantasies relating to early developmental stages, especially related to the mother-child interaction and hopeless dependency. He believed that the treatment situation requires a regression (adaptive or maladaptive) to early life stages, suggesting that the quality and degree of conflict that reemerges and past solutions to early conflicts will affect the quality of the adaptation to treatment. The patients will do poorly unless he has developed a particularly gratifying infantile mutuality with his mother who engendered a deep sense of basic trust, and hope which persists in the face of severe frustration.

Most investigators have focused on the social environment of the patient undergoing dialysis, citing relationships with staff and family. Foster et al.[141] correlated survival with affiliation with the Roman Catholic faith, continued presence of both parents, as well as low mean blood urea nitrogen levels. Length of survival correlated with the constraint scale on the Miller-Quinlan Boundary Image Test. Gillum and Barksy[142] suggested that compliance depended upon four factors: (1) psychological; (2) environmental and social; (3) characteristics of the treatment regimen: and (4) patient-physician interaction. DeNour and Czaczkes[143] predicted adjustment to dialysis in terms of compliance with diet, rehabilitation to social and work situations, and the patient's psychological condition as reflected by four aspects—depression, suicidal tendencies, anxiety, and psychotic complications. In comparing results on the research unit with other groups, they found the studied patients fulfilled their potential for adjustment to a greater degree than the controls, who showed more depression and more noncompliance. They suggested that this related to the presence of a psychiatrist and a social worker on the unit but questioned whether this was the result of direct interactions with patients or through indirect work with physicians and staff. Marshall[144] addressed the effective use of a psychiatric consultant on a dialysis unit in group meetings of patients, staff meetings, the evaluation of patients, and in ward routines. MacNamara[145] identified the role of the social worker on the dialysis and homotransplant units working with transplant donors and recipients. She found that the focus of psychiatrists has frequently been only on the hospital course of the patient, with less attention to the family, donors, and even the staff. First and foremost, she felt that the essential need imposed by the illness on the patient was one of self-control. Patients were concerned about the reactions of spouses and children; loss of status; deprivation of formerly gratifying activities, such as eating, drinking, sexual relations; emotions of anger, guilt, and anxiety; and, especially, in finding outlets for tension and aggression. Cramond et al.[146] defined the role of the psychiatrist as: (1) assessing and assisting patients, staff, and family responses under stress; (2) educating staff as to the emotional responses of patients and families to the frequent changes in staff; (3) selection of patients for dialysis and transplant; (4) involving the community in the selection process of dialysis candidates; and (5) working with patients and families about the anxieties and hopes regarding transplant. Shambaugh and Kanter[147] studied spouses under stress, noting a progressive lessening of panic and denial and increasing openness and interaction leading to a sense of emotional separateness from partners. This would seem to be a double-edged sword were it to result in withdrawal from the partner's needs.

HOME DIALYSIS

In order to accommodate the increasing numbers of individuals requiring dialysis, with its expense and the inconveniences imposed upon families and patients, home dialysis has become increasingly common. It is not without its specific hazards and specific problems. Smith et al.,[148] in discussing the advantages and disadvantages, noted that the idea of home dialysis needs to be part of the initial contract with the patient. Patients with whom this had not been discussed had difficulty in transferring from the hospital to the home situation. Also noted were the frustrations of patients and staff over delays caused by administrative decisions, obtaining the equipment, and educating patient and spouse. Success or failure depended upon not only the presence of a spouse, but of an individual capable of withstanding the heavy responsibility and onerous duties imposed. Brown et al.[149] identified four factors relating to the success of home dialysis: (1) extent of change in physical and emotional state secondary to the disease, (2) source and extent of financial support, (3) role and relationship of helper to the patient, and (4) importance that the patient perceived dialysis had to his daily life. Success depended on the recognition by patient and spouse of the imposing roles demanded by dialysis that were incompatible with preexisting roles and the ability to accept these changed relationships. Success also depended on an ability to gain a sense of independence from the machine and redevelopment of social contacts and interests. Staff, as well as patients and families, should realize that a full-time job is neither important nor possible for all dialysands. Blagg et al.[150] focused on the physical complications of dialysis previously mentioned and emphasized problems with anticoagulation, infections, shunts and fistulas, and equipment in home dialysis. He noted that psychological problems were greater in the young than in the old, who had less difficulty adjusting to the rigid schedule demanded by dialysis. Fishman and Schneider[151] reported on adjustment to home dialysis as relating to psychometric variables established during the first week of dialysis rather than to background variables. For the patient, elevated Minnesota Multiphasic Personality Inventory and MAACL scores on anxiety, depression, and hostility scales correlated with more numerous complaints of physical symptoms on dialysis. For the patient's relative, high scores on anxiety, depression, hostility, competitiveness, and introversion likewise correlated with more complaints of physical symptoms while the patient was on dialysis. First year on dialysis adjustment correlated with present problem-solving ability, rather than past learning, as measured by the Shipley-Hartford I.Q. Scale. However, the physical health of the patient after the initial week on dialysis did not correlate with emotional adjustment but with survival.

TRANSPLANT

Although the sociopsychobiological aspects of transplants have frequently been grouped with those of dialysis, there are specific additional problems relating to the donor or the cadaver donor's family and his relationship to the recipient.[152] Again, this is a transitional relationship with changes occurring over time. There is first anxiety over finding a donor, then over making a specific request of the donor, the multiple pressures on the donor—both internal (obligation) and external (the family)—the sense of obligation of the recipient to donor or donor's family, the sense of guilt by the recipient in the event of rejection, the specific hazards of immunosuppressant and steroid therapy to the physical and emotional state of the patient, the changing focus of attention from the donor at one stage to the recipient, and, finally, the ordeal of second and even third transplants in the event of rejection.[153–155]

Psychotherapy with patients on chronic hemodialysis is not only possible but necessary and involves not only the patient, but family, staff, and potential donors and their families. Hence, the complexities are great in terms of who is the identified object for therapy and who is the identified therapist at any point in time. There is also the question of individual therapy in addition or as opposed to group therapy. There is always the ethical issue of confidentiality and the almost certain infringement on the usual patient-physician relationships. Therapy will follow and relate to the stresses of dialysis as have been identified above. These include: (1) alteration in body concept by threatened loss, dysfunction, and presence of shunt; (2) dependency on machine; (3) threat of death; and (4) frustration in coping with drives (aggression) or loss of drives (sexual). Therapy addresses denial, the marked ego restriction and personality impoverishment observed in these patients. The extent of therapy will depend on the patient's resistance, tolerance for increased anxiety, and ability to form interpersonal relationships and the capacity of the therapist to get involved with life-threatening and debilitating problems. The focus of therapy is frequently that of addressing: (1) the issue of dependence-independence, (2) bringing out and channeling aggression, (3) coping with the threat of death; (4) acceptance of time-limited regression, and (5) accepting an altered sense of body image.[53]

As implied in the preceding overview, the phenomena of dialysis and organ transplant occur in an environment that transcends the usual physician-patient dyad that focuses on specific physical or emotional problems; rather, it involves many individuals and many problems relating to modern society and technology and its values that directly and indirectly affect the patient-physician interaction. These are best considered by Fox and Swazey[156] in *The Courage to Fail.*

The Family and Illness

Throughout the preceding sections, we have focused on the indivdual's experience of illness as occurring in and relating to an environment, dependent not only on his past existence but on the support of those individuals around him, most of all the family. In more recent times, we have come to think and speak less of illness in the individual and more about illness in and of the family. For illness, whether it is specified as being in a specific individual or not, seems always to relate to preceding or concurrent illness in the family. When illness occurs in the family, Anthony[157] observed: (1) changes in intrafamilial dominance, (2) a reevaluation of family member roles, (3) shifts in the strength and directions of feelings between family members, (4) alterations in sexual patterns, (5) new patterns of maintaining discipline, and (6) reordering of home routines. Illness and incapacitation of the father resulted in his becoming a relative nonentity, with a disregard for his rulings. Even upon recovery, he failed to regain all of his former dominance. Jackson[158] noted four patterns of adjustment to the crisis of illness: (1) the family may return to its normal level of adjustment; (2) the family may fail to recover for a while, if it has previously been a poorly organized unit; (3) with repeated illness, the lack of family interaction is chronically impaired, with further deterioration after each episode; and (4) the level of interaction is frequently higher after illness. Koos[159] described the extrafamilial effects of illness as withdrawal from active contact with the outside world, so that affiliations and relationships are gradually discarded. Shame is important in bringing about such withdrawal from active contact. This may become amalgamated with guilt reactions already provoked in individual family members as a consequence of assumed responsibility for the illness. Parsons and Fox[160] viewed illness as a form of deviant behavior and as an escape from the pressures of everyday life. Small families are vulnerable to the strains of illness, and members exploit it. Frequently, it "provides" a solution for life problems of individual family members. Families overeact to the passive, dependent nature of illness and its inferior child-like status by being more sympathetic, supportive, indulgent, and persuasive than they need to be, because they project their own regressive needs on the sick individual. Thus, becoming sick entails the learning of a sick role. Anthony, viewing illness in the family as a challenge, adopted Toynbee's analysis of growth, breakdown, and disintegration in social groups as including the potential for: (1) growth and differentiation, (2) breakdown and rally, and (3) rout and disintegration. Spiegel[161] identified three stages of accommodation of a family to illness in one of its members. The first is one of manipulation in which the family exercises role induction measures, such as coercing, coaxing, evaluating, unmasking, and provoking, only to be met by the patient's counterinduction or neutralization measures of defying, withholding, denying, masking, and postponing. Subsequently, role reversal techniques will be used which may lead to role modification, using measures such as joking, referral, exploring, compromising, and consolidating.

These studies emphasize that the care of the patient with a chronic illness necessitates care and attention of the family as well. Oftentimes, family members are left to shift for themselves under the burden of illness, isolated both from the attention to the patient by the physician or the concern of other family members and friends. Group and family therapeutic methods are frequently useful in detecting and alleviating distress resulting from illness in the family. Individual attention by the physician and/or consulting psychiatrist, however brief, may serve to elicit unsuspected tensions and conflicts within the family. No evaluation or treatment of an individual is complete until at least one other member of the family has been interviewed.

Summary

The approach to the patient (Table 20.11) with illness resulting in chronic disability demands first a knowledge of the patient's previous life situation, his early development, his adjustment to the stresses of that environment, the major behavior and personality characteristics that developed in that environment, the present life situation of the

Table 20.11
Role of the Liaison Psychiatrist

1. Know the patients:	Listen to them.
2. Know the field:	Have an internship.
3. Know the staff:	Eat with them.
4. Be seen:	Go on the ward.
5. Be available:	At office and home.
6. Know your limits:	They want you for *your* expertise.
7. Make no promises:	Above what you can give.
8. Communicate simply:	In English.
9. Stick to empirical data, not theory:	Theory is fine in conferences.
10. Be ethical:	Confidentiality.

person[162] when he became ill, his reactions to the acute and convalescent phases of illness, and an assessment of the environmental resources available to the individual at the present time, especially significant others. Most important, perhaps, is the patient's capacity[163] for optimism and faith in learning new ways for survival.

References

1. Kimball, C. P.: Conceptual developments in psychosomatic medicine: 1939–1969. Ann. Inter. Med. *73:* 307, 1970.
2. Kimball, C. P.: The languages of psychosomatic medicine. Psychother. Psychosom. *28:* 1, 1977.
3. Grinker, R. R., editor: *Toward a Unified Theory of Human Behavior: An Introduction to General Systems Theory*, 2. New York, Basic Books, 1967.
4. Heller, J.: *Something Happened.* New York, Random House-Ballantine Books, 1975.
5. Shapiro, D.: *Neurotic Styles.* New York, Basic Books, 1965.
6. LeVine, R. A.: *Culture, Behavior and Personality.* Chicago, Aldine Publishing Company, 1973.
7. Holmes, T. H., and Rahe, R. H.: The social readjustment rating scale. J. Psychosom. Res. *11:* 213, 1967.
8. Coddington, R. D.: The significance of life events as etiologic factors in the diseases of children. I. J. Psychosom. Res. *16:* 7, 1972.
9. Paykel, E. S., Prusoff, B. A., and Uhlenhuth, E. H.: Scaling of life events. Arch. Gen. Psychiatry *25:* 340, 1971.
10. Schmale, A. H.: Relationship of separation and depression to disease. I. A report on a hospitalized medical population. Psychosom. Med. *20:* 259, 1958.
11. Sapira, J. D., Scheilp, E. T., Moriarty, R., and Shapiro, A.: Difference in perception between hypertensive and normotensive populations. Psychosom. Med. *33:* 239, 1971.
12. Reiser, M. F.: Theoretical considerations of the role of psychological factors in pathogenesis and etiology of essential hypertension. Bibl. Psychiatr. *144:* 117, 1970.
13. Rahe, R. H.: Stress and strain in coronary heart disease. J. S. C. Med. Assoc. *72:* 7 (Suppl. 2), 1976.
14. Alexander, F.: *Psychosomatic Medicine.* New York, W. W. Norton, 1950.
15. Bridger, W. H.: Sensory discrimination and autonomic function in the newborn. J. A. Acad. Child. Psychiatry *1:* 67, 1962.
16. Mirsky, I. A.: Physiologic, psychologic and social determinants in the etiology of duodenal ulcer. Am. J. Dig. Dis. *3:* 285, 1958.
17. Weiner, H., Thaler, M., Reiser, M. F., and Mirsky, I. A.: Etiology of duodenal ulcer. I. Relation of specific psychological characteristics to rate of gastric secretion (serum pepsinogen). Psychosom. Med. *19:* 1, 1957.
18. Friedman, M., and Rosenman, R. H.: Association of specific overt behavior pattern with blood and cardiovascular findings. J.A.M.A. *169:* 1286, 1959.
19. Dunbar, H. F.: *Emotions and Bodily Changes: A Survey of Literature on Psychosomatic Interrelationships.* New York, Columbia University Press, 1954.
20. Ruesch, J.: The infantile personality: The core problem of psychosomatic medicine. Psychosom. Med. *10:* 134, 1948.
21. Nemiah, J., and Sifneos, P.: Affect and fantasy in patients with psychosomatic disorders. In *Modern Trends in Psychosomatic Medicine*, O. W. Hill, editor, vol. II, chapter 2, pp. 26–34. London, Butterworths.
22. Marty, P., and De'Uzan, M.: La "pensée opératoire." Rev. Franc. Psychoanal. *27:* suppl. 1345, 1963.

23. Engel, G. L.: Studies of ulcerative colitis. V. Psychological aspects and their implications for treatment. Am. J. Dig. Dis. *3:* 315, 1958.
24. Kernberg, O. F.: Prognostic considerations regarding borderline personality organization. J. Am. Psychoanal. Assoc. *19:* 595, 1971.
25. Grinker, R., Werble, B., and Drye, R.: *The Borderline Syndrome.* New York, Basic Books, 1968.
26. Engel, G., and Schmale, A.: Psychoanalytic theory of somatic disorder: Conversion, specificity and the disease-onset situation. J. Am. Psychoanal. Assoc. *15:* 344, 1967.
27. Rabkin, J. G., and Struening, E. L.: Life events, stress and illness. Science *194:* 1013, 1976.
28. Cassem, N. H., and Hackett, T. P.: Psychiatric consultation in a coronary care unit. Ann. Intern. Med. *75:* 9, 1971.
29. Kornfeld, D. S., Zimberg, S., and Malm, J. R.: Psychiatric complications of open-heart surgery. N. Engl. Med. *273:* 287, 1965.
30. Seligman, R., Macmillan, B. G., and Carroll, S.: The burned child: A neglected area of psychiatry. Am. J. Psychiatry *128:* 84, 1971.
31. Engel, G. L., and Romano, J.: Delirium: A syndrome of cerebral insufficiency. J. Chronic Dis. *9:* 260, 1959.
32. Kimball, C. P.: Delirium. In *Current Therapy*, H. F. Conn, editor, pp. 833–835. Philadelphia, W. B. Saunders, 1974.
33. Kahana, R. J., and Bibring, G. L.: Personality types in medical management. In *Psychiatry and Medical Practice in a General Hospital*, N. Zinberg, editor, pp. 108–123. New York, International Universities Press, 1964.
34. Greene, W. A., Conron, G., Schalch, D. S., and Schreiner, B. F.: Psychological reactions with changes in growth hormone and cortisol levels: A study of patients undergoing cardiac catheterization. Psychosom. Med. *32:* 599, 1970.
35. Quinlan, D. M., Kimball, C. P., and Osborne, F.: The experience of open heart surgery. IV. Assessment of disorientation and dysphoria following cardiac surgery. Arch. Gen. Psychiatry *31:* 241, 1974.
36. Klein, R.: Behavioral patterns and catecholamine excretion in acute myocardial infarction (abstract). Psychosom. Med. *31:* 449, 1969.
37. Klein, R. F., Kliner, V. A., Zipes, D. P., et al.: Transfer from a coronary care unit. Arch. Intern. Med. *122:* 104, 1968.
38. Engel, G. L.: *Psychological Development in Health and Disease.* Philadelphia, W. B. Saunders, 1962.
39. Mechanic, D.: Response factors in illness: The study of illness behavior. Soc. Psychiatry. *1:* 11, 1966.
40. Lindemann, E.: Symptomatology and management of acute grief. Am. J. Psychiatry. *101:* 141, 1944.
41. Pratt, J. H.: The "home sanatorium" treatment of consumption. Boston Med. Surg. J. *154:* 210, 1906.
42. Bilodeau, C. B., and Hackett, T. P.: Issues raised in a group setting by patients recovering from myocardial infarction. Am. J. Psychiatry. *128:* 105, 1971.
43. Agle, D. P., Baum, G. L., Chester, E. H., et al.: Multidiscipline treatment of chronic pulmonary insufficiency. I. Psychological aspects of rehabilitation. Psychosom. Med. *35:* 41, 1973.
44. Castelnuovo-Tedesco, P.: *The Twenty-minute Hour: A Guide to Brief Psychotherapy for the Physician.* Boston, Little, Brown and Company, 1965.
45. McKegney, F. P., and Lange, P.: The decision to no longer live on chronic hemodialysis. Am. J. Psychiatry *128:* 267, 1971.
46. Croog, S. H., and Levine, S.: Social status and subjective perceptions of 250 men after myocardial infarction. Public Health Rep. *84:* 989, 1969.

47. White, K.: Angina pectoris and angina innocens. Psychosom. Med. *17:* 128, 1955.
48. Engel, G. L.: Conversion symptoms. In *Signs and Symptoms: Applied Physiology and Clinical Interpretation*, C. M. MacBryde, editor, ed. 5, chapter 26. Philadelphia, J. B. Lippincott, 1969.
49. Hamburg, D., Hamburg, B., and deGoza, S.: Adaptive problems and mechanisms in severely burned patients. Psychiatry *16:* 1, 1953.
50. Visotsky, H. M., Hamburg, D. A., Goss, M. E., and Lebovits, B.: Coping behavior under extreme stress. Arch. Gen. Psychiatry *5:* 27, 1961.
51. Friedman, S. B., Mason, J. W., and Hamburg, D. A.: Urinary 17-hydroxycorticosteroid levels in parents of children with neoplastic disease: A study of chronic psychological stress. Psychosom. Med. *25:* 364, 1963.
52. Janis, I. L.: *Psychological Stress: Psychoanalytic and Behavioral Studies of Surgical Patients.* New York, John Wiley & Sons, 1958.
53. Kaplan De-Nour, A.: Psychotherapy with patients on chronic hemodialysis. Br. J. Psychiatry *116:* 207, 1970.
54. Adams, J., and Lindemann, E.: Coping with long-term disability. In *Coping and Adaptation*, G. V. Coehlo, D. A. Hamburg, and J. E. Adams, editors. New York, Basic Books, 1974.
55. Hamburg, D. A., and Adams, J. E.: A perspective on coping behavior: Seeking and utilizing information in major transitions. Arch. Gen. Psychiatry *17:* 277, 1967.
56. Murphey, E., et al.: Development of autonomy and parent-child interaction in late adolescence. Am. J. Orthopsychiatry *33:* 643, 1952.
57. Chodoff, P., Friedman, S., and Hamburg, D.: Stress, defenses and coping behavior: Observations in parents of children with malignant disease. Am. J. Psychiatry *120:* 743, 1964.
58. Schoenfield, B., Goldberg, I., Carr, A., and Peretz, D.: *Anticipatory Grieving.* New York, Columbia University Press, 1974.
59. Kiely, W. F.: Coping with severe illness. Adv. Psychosom. Med. *8:* 105, 1971.
60. Lipowski, Z. J.: Physical illness, the individual, and the coping process. Psychiatry Med. *1:* 91, 1970.
61. Davis, F.: *Passage through Crisis: Polio Victims and Their Families.* New York, Bobbs-Merrill, 1963.
62. Andreason, N. J., Noyes, R., Hartford, C., Grodland, G., and Proctor, S.: Management of emotional reactions in seriously burned adults. N. Engl. J. Med. *286:* 65, 1972.
63. Seligman, R.: Emotional responses of burned children in a pediatric intensive care unit. Psychiatry Med. *3:* 59, 1972.
64. Quinby, S., and Bernstein, N.: Identity problems and the adaptation of nurses to severely burned children. Am. J. Psychiatry *128:* 58, 1971.
65. Quindlen, E. A., and Abram, H. S.: Psychosis in the burned patient: A neglected area of research. South Med. J. *62:* 1463, 1969.
66. O'Connor, J. R.: Traumatic quadriplegia: A comprehensive review. J. Rehabil. *37:* 14, 1971.
67. Rusk, H.: *Rehabilitation Medicine.* St. Louis, C. V. Mosby, 1964.
68. Tromby, C.: Principles of operant conditioning relating to orthotic training of quadriplegic patients. Am. J. Occup. Rehabil. *49:* 592, 1968.
69. Albrecht, G. L., editor: *The Sociology of Physical Disability and Rehabilitation.* Pittsburgh, University of Pittsburgh Press, 1976.
70. Nagler, B.: Psychiatric aspects of cord injury. Am. J. Psychol. *107:* 49, 1950.
71. Shoutz, C.: Severe chronic illness. In *Psychological Practices with the Physically Disabled*, J. Garrett and E. Levine, editors. New York, Columbia University Press, 1962.
72. Masterman, L.: *Psychological Aspects of Rehabilitation.* Kansas City, Mo., Community Studies, Inc., 1961.

73. Kaplan, L., et al.: *Comprehensive Follow-up Study of Spinal Cord Dysfunction and Its Resultant Disabilities*. New York, New York Institute of Rehabilitation Medicine, New York University Medical Center, 1966.
74. Mueller, A.: Personality problems of the spinal cord injured. J. Consult. Psychol. *14:* 189, 1950.
75. Siller, J.: Psychological situation of the disabled with spinal cord injuries. Rehabil. Lit. *30:* 290, 1969.
76. Rabinowitz, H.: Motivation for recovery: Four social psychologic aspects. Arch. Phys. Med. Rehabil. *42:* 799, 1961.
77. Levenson, B., and Green, J.: Return to work after severe disability. J. Chronic Dis. *18:* 167, 1965.
78. MacRae, I., and Henderson, G.: Sexuality and irreversible health limitations. Nurs. Clin. North Am. *10:* 167, 1975.
79. Hanson, R. W., and Franklin, M. R.: Sexual loss in relation to other functional losses for spinal cord injured males. Arch. Phys. Med. Rehabil. *57:* 291, 1976.
80. Wing, J. K.: Social and psychological changes in a rehabilitation unit. Soc. Psychiatry *1:* 21, 1966.
81. Goldiamond, I.: Coping and adaptive behaviors of the disabled. In *The Sociology of Physical Disability and Rehabilitation*. G. L. Albrecht, editor, chapter 5, pp. 97–138. Pittsburgh, University of Pittsburgh Press, 1976.
82. Goldiamond, I.: Toward a constructional approach to social problems. Behaviorism. *2:* 1, 1974.
83. Storey, P. B.: Brain damage and personality change after sub-arachnoid hemorrhage. Br. J. Psychiatry *117:* 129, 1970.
84. Browne, T. R., and Poshanzer, D. C.: Treatment of strokes. N. Engl. J. Med. *281:* 594, 650, 1969.
85. Ford, A., Katz, S., Chin, A., and Newill, V.: Prognosis after strokes. I. A critical review. Medicine *45:* 223, 1966.
86. Goldstein, K.: The effect of brain damage on the personality. Psychiatry *15:* 245, 1952.
87. Feldman, D. J., Unterecher, J., Lloyd, K., Rush, H. A., and Toole, A.: A comparison of functionally oriented medical care and formal rehabilitation in the management of patients with hemiplegia due to cerebrovascular disease. J. Chronic Dis. *15:* 297, 1962.
88. Engel, G. L.: Psychogenic pain and the pain-prone patient. Am. J. Med. *26:* 899, 1959.
89. Szasz, T.: *Pain and Pleasure*. New York, Basic Books, 1975.
90. Egbert, L. D., Battit, G. E., Welch, C. E., and Bartlett, M. K.: Reduction of post-operative pain by encouragement and instruction of patients. N. Engl. J. Med. *27:* 825, 1964.
91. Zborowski, M.: Cultural components in responses to pain. In *Sociological Studies of Health and Illness*, D. Apple, editor, pp. 118–133. New York, McGraw-Hill, Blakiston Division, 1960.
92. Hardy, J. D., Wolff, H. G., and Goodell, H.: *Pain Sensations and Reactions*. Baltimore, Williams & Wilkins, 1952.
93. LeShan, L. I., and Worthington, R. E.: Personality as factor in the pathogenesis of cancer: A review of the literature. Br. J. Med. Psychol. *29:* 49, 1956.
94. LeShan, L. I.: An emotional life-history pattern associated with neoplastic disease. Ann. N. Y. Acad. Sci. *125:* 780, 1966.
95. Thomas, C. E., and Greenstreet, R. L.: Psychobiological characteristics in youth as predictors of five disease states: Suicide, mental illness, hypertension, coronary heart disease and tumor. Johns Hopkins Med. J. *132:* 16, 1973.
96. Harrower, M., Thomas, C., and Altman, A.: Human figure drawings in a prospective study of six disorders. J. Nerv. Ment. Dis. *161:* 191, 1975.
97. Kissen, D. M., Brown, R. I. F., and Kissen, M.: A further report on personality and

psychosocial factors in lung cancer. Ann. N. Y. Acad. Sci. *164:* 535, 1969.

98. Goldfarb, C., Driesen, J., and Cole, D.: Psychophysiologic aspects of malignancy. Am. J. Psychiatry *123:* 1545, 1967.
99. Koroljow, S.: Two cases of malignant tumors with metastases apparently treated successfully with hypoglycemic coma. Psychiatr. Q. *36:* 261, 1962.
100. Mueller, P., and Watkin, D.: Plasma unesterified fatty acid concentration in neoplastic disease. J. Lab. Clin. Med. *57:* 95, 1961.
101. Cardon, P. V., Jr., and Miller, P. S.: A possible mechanism: Psychogenic fat mobilization. Ann. N. Y. Acad. Sci. *125:* 924, 1966.
102. Hackett, T. P., Cassem, N. H., and Raker, J. W.: Patient delay in cancer. N. Engl. J. Med. *289:* 14, 1973.
103. Henderson, J. G.: Denial and repression as factors in the delay of patients with cancer presenting to the physician. Ann. N. Y. Acad. Sci. *125:* 856, 1966.
104. Hinton, J.: Bearing cancer. Br. J. Med. Psychol. *46:* 105, 1973.
105. Milton, G. W.: Thoughts in the mind of a patient with cancer. Br. Med. J. *4:* 221, 1973.
106. Solzhenitsyn, A.: *Cancer Ward.* Harmondsworth, England, Penguin Books, 1972.
107. Renneker, R., and Cutler, M.: Psychological problems of adjustment to cancer of the breast. J.A.M.A. *148:* 833, 1952.
108. Asken, M. J.: Psychoemotional aspects of mastectomy: A review of the literature. Am. J. Psychiatry *132:* 56, 1975.
109. Nagy, M. H.: The child's view of death. J. Genet. Psychol. *73:* 3, 1948.
110. Moore, D. C., Holton, C. P., and Marten, G. W.: Psychologic problems in the management of adolescents with malignancy. Clin. Pediatr. *8:* 465, 1969.
111. Norton, J.: Treatment of a dying patient. Psychoanal. Study Child *18:* 541, 1963.
112. Stehlin, J. S., and Beach, K. H.: Psychological aspects of cancer therapy: A surgeon's viewpoint. J.A.M.A. *197:* 100, 1966.
113. Davies, J., Quinlan, D. M., McKegney, F. P., and Kimball, C. P.: Organic factors and psychological adjustment in advanced cancer patients. Psychosom. Med. *35:* 464, 1973.
114. Schonfield, J.: Psychological factors related to delayed return to an earlier life style in successfully treated cancer patients. J. Psychosom. Res. *16:* 41, 1972.
115. Bilodeau, C. B., and Hackett, T. P.: Issues raised in a group setting by patients recovering from myocardial infarction. Am. J. Psychiatry *128:* 73, 1971.
116. Yalom, I. D.: The terminally ill with cancer find support in group therapy: Roche report. Front. Psychiatry *40:* 7, 1977.
117. Ramsey, P.: Choosing how to choose: Patients and sparse medical resources. In *The Patient as Person.* New Haven, Yale University Press, 1970.
118. Sand, P., Livingston, G., and Wright, R. G.: Psychological assessment of candidates for a hemodialysis program. Ann. Intern. Med. *64:* 602, 1966.
119. Abram, H. S.: The psychiatrist, the treatment of chronic renal failure, and the prolongation of life. II. Am. J. Psychiatry *125:* 157, 1969.
120. Reichsman, F., and Levy, N. B.: Problems in adaptation to maintenance on hemodialysis: A four year study of 25 patients. In *Living or Dying: Adaptation to Hemodialysis,* N. Levy, editor. Springfield, Ill., Charles C Thomas, 1974.
121. Wakim, K. G.: The pathophysiology of dialysis equilibrium syndrome. Mayo Clin. Proc. *44:* 406, 1969.
122. Tyler, H. R.: Neurologic disorders seen in uremic patients. Arch. Intern. Med. *126:* 781, 1970.
123. Savoy, G. M., Yium, J. J., Jordan, P. H., and Guinn, G. A.: Hyperparathyroidism in patients in chronic hemodialysis. Am. J. Surg. *126:* 755, 1973.
124. Raskin, N. H., and Fishman, R. A.: Neurological disorders in renal failure. N. Engl. J. Med. *294:* 204, 1976.

125. Mahurkar, S. D., Salta, R., Smith, E. C., Dhar, S., Meyers, E., and Dunea, G.: Dialysis dementia. Lancet *1:* 1412, 1973.
126. Alfrey, A. C.: The dialysis encephalopathy syndrome. N. Engl. J. Med. *294:* 184, 1976.
127. Shea, E. J., Bogdan, D. F., Freeman, R. B., and Schreiner, G. E.: Hemodialysis for chronic renal failure. IV. Psychological consideration. Ann. Intern. Med. *62:* 558, 1965.
128. Abram, H. S.: The psychiatrist, the treatment of chronic renal failure and the prolongation of life. I. Am. J. Psychiatry *124:* 1351, 1968.
129. DeNour, A. K., Shaltiel, J., and Czaczkes, J. W.: Emotional reactions of patients on chronic hemodialysis. Psychosom. Med. *30:* 521, 1968.
130. Beard, B. H.: Fear of death and fear of life. Arch. Gen. Psychiatry *21:* 373, 1969.
131. Short, M. J., and Wilson, W. P.: Roles of denial in chronic hemodialysis. Arch. Gen. Psychiatry *20:* 433, 1969.
132. Halper, I.: Psychiatric observations in a chronic hemodialysis program. Med. Clin. North Am. *55:* 177, 1971.
133. Abram, H. S., Moore, G. L., and Westervelt, F. B.: Suicide behavior in chronic patients. Am. J. Psychiatry *127:* 1199, 1971.
134. Goldstein, A. M., and Reznikoff, M.: Suicide in chronic hemodialysis patients from an external locus of central framework. Am. J. Psychiatry *127:* 1204, 1971.
135. Glassman, B. M., and Siegel, A.: Personality correlates of survival in a long-term hemodialysis program. Arch. Gen. Psychiatry *22:* 566, 1970.
136. DeNour, A. K., and Czaczkes, J. W.: Personality factors in chronic hemodialysis patients causing non-compliance with medical regimen. Psychosom. Med. *34:* 333, 1972.
137. Lindner, A., Charra, B., Sherrard, D. J., and Scribner, B.H.: Accelerated atherosclerosis in prolonged maintenance hemodialysis. N. Engl. J. Med. *290:* 697, 1974.
138. Lim, V., and Fang, V. S.: Gonadal dysfunction in uremic men. Am. J. Med. *58:* 655, 1975.
139. Levy, N. B.: Sexual adjustment to hemodialysis and transplantation. In *Living or Dying: Adaptation to Hemodialysis.* Springfield, Ill., Charles C Thomas, 1974.
140. Viederman, M.: Adaptive and mal-adaptive regression in hemodialysis. Psychiatry *37:* 68, 1974.
141. Foster, F. G., Cohn, G. L., and McKegney, F. P.: Psychobiologic factors and individual survival on chronic renal dialysis: A two-year followup. I. Psychosom. Med. *35:* 64, 1973.
142. Gillum, R. F., and Barsky, A. J.: Diagnosis and management of patient noncompliance. J.A.M.A. *228:* 1563, 1974.
143. DeNour, A. K., and Czaczkes, J. W.: The influence of patient's personality on adjustment to chronic dialysis: A predictive study. J. Nerv. Ment. Dis. *162:* 323, 1976.
144. Marshall, J. R.: Effective use of a psychiatric consultant on a dialysis unit. Postgrad. Med. *55:* 121, 1974.
145. MacNamara, M.: Psychosocial problems in a renal unit. Br. J. Psychiatry *113:* 1231, 1967.
146. Cramond, W. A., Knight, P. R., and Lawrence, J. R.: The psychiatric contribution to a renal unit undertaking chronic haemodialysis and renal homotransplantation. Br. J. Psychiatry *113:* 1201, 1967.
147. Shambaugh, P. W., and Kanter, S. S.: Spouses under stress: Group meetings with spouses of patients on hemodialysis. Am. J. Psychiatry *125:* 928, 1969.
148. Smith, E., McDonald, S., Curtis, J., and deWardener, H.: Hemodialysis in the home. Lancet *1:* 614, 1969.
149. Brown, T. M., Feins, A., Parke, R., and Paulus, D.: Living with long term dialysis. Ann. Intern. Med. *81:* 165, 1974.

150. Blagg, C., Hickman, R., Eschbach, J., and Schribner, B.: Home hemodialysis: Six years' experience. N. Engl. J. Med. *283:* 1126, 1970.
151. Fishman, D., and Schneider, C.: Predicting emotional adjustment. J. Chronic Dis. *125:* 99, 1972.
152. Kempf, J.: Renal failure, artificial kidney, and renal transplant. Am. J. Psychiatry *122:* 1270, 1966.
153. Short, M., and Harris, N.: Psychiatric observations of renal homotransplantation. South. Med. J. *62:* 1479, 1969.
154. Kempf, J., Bermann, E., and Coppolillo, H.: Kidney transplant and shifts in family dynamics. Am. J. Psychiatry *125:* 1485, 1969.
155. Eisendrath, R.: The role of grief and fear in the death of kidney transplant patients. Am. J. Psychiatry *126:* 381, 1970.
156. Fox, R. C., and Swazey, J.: *The Courage to Fail: A Social View of Organ Transplants and Dialysis.* Chicago, University of Chicago Press, 1974.
157. Anthony, E. J.: The impact of mental and physical illness on family life. Am. J. Psychiatry *127:* 138, 1970.
158. Jackson, D.: Family interaction, family homeostasis and some implications for conjoint family psychotherapy. In *Individual and Familial Dynamics*, J. Masserman, editor. New York, Grune & Stratton, 1959.
159. Koos, E.: *Families in Trouble.* New York, King's Crown Press, 1946.
160. Parsons, T., and Fox, R.: Illness, therapy and the modern urban American family. J. Soc. Issues *8:* 31, 1952.
161. Spiegel, J.: The resolution of role conflict within the family. In *The Patient and the Mental Hospital*, E. Greenblatt, D. Levinson, and R. Williams, editors. Glencoe, Ill., Free Press of Glencoe, 1957.
162. Ramsey, P.: *The Patient as Person.* New Haven, Conn., Yale University Press, 1974.
163. Frank, J. D.: *Persuasion and Healing.* Baltimore, Johns Hopkins University Press, 1973.

CHAPTER 21

Noncooperation: An Examination of Factors Leading to Nonadherence in a Hypertension Clinic

OVERVIEW

Based upon a review of patients referred because of difficulty in following treatment protocols for the control of elevated blood pressure, seven major factors and a number of elements composing these were identified as significant, when matched with a contrasting sample of patients attending the same clinics not referred for difficulty in following treatment plans. It is suggested that these factors assist the physician and his staff in identifying the particulate element or factor in noncompliance of the individual patient, which can then be addressed specifically. Several examples of such interventions are identified. The extension of this model to other clinics, with appropriate modifications for specific problems, may have similar utility.

METHODS

Over a 5-year period, 87 patients were referred to the author from a hypertensive clinic because of difficulty in adhering to an antihypertensive regimen. These patients were interviewed intensively one or more times. Many were followed over the course of several years as they returned to the clinic for periodic review. During this study, a number of commonly presenting elements were identified. Subsequently, these were clustered into six factors. A chart review, followed by random interviews, was then made of 87 patients also attending the hypertensive

Modified version (and reproduced with permission) of article from Psychiatric Journal of the University of Ottawa 5: 4, 1980; copyrighted by the University of Ottawa Press.

clinic but not referred for nonadherence in an attempt to determine whether significant differences could be identified vis-à-vis the identified nonadhering group (Table 21.1). There were no differences observed between the two groups as to race, sex, age, marital status, or social class.

Among the elements of nonadherence cited in the early phase of this study were complaints relating to effects of medication, understanding of instructions, trust in physician, salt restriction, diet, weight control, smoking, drinking of alcoholic beverages, exercise, work, marital circumstances, emotional feelings expressed as anxiety, despair, sadness, hopelessness, dependency, sense of urgency, and burden (Table 21.2).

These, with others, were subsequently grouped into six factors, identified as: (I) physician-patient communication; (II) experienced side effects of medication; (III) sense of well-being; (IV) depression; (V) acceptance of sick role; (VI) hearsay. A seventh factor, not originally included but subsequently observed with frequency on inpatient services, is included as: (VII) fear of and refusal to undergo diagnostic

Table 21.1
Noncooperation Study in a Hypertension Clinic

1. 87 patients attending hypertension clinic were referred for noncompliance.
2. Based on interviews, six factors were identified.
3. 87 patients attending hypertension clinic were not referred—charts evaluated for same factors.
4. Significant differences cited.

Table 21.2
Elements of Noncooperation

I. Complaints about medication
II. Failure to keep appointments
III. Inability to reduce
IV. Inability to restrict salt intake
V. Inability to reduce smoking
VI. Inability to reduce intake of alcohol
VII. Failure to develop an exercise protocol
VIII. Work pressures
IX. Marital conflicts
X. Social conflicts
XI. Denial of illness
XII. Chronic anxiety
XIII. Sense of urgency
XIV. Sense of burden
XV. Depression

procedures. These, together with the elements common to them, are identified in Table 21.3. The p values for each factor as identified by chi-square are indicated in Table 21.4. All six showed significant differences between the subject and contrast populations, with factors I (communication), II (side effects), and IV (depression) revealing the greatest deviance.

DISCUSSION OF RESULTS

The initial identification of elements and the subsequent grouping of the more commonly presenting ones under factors allowed us specifically to identify the major alleged component in an individual's nonadherence. Our understanding of nonadherence in these terms led directly to the isolation of one or more specific factors and their elements and, hence, to specific points of intercession in counteracting these obstacles. Examples for each one of the seven factors are discussed.

Physician-Patient Communications. Cited most frequently under this factor was failure to take medicine regularly because of fear of side effects which had been communicated to the patient by the physician when writing a prescription for the antihypertensive medication. Although methods of informing patients about side effects vary greatly, we were impressed in our survey of prescribing habits among physicians that many recited diligently every conceivable side effect that could possibly occur. It was an impression that some did this as if to satisfy

Table 21.3
Factors in Noncooperation

- I. Physician-patient communication
  - A. Communication of side effects of medication
  - B. Physician displeasure
  - C. Patient lack of understanding
- II. Experienced side effects of medication
  - A. Orthostatic hypotension
  - B. Depression
  - C. Decrease in cognitive functions
  - D. Impotence
- III. Sense of well-being
  - A. Denial
  - B. Absence of symptoms
- IV. Depression
  - A. Helplessness/hopelessness
  - B. Will not do any good
- V. Acceptance of sick role
  - A. Benefits
- VI. Hearsay
- VII. Fear of diagnostic procedures

Table 21.4
Chi-square of Factors: Correlations

Factor	S*	C	P
Factor I: Communication	40	13	
	47	74	.001
Factor II: Side effects	65	45	
	22	42	.001
Factor III: Sense of well-being	35	20	
	52	67	.05
Factor IV: Depression	49	23	
	38	64	.001
Factor V: Sick role	43	57	
	44	30	.05
Factor VI: Hearsay	53	39	
	34	48	.05
Factor VII: Fear of procedures	Not measured		

* S, subject population; C, contrast population.

some external and coercing authority. The patient frequently remembered the most infrequent and frightening side effect that was mentioned. Examples were the possibility of lupus erythematosus, depression, lethargy, confusion, and impotence. The latter was the element most commonly cited by men, not unexpectedly. The idea that "Informed Consent May Be Hazardous to Health" has recently been addressed by Elizabeth F. Loftus and James F. Fries of the Center for Advanced Study in the Behavioral Sciences in an editorial in *Science*.[1] So far as doctor-patient communication goes, it is more likely the quality of the relationship that affects patient acceptance of a particular regimen rather than the specific content.

Lethargy and confusion were feared by all, but there was the suggestion that these were of particular concern to the aging. Despite the seeming ability of some patients to screen out potentially disturbing stimuli through a process of denial or conditioning,[2] it seems that patients with hypertension, in contrast to some other groups, paradoxically, are especially disturbed by anything interfering with perceptual and cognitive processes. The screening-out process seems to be more one at the cognitive, as opposed to the perceptual, level, inasmuch as physiological responses in the cardiovascular system may be recorded at the same time the patient is denying that an external factor is disturbing.[3] This is corroborated, perhaps, by the frequently recorded patient impression that a doctor was displeased with them, although his verbal statements suggested nothing of the kind. Yet, there would be no question about this in the patient's mind. Such displeasure was apparent to the patient by a look, a tone of voice, or an abruptness. So preoccupied was the patient with this that he or she failed to hear or understand the rest of the doctor's comments.

Lack of understanding of what a physician is communicating is so common as to be a banality. Many studies have been made of this. In the last analysis, this element alone requires splitting into particulate parts for further understanding and identification. It does not seem to relate only to the inevitable medical jargon that professionals bring into the discussion with the patient. It relates also to the disparity between the physician's ordinary vocabulary of four- and five-syllable words and the patient's two- and three-syllable ones. Patient receptivity is a major element and probably relates to the shock of diagnosis, anxiety, specific fears, and other factors interfering with perceptual and cognitive functions at the time of interview, diagnosis, and instruction. Some failure in receptivity may relate to the medication that the patient is presently taking.

Experienced Side Effects of Medication (Table 21.5). Of first importance in this discussion was the difficulty in always understanding whether the side effects experienced by the patient actually related to the medication or were fantasied. In other words, how likely were the possible side effects to be subjectively experienced by the patient through the process of suggestibility? This is frequently a difficult differentiation to make in a clinical situation and should always be made with humility on the part of the physician. When this is part of the physician's consideration, he or she will do well to focus on a particulate analysis of the symptom before cavalierly accepting it as a verified side effect or a specious one based on suggestibility. The preciseness with which the patient describes the symptom, together with a congruent affect, suggests greater likelihood of a verifiable

Table 21.5
Side Effects of Common Antihypertensive Drugs

Drug	Common Effects	Severe Effects
Diuretics Thiazide Lasex	Polyuria, nocturia Uric acid	Hypokalemia (cramps, lassitude) Impotence Diabetes Gout
Aldactone	Gastrointestinal upset, nausea Dyspepsia, gynecomastia Impotence	Hyperkalemia Renal disease
Aldomet	Nasal stuffiness Depression, weakness Tiredness, fatigue Diarrhea	Hepatitis
Clonidine	Depression	Hypertension when stopping
Prazosin	Lassitude, fatigue	
Hydralazine		Lupus Arthralgias Arrhythmias Angina
Guanethidine	Depression Orthostatic hypotension	
Reserpine	Gastric distress Ulcers	Depression
Inderol	Drowsiness Diarrhea Nightmares	Asthma Congestive heart failure Bradycardia

physiological component. Appropriate to this consideration is a recent article by Haynes et al. in the *New England Journal of Medicine*,[4] indicating that in a screening program for hypertension there was increased absenteeism from work after detection and labeling of hypertensive patients. This was in comparison to a contrasting group in which the individuals were not notified immediately about their elevated blood pressures and in which an increase in absenteeism did not occur.

In our experience, it seemed that the more potentially threatening the side effect was, the more susceptible the patient was to thinking he might have experienced it. In other words, upon questioning a patient with a complaint of "impotence," it could be identified that: "yes, he had an episode of failure to have an erection since he had taken the medication." On further interviewing, however, it occurred that this had been experienced after an evening of drinking alcohol and that he had had similar experiences at other times prior to antihypertensive medication. In this situation, it is apparent that a patient is all too likely to ascribe to a new medication symptoms which he has previously experienced.

There are, of course, *real* side effects to many of the hypertensive medications that affect patient adherence. First among these is the previously identified fear that patients with hypertension seem especially wary, i.e., decreases in cognitive function. This is experienced by feelings of fuzziness, less attentiveness, difficulty concentrating, and of not being one's self.[5] These were most notable in the aged. Frequently, the experience of these symptoms were in the context of a more complex situation. A typical scenario was that Mrs. T. had recently changed physicians because of the retirement of Dr. E. who had been her doctor for many years. Now she was going to Dr. R. who had changed all her medicine, saying that what she had received from Dr. E. was not doing an effective job. Dr. R. put her on "more potent" medication and "was going to get her under control." On this new regimen, Mrs. T. felt "frightened and displaced." She experienced "dizziness, difficulty in thinking, and depression." She became incontinent. She felt she "was falling apart." In this situation, it was difficult to untangle some of the symptoms experienced by Mrs. T. from the effects of the medication and those of Dr. R. on her sense of well-being. Nevertheless, it is important to stress the sensitivity of older individuals to the effect of antihypertensive medications on different systems. First is the further detection and investigation of symptoms relating to autonomic dysfunction. These include orthostatic hypotension, a sense of instability, incontinence, impotence, and gastrointestinal function.

Sense of Well-being. For whatever reason, it remains a reality that many patients with hypertension are unaware of symptoms relating to it. In these individuals, elevation in blood pressure has been identified on routine checkups without previous complaints of symptoms that could be ascribed to the elevation. Although initially concerned, based on their physician's recommendations, these asymptomatic individuals, rather than becoming preoccupied with the diagnosis, tend to dismiss the potential seriousness of it and fail to follow a therapeutic regimen. It was difficult to elicit the extent that this reaction related to the physician's communication. In fact, many of these individuals had difficulty in identifying just what it was that the physician had told them regarding their elevated blood pressure. Those who did, recalled the conversation vaguely in such terms as "he told me not to worry, I would be all right, just to take it a bit easier, that's all." Although this conversation seems veritable enough and certainly has been witnessed by us, it seems, at least among our clinic physicians, less than typical. Rather, our physicians seem most assiduous in spelling out the details of hypertension and its treatment both vigorously and vividly. On this basis and as corroborated by our interviews, the most common explanation for this reaction is the process of denial. The use of the relatively primitive defense of denial by patients with hypertension has long been identified in this group of patients. It is an especially interesting phenomenon which requires longitudinal studies. One hypothesis postulated by some of us working with hypertensive patients is based on seeing patients at different stages of hypertension.[6] In the earliest stage, the individual, usually an adolescent, predisposed to essential hypertension manifests a lability of arousal and mood frequently associated with a lability of blood pressure. This individual is likely to show lower than normal readings in a resting state but markedly elevated systolic and diastolic readings when given a task that involves interaction (e.g., interviewing) with another. This is unrelated to content. In this situation, the predisposed individual seems extremely vulnerable to the environment, especially so far as the cardiovascular system is concerned. In a later stage of established hypertensive levels, this demonstrated liability to external stimuli seems to change. In this stage, there appears the aforementioned screening out of stimuli, which seems to be more at a cognitive and affective, as opposed to a perceptual, level. The provoking environmental stimuli or social interactions are denied. They continue to be denied, even when called to the individual's attention. Paradoxically, this individual, while denying the relationship identified above, nevertheless frequently expresses in words that: "If such and such happens, it will make my blood pressure go way up."[7] It is important to note the object of vexation almost always relates to another individual, usually a family member or intimately known person. At yet a later stage of hypertension, there are alterations in states of consciousness and cognitive functions which relate directly to compromises in the involved organ systems and reflect dysfunctions within these. Again, the patient's idea of the problem more frequently relates to the specific organ system, i.e., the heart, the kidney, or the "head," in contradistinction to hypertension.

Nevertheless, the idea that a sense of well-being, whether it is through a failure of perception or cognition or is indeed based on lack of symptoms, is a real phenomenon among patients with hypertension and correlates as a major factor in and of itself in nonadherence to a treatment program. This is not unknown with other illnesses and diseases. Charney et al.[8] have noted nonadherence in a pediatric practice in which a 10-day course of oral penicillin was prescribed after the identification of β-streptococci on throat cultures of symptomatic children. Despite careful verbal and written instructions to parents, few families were able to complete the full 10-day course. This was also true for the families of physicians and even in the circumstance when both parents were physicians. Once the child was asymptomatic, the administration of tablets became more erratic.

Depression. The relationship between worsening and exacerbation of hypertensive episodes in patients with this illness has frequently been commented on, but never satisfactorily documented. In this series of patients, depression was significantly manifested by patient self-reports and was closely related to difficulty in adherence to an antihypertensive regimen. The depression was frequently portrayed by the expression of feelings of helplessness—"Nothing that I do will make any difference"—and of hopelessness—"There isn't anything or anyone that can make a difference."[9] This was an initial reaction of a number of patients to the first diagnosis of hypertension. It was as if they threw up their arms and gave up. For some, it was experienced as almost a release from a constant sense of burden, pressure, and the sense of "being put upon." These individuals literally gave up and became the opposite of their customary conscientious, striving-against-great-odds selves. Dependency needs were acknowledged, but usually there were few identifiable resources or persons to satisfy them. They saw no use in taking the medication, saying that: "It would not do any good"; "They had it (hypertension) now, and things would only get worse." On further examination, this group did indeed identify individuals who had been under stress of chronic duration which they had seemingly borne well without external signs or symptoms of great perturbation. "It had finally been too much"; "It was no use"; "Nothing (they) had done had succeeded." Having given up on whatever great endeavor or project they had persisted in, they found no other interest or commitment. They were bothered by "minor" bodily symptoms, which brought them to the physician and diagnosis. More often than not, they seemed lethargic, complained of only wanting to sleep, found themselves constantly snacking without any real enjoyment and their weight increasing, went through the motions of sex without any feeling or interest, and identified that they did not really have any interest in other people or their problems. With the doctor, they seemed initially unconcerned, meekly accepting the diagnosis and the treatment protocol. This, of course, is in marked contrast to their feelings and subsequent expression made to the consultant to whom they were referred after failure to follow a therapeutic protocol. Although not a subject of this report, this group did extremely well in brief psychotherapy combined with tricyclic antidepressants, frequently with a return of their blood pressure to normotensive levels. That this group was "hypertensive prone" was identified by the high prevalence of hypertension in the family history.

Acceptance of the Sick Role. Patients falling into this group were not unlike those in the previous one, except they were lacking in depressive symptoms. It was as if, with the initial diagnosis of hypertension, they had said to themselves, "That's it; I don't have to do this anymore. I'm just going to give it all up and relax. I've worked hard all my life, taken care of everyone else; now I'm going to let them take care of me. There are still things I want to do, fishing, hunting, travel. I'm not going to worry anymore." Their explanations for their difficulty with following the hypertensive regimen overlapped with several other factors, notably fear of side effects and sense of well-being. Attributing their diagnosis of hypertension as related to the stresses of their employment and sometimes home, they felt their salvation lay in "cutting back, retirement, getting some fun out of life before it was too late." They were assiduous in their efforts in looking into the possibilities of obtaining workman's compensation, early retirements, and other health and social benefits which they felt were their due. They were reluctant to take medications because they did not "think this was the answer," "feared side effects," and did not want to feel "other than myself—like a zombie, like some of my friends." Underlying refusal to follow a routine in some cases seemed to be a fear that they might get better too soon and risk losing their rosy view of the future, namely early retirement, release from the simultaneous burden of and monotony of factory employment.

Hearsay. This factor identifies the contaminatory effect of others on patients with hypertension. It begins something like this. A newly diagnosed patient or one who has recently changed physicians returns home and is talking across the fence to her neighbor. The response is: "Your doctor told you that! You should go to my doctor. He'd tell you just the opposite. I really think you should get another opinion. You know you can't be too careful about something like hypertension." Or from the mother-in-law: "I knew something was wrong with you, didn't I say so, but you'd better be careful. You're sure that doctor knows what he's doing? When Sally had trouble like this, she was told just to give up, that's all—give up work, slow down, take it easy, let someone else do the lugging and shopping and all that. Relax, take it easy. And above all, don't get loaded down with all those expensive drugs." Or the supporting spouse: "Oh, I wouldn't worry about a thing; just take it easy. We'll all help you out. Just relax, the trouble with you is you worry about every little thing. You're always worrying. No one can relax around you. That's the trouble. Just relax. Where the hell are my fishing hooks, anyway? Gee, I never can find anything around here. Why can't we keep this place in better order?"

In this series, there was no question but what the attitude of significant others affected a patient's commitment to the treatment advised by the physician. Hypertension, especially, it would seem is a subject which exercises a great many individuals and for which there are conflicting or at least alternative approaches depending on the sophistication of medical practice and the local folklore of lay populations in various segments of the country and world. We need only review the various regimens that have characterized this area of medicine over the past quarter century to note the fervor and commitment that are generated by one approach as opposed to another. When we add the medical folklore of a subculture, we identify treatment strategies for which there are as many proponents as there are for those of legitimate medicine. The former are tried and are in use in large parts of our population, frequently by the practitioners of "Roots."[10]

Fear of Diagnostic Procedures. More recently, among an inpatient population, we have been requested to counsel patients refusing diagnostic procedures in the investigation of their hypertension. These are usually younger persons, frequently women. The procedures that seem to be most threatening are the invasive ones, such as an intravenous pyelogram or a renal arteriogram. These women are adamant in their fear of having a "foreign" substance put in them. Their first objection is on rational grounds that they may have a reaction to the dye, which "the doctor said might happen" or which "actually did happen to one of my friends." Sometimes they hedge by saying, "What good would it do, anyway? I'm not going to have surgery 'nohow,' and there's no way I'm going to have any kidney thing done." Beneath this are all the fears of needles and of violation to the body image. The body image of the patient with hypertension seems to be peculiarly threatened, which is manifested by a need for distinct demarcation from others. There is a fear of getting too close. This is also conveyed in emotional and cognitive ways, as may be seen in some as a lack of capacity for closeness and intimacy. These observations are subject to a number of interpretations. For this chapter, it suffices that this phenomenon is recognized and respected by the physician. Most simply, it can be explained as a way in which individuals with hypertension learn to protect themselves from real, fantasied, or imminent assaults, physical or verbal, from without. There is the sense of keeping a "safe distance."

Other factors identified but not measured included the following:

Excessive Use. A small number of individuals used antihypertensive medication irregularly and indiscriminately. When they "felt" their blood pressure going up, they would "take a handful of pills." Others felt "If one pill was good, two would be better."

Other Fears. Following the invasive theme under factor VII, some patients felt all antihypertensive medication was "poison." "It did things to you, changing your body and your mind."

The Doctor Again. Some saw the doctor as "merely interested in the medication, not me." "He cared more about my blood pressure than me." "All he cared about was getting me in and out of there (office)." "He didn't want to see me often enough." "How was I to stay on the stuff, if he wasn't seeing me?" "I couldn't tell if it was doing any good or not."

Other Problems. As part of the denial process, some patients said they "really couldn't be bothered." "It wasn't important in terms of everything I had to do." "I have too many other problems to worry about myself." "I got all these kids, my husband's unemployed. I'm the only one that can work." "I feel better, anyway, when I'm not worrying about myself." "Those drugs cost too much money, anyway, and I don't have any way of knowing if it's doing any good."

EFFECTING COMPLIANCE (TABLE 21.6)

As this chapter has attempted to suggest, effecting compliance comes first by a careful analysis of the problem. By identifying and investigating the factors suggested above through a general interviewing approach, (see Chapter 2) the particulate element(s) can be discerned and subsequently explored in terms of the patient's feelings (anxiety, sadness, anger, thoughts-fears—real and fantasied, expectations, and other attitudes). In effecting compliance, attention to each of these factors and elements suggests remedial approaches on the part of the physician. Some of these are obvious and follow from attention to the usual doctor-patient relationship and communication. Others may demand some transformation of the usually conceptualized doctor-patient relationship. For example, for many patients, especially those with hypertension, the sense of autonomy—of being in control of oneself, specifically in control of cognitive processes of understanding and decision making—is all important.[11] These patients do much better with adhering to an antihypertensive protocol when they are given responsibility in deciding the best regimen for themselves. When they feel that they are participating in setting up the approach and have understanding of the alternatives, an opportunity to select one as opposed to another (with the advice of the physician), compliance improves. This will vary with

Table 21.6
Effecting Cooperation

I. Communication	IV. Depression
Informed consent	Other factors
Simple instructions	Association with exacerbation
Time	Therapy
Follow-up	V. Sick role
Support	Personality
II. Side effects	Therapy
Follow-up	VI. Hearsay
Instruct how to avoid	Effecting trust
III. Sense of well-being	VII. Invasive diagnostic procedures
Education	Education
Follow-up	Psychotherapy
Denial	

different stages of hypertension. In the latter stages, when cognitive processes are interfered with because of increasing dysfunction of one or more organ systems, patients may need to relinquish some of the decision-making process to others. At other times, other conditions, such as depression or lack of knowledge, interfere with the individual exercising what might be called informed autonomy. In these situations, the depression or lack of knowledge will need to be approached in its own right.

A major element, which might be viewed as a process indigenous to medicine and which seems especially important in the case of the patient with hypertension, is frequent follow-up and supportive reassurance if maximum benefits are to result from treatment. This reinforcement is especially significant for patients with hypertension who respond favorably to encouragement and a good report by the physician.

Notable in this study is the response of patients to physicians' identification of side effects in the service of informed consent. Our view based on this study is that the question of informed consent is not so much that it is done, but how it is done. First, it must be done in such a way that the patient truly understands not only the nature of the side effects and their permanence or transitoriness, but the percentage of risk. Mere terms or numbers are not enough communication for most of us. Furthermore, many side effects develop gradually and can be identified early in their course, thereby avoiding more cataclysmic events. There is no substitute for instruction in the recognition of signs and symptoms.

Psychiatric Assistance. A sense of well-being is a most difficult phenomenon to counteract. It demands not only identification and education, but it necessitates recognition of the phenomenon of denial and therapeutic skills to confront and assist the patient in working through this psychological defense. In its most severe form, the specific skills of a psychotherapist will be required. Similarly, the confirmation of a *real* depression will frequently demand consultation with a psychiatrist, who may work through the physician in his care of the patient. Attention to the fact that exacerbation of hypertension frequently relates to periods of depression will result in psychotherapeutic, and, in come cases, psychopharmacological, approaches to the patient. The assumption of the sick role[12] is a complex factor, which will also need to be identified and addressed by the physician, frequently with the assistance of a psychiatrist.

Confronting the Demons. The physician, in treating his patient with hypertension, is most up against it when he is confronted with hearsay evidence. In the simplest analysis, it frequently comes down to his word against the others. This is usually based in trust, which I suspect has something to do with both persuasion and healing.[13] Finally, in a literal and cognitive world, one cannot say enough about education, the need for and the execution of it. It is not as simple as our public education programs, especially in hypertension, have suggested. Public screening programs based on education have not proven, thus far, cost efficient.[14] Perhaps our approaches in education are overly didactic, coercive, and rigid. It would seem as though public health doctrine has always been a bit, "Thou shalt. . . . " As therapists and physicians, we might do better with metaphor[15, 16] or soliloquys "overheard" by the patient as ways of giving the patient a sense of our deliberations in their behalf.

EXTRAPOLATION TO OTHER CLINICS

A preliminary attempt has been made to extend this model of identifying general factors and their relating elements to other clinics based upon our activities in them. Each factor identified within this report seems to hold up and is useful in identifying the particulate component of failure to follow a specific medical regimen or protocol. In addition, other elements are identifiable in each clinic specific to that specialty and its diagnostic and therapeutic procedures (Table 21.7). Further studies are indicated to identify these more specifically. Once this has been accomplished, it should be relatively easy to compile a specific checklist pertinent to each clinic for identifying the area of difficulty in following a treatment plan. Once this area has been identified, it becomes the focus for further examination and discussion between the physician and/or physician's assistant and the patient.

Table 21.7
Selected Elements of Noncooperation in Other Clinics

Oncology
Fear of change in body image
Fear of change in mental status
Feelings of futility
Psychiatric
Fear of mind control
Displeasure with altered mood/cognitive state
Cardiac
Trouble getting blood levels (prothrombin)
Fear of bleeding to death
Contraception
Fear of cancer
Wish to get pregnant
Denial of planned sex
Infectious disease
Sense of well-being
Dental
Fear of pain
Arthritis
Emphasis on activity
Maintaining conflictual relationships
Side effects

References

1. Loftus, E. F., and Fries, J. F.: Informed consent may be hazardous to health (editorial). Science *204:* 1, 1979.
2. Sapira, J. D., Scheilp, E. T., Moriarty, R., et al.: Differences in perception between hypertensive and normotensive populations. Psychosom. Med. *33:* 239, 1971.
3. Williams, R. B., Jr., Kimball, C. P., and Willard, H. N.: The influence of interpersonal interaction upon diastolic blood pressure. Psychosom. Med. *32:* 194, 1972.
4. Haynes, R. B., Sackett, D. L., et al.: Increased absenteeism from work after detection and labelling of hypertensive patients. N. Engl. J. Med. *299:* 741, 1978.
5. Graham, R. M., and Pettinger, W. A.: Medical intelligence: Drug therapy—Prazoin. N. Engl. J. Med. *300:* 232, 1979.
6. Reiser, M. F.: Theoretical considerations of the role of psychological factors in pathogenesis and etiology of essential hypertension. Bibl. Psychiatr. *114:* 117, 1970.
7. Grace, W. J., and Graham, D. T.: Relationship of specific attitudes and emotions to certain bodily diseases. Psychosom. Med. *14:* 243, 1952.
8. Charney, E., Bynum, R., Eldredge, D., et al.: How well do patients take oral penicillin? A collaborative study in private practice. Pediatrics *40:* 188, 1967.
9. Engel, G. L., and Schmale, A. H.: Psychoanalytic theory of somatic disorder: Conversion, specificity and the disease-onset situation. J. Am. Psychoanal. Assoc. *15:* 344, 1967.
10. Kimball, C. P.: A case of pseudocyesis caused by "Roots." Am. J. Obstet. Gynecol. *107:* 801, 1970.

11. Beauchamp, T., and Childress, J.: The principle of autonomy. In *Principles of Biomedical Ethics*, chapter 3. New York, Oxford University Press, 1979.
12. Kasl, S. V., and Cobb, S.: Some psychological factors associated with illness behavior and selected illnesses. J. Chronic Dis. *17:* 325, 1964.
13. Frank, J. D.: *Persuasion and Healing.* New York, Schocken Books, 1961.
14. Weinstein, M. C., and Stason, W. B.: Allocating resources for hypertension. Hastings Center Rep. *7:* 24, 1977.
15. Friedman, M.: Qualities of patient and therapist required for successful modification of coronary-prone (type-A) behavior. Psychiatr. Clin. North Am. *2:* 243, 1979.
16. Sontag, S.: *Illness as Metaphor.* New York, Farrar. Strauss, & Giroux, 1977.

CHAPTER 22

Death and Dying: A Chronological Discussion

OVERVIEW

In this discussion, we examine some of the factors that are operating in our patients, their families, and ourselves in our mutual confrontations with death and processes of dying. We have oriented our observations in a chronological framework, suggesting that attitudes toward death are to a large extent derivative of those toward life and reflect the individual's evolving formulations of these. In great measure, these seem to follow universal concepts specific to age groups. To a lesser extent, especially correlating with age, the experience of dying and of confronting death seems to be modified by the idiosyncratic experiences of the individual. It is also suggested that the individual, the family, and the professional staff caring for the patient have active work to do in anticipating and participating in the grieving process that begins antemortem. This process itself varies according to both the age and the personal experiences of the individual. Professional workers dealing with the daily confrontation with dying that constitutes the practice of medicine are viewed as needing to ascertain their own attitudes toward death in order to assist a patient in exploring his own feelings and in working with the patient and his family in an active grieving process.

DEATH AND DYING: A CHRONOLOGICAL DISCUSSION

The attention of society in general and medicine in particular during the past decade has turned more and more to a consideration of how people die.[1-3] The reasons are multiple, and, so far as the societal

---

Modified version (and reproduced with permission) of article from Journal of Thanatology 1: 42–52, 1971.

attitude in general is concerned, it is natural to speculate that this is intimately related to the syndrome called the Age of Anxiety.[4–6] In medicine, however, much of the anxiety generated by health personnel seems to have been influenced by a number of changes in the practice of medicine. More people die in hospitals than formerly. Greater technological skills are keeping people alive. This results in a state directly observable in patients suffering from chronic diseases such as cardiac, renal, and pulmonary conditions and cancer, where it is almost commonplace to think in terms of pacemakers, open heart surgery, valve replacement, transplantation, hemodialysis, transplantation, prolonged assistance with mechanical respirators, and intermittent irradiation and chemotherapy. Patients from these groups, who are rarely cured, return to the hospital periodically for further treatment, sometimes routine, but often in acute if not terminal distress. The hospital staff working with these patients is forced to deal with the attitudes, feelings, and behavior of the patient with a chronic illness who is constantly threatened with the proximity of death. On closer observation, however, experience suggests that the real issue is less that of the inevitability of death and more the process of dying, involving as it often does the relatively rapid deterioration of both physical and mental functioning and control in association with pain and other discomfort, oftentimes introduced by the treatments themselves. A closer examination of the attitudes, feelings, and behavior of these patients may lead the investigator to formulations that can assist health workers directly participating in the care and treatment of these patients. Various investigators have been concerned with how patients are prepared for, react to, and adjust to specific procedures. In these reports attention has been focused on the anxieties, depressions, and denial of the patient (see Chapter 19),[7] as well as such factors as the procedure[8, 9] the hospital environment,[10] and specific rehabilitation factors.[11]

From some of these studies, the impression is given that the factor of age may be an important one in determining attitudes about illness, dying, and death. In this Chapter we describe, on the basis of observing patients with life-threatening and chronic illnesses of all ages, attitudes toward death that we believe to be characteristic for specific age groups and which seem of pertinence in our relating to the dying patient.

Children

Several authors[12–16] have investigated the attitudes of children under 10 toward death and have noted that they vary greatly from those of adults. Partly this would seem to stem from the ability of the child to tolerate the juxtaposition of opposites in his mind simultaneously, an example of Piaget's[17] preoperational thinking. For the child up until the age of 6, reality is often in the power of words, and a verbal denial of the fact is tantamount to proof that the fact does not exist. Later, the child may verbalize death as the "going away" of the loved one. This is verbalized with the belief that this is only a temporary absence and that the "bad mommy or daddy" will return after a few days as they always have before. The child often verbalizes ideations of his own death in terms of "going away" and making "mommy and daddy sorry." These are fantasies that continue to exist at one level of thinking at every age, but usually they are not verbalized or actually acted on as being true. It is not uncommon for the "bad" parent to threaten a chronically disobedient child with banishment of either the child or the parent in terms of death. Guilt introduced and emanating from such statements becomes retained in the subsequent metamorphosing concepts of death derived by the individual. Kornfeld et al.[10] and Abram[8] explained the absence of psychotic disturbances in children under the age of 10 undergoing open heart surgery on the basis that the permanency of the death concept has not been arrived at in the thinking of the child; hence, the anxiety, presumed to be a factor in the etiology of psychosis, is less.

No doubt there is an interim phase, as far as death concepts are concerned, between 6 and adolescence. The child of latency age has an active fantasy life dealing with violence and aggression, which is both verbal and pictorial. Children of this age may become preoccupied with death and killing, but these preoccupations are usually at a great distance from their own lives in terms of actuality and reality. The active life and death game as embodied in "cowboys and Indians" or "cops and robbers" puts the concept of death—the falling down with the hand over the mortal wound—into one more consistent with adult concepts. But active children cannot long remain either immobile or endure being buried. They provide their own active antidote to death by a resurrection—reversing roles and changing games. The burials of dead birds and animals become ritualized events, although still at an emotional distance from the child, except in the case of the pet for which a very real sense of loss and the ensuing grieving process may occur. Pets, however, are replaceable even to the point of receiving identical appellations.

Adolescents

In adolescence,[18] death becomes closer in terms of deceased relatives, particularly grandparents. As long as they are not parents, and the attachment has not been intense, the adolescent is buffered by family and societal attitudes. When these are parents or peers, reactions do occur, and the adolescent, in order to accept the death, may have to learn how to grieve. If this is not done, displacement of the grief feelings may become manifested in ways directly jeopardizing the adjustment of the youth.[19]

Observations of adolescents with diseases such as diabetes,[20] hemophilia,[21] Hodgkins disease,[22] and cardiac abnormalities (see Chapter 17) serve to suggest specific attitudes toward death that are probably more characteristic of the age than of the illness. These youths are primarily concerned about body image and any imperfection in it. An imperfection is what above all they wish to keep concealed. Inasmuch as illness is an imperfection, they are inclined to act as if the disease and illness do not exist. They do this to the point of actually denying the disease, participating in contraindicated activities, and refusing to follow rules that have been prescribed by parents and physicians. They deny illness, but they also deny death, even those who have undergone long debilitating courses. This denial of death seems to have as its basis an inability to accept the fact of not being, of one's own mortality.

Defenses against mortality are everywhere apparent in this age group. The desire to live in terms of taking chances and risks is nowhere more apparent. It is vaguely phrased in such terms as: "This is my life, and I am going to live it now." A sense of future is vague and otherwise cannot be formulated in terms of more than a year or two. Whether one is alive 4 or 5 years hence does not seem to matter, because it is inconceivable both that one would be dead or what life would be like if alive. Death-defying attitudes and acts, however, are everywhere counterphobically present. Death is used as a weapon to punish parents and surrogate parents and to gain the empathy and respect of the peer group. The concept here is the active or dynamic nature of death, the effect that it has on others, and much less the ultimate significance of it for the self. Even in suicidal depressions, in which the emptiness and nothingness of life and the world are everywhere apparent,[23] the act of suicide[24] seems to be an attempt to live, to gain significance, to attain meaning. Suicide in this age group seems an attempt to deny the fact of death. Some have viewed psychosis, especially schizophrenic reactions, as representing the inability of the individual to come to terms with the culturally prevailing terms of death, as an inability to accept these and especially one's own mortality, and as the ultimate defense against death (J. H. Wall, personal communication).[3, 25, 26] The high incidence of psychotic disturbances occurring in adolescents and young adults may represent not only the result of the anxiety engendered from an inability to adjust to and resolve conflicts of life, but also an inability to adjust to and resolve conflicts and ideas of death.

The problem of coping with the anxieties of death, particularly as they exist in children, adolescents, and young adults who have experienced an early parental death, has led many investigators[19, 27–29] to note a high incidence of behavioral disorders and physical disability in this population. With the early death of a parent, there may be something in the child or youth that no longer grows, no longer evolves. He has lost the identifying object about which he has learned to mold his growth and behavior. The result may be a defense against the inner loss, an attempt to deny the loss or to replace the loss. At various ages, we have observed young adults with depressive reactions. We noted their inability to project themselves into the future because they had no model upon which to base this projection, inasmuch as the parent of the same sex had died at the same age the patient was presently. These were individuals who had enjoyed an involved or symbiotic relationship with that parent.

Adults in Health and Illness

With the late twenties and the resolution of the ambivalence of adolescence, an adult concept of death matures. The individual tends symbolically and literally to acknowledge his mortality with marriage and procreation. He is caught up with living in the present. He has begun to make the ever-increasing differentiation as to who he is and to identify[30] in terms of what he does and what effect he has on others. The adult is more cautious and usually gives up at least active death-defying actions.

For the woman, 30 is approached with some of the anxiety, if not more so, of death. She views it as a distinct turning point of her life, widely separated from her years of spontaneity. Her family is often completed. She has not the life-resurrecting yearly birth to look forward to in order to reaffirm her womanhood and life itself. Her success in these years seems to be how much she is able to accept her lost youth and simultaneously to separate herself from her children. In our present society, the woman may have set aside the completion of her adolescence, during which time the anxieties of illness and death are first actively coped with, in favor of marriage and adult responsibilities. Now in her thirties, she may be faced with these anxieties and dependencies over separation and identity that she has not previously coped with and which now may become a major task for resolution. Central to this resolution are her attitudes toward life, and its meaning becomes encompassed in the process of procreation, which may be the most death-defying act humans have available to them. With contraception and the limitation of families, this defense is no longer available and may account for the increasing depressions that we see among women in their early thirties.

It is just in this relation to her procreative function that the woman has a particularly difficult task[1] in confronting a death-threatening event during the middle years. She cannot do so without the almost overwhelming guilt engendered by her abandonment of her children in death. This is a guilt that is given very real substance by her actual abandonment of them during life at the time of illness. It is not easy for her to plan in terms of a surrogate figure to substitute for her either during or after death. She cannot abandon home or children to another with ease. Many of the problems observed in families in which the mother is chronically ill and/or dying arise over conflicts with the surrogate figure, whether a professional housekeeper or a relative. The guilt about neither being able to care for nor living to see her children reach maturity is frequently associated with a severe depression that interferes with medical management. Features of this depression may be regression and giving-up.[31] With these reactions are, frequently, manifestations of hostility and resentment, which may be directed toward spouse, children and other relatives. These feelings often persist, even when a facade of endurance, acceptance, and cheerfulness exists. Men and women may both need help in maintaining the facade that they have adopted, while at the same time being given permission to ventilate to someone in the sanctity of their room their deeper and more troubled feelings. This task frequently falls to the health worker. More often than not, the health worker may need to solicit, probe, and therefore give permission to the patient to complain, cry, and vent his anger. A sense of life's purpose can develop out of one's confrontation with the fact of death. For both the woman and the man in their thirties, this issue is often solved de facto by the presence of children. Some men have the added direction of profession and sense of accomplishment to be attained, which is in itself death defying.

With this partial, albeit successful, conquering of death fantasies, it is ironic that the ogre of illness and disease steps up its pace. The years of hypertension, arthritis, peptic ulcer, the early coronaries, and cancer come quickly. With the forties and illness, also comes death. There is death on many sides. Colleagues drop dead or develop cancer. Counterphobic behavior attempts to deny these facts with dieting, exercising, and abrupt changes of habit. Attitudes toward death during the middle years[32] reflect the values held by society and the family toward life during the same period. The provision for and care of the young children constitute the primary concern of most adults from 35 to 50. The individual faced with death at this time has real work to do in the preparation for his death.[1] He needs to know that his affairs are in adequate shape to provide for the care of his young. He may wish to provide for or identify, usually from his family group, a surrogate figure to offer as a model for sexual, moral, and professional identity. He may then die with the knowledge that there is a reasonable chance for the nurturance and guidance of his progeny to adulthood.

Older Adults

The pace of the acceptance of death is stepped up with the onset of the fifties and sixties and given emphasis by retirement, which for many is identified closely with death. How retirement and the ensuing readjustments are negotiated by the individual seem to determine to a very great extent whether or not death occurs at this time.[33] Each day, now, may be the last, and there is increasing emphasis by the individual on "one last visit" or "at least once before I die." The opportunity to reminisce is cherished, as is the experience of some long sought-after ambition. There seems to have developed a will to live, almost consciously arrived at, with one's infirmities. Objects, especially material objects are held onto with firm resolve, as though each is a vital part of self and existence. Children become for many the identification of their afterlife on earth. The severest conflict in old age seems to be the ambivalence of seeing oneself replaced by the next generation, especially when this means becoming dependent and being cared for by them. The fear of compromising their children's lives both emotionally and financially and the giving up of their own role is not easy to resolve. For many at this time, life may become more frightening than death and illness, and the process of dying may be viewed as a necessary interlude before the finality of departure. Illness is endured and accepted and not always fought. The presence of depression itself may be exacerbated or precipitated by losses—spouse, home, independence, children—all of which are viewed as symbolic parts of self.

Life after Seventy

After 70, there becomes in many cultures a kind of status associated with living. One lives not so much in fear of death as in defiance of it. This attitude may exist despite a superficial avowal and cataloguing of the infirmities of age, with such vocalizations as, "I wish it were over," "The Lord should take me," etc. An increasing awareness of one's incompetence, failing, and internal decompensations—the wearing out of organs, bodies, mind, and spirit—may presage the actual death. Daily the erosion and ravages of life are incessantly attendant with new losses and infirmities.

It is impossible either to contemplate our own concepts of death or understand those of others without a point of departure, which is, of course, our concepts about life. Whether or not the developing personality has successfully completed the resolution of conflicts for each age will influence where he is fixated in terms of his negotiations with death. Hence, an understanding of the individual[34] is a necessary prelude for working with the patient engaged in a life and death struggle. For some patients, the fear of dying may be overshadowed by a greater fear of the compromised existence enforced by the disease. Preliminary studies suggest that attitudes toward death and dying and how they are defended against in patients facing open heart surgery correlate with outcome as far as mortality and morbidity.[35] In patients undergoing hemodialysis and renal transplantation, denial of affect has been noted by several investigators.[1, 9] In patients with cancer,[36, 37] the anxieties seem to depend more on premorbid personality and "generational age"[38] than response to the disease.

Care of the Patient

Although attitudes toward death differ from individual to individual and from age to age, there are considerations in the care and treatment of the dying patient[1, 39–42] of any age which are of importance to the clinician.

1. Any hospitalized patient, regardless of the illness, has, as a part of that illness, anxiety regarding possible vulnerability and mortality.

2. As a part of illness, the individual goes through a grieving process[43, 44] for himself that includes guilt, anger, fear, depression, and ideations, rational or irrational, about himself and the world. This grieving may be about what is, what may be, or what might have been. Because the resolution of the grieving process is achieved at least partially by the opportunity to ventilate and thereby externalize or objectify vague, internal feelings, giving the patient the permission and providing the opportunity for the patient to talk about his illness become a crucial part of care and therapy. To do this most effectively, a knowledge of grieving is important.

3. In assisting the patient to grieve for himself, it is at all times necessary to keep in mind the specifically personal nature of this grief. The grieving is for his pain, his losses, his past being, and what his future being might have been.

4. The grieving process occurring in the individual is also occurring, even ante mortem in the family.[45, 46] And as the individual needs permission and opportunity to grieve, so too does the family. It is well to remember that the family's grief is as much for itself as it is for the departing member, inasmuch as it is in part a death of the family. In assisting family grieving, it is useful in one's relationships with family members to focus on how it is for *them*, what *they* have been through,

and what *they* will have to look forward to. By this approach, the family is given the permission and opportunity to take itself as object of its grief and to give expression to its feeling as apart from its feeling for the ill member. By providing an opportunity for this objectification, oftentimes the family, freed from its own unresolved conflicts, is able to give more of itself in objective terms during the last days, weeks, or months of illness of the dying member.

5. Perhaps the greatest fear that the patient has concerning his illness, especially if he is aware of its potential "fatality," is the dread of being left alone.[47] This is a very real fear and one that is likely to occur in the hospital when the staff has run out of procedures to do for the terminally ill patient. These patients do not fear the end of possible procedures, indeed they often welcome it, but they do fear the loss of human contact, both professional and familial. It is at this time in the course of illness, when the ill begin to experience their own hopelessness and the family theirs, that the living begin, at first unconsciously, to place distance between themselves and the dying.

6. The physician, nurse, and other members of the professional staff,[48, 49] especially after long involvement with a patient or continuing involvement with many terminal patients, may also need the opportunity to objectify their feelings about illness and death, both in general and in particular. This is frequently successfully done by staff group meetings especially for this purpose. It is also frequently accomplished by sublimation through professional peer groups that discuss therapeutic triumphs and failures. Members of the clergy are more and more often viewed as important components of the team treating the chronically and terminally ill patient. Their contribution is frequently one of adding the dimension of hope, not only for the patient, but for the staff.[50]

References

1. Bowers, M. K., Jackson, E. N., Knight, J. A., and LeShan, L.: *Counseling the Dying*. New York, Thomas Nelson & Sons, 1964.
2. Mitford, J.: *The American Way of Death*. New York, Simon and Schuster, 1963.
3. Lasagna, L.: *Life, Death, and the Doctor*. New York, Alfred A. Knopf, 1968.
4. Wheelis, A.: *The Quest for Identity*. New York, W. W. Norton, 1958.
5. May, R.: *The Meaning of Anxiety*. New York, Ronald Press, 1959.
6. Branch, C. H. H.: Anxiety—A key to personality. In *Aspects of Anxiety*, preface. Philadelphia, J. B. Lippincott, 1968.
7. Janis, I. L.: *Psychological Stress: Psychoanalytic and Behavioral Studies of Surgical Patients*. New York, John Wiley & Sons, 1958.
8. Abram, H. S.: Adaptation to open heart surgery: A psychiatric study of response to the threat of death. Am. J. Psychiatry *122:* 659, 1965.
9. Kempf, J. P.: Renal failure, artificial kidney and kidney transplant. Am. J. Psychiatry *122:* 1270, 1968.

10. Kornfeld, D. S., Zimberg, S., and Malm, J. R.: Psychiatric complications of open heart surgery. N. Engl. J. Med. *273:* 287, 1965.
11. Knox, S. J.: Psychiatric aspects of mitral valvotomy. Br. J. Psychiatry *109:* 656, 1963.
12. Nagy, M. H.: The child's view of death. J. Genet. Psychol. *73:* 3, 1948.
13. Moellenhoff, F.: Ideas of children about death. Bull. Menninger Clin. *3:* 148, 1939.
14. Schilder, P., and Wechsler, D.: Was weiss Kind vom Korperinneren? Int. Z. Psychoanal. *20:* 93, 1934.
15. Natterson, J. M., and Knudson, A. G., Jr.: Observations concerning fear of death in fatally ill children and their mothers. Psychosom. Med. *22:* 456, 1960.
16. Carter, R. E.: Palliation of childhood cancer. In *Palliative Care of the Cancer Patient*, R. C. Hickey, editor, chapter 27. Boston, Little, Brown and Company, 1967.
17. Piaget, J.: *The Child's Conception of the World*, p. 39. New York, Harcourt, Brace, 1929.
18. Kastenbaum, R.: Time and death in adolescence. In *The Meaning of Death*, H. Feifel, editor, pp. 99–113. New York, McGraw-Hill, Blakiston Division, 1959.
19. Birtchnell, J.: The possible consequences of early parent death. Br. J. Med. Psychol. *421:* 1, 1969.
20. Hinkle, L. E., and Wolf, S.: A summary of experimental evidence relating life stress to diabetes mellitus. J. Mt. Sinai Hosp. *19:* 537, 1952.
21. Agle, D. P.: Patients with hemophilia and related states. Arch. Intern. Med. *114:* 76, 1964.
22. Greene, W. A., Jr., Young, L. E., and Swisher, S. N.: Psychological factors and reticuloendothelial disease. Psychosom. Med. *18:* 284, 1956.
23. Kierkegaard, S.: *The Sickness unto Death*. Garden City, N.Y., Doubleday, 1955.
24. Zilborg, G.: Differential diagnostic types of suicide. Arch. Neurol. Psychiatry *35:* 270, 1936.
25. Feifel, H.: Attitudes toward death in some normal and mentally ill populations. In *The Meaning of Death*, H. Feifel, editor, pp. 114–130. New York, McGraw-Hill, Blakiston Division, 1959.
26. Stern, M.: Fear of death and neurosis. J. Am. Psychoanal. Assoc. *16:* 3, 1968.
27. Brown, F.: Childhood bereavement and subsequent psychiatric disorders. Br. J. Psychiatry *112:* 1035, 1966.
28. Granville-Grossman, K. L.: Early bereavement and schizophrenia. Br. J. Psychiatry *112:* 1027, 1966.
29. Brown, F., and Epps, P.: Childhood bereavement and subsequent crime. Br. J. Psychiatry *112:* 1043, 1966.
30. Erikson, E. H.: *Childhood and Society*, p. 269. New York, W. W. Norton, 1963.
31. Engel, G. L., and Schmale, A. H., Jr.: Psychoanalytic theory of somatic disorder: Conversion, specificity, and the disease onset situation. J. Am. Psychoanal. Assoc. *15:* 344, 1967.
32. Levinson, D.: *The Seasons of a Man's Life*. New York, Alfred A. Knopf, 1978.
33. Lieberman, M. A.: Observations on death and dying. Gerontologist *16:* 70, 1966.
34. Kempf, J. P.: Renal failure, artificial kidney and kidney transplant. In *The Meaning of Death*, pp. 237–249. New York: McGraw-Hill, Blakiston Division, 1959.
35. Kimball, C. P.: A predictive study of adjustment to cardiac surgery. J. Thorac. Cardiovasc. Surg. *58:* 891, 1969.
36. LeShan, L., and LeShan, E.: Psychotherapy and the patient with a limited life span. Psychiatry *24:* 318, 1961.
37. Lion, J. R., and Hackett, T. P.: Forewarnings of illness: Predictions and premonitions in cancer patients. Am. J. Psychiatry *125:* 99, 1968.
38. Davies, R., Quinlan, D., McKegney, F. P., and Kimball, C. P.: Organic factors and psychological adjustment in advanced cancer patients. Psychosom. Med. *35:* 464, 1973.

39. Norton, J.: Treatment of a dying patient. Psychoanal. Study Child *18:* 541, 1963.
40. Hinton, J. M.: The physical and mental distress of the dying. Q. J. Med. *32:* 1, 1963.
41. Evans, A. E.: If a child must die. N. Engl. J. Med. *278:* 138, 1968.
42. Noyes, R.: The dying patient. Dis. Nerv. Syst. *28:* 790, 1967.
43. Siggins, L. D.: Mourning: A critical survey of the literature. Int. J. Psychoanal. *47:* 14, 1966.
44. Engel, G. L.: Is grief a disease? A challenge for medical research. Psychosom. Med. *23:* 18, 1961.
45. Marshall, J. R., Abroms, G. H., and Miller, M. H.: The doctor, the dying patient and the bereaved. Ann. Intern. Med. *70:* 615, 1969.
46. Friedman, S. B., Chodoff, P., Mason, J. W., and Hamburg, D. A.: Behavioral observations on parents anticipating the death of a child. Pediatrics *32:* 610, 1963.
47. Weisman, A. D., and Hackett, T. P.: Predilection to death. Psychosom. Med. *23:* 232, 1961.
48. Eissler, K. R.: *The Psychiatrist and the Dying Patient,* p. 243. New York, International Universities Press, 1955.
49. Aring, C. D.: Intimations of mortality: An appreciation of death and dying. Ann. Intern. Med. *69:* 137, 1968.
50. Pruyser, P. W.: Phenomenology and dynamics of hoping. J. Sci. Study Religion *3:* 86, 1963.

CHAPTER 23

The Psychotherapeutic Interview

THE BEGINNING OF THE INTERVIEW

Medical psychotherapy is based in the physician's capacity to establish an empathic confidential relationship with his patient. Therapy begins even before the initial contact, inasmuch as the relationship is influenced by the patient's expectations of the physician. These expectations come from the patient's awareness of the physician's professional and social reputation as acknowledged in the community and by the referring source (whether from another physician, a patient, or another source.) A knowledge of the referral source is helpful to the physician in assessing the initial expectation of the patient. During the course of the professional relationship, the expectation may stand in need of clarification and modification. Once the initial relationship has been consummated by personal, written, or telephone contact, the stage is formally set for the development of the patient-physician contract.

THE CONTRACT

The contract begins with implicit and explicit agreements between patient and physician. Both informally agree upon the nature of the contract. This begins with the identification and clarification of the patient's purpose in seeking professional help and care. The explicit purpose may be clear cut (for example, a patient requiring sutures for

---

Modified version (and reproduced with permission) of chapter in *Basic Psychiatry for the Primary Care Physician*, H. S. Abram, editor. Boston, Little, Brown & Company, 1976.

a laceration) or complex (for example, a patient whose initial complaint of insomnia reflects underlying emotional problems). In the latter case, the nature of the patient's problems may require considerable assessment extending over the course of several interviews during the early treatment phase. Nevertheless, the nature of the contract centers around the patient's presenting complaint and remains centered on that complaint until therapy is terminated or until by mutual agreement the contract is altered.

The implicit nature of the contract is less precise and rests upon the conscious and unconscious expectations of the two individual parties involved. Frequently, especially when there is a disparity between these two parties, these implicit expectations will need to be clarified during the course of therapy. Implicit expectations are partly socially defined and partly stem from idiosyncratic personal expectations of the two parties, for example, the patient's need to see the physician as a surrogate parent or the physician's need to see himself in that capacity. It may take the physician some time to assess the patient's implicit expectations. The physician is then faced with the question of either reinforcing or changing these expectations. Usually, this decision will be based on the extent to which the expectations realistically enhance or interfere with therapeutic objectives. The physician needs to examine for each of his patients his own subjective and objective interest in the patient and his problem and how these affect his care of that patient.

THE PATIENT-PHYSICIAN RELATIONSHIP AND PERSONALITY

From the patient-physician contract develops the relationship from which formulation, diagnosis, and therapy then proceed. This relationship will depend upon the personality and behavioral characteristics of the two individuals, which also have shaped to a great extent the explicit and implicit expectations identified above. It is useful for the physician to identify major personality traits in his patient, as well as to be aware of how his own predominant personality characteristics interact with those of other people. For some physicians, it may be enough to utilize some idiosyncratic formulations that have developed spontaneously out of their own experiences. For others, using more formal conceptualizations—such as Shapiro's *Neurotic Styles*,[1] Kahana and Bibring's "Personality Types in Medical Management,"[2] or Friedman and Rosenman's behavior pattern type A (for some patients with coronary artery disease)[3]—may be of help. It is important that the physician does not view these formulations as pathological diagnoses;

rather, he should use them in understanding his patient. Most simply, personality profiles and behavior patterns may be seen as identifying characteristic ways in which an individual reacts to and handles basic emotions or feelings (e.g., anxiety, sadness, anger, pleasure, pain) precipitated by environmental stresses and events. These reactions may indicate adaptive defenses and coping patterns. At other times they may be overdetermined and exaggerated, resulting in behavior that may complicate medical evaluation and treatment, e.g., the angry impulsive individual who threatens to sign out of the hospital when subjected to anxiety-provoking procedures; the cardiac patient who tends to deny that he has had an infarct by working even harder after discharge; the usually independent patient who requires constant attention for his complaints and demands after hospitalization; or the controlling individual who counters anxiety by requiring detailed and precise explanation of everything the doctor plans. Sensitivity to emotional reactions and the varying ways in which different types of individuals handle these reactions allows the physician to identify these patterns early in the course of his relationship with the patient and to adjust his own reactions to the patient's specific response. Careful explanation of hospital routine and procedures to be done by physicians and hospital personnel will allay many fearful reactions. The extent to which the physician acquires skill in assessing his patient's style will frequently determine the success with which he is able to conduct a satisfactory interview and examination (see Chapter 2).

EXPLAINING THE COMPLAINT

The interview begins by identifying the patient's problem as a symptom or sign. A symptom is always subjective, inasmuch as it is a feeling, a hurt or pain. It is determined by factors that may be subsequently considered using biological, social, and psychological concepts. As a feeling, the symptom is colored by the patient's explicit and implicit expectations of the treatment situation, his reactions to it based on previous and present experiences, and his knowledge of the symptom's potential implications. The physician's interest is documented by his ability to attend to the patient's description of the symptom by listening, observing, and voicing concern by the questions he asks. The questions are determined by the physician's ability to ascertain what might be called the geometric configurations of the symptom. The physician begins to assess when and where the patient first became aware of the symptoms, as well as the symptom's specific intensities and fluctuations in time influenced by factors such as position, state of consciousness, and environmental setting. He notes that it is associated with other symptoms; that it has developed in a specific environmental setting and time in the patient's domestic, social, and professional life; and that the patient has reacted to it in one or more ways and has ascribed it to one cause or another.

A model useful to the physician in evaluating a patient's symptom is the journalist's "who, where, what, when, and how." *Who* is the patient? *Where* is he in the life cycle when the symptom or sign occurred? *What* is its meaning? *When* and *how* has it occurred in relationship to the patient's activities? As the physician gathers data about the symptom, he may begin to conceptualize it in terms of those language models developed in the course of his training: biological, social, and psychological. Each of these categories is essential in the complete evaluation. For most physicians, the biological model is the best developed and, consequently, the most readily utilized. A socioenvironmental model can be accepted with comparative ease of transition by the physician if correlations between symptom and environmental relationships can be identified readily, e.g., the occurrence of headache and an epidemic of encephalitis. It may be more difficult to derive and accept the relationship of a mother's headache to her whining 2-year-old child and demanding spouse at 6 o'clock in the evening. Most difficult to associate is the headache with an unconscious conflict in the woman whose own marriage is beginning to assume the turbulence of that of her parents when she was a child. However, it is essential that the physician consider each of these conceptual approaches in his investigation of the system.

In considering the evaluation of the symptom from the approaches suggested above, it is helpful for the physician to remain aware that a symptom is a feeling, not a biological, social, or psychological phenomenon in and of itself, and that these three conceptual orientations may be viewed as different languages, each with its own intrinsic logic from which a compatible methodology has been developed to investigate the symptom. At times, one approach will prove more satisfactory in terms of remediation than another. At other times, one or more approaches may be required if full remediation is to be achieved. It is within this context that full evaluation of the symptom from each one of these approaches is seen as a part of medical psychotherapy rather than a simpler psychological explanation of the symptom, inasmuch as this fuller evaluation addresses itself to the patient and his problem rather than existing as independent from the patient. This concept is essential in medical psychotherapy.

Inherent in the interview process and the analysis of the symptom are psychological techniques that even as they aid the physician in evaluating the nature of his patient's problems, are also therapeutic. During the course of the analysis of the symptom, the physician's objectives include helping the patient *clarify* what he means in describing the vectors of the symptoms: How is the symptom best described in terms of location, intensity, and feeling? When and where was it first experienced? In the process of clarification, the symptom can be *objectified* by the physician into a greater symptom universe that will allow him to consider it from biological, social, and psychological perspectives. During the course of evaluation, the doctor, in his age-old role of teacher, helps the patient achieve understanding by his *didactic* explanations of the symptom. In relating with the patient in this way, the physician supplies a *supporting structure* for the patient, confidently communicating that full understanding will lead to therapeutic approaches. Out of this process the patient derives hope, the sine qua non of the therapeutic process. It is important to note that the supportive aspects of interviewing and therapy are most effective when they are an intrinsic part of the interview, rather than when they are consciously applied external to the data-gathering process, when they are more likely to be viewed as gratuitous or less genuine. At times, it may be necessary for the physician to obtain the counsel of other professional persons (psychiatrists, social workers, clergymen) or social agencies in assisting his patient through a specific crisis.

LIFE CYCLES

In addition to objectifying the symptom, the interview process is addressed to finding out who and where the patient is in his present life cycle. The physician can gain much assistance by becoming familiar with life cycle models, as suggested by Erikson.[4] Such a chronological approach to patients and their problems is often helpful in directing the physician's attention to the most likely explanation of what a symptom may mean biologically, socially, and psychologically. For any given patient problem, the physician develops biases intuitively which must be subjected to a conscious testing of their probability. For example, a 19-year-old, black, single woman presenting with abdominal pain will elicit from the physician a number of tentative biological, social, and psychological hypotheses on an epidemiological and statistical basis that may direct him to the most likely explanation of not only the symptom but also to what else may be going on in the life of the patient. In this situation, the physician may spontaneously think of sickle cell disease, tubal pregnancy, or appendicitis in a biological frame of reference; the illnesses of economic and social poverty, such as malnutrition, addiction, pelvic inflammatory disease, and parasitic infestations in a social framework; and conflicts regarding family, boyfriends, childbearing, career development, and racial discrimination in a psychological framework. These and other hypotheses will be strengthened or weakened by the physician's ability to attend to the setting in which the symptom has developed.

ONSET OF ILLNESS

Attention to the onset of illness will lead the physician to a consideration of how environmental and psychological factors relate with biological ones in determining the time and manner in which the illness was manifested. Rather than thinking of these factors primarily in a casual or etiological context, the physician will gain more assistance in viewing them as complicating factors of the biologically considered illness that will need to be addressed in the therapy of the patient. For example, after the acute diagnostic and treatment phase of a 40-year-old, white, married business executive with a documented myocardial infarction, it may be an imperative part of subsequent therapy for the physician to explore with the patient his marital and professional situation, as well as his characterisic behavioral patterns, if optimal therapy is to occur. In this exploration the physician may discover that the illness has occurred at a critical juncture in the patient's life. The patient may have recently experienced profound marital problems as well as adverse business conditions after years of conscientious and industrious work that led to what had all the earmarks of professional, social, and economic success. Without helping the patient acknowledge and begin to find ways of untangling these issues, and perhaps modify his previous behavior pattern, the physician will be negligent in addressing himself to the full therapeutic field necessary for this man's rehabilitation and convalescence. Awareness of the association between loss and onset of illness, as observed by Holmes and Rahe[5] and Engel and Schmale,[6] is necessary for the physician who addresses himself to total patient care.

SOCIAL AND ETHNIC DIFFERENCES

Knowledge of and sensitivity to ethnic, racial, and social differences in the description of, manifestation of, and reaction to symptoms also assist the physician in evaluating his patient. Folk medicine has taught us that other medical systems have different ways of viewing symptoms and different explanations for their presence.[7] When working with patients from other backgrounds, it is important to learn whether they adhere to a belief in a particular folk medicine and, if so, how that form of medicine may explain the patient's symptom. For the physician using a Western orientation toward disease, his major task in treating such a patient may be finding a means whereby he can acceptably translate the patient's symptom and its treatment into Western terms and methods that do not clash with firmly held beliefs of his patient. The physician may learn that a patient requires the therapeutic techniques of both systems if complete healing is to occur. Navajo Indians have become quite responsive to Western medical prractitioners, especially if they also participate in the ceremonial practices of the Navajo medicine man or Singer. Similar observations have been made among rural Southern blacks believing in "root" medicine, a derivation of Voodoo practices, and among those Appalachian whites in the hill country of Kentucky and Tennessee who belong to snake-handling cults. Although the therapeutic potential of folk medicine cults is presently under systematic evaluation, especially that of utilizing indigenous herbs, physicians who have studied transcultural or intercultural medicine consider that a patient's belief in a given therapeutic approach frequently has much to do with its success.[8]

Patients' external reactions to symptoms[9] vary according to their ethnic origin, with Mediterraneans generally more expressive than Nordics of their emotional reactions. The stiff-lipped upper-class Englishman may express compartively little emotion while describing his chest pain rather precisely. In contrast, the Italian mother may express considerable emotion with tears while manifesting her abdominal pain, with little coherence in her verbal description of it. Similarly social class imposes both semantic and emotional constraints on describing, manifesting, and reacting to symptoms, which vary from culture to culture.

STAGES OF ILLNESS

As the physician follows patients through illness, he begins to identify stages of illness that have similar patterns of reaction in different patients. We have previously identified the onset of illness stage. Next there occurs the acute phase, in which there may be considerable urgency, depending on the nature of the illness. This stage requires rapid evaluation and decision, processes that cause considerable anxiety not only for patients and their families but also for the professional personnel involved. Elaborate and frequently painful procedures may be required, which increase anxiety. With specific procedures (e.g., cardiac catheterization)[10] and particular environments, investigators have identified relatively similar reaction patterns. An example is the so-called intensive care unit syndrome,[11] in which the highly anxious patient in a strange and foreign environment, with a mental state further compromised by analgesic and sedative agents, becomes increasingly detached from reality, confused, disoriented, and delusional. The evaluation and treatment of such a patient require attention not only to biologically conceptualized factors but also to environmental (including professional staff and family) and psychological ones. The acute phase, at least for coronary artery disease patients,[12] beginning with anxiety directly relating to pain and the severity of illness, gradually is replaced by a phase of sadness or depression. Whereas in the first stage the patient's reaction to anxiety may be impulsive, during the second stage the behavior may be more characteristic of his premorbid behavioral patterns. Because both anxiety and sadness may lead to behavior that directly interferes with treatment and recovery, it behooves the physician and his staff to evaluate the emotions and behavior of such patients and their families regularly and to be ready to intercede with appropriate antianxiety and antidepressive measures.

A third or convalescent stage is recognized that may be characterized as a grieving stage, that is, a grieving because of one's changed health and situation, and one in which the individual begins to accept the fact of illness and its consequences, not only intellectually but emotionally. This requires expression of feeling, especially those unpleasant ones of anxiety, sadness, and anger. Until a patient has done this, he will be unable to complete the process of grieving requisite for negotiating the rehabilitative tasks for family, social, and professional adjustment that lie ahead. In order to go through the grieving stage, the patient requires the firm guidance of the caring physician and professional staff. First, patients require the opportunity and permission to ventilate emotion, which may be uncomfortable for both the family and staff. Second, the patient will need the assistance of the staff in sorting out appropriate from inappropriate defenses and reactions to these emotions as they relate to optimal adjustment. Third, the patient may need the assistance of other professional counselors and agencies in affecting rehabilitation processes involving family, social, and professional readjustments.

Many patients during acute illness experience altered states of consciousness. These patients require a different level of interaction with the family and professional staff. If consciousness is severely compromised, the approach must be a fairly simple and concrete one that will help the patient gain a firmer hold on reality. For example, the patient who experiences confusion and disorientation will require the assistance of the professional staff in reestablishing contact with the world around him in terms of who he is, where he is, what has happened to him, and what is expected of him. This may require frequent repetition of instructions by a careful attendant who will not become overly complex in his or her explanations.

Following the three stages of reaction to illness outlined above, some patients will require prolonged counseling of a time-limited nature in negotiating the tasks of the fourth stage of illness, the rehabilitation phase. This phase occurs as the individual reemerges into the home, social, and work environments with his altered sense of self. During this stage, the patient requires help in assessing new patterns of coping with the complex problems that are a part of life's progress and that are further complicated by the altered physical and emotional processes of the individual. Limited but frequent counseling is very much the province of the physician in his attempt to assist the patient in making a satisfactory adjustment. Although the attention of the physician will continue to be focused on the patient and his illness, it must at all times attend to the patient's life stage, reaction to illness, family, social, and professional tasks.

AN EXAMPLE OF EVOLVING PSYCHOTHERAPY

With many patients presenting to physicians with symptoms that suggest somatic dysfunction, it soon becomes obvious that the symptom relates primarily to a social or psychological situation, that is, in conversion reactions. For example, a 42-year-old married mother of four and private duty nurse presented with constant pain in the perineal region. Extensive gynecological and urological procedures were negative. A review with the patient of her current life situation revealed that she had recently experienced sleep, appetite, and libidinal changes. In addition, she found herself more irritable and preoccupied with feelings of discontent about herself and her family, fears of what the future held for her, and ideations of usefulness. She ascribed these disturbances and feelings to her perineal pain. Further interviews revealed that the symptom had developed shortly after she had completed caring for an elderly man who was the same age as her father. The man had carcinoma of the prostate gland and required daily catheterizations by the patient. She nursed him for the last 6 months of his life, during which time she developed strong feelings ("like those of a daughter") for him. After he died, she did not return to work but became preoccupied with what she felt were the first signs of menopause. She had grown away from her husand, a busy executive who over time had become less interested in her sexually as well as emotionally. At the same time she was disturbed by a change in her sexual feelings, which she had previously suppressed. Her older children were in the process of leaving home. The oldest daughter was recently married and was expecting a baby. Two other girls were at college. The youngest boy, 15, was never at home. She felt alone and abandoned. There was not enough to do, and what she tried no longer interested her.

As she talked, she became aware of her depression and began to relate it to circumstances in her life other than the presenting symptom. She gained some immediate help from a tricyclic antidepressant drug as she began to explore with the physician possible changes in her life. Her husband began to participate in alternate interviews, and together they began to plan weekend trips away from home. He began to spend more time at home. Cautiously they began to discuss their sexual disaffection. Over a period of time she was able to suggest that the perineal pain, which had receded, perhaps was related to her concerns about her fear of menopause and in some way to the painful task of catheterizing her patient. Over the ensuing years she has experienced an exacerbation of the pain at times of particular stress, e.g., when her daughter gave birth, when her youngest unmarried daughter went on birth control pills, when a brother died, and when her husband went away on a business trip. During the first 6 weeks of contact the physician saw the patient weekly, thereafter biweekly for the remainder of 6 months, whereupon he saw her every 3 months for a year, and since then at 6-month intervals, the patient's course remaining stable (except for the episodes noted above) over 5 years.

In this case, therapy was never intensive. The symptom was the patient's ticket of admission. At first she was unable to admit that her depression was possibly related to her symptom; later, as she began to examine her life field, she realized that the depression did relate to it. Subsequently she began to feel some hope and began to utilize former adaptive patterns in engaging in domestic, social, and professional activities, partly by modifying her previous compulsive patterns and partly by achieving some insight into why she experienced certain feelings when there were changes in her environment. Throughout the course of therapy, the physician was there, staying where the patient was, utilizing various adjunctive approaches as they seemed pragmatically indicated, sometimes gently guiding, but largely sharing the patient's cautious progress through a time of accelerated transition in life. *Staying with the patient in the patient's here and now is the hallmark of medical psychotherapy.* At various times during the course of therapy, the physician utilized differing conceptual approaches in attending to the patient's problem and its remediation, using psychological, social, and biological constructs in turn as each seemed appropriate.

References

1. Shapiro, D.: *Neurotic Styles*. New York, Basic Books, 1965.
2. Kahana, R. J., and Bibring, G. L.: Personality types in medical management. In *Psychiatry and Medical Practice in a General Hospital*, N. E. Zinberg, editor. New York, International Universities Press, 1964.
3. Friedman, M., and Rosenman, R. H.: Association of specific overt behavior pattern with blood and cardiovascular findings. J. A. M. A. *169:* 1286, 1959.
4. Erikson, E.: Eight ages of man. In *Childhood and Society*, ed. 2, p. 247. New York, W. W. Norton, 1963.
5. Holmes, T. H., and Rahe, R. H.: The social readjustment rating scale. Jr. Psychosom. Res. *11:* 213, 1967.
6. Engel, G. L., and Schmale, A. H.: Psychoanalytic theory of somatic disorder: Conversion, specificity and the disease-onset situation. J. Am. Psychoanal. Assoc. *15:* 344, 1967.
7. Fabrega, H., Jr., and Silver, D. B.: *Illness and Shamanistic Curing Zinacantan: An Ethnomedical Analysis*. Stanford, Stanford University Press, 1973.
8. Frank, J. D.: *Persuasion and Healing: A Comparative Study of Psychotherapy*. Baltimore, Johns Hopkins University Press, 1961.
9. Zborowski, M.: Cultural components in responses to pain. J. Soc. Issues *8:* 16, 1952.
10. Greene, W. L., Conron, G., Schalch, D. S., and Schreiner, B. F.: Psychological reactions with growth hormone and cortisol levels: A study of patients undergoing catheterization. Psychosom. Med. *32:* 599, 1970.
11. Blachly, P., and Starr, A.: Post-cardiotomy delirium. Am. J. Psychiatry *121:* 317, 1964.
12. Cassem, N. H., and Hackett, T. P.: Psychiatric consultation in a coronary care unit. Ann. Intern. Med. *75:* 9, 1971.

CHAPTER 24

Psychotherapeutic Intervention in Acute Medical Situations

OVERVIEW

Psychotherapy in the extreme medical situation is an extension of the interviewing process. The interviewer must expeditiously and sometimes briefly assist the patient in elaborating his complaint, obtain information about the development of the complaint, and assess the patient's reactions to it. Past history, developmental patterns, reactions to previous illness and crises, the patient's present life situation, and past and present relationships may all be relevant and require evaluation. The interactive process requires that the therapist call upon specific knowledge as he engages with the patient, facilitates the expression of concern, and appropriately reassures, instructs, prepares, clarifies, and leads the patient to some insight about his altered state. Attention to the affective correlates of acute illness can enhance convalescence and the rehabilitative process.

DEFINITIONS

In discussing psychotherapeutic processes in patients in the acute phases of illness, it is first necessary to identify the territories to be explored. The acute situation can be defined as inclusive of the period of time and the place in which the patient becomes ill and is taken for

---

Modified version (and reproduced with permission) of article from General Hospital Psychiatry *20*: 150–155, 1979; copyrighted by the Elsevier-North Holland Publishing Company.

treatment and diagnosis: the time may include the critical state in which there is question about survival and the immediate convalescent period; the place may be a clinic, emergency room, or hospital ward. This acute or critical state is often experienced as if one were in a foreign culture, in different and usually unfamiliar environments and among strangers. The individual in the acute situation is isolated from familiar contacts such as family and is exposed to the difficulties of adjusting to the emotional reactions of others. Therapy is defined in a relatively broad sense, focusing on what transpires in the relationship between the patient and the many individuals attending the patient, including diagnostic and therapeutic procedures. Psychotherapy is discussed in the narrower sense of specific techniques utilized by a psychiatrist or communicated by him to other individuals attending the patient.

THE LIAISON CONSULTANT

A common denominator and multiple extrapolations may be developed from different illness situations, but the liaison psychiatrist must also have specific knowledge about specific illness situations to be optimally effective as a therapist. The focus in this discussion is on the patient with cardiovascular disease, based on investigations of patients sustaining myocardial infarctions and those undergoing cardiovascular surgery (see Chapter 19).[1]

The fundamental knowledge for implementation of any therapy comes from the patient. The knowledge that we have of psychotherapy is based on experience with approaches and processes. Psychotherapeutic skill comes from practice and innate ability. The knowledge of situations and specific illnesses serve as a framework to orient the physician to the form or dimensions that an experience with a specific patient may take. Because knowledge of the patient is derived from talking with the patient, psychotherapy also commences at this time. The demonstration of an effective interview technique by the liaison consultant to primary care personnel will enhance a psychotherapeutic orientation to the patient from the time of his initial contact with the health services (see Chapter 2).

THE PATIENT

Because the consultant meets the patient somewhere along the spectrum of illness after the acute process has begun—sometime in the course of the relationship with the patient or in supervision of others in this work—the consultant will need to relive with the patient these early moments: How did he first become aware of the symptom(s)? When? Where is he? With whom? What did he experience? What did he feel? What did he do? Through this process, the consultant begins to understand how this individual reacts to catastrophic events, how he copes emotionally, and how he utilizes defenses and reasoning powers. He also learns about the patient's orienting and arousal states. This stands the consultant in good stead in his future work. At the same time, he has accomplished a primary aspect of therapy, that is, getting the patient to talk about himself, especially about his feelings. In the dependent state, the patient is also more able to talk about how he behaved and how he has coped actively with his problem in the past and has the ability to cope similarly now.

In this preliminary exploration, the consultant has picked up much factual information that will assist him in identifying specifics about the patient and his illness. He has been able to assess his patient's present feeling state, his defenses and their effectiveness and limitations, and his specific coping activities. The therapist has also obtained a good description of the symptoms and their progress and of what the patient was doing, with whom, and what other events were occurring in the proximal onset situation. He will also have gleaned a bit of data about the patient's recent past in terms of marital, social, and work activities. He will have identified not only the symptom—pain, dyspnea, fever, cough, and so on—but also the patient's tolerance for it, as well as his fears and present rationalizations.

ANXIETY

In the immediate present, whether in the emergency room or the intensive care unit, the patient and the therapist are in a similar situation. They are both dangling on the thread of a decision regarding the pathophysiological process, in which the prevailing emotion is anxiety.[2] It will persist until something definite has occurred. The anxiety relates to the present (i.e., what is—the pain, the strange environment, the diagnostic procedures, including the interview), the future (i.e., what could be—the heart attack, the embolism, cancer, pneumonia), and the possible consequences (death, invalidism, deformity, loss of status). Previous investigations suggest that, throughout the acute phase of illness, the patient is more concerned about his discomfort (the pain of living) than about death. Concern about dying and death is a luxury that is afforded when other feelings are less acute. This occurs later on.

Much of the anxiety experienced from outside the body relates to the environment, which is a strange and changing one in the acute situation. The environment begins to change at the time of symptom onset. Depending on the physiological changes, there may be perceptual distortions in feelings about the body or of the pain, in vision, hearing, and tactile sense. These perceptual distortions will influence cognition and may be accompanied by various emotional sensations, such as anxiety and specific fears. The patient defends himself against these by a variety of characterological maneuvers. A common one is the sense of distancing onself from what is happening and from the environment.

ALTERED STATES OF CONSCIOUSNESS

This is the initial stage of an altered state of consciousness that may progress, wax and wane, or exist ephemerally.[3, 4] An awareness of this by the therapist will allow him to moderate the extent and intensity of his interaction. It will also stimulate him to seek the source of this alteration—whether it relates to the anxiety about the pain or the environment or to specific pathophysiological effects of the illness or its treatment with analgesics, hypnotic sedatives, and antianxiety agents.

A patient in such a state requires an altered approach in interaction: a structuring one, a limited one, but a frequent one. The patient should not be left alone, especially if he is apprehensive and agitated. Reassurance should be given in simple, direct, and matter-of-fact terms, often best accomplished by aides. They need only emphasize the identity of the patient, where he is, what has occurred, that things will be all right, who the attendant is, and that she is going to stay. Repetition of such details is important. Delusions and hallucinations are usually ego alien and are handled well by the patient with a bit of reinforcement by the aide or the physician. Small amounts of butyrophenones administered orally and frequently over a 3- to 4-hour period will often ameliorate agitation, although this is not a replacement for the interaction described above. Once an adequate amount has been determined, dosage is repeated at regular intervals over the next 7 to 10 days. Recognizing and treating early deficits in the cognitive functions of attention, orientation, and memory as well as increasing emotional lability will help prevent the delusions, hallucinations, and agitation of advanced delirium.

THE ENVIRONMENT

The initial reaction of anxiety by most patients to the distress of symptoms is exacerbated by the environment in which the patient is attended.[5] As noted, these are alien environments, unfamiliar to most patients. They are alien in every sense: sound, sight, touch, smell, taste, and proprioception. Even for the alert, oriented, and well, these alien environments, crowded with patients and personnel, can convey a sense of the unreal and lead to disorientation and depersonalization. Compounding the patient's anxiety about himself is an aura of anxiety indigenous to these units. Ambulances scream into the unloading docks, to which a stream of personnel are mobilized. The instruments of medical progress are mobilized for initial sustenance of life, while multiple diagnostic procedures are instituted. The atmosphere is rife with the sounds of monitors, suction machines, patients' moans, and their families' lamentations. The loudspeakers signal the harried staff and announce the imminent arrival of new victims of tragedies for whom new forces must be mobilized. The stretcher-ridden patient waits for first one and then another consultant or technician for what must seem like an eternity.

After triage, initial diagnosis, and preliminary treatment, the patient is transferred to a new and equally foreign environment, which causes a new uncertainty and increased anxiety. Most patients, other than the cardiovascular surgery patients, have had little experience with an environment such as that of the coronary care unit. In this arena of uncertainty, the individual is often at the threshold between two worlds, that of the painfully living and that of the unknown dead. It is an arena in which resignation is not unknown. The previously interviewed cardiovascular patient has had some preparation for this environment; in many places, he has been exposed to this unit in the preparation for surgery. Such is not, however, the experience of myocardial infarction patients. There has been no time to identify those patients at greater risk for specific emotional reactions to illness nor for the remedial intervention that specific risk factors might indicate. The anxiety developing in the emergency area continues to mount over the first several days and continues to correlate with the severity of symptoms related to the disease process. Attempts to modify this pattern pharmacologically through analgesics or hypnotics frequently increase the anxiety by leading to greater confusion in this strange environment. During this early experience in the intensive care unit, the combination of high anxiety and unfamiliarity fosters greater levels of confusion, anxiety, and sense of depersonalization in susceptible individuals. Crucial for the well-being, if not the life, of the patient is attention, first, to the detection of confusion and, second, to reorienting procedures.

As the patient moves out of the anxiety phase, where the primary defense is denial, he begins to demonstrate other behaviors that are characteristic of his premorbid patterns in reaction to stress.[6] A patient who is usually demanding and plaintive may demonstrate these behaviors in an exaggerated form. Recognizing that this is based upon anxiety and uncertainty will lead the staff to take time in helping the patient structure his life. Rather than respond to the patient's demands ad lib, it is helpful to assure the patient that someone, preferably the same individual on each shift, will attend the patient at fixed intervals. Another patient may respond to anxiety with irritability, anger, and hostility, manifested by threatening and menacing behavior; this calls for immediate, matter-of-fact setting of limits by the individual in charge. An individual who is suspicious by nature will become more so during times of acute stress; staff can minimize this by giving precise, clear, and simple statements about what is happening. The obsessive individual will respond to the staff's recognition of the patient's concern for precision, detail, and exceptions. If changes are to take place in the patient's schedule, he should be fully apprised well beforehand and given an explanation. The hysteric, on the other hand, will only become more anxious and concerned with detailed explanations. Rather, he requires frequent reassurance and simple explanations. Another patient may become almost mute and withdrawn; in this case, patient and extended efforts of a staff member to penetrate this defensive style are required. Confrontation techniques may occasionally reduce the resistance of these individuals, although they may antagonize others.

During the second phase of the intensive care unit experience, the major affect is one of sadness, sometimes anger at self, sometimes resignation manifested by behavior based upon characterological defenses. Although self-limited in some, this affect extends well into the convalescent phase in others and, if left unattended, may evolve into or be superseded by a frank depression after convalescence, which accounts for much of the morbidity associated with the postinfarction period.[7] Protracted sadness that remains unexplored, unmobilized, and verbally unexpressed may become latent and appear as fatigue, listlessness, helplessness, and hopelessness. At the initial phase, it resembles the "giving-up—given-up" state with its expressions of helplessness-hopelessness; its verbalization of, "It's all too much; I can no longer cope", its physical posture of bowed head, turned-down mouth, and thrown-down palm-upward outreached arms and hands; its preoccupation with the past and its tragedies; its failure to identify a future; and its sense of disengagement or retreat from the present and those within it.[8]

The physiological characteristics of this in limbo state may be potentially adaptive or maladaptive for the patient. This state can also be viewed as a conservation-withdrawal state that follows the acute stress the patient has thus far survived.[9] It is characterized (1) physically by a turning away from staff and family, a reduced appetite, and an increased sleep pattern and (2) verbally by a patient saying, "All I want to do is sleep. I've been through so much. Now, I just want to turn toward the wall and sleep." The sleep and fatigue are real. It is estimated that in the acute care units, patients sleep about 4 hours out of 24. In the convalescent units, it is not unusual to observe patients who sleep up to 19 hours per day. Usually, these patterns last 2 to 5 days. The role of the liaison therapist at this time is to assist in documenting the state and to advise the attending staff, especially physicians and surgeons, to leave the patient alone.

CONVALESCENCE

The remainder of the convalescent period is devoted to taking stock of what has happened. Based on this appraisal, preparations and plans for the rehabilitation phase begin. During this period, there are occasional exacerbations and complications of the underlying illness, which will set the patient back, again raise doubts, fears, and anxieties, and occasionally lead to resignation, which will require identification and exploration.

The first part of the convalescent period allows the therapist to review and bring together the various aspects of self-grieving that the individual has experienced for the real and partial loss of self.[10] In this grieving process, the patient is helped to review prior experience and feelings about the illness, with opportunities to vent those feelings and to associate them with similar feelings about various past losses.

Dreams, often exacerbated by hypnotic sedatives at this time, are frequently of these past vulnerabilities, with their manifest content of the experience. Rather than provoking anxiety, such recollections and reminiscences can bring about resolution and a greater sense of tranquility. This is a time when the past meets the future, and the insecurities that the patient has experienced in the past are projected on that future. The concerns are real and must be separated from the overdetermined emotions in which they are invested because of unresolved conflicts of the past.

GROUP PROCESSES

The real concerns about the future may often be bridged effectively and satisfactorily in group processes during the convalescent phase.[11] These groups are conducted in the hospital with spouses and sometimes other family members. They may include all or selected members of the therapeutic team. The content is frequently didactic in relation to common problems faced by all: diet, exercise, sexual activity, and medicine. Anticipations and apprehensions common to all spouses are aired in these discussions as a step toward their alleviation. Illness of the individual is also illness in the family, and, although therapy for the patient may result in his return to health, it does not guarantee a return to health of the family. Illness of the individual causes dysfunctions within the family that require attention. Adolescents react to the illness of a parent with various behaviors, including anxiety, distrust, withdrawal, alliances outside of the home, defiance, and occasionally self-destructive behavior. Young children, watching the disintegration of previous stable family patterns, may show regressive behavior and develop symptoms of childhood neurosis: tics, thumb sucking, enuresis, fear of school and other phobias, and sleep disturbances, including nightmares. One or more family sessions may result in the release of muted affects centered around internalized and unresolved conflicts that the illness has aroused.

Preparation of both patient and family for the homecoming[12] is an essential component of therapy after the acute situation. In general, it will reflect other transitions, entrances, and exits encountered in the journey through life. In short, it will be full of unrewarded expectations and rich in unexpected complications. Reengagement with significant others will be more and less than what was anticipated. The individual's and the family's sense of vulnerability will take a long time to heal. If time is taken at this point by the attending physician and his liaison consultant, much of the morbidity that has been identified in the postinfarct and postsurgical course will be better understood and more effectively addressed.

REHABILITATION

Ahead of the patient and his family lies the rehabilitation course of illness. Factors relating to therapeutic efforts will depend on severity of the individual's physical condition; the extent to which effective grieving has occurred; the openness of communication in the family; the presence of supportive social structures, including immediate family, extended family, friends, and work; other social institutions, such as rehabilitation facilities and church groups; and the patient's personality and his capacity for hope. Many correlations have been drawn between individual behavior patterns and proneness to coronary artery disease.[13] The profile includes a man in a rush, with a chronic sense of urgency and a repressed sense of anger, who is competitive, controlled, and industrious—in short, an individual with raised arm and clenched fist, living by a stop watch. Whether or not every individual reflects this image superficially or internally, by the time of discharge the physician-therapist will have had time to assess the behavioral patterns and personality styles of his patient and family and to identify to what extent they compromise maximum rehabilitation. Continuing assessment will identify to what extent therapy may assist modification of patterns detrimental to the health of the individual during the rehabilitation period. It may be desirable to learn new approaches and skills for maximum rehabilitation, in which event psychotherapy may be an important adjunct in helping the patient to confront his feelings and review his defense patterns.

SUMMARY

The experience of a patient sustaining an acute illness has been reviewed by following him through the environments in which he is treated and identifying the sequence of stages from his and the staff's emotional and behavioral perspective. It is suggested that effective therapeutic intervention depends upon the attention given to the patient by the primary health team with the assistance of the liaison therapist-physician and relates positively to the successful rehabilitation of the individual.

References

1. Kimball, C. P.: Psychological aspects of cardiovascular disease. In *American Handbook of Psychiatry*, D. X. Freedman and J. Dyrud, editors, vol. IV, pp. 608–617. New York, Basic Books, 1975.
2. Cassem, N. H., and Hackett, T. P.: Psychiatric consultation in a coronary care unit. Ann. Intern. Med. *75:* 9, 1971.
3. Engel, G. L., and Romano, J.: Delirium, a syndrome of cerebral insufficiency. J. Chronic Dis. *9:* 260, 1959.
4. Kimball, C. P.: Delirium. In *Current Therapy*, pp. 833–835. Philadelphia, W. B. Saunders, 1974.
5. Kornfeld, D. S., Zimberg, S., and Malm, J. R.: Psychiatric complications of open heart surgery. N. Engl. J. Med. *273:* 287, 1965.
6. Kahana, R., and Bibring, G.: Personality types in medical management. In *Psychiatry and Medical Practice in a General Hospital*, N. E. Zinberg, editor, pp. 108–123. New York, International Universities Press, 1964.
7. Croog, S. H., and Levine, S.: Social status and subjective perceptions of 250 men after myocardial infarction. Public Health Rep. *84:* 989, 1969.
8. Engel, G. L., and Schmale, A. H.: Psychoanalytic theory of somatic disorder: Conversion, specificity, and the disease onset situation. J. Am. Psychoanal. Assoc. *15:* 344, 1967.
9. Engel, G. L.: *Psychological Development in Health and Disease*. Philadelphia, W. B. Saunders, 1962.

10. Lindemann, E.: Symptomatology and management of acute grief. Am. J. Psychiatry *101:* 141, 1944.
11. Bilodeau, C. B., and Hackett, T. P.: Issues raised in a group setting by patients recovering from myocardial infarction. Am. J. Psychiatry *128:* 73, 1971.
12. Pinter, H.: *The Homecoming*. London, Methuen, 1965.
13. Friedman, M., and Rosenman, R. H.: Overt behavior pattern in coronary disease: Detection of overt behavior pattern A in patients with coronary disease by a new psychophysiological procedure. J.A.M.A. *173:* 1320, 1960.

CHAPTER 25

Determinants of Ethics in a Personal Medicine

OVERVIEW

In this chapter, I shall discuss the subject of medical ethics in terms of those values and qualities that are intrinsic to the profession of medicine and the individual engaged in its practice. Whereas we may find that there exist some similarities to the ethics of other professions and disciplines as well as to all aspects of human life, this emphasis on the intrinsic values may give us a better idea of what medical ethics is as opposed to the application of moral and ethical systems derived from other disciplines, including theology and philosophy. Such traditions only to a limited extent touch on those of a specific profession. Within each profession there develops an *evolution* of value systems unique to that profession and based upon the specific experiences of the generations that constitute that profession.

PERSONAL VERSUS PUBLIC MEDICINE

In speaking of medical ethics, I would go somewhat further in suggesting that there are two major parallel divisions within the health field. I label these the personal and the public medicine (health).[1] Personal medicine is that aspect of medical practice that is based upon the personal rendering of care, diagnosis, and treatment for the individual with a self-identified health problem. It is personal and most

---

Modified version (and reproduced with permission) of article from Medical Clinics of North America 61: 867–877, 1977; copyrighted by the W. B. Saunders Company.

frequently conducted between a physician and a patient. Public medicine, on the other hand, is a corporate enterprise and covers the spectrum that includes and, at one time or another, has been identified as public health, preventive medicine, epidemiology, community health, environmental medicine, and, more recently, medical ecology. The very proliferation of these names suggests a certain discomfort of society with these terms. A further examination identifies that the terms are not all of the same class. Epidemiology suggests a methodological approach to health phenomena and, as such, is part of other disciplines, many of which impinge on a personal medicine. One might even suggest that it is ethically incumbent upon the physician to view every individual from an epidemiological perspective at some phases of both diagnosis and treatment. On the other hand, the term preventive medicine makes little sense when subjected to further analysis. In its most liberal sense, it suggests that medicine can be prevented by attending to potential health problems before they require the remedial effects of a personal medicine. Even were this achievable, there would still be problems outside the purview of preventive medicine for which a personal medicine would be needed, e.g., problems associated with living that invariably come to the physician but which are not directly associated with a primarily biological or psychological approach. The proliferation of terms identifies an ambiguity that not only concerns public medicine but also directly concerns the personal medicine, a concern that is rarely addressed. At this point in history, what has always been a tenuous balance between the personal and the public medicine is emerging as a central issue in both areas, if only because they increasingly share the public concern and the health dollar. This concern is reflected further in the differences in ethical orientations between a personal medicine as opposed to a public medicine. In Western society, at least, it has become increasingly obvious that private medicine exists largely at an expense to the public sector. This issue is demonstrated both in what has become the public education of the physician as well as in the public support of many of the facilities that personal medicine utilizes in diagnosis and treatment. Consequently, the increasing intrusion of public medicine into a personal medicine is inevitable and will result in an increasing societal influence over what goes on in the personal sector. The issues of the regulation and distribution of health and medical resources, including the production and dispersement of physicians, have become ones of public concern and legislation.[2] These issues, including those such as population control, either by limited production or the limitation of life support systems, become issues of societal values as distinct from those of the individual physician and his patient. These issues, which deserve public debate, more often are resolved by legislation on the basis of what has spontaneously evolved, rather than by deliberate attention to the ethics of the evolving problem, e.g., abortion. The resolution is less based in individual ethical concerns and more dictated by societal exigencies out of which a new social morality may develop.

Although the ethics of a public medicine is not the major thesis of this chapter, the ethics of a personal medicine needs to be viewed within the light of this backdrop. Specifically, the so-called ethics of medicine is being redressed by an impersonal social system concerned with statistics and numbers, whose value system is frequently out of step with the ethics of a personal medicine that is concerned with the individual ethical values of a patient coming with a specific need to a caring physician.

THE PHYSICIAN

Because both the physician and the patient are also members of the larger society, it is inevitable that each alone and sometimes together will find himself in conflict between the ethics of personal and public medicine. For the emerging student of medicine today, a major ethical dilemma can be that of deciding toward which end of the spectrum his innate values lead him. He needs to question which is most in accord with his ethical sense of self, an orientation and investment in the personal care of the individual or involvement in a larger sphere where decisions based on problems affecting the lives of great numbers may only indirectly and nonspecifically touch upon the life of a given individual. This is perhaps the most vital decision that the emerging physician needs to make. It is a decision that is primarily based upon individually derived ethics. Thus, the first ethical task of the physician is to review his/her own value system. Similar to everything else in life, this begins with a review of the development of the individual's moral development and an acceptance of the point at which he has settled or coalesced along a hypothesized evolutionary spectrum of moral development. Piaget[3] has initiated such a scheme based upon his empirical observations of children, which Lawrence Kohlberg[4] has discussed (Table 25.1). Such a scheme is not unlike that of Erikson's (Table 25.2) maturational one.

My own predilection is such that I see these essentially socially and cognitively conceptualized schemes as incomplete without including an affectually conceptualized one. In other words, I suggest that an individual's derived value system is only partly derived from the external environment, but depends on his own innate substrate and what sys-

Table 25.1
Stages in the Development of Moral Judgment*

1. Orientation to punishment and reward and to physical and material power.
2. Hedonistic orientation with an instrumental view of human relations. Beginning notions of reciprocity, but with emphasis on exchange of favors—"You scratch my back and I'll scratch yours."
3. "Good boy" orientation: seeking to maintain expectations and win approval of one's immediate group; morality defined by individual ties of relationship.
4. Orientation to authority, law, and duty to maintaining a fixed order, whether social or religious, which is assumed as a primary value.
5. Social contract orientation, with emphasis on equality and mutual obligation within a democratically established order, e.g., the morality of the American Constitution.
6. Morality of individual principles of conscience that have logical comprehensiveness and universality. Highest value placed on human life, equality, and dignity.

* From Kohlberg, L.: A cognitive-developmental approach to moral education. Humanist *32:* 13–16, 1972.

tems are most easily integrated with it. An individual's ethics is not based only on what one is taught to believe or even wishes to believe[6] but also on the integration of cognitive with conative behavior. In other words, ethical attitudes may be of less significance if they do not gain expression in action or works. The essential intermediary here depends on the individual's personality, which gives structure to his cognitive processes and conative acts. Whether one reaches a greater or lesser psychosexual stage of development, cognitive stage of abstraction, or social interactive stage of relatedness with others will individually and together determine the level of maximum ethical functioning. For society as a whole, further research into the multiple factors affecting ethical development in the individual, as well as within a society, will assist us globally as well as individually to know the ethical base from which we start in our approach to both personal and public medicine. This, I submit, is the primary ethical principle for the physician. It is not dissimilar from the old maxim, "Physician, know thyself!"

PERSONAL MEDICINE

Since the practice of a personal medicine essentially involves two individuals, there is the further consideration of the interaction of the potentially differing value systems seen in each one. I suppose this is what is hinted at, but not directly discussed, in our controversies about minority groups being treated by their own members. The premise here

Eight Ages of Man*

VIII. Maturity								Ego integrity vs. despair
VII. Adulthood							Genera-tivity vs. stagnation	
VI. Young adulthood						Intimacy vs. isolation		
V. Puberty and adolescence					Identity vs. role confusion			
IV. Latency				Industry vs. inferiority				
III. Locomotor-genital			Initiative vs. guilt					
II. Muscular-anal		Autonomy vs. shame, doubt						
I. Oral sensory	Basic trust vs. mistrust							
	1	2	3	4	5	6	7	8

* From Erikson, E. H.: Eight ages of man. In *Childhood and Society*, ed. 2, Chapter 7, pp. 247–274. New York, W. W. Norton, 1963.

would be that personal medicine is more likely to be more caring and, hence, more effective when the value systems of the physician and patient are more nearly the same. Whether or not this works in practice may be another matter, but the inherent concept is that a personal medicine or even a public medicine cannot be practiced without an intimate knowledge of the individual's background and personal habits.

KNOWING

The concept of empathy is a difficult one, and the term is fiercly abused by many using it. It is perhaps important to pause here to consider it because I submit that it is intrinsic to the values of a personal medicine. The standard definition of empathy as the ability to put oneself in the other's shoes in attempting to feel what he does is a noble one. Being noble, it is difficult to achieve. It is also questionable as to what value it serves by having two individuals in the same pair of shoes, so to speak, at the same time. I would rather see this complex term defined more in terms of the ability of the physician to sense and bring out the feelings of his patient. A further component essential to empathy, I suggest, is the ability of the physician to communicate to his patient a sense of himself as also mortal, subject to similar discomforts, and living in the same world. This is, of course, difficult to achieve and frankly ludicrous when there is a marked discrepancy between cultural and social backgrounds. In a personal medicine, empathy is perhaps the third ethical principle, for without it there can be no relationship and little attending.

CONFIDENTIALITY

With empathy and attending, the patient has the opportunity for expression of concerns and ventilation of feelings, which are accomplished with increasing freeness when the physician and patient are able to relax within the confidentiality of the relationship. This serves to overcome the initial reticence and inhibitions of each and provide an intimacy unknown and unshared in most other human contacts. The stuff about which medical communications are made is entirely personal, whether it is factual, in terms of the description of a mass or pain, or subjective, in terms of a feeling. It is of the patient and belongs to him; is shared with the physician in the strictest confidence without which it could be used wittingly or unwittingly to assure his vulnerability. This concept of confidentiality goes beyond signed permission to relate to others information communicated by the patient to the physician. This mere consent must in no way lead to the compromise of confidentiality. What is communicated in a consent release must be objective and totally satisfactory to the patient. Furthermore, it is inherent on the part of the physician to make his patient aware of possible risks to the patient of releases of this information.

FACILITATION OF EMOTIONAL EXPRESSION

Part of the physician's duty is to relieve anxiety and fear that the suffering patient brings with him in his concern about himself. Part of this relief is obtained through the physician's ability to attend, empathize, and, in so doing, bring out as complete a story about the patient and his complaint as possible in an intimate and confidential setting. Through this opportunity, the patient more clearly identifies what his complaint is to the physician as well as to himself. The patient also begins to express his feelings, the anxieties, fears, sadness, guilt, and shame that are associated with illness. This aspect of the relationship is intrinsic to the ethical dimensions of the physician's role, for it is part of caring for the whole individual. It is a component that is increasingly compromised in the dilemma between a public and a private medicine.

TEACHING

When the relationship between patient and physician has evolved on the basis of the above dimensions, a new role evolves for the doctor, that of teacher.[7] His obligation as a teacher becomes a fifth intrinsic ethical dimension for the physician. This is one of the areas in which a personal medicine bridges with a public medicine, that is, health education. It is a further way of alleviating anxiety by identifying for the patient what is known, regardless of the severity, of the disorder. The identified illness then becomes something tangible that the patient, in therapeutic alliance with the physician, can objectively approach and with which he can contend. This enucleation and distinction of the phenomenon intrinsic to medicine puts a negotiable distance between the patient and his illness. The ramifications of this Cartesian mind-body separation are many but will not be further considered here. What is of importance in the ethical role of the doctor is that both the physician and his patient see him as a teacher who can skillfully educate and instruct the latter in understanding the illness in terms of (1) those things that will affect it adversely or propitiously; (2) what changes may be necessary in his personal, social, and professional life; and (3) the effects of this illness on significant others. Teaching is a fifth ethical principle of the physician.

INFORMED CONSENT

This principle of teaching is intimately related to that of informed consent.[8] Rather than as a defense, the physician uses education to inform the patient about the latter's illness and counsels the patient as to the directions or alternatives to follow. This is a mutual process, inasmuch as the physician cannot lead unless the patient is willing to follow. The patient is not willing to follow unless he has developed confidence in the physician through the patient-physician relationship. This confidence will depend on the basic trust of which each is capable and which is intrinsic to the development of each. It is further nurtured or deviated by experiences with significant other helping individuals over the course of a life-time. Trust and confidence are neither blind nor static. They rest on candor and truth, but a candor and truth that are delivered in a neutral and appropriate way for the individuals involved. In the ideal situation, informed consent is not primarily directed at the requisite signature of the patient on a piece of paper giving permission to the physician to carry out one or another procedure. Rather it is based on the mutual agreement of patient and physician to follow a course of action in terms of an illness that makes not only appropriate medical sense in terms of the biological considerations, but social and psychological sense in terms of the intrinsic responsibilities, goals, and other values of the individual. This is of sufficient proportions to consider as a sixth principle of the ethics of a personal medicine.

CONTINUITY

The subsequent tasks of the doctor in his relationship with the patient that have ethical dimensions include the maintenance of that relationship over time. A commitment for care based on confidentiality and intimacy has been made, and it is the responsibility of the physician to maintain that care through whatever adversities affect the relationship until the responsibility is transferred by mutual consent to another individual. Such maintenance of care implies availability, notification to the patient at times of absence from his/her work, providing for an acceptable physician to substitute for him/her during these absences, and the follow-up of the patient periodically whether or not the patient explicitly desires it. Whereas these might be considered part of the technical aspects of practice, they are based on an ethical commitment of the physician to not only the patient, but also to him/herself. This constitutes a seventh principle of ethics.

ETHICS AS A CONCEPTUAL APPROACH

Thus, we can view a personal medical ethics as intrinsic to the profession in the implicit and explicit contract between the patient and the physician. As such, it represents an approach, rather than a rigid set of "Thou shalts!" and "Thou shalt nots!" The approach is a process and, as such is not one of doing things according to rigid prescription but of knowing what to do at the right time. This is done by posing the significant hypotheses as the relationship unfolds. Only by so doing will the physician attune his observational processes to obtaining the objective data that will confirm or negate his hypothesis. In this way, the scientific method is an integral aspect of medical practice and, as such, its use is an eighth major ethic intrinsic to medical practice. It seems necessary at this time in history to stress that the scientific method is not nearly so much that of a process occurring at the wet bench in the laboratory, where the emphasis is on a different kind of observational technique, as it is a process of thinking about a patient at the bedside, in the consulting room, and for many long hours thereafter.

PERSONAL VERSUS SOCIETAL ETHICS

These questions, as I have indicated above, do not involve only those relating to the biological problem but to all aspects of the life of the patient. A patient is only arbitrarily conceptualized in terms of various disciplines. Medicine uses these orientations in attempting to analyze the problem. But, in approaching a problem, medicine becomes synthetic and directs its treatment in terms of the patient. At this juncture, the individual's value system, which is as intrinsic a part of his life as any other arbitrarily isolated part, needs to be addressed in terms of what is acceptable or unacceptable or, more concretely, what makes sense or no sense in that individual's life. In this situation, the physician assists the patient in analyzing and, through instruction, becomes a counselor who assists the patient in a decision-making process. One is reminded of the Hippocratic statement in the book of *Aphorisms*: "Life is short and the (healing) art is long; the opportunity (to administer remedies) fleeting, experiment is dangerous, the decision difficult.... One must not only do the right thing oneself, but make the patient and all about him concur.... You must not only do the proper thing, but do it at the right time."[9] Such an approach introduces an uncomfortable relativism into medicine that will oftentimes lead to discomfort on the parts of both the physician and the patient. In order to avoid this, at least in the moments of illness, the physician first needs to be objective and comfortable with this relativism. He needs to see this as deriving from the situation at hand rather than in terms of prejudgments. In order words, he cannot assist in an individual decision regarding the care of an aged patient on the basis that he feels a useful life ends at 70. Such a bias, whatever its basis or potential merit in other considerations, is anathema to the resolution of the individual case in terms of the physician's ethics in a personal care medicine. On the other hand, this physician's view might have an ethical basis in a public medicine (health) policy in which a society or a world bases its potential for survival or some other derived value on the optimal care of the young, essentially at the expense of the aged patient.

Many of the problems that have been identified as ones of medical ethics relate to a public medicine (health) as opposed to a personal medicine. As such, they are not really intrinsic to a personal medicine but derive from the values of a society that change over time and are ultimately based on the survival of that group or society (itself an ethical value, but a societal one). Thus, although there exist ethical bases for the attitudes adopted toward population control (whether these be contraception, abortion, euthanasia for the defective or aged, selection of patients for scarce resources, distribution of physicians, or suicide), they are of a societal nature and are only partially reflected, if at all, in the doctor-patient relationship and contract. In the latter, both the doctor and the patient may frequently be in conflict within themselves over attitudes based on a societal position as opposed to an individual one. These values reflected by a society's approach to such issues only indirectly reflect those of its individual members. They are pragmatic for that society's survival (in one sense or another), the same as an individual's values may ultimately derive from a sense pragmatic for his own survival. In either case, this does not mean that there may not be internal conflict between an individual's or a society's pragmatic decisions (what is best at a particular time) as opposed to a more usual ethic.

It is of the utmost importance that neither the physician nor the patient confuse what might be identified as his societal ethic with that of a personal ethic that is based in a patient-doctor relationship. This is an ethic based on a fundamental belief in the autonomy (a ninth principle) of the life of the individual, which may be necessarily compromised in a social situation. This is not to say that there is no place for altruism in the individual's personal life in terms of decisions made about himself. There is every place for altruism, and such an issue needs to be evaluated objectively with the physician in this relationship. This altruism, however, must be seen as only partially derived from the sense of a societal altruism[10] but also from an ethic based on the sense of self-integrity. It is at times when the patient's personally derived ethic comes in conflict with a societally derived ethic that the greatest dilemma for the physician is posed. This is probably most often around the issue of suicide and formerly around abortion, if only because the individual at once is both of society and out of society (in terms of the contemplated act). It involves others and, hence, has an effect on others and society that society may have a need to protect. In such situations, there inevitably comes a time when the physician draws the line between his actions based on a commitment to the patient and those based on his membership in society. Legal formulations aside, which is not to say they are without merit and do not reflect a societal position, the resolution remains that of the physician.

Societally derived resolutions of ethical dilemmas may be more clearly addressed, especially if it is possible to derive in a historical sense the evolution of its ethical development. In the democracies of Western society, I view this as toward the maximum autonomy for individual decision making, which allows an equal autonomy for any other affected or potentially affected individual. There is, of course, more restraint than license implied in such a formulation. The ethics of a society, as I suggested before, probably relate to its (majority opinion) survival. Whatever and however, the societal ethics relating to medical (health) issues are necessarily addressed in terms of where that society is at a given time in terms of its internal and external pressures. Thus, ethics will reflect the changing values of a society based on its accommodation to a survival principle with as little (in a democratic society) imposition as possible on individual autonomy. Society will or will not eventually permit contraception and abortion, depending on whether the population is markedly expanding and threatening other values such as the "quality" of life, or threatening a marked decrease in economic survival or even racial or ethnic extinction. On this level, a public medicine policy will be determined on the basis of broad social and political factors occurring over time that effect change in (1) societal and (2) individual values. I do not believe that a humane physician cannot take part in these discussions of a public medicine policy. However, it should be apparent to him and to the public that this is at a different level and of another order than the ethics of a personal medicine that I have identified above.

VALUE OF PHILOSOPHICAL AND THEOLOGICAL CONTRIBUTIONS TO MEDICAL ETHICS

To some extent, the practitioner of a personal medicine may utilize many of the analytic modes fashioned by philosophical and theological traditions in examining some of the factors operating in his personal medicine decision-making activities. These will serve as consciousness-raising models alerting the physician to some of the bases upon which he makes operational decisions. In many instances, such an identification may indeed lead him to question, if not change, his decisions or approach. For instance, in a personal medicine, it is questionable to what extent "a greatest good for the greatest number" principle should operate, if at all. In other words, the consequences of action based on such a principle would often be distinctly different for the individual vis-à-vis the society.[11] Similarly, although more complex, is "the sanctity of life" principle. One cannot go very far with the concept until such questions as the definition of humanness and the quality of life are raised. Immediately, we are on the verge of discordancy between the possible answers forthcoming in terms of the quality of life of the individual in terms of the patient and the quality of that life as viewed in societal terms. We might extend this to suggest that we have little, if any, empirical data on the quality of life of the comatose individual, inasmuch as we do not know what is going on, in that life (mind). Yet, we are influenced by societal definitions in accepting a value system that may frequently be at odds with that of the individual and of a personal medicine. Societal values place higher evidence on achievement, specific ages, health as opposed to illness, status (social, economic, position), creativity, fame, and productivity, all of which may have little to do with a personal medicine that most often addresses individual illness, in the poverty stricken, and the disenfranchised.

The physician may be frequently influenced in his care of patients by other factors, such as pain and the degree of suffering. Particularly in our society, there is a sense that one should not have to suffer, although other societies have acknowledged suffering as an obligatory part of daily living. However, around the patient with chronic illness, we have often developed a concept that one should not have to suffer and should be relieved of and even helped out of his misery. There is the possibility that such an emphasis may operate to a greater extent than it is generally thought to in the care of the patient.

More recently, we have before us the idea of a living will, defining under what circumstances the writer would no longer want to live. Beneath its candor is a certain absurdity in that until one has lived through something, one cannot know it. There are many situations I have observed or been told about that I would not desire to live through, but as a physician caring for severely ill patients, I know that patients have had similar thoughts in a well state. This does not mean that they have the same thoughts in the present state or would have the same thoughts 2 weeks or 6 months from the present time in a partially rehabilitated state. A corollary of this type of thinking is the physician who would do for his patient what he would do for a member of his family or would want done for him. In the first instance, we need to ask how he can presume to know what another would want in terms of himself. In the second, we would need to ask how he knows what he would want. A final ethical value for the physician is humility.

SOCIETAL VERSUS INDIVIDUAL ETHICS

There is another area in which ethically derived principles of society conflict with individual ones. This dilemma is perhaps best joined in the issue of suicide in Western society. (In some societies, suicide has been societally accepted and probably reinforced). The question of suicide as an individual right is, of course, first one based on legal rights. However, whether it is ethically right for one to commit suicide is another matter, inasmuch as suicide directly affects significant others as well as society as a whole. From a psychological perspective, we know that suicide frequently is directed at another or others as a way of bringing discomfort to him/her or them. The consequences frequently are longer lasting and greater than either the individual or others (advocates) might suspect. The question here is not whether the individual needs to protect himself, in this case his rights of autonomy, but whether society has a need to protect itself and others from the consequences of such an act. To what extent does society have a right to protect itself from an act of one of its members when that act may grievously distort the social structure by leading, as experience has shown in some instances, to a "wave of suicides" or a devaluation of life within that society?

In a somewhat similar way, the societal attitudes toward abortion may be at variance with a personal ethics based on consequences, definitions of life, quality of life, etc., when abortion might threaten the survival indirectly (economic) or directly (eventual extinction) of a society or the "reverence for life" that society needs in order to conduct its affairs humanely.

In these and other situations, the dilemma for the physician in personal medicine is frequently great, regardless of what his own value system may be, inasmuch as he must determine at what point he can (should) desist from being the counselor of the patient and serve as the protector of the state.

RETURNING TO A PERSONAL MEDICINE

In closing this deliberation, I return to the intrinsic ethics of a personal medicine and consider the matter of *intimacy*. Perhaps, in no other relationship is there the potential for as much intimacy as there is between the doctor and patient. Our attention is drawn to the Hippocratic Oath[12] (Table 25.3). Read it sometime! It is a most contemporary document. It addresses the excesses and abuses of a personal medicine that are still with us. Intimacy allows for the maximum of communication between physician and patient necessary for the accumulation of the empirical data upon which medicine is practiced. The physician has more access to the patient's mind and body than any other individual. This occurs at a time of distress when the patient is especially vulnerable. Such an individual is at maximum risk and vulnerable (willingly or unwillingly) to another. This intimacy is essential to the therapeutic situation if the patient is to receive maximum care and attention. Only in such a situation based on trust and confidence can the patient divulge the data necessary for the physician to attend to his needs. In doing so, the patient knowingly places himself at maximal

Table 25.3
The Hippocratic Oath*

"I swear by Apollo the physician, and Aesculapius, and Health, and All-heal, and all the gods and goddesses, that, according to my ability and judgment, I will keep this Oath and this stipulation: to reckon him who taught me this Art equally dear to me as my parents, to share my substance with him, and relieve his necessities if required; to look upon his offspring in the same footing as my own brothers, and to teach them this Art, if they shall wish to learn it, without fee or stipulation; and that by precept, lecture, and every other mode of instruction, I will impart a knowledge of the Art to my own sons, and those of my teachers, and to disciples bound by a stipulation and oath according to the law of medicine, but to none others. I will follow that system of regimen which, according to my ability and judgment, I consider for the benefit of my patients, and abstain from whatever is deleterious and mischievous. I will give no deadly medicine to any one if asked, nor suggest any such counsel; and in like manner I will not give to a woman a pessary to produce abortion. With purity and with holiness I will not cut persons laboring under the stone, but will leave this to be done by men who are practitioners of this work. Into whatever houses I enter, I will go into them for the benefit of the sick, and will abstain from every voluntary act of mischief and corruption; and, further, from the seduction of females or males, of freemen and slaves. Whatever, in connection with my professional practice or not in connection with it, I see or hear, in the life of men, which ought not to be spoken of abroad, I will not divulge, as reckoning that all such should be kept secret. While I continue to keep this Oath unviolated, may it be granted to me to enjoy life and the practice of the Art, respected by men, in all times! But should I trespass and violate this Oath, may the reverse be my lot!"

* From Hippocrates: The Oath. In *Greek Biology and Medicine*, H. O. Taylor, editor, pp. 34–36. Boston, Marshall Jones, 1922.

risk. Essentially, he is exposing his defects and deficiencies, which can be used by the physician in his societal role, wittingly or unwittingly, to take advantage of the patient. This may occur through carelessness in matters of confidentiality, whether these are by leaving records around or by careless remarks. Because of his humaneness, the physician may find that his affections may put him at risk of compromising his professional relationship with a patient and placing his patient in a compromised situation. This degree of intimacy between physician and patient may take many forms. A physician can become overinvested in a patient's personal life and take it upon himself to advise in matters that go beyond his concern, knowledge, or competence. Physicians may promise more than they or perhaps anyone else can realistically give in the way of emotional and social support. Physical intimacy with a patient is not uncommon, nor is it not understandable. Its roots are based on a mutuality between an individual (physician) wishing to give something "substantive" and a patient wishing to receive a tangible expression of care. The classical characterization of it is the laying on of hands. More rarely this may intimate and evolve into something more in terms of fantasied or actual sexual activity. This was not unforeseen by Hippocrates and is still a matter of contemporary controversy in our profession. Despite attempts by some to give a therapeutic and even an ethical basis for such actions, it seems to me that this remains in complete violation of the implicit and explicit trust invested in the concept of the patient-physician relationship by all parties concerned—patient, physician, and society.

Intimacy is not only physical but transcends the usual ego boundaries between the individuals involved. As such, it may seem seductive in promising more involvement than can possibly be maintained and/or infringing upon areas outside the competent concern of the physician. On the other hand, a patient in the course of treatment may violate the unwritten ethic of the relationship by intruding in one way or another

Table 25.4
Ethical Dimensions of the Physician

1. Physician, know thyself!
2. Physician, know thy patient!
3. Empathy
4. Confidentiality
5. The doctor as teacher
6. Informed consent
7. Commitment for continued care
8. Use of the scientific method
9. What is right for the patient
10. Humility

into the personal life of the physician, a problem that always requires maximum delicacy and firmness in resolving. Over time it behooves the physician to acquire the experience and skill that will assist him in negotiating these situations.

Lastly, intimacy is a rare privilege. Perhaps only the physician has the opportunity to share this relationship with many individuals. It serves to enhance his view of humanity and, consequently, has the potential for increasing his own humanity (Table 25.4).

SUMMARY

In this discussion, I have suggested that the intrinsic basis of a personal medical ethic derives from the patient-physician relationship in matters of health and illness. In so doing, I have suggested that an ethical bases for a personal medicine are: (1) awareness by the physician of his(her) motivations, abilities, and competence; (2) the physician's ability to get to know as much about his/her patient as a person as s/he would about the complaint; (3) the physician's capacity for empathy that will facilitate (2); (4) the physician's ability to maintain the confidentiality of the doctor-patient relationship; (5) the physician's obligation to be a teacher to his(her) patient; (6) the physician's obligation to inform the patient of what s(he) is doing and is planning to do; (7) the physician's obligation to continue his(her) care of the patient; (8) the physician's commitment to a scientific (or analytic) approach to the patient and his problems; (9) the physician's capacity for helping his(her) patient reach decisions most appropriate for that individual's illness and life; and (10) the physician's awareness of his(her) own humanness and limitations.

Thus, I propose that medicine is a matter of ethics. Ethics in terms of the individual (patient or physician) is not a matter of cognitive processes alone, but also of an emotional tolerance of the individual for internal conflict between the cognitive and emotional aspects of the self as well as the external conflict between the resolved individual position, its conative acts, and society's.

References

1. Kass, L. R.: Regarding the end of medicine and the pursuit of health. Public Interest *40:* 11, 1975.
2. Hardin, G.: The tragedy of the commons. Science *162:* 1243, 1968.
3. Piaget, J.: *The Moral Judgment of the Child.* Glencoe, Ill., Free Press of Glencoe, 1948.
4. Kohlberg, L.: A cognitive-developmental approach to moral education. Humanist *32:* 13, 1972.
5. Erikson, E.: Eight ages of man. In *Childhood & Society*, Chapter 7. New York, W. W. Norton, 1963.

6. James, W.: The will to believe. In *Essays in Pragmatism*, A. Castell, editor. New York, Hafner, 1948.
7. Tosteson, D.: The right to know: Public education for health. J. Med. Educ. *50:* 117, 1975.
8. Beecher, H. K.: Medical research and the individual. In *Life or Death: Ethics and Options*. Seattle, University of Washington Press, 1968.
9. Hippocrates: Aphorisms. In *Greek Biology and Medicine*, H. O. Taylor, editor, p. 32. Boston, Marshall Jones, 1922.
10. Wilson, E. O.: *Sociobiology: The New Synthesis*. Cambridge, Mass., Harvard University Press, 1975.
11. Mill, J. S.: Utilitarianism. In *The English Philosophies: From Bacon to Mill*. New York, The Modern Library, 1939.
12. Hippocrates: The Oath. In *Greek Biology and Medicine*, H. O. Taylor, editor, pp. 34–36. Boston, Marshall Jones, 1922.

PART

4

USING THE CLINICAL CASE METHOD IN THE BIOPSYCHOSOCIAL APPROACH

CHAPTER

26

Educational Methods

Techniques of Interviewing: Introducing the Patient to the Student*

In Chapter 2, "Interviewing and the Meaning of the Symptom," we outlined a general approach to interviewing patients. This approach is considered essential in examining the patient's symptom or complaint from three perspectives: the organic, the psychological, and the social or environmental. In that chapter was suggested a methodology by which the student physician could learn to identify the multidimensional meaning of the symptom by examining the relationship of the patient's symptoms to the events currently taking place in the patient's life, his present mental and psychological status, predisposing personality characteristics, and the organic basis of the symptom.

It is the purpose of this discussion to suggest a format for the teaching of a course in general interviewing to students and house officers.

MATERIAL

The patients utilized in the exercises described may be selected from any population. They may be inpatients or outpatients on any of the

* Modified version (and reproduced with permission) of article from Psychiatry in Medicine *1*: 167–170, 1970; copyrighted by Greenwood Periodicals.

services of the hospital. Most often, and especially in the initial phases of this course, it is best to select patients on the basis of their ability and willingness to participate. Interviewing may be done at the bedside, in a nearby conference room, or in an outpatient office. It is best to reserve acutely ill and disoriented patients for special exercises toward the end of the course.

Students participating in this course are commencing their Introduction to Clinical Medicine course, their internship, or their residency. Experience suggests that students should work with a preceptor in groups of six to eight. More than this number tends to interfere with bringing closure to topics discussed in the seminars that follow the interviews. Furthermore, six to eight students may comfortably gather around a bed or in a patient's room, whereas more than this leads to distractions interfering with hearing and observation.

Preceptors are selected on the basis of their general interest in this approach to interviewing and their willingness to participate in an ongoing workshop in which to discuss and experiment with new approaches to interview instruction. The model of the faculty workshop is similar to the student groups, limited to six to eight faculty members who participate in deriving the approaches to the interviewing process that will be used with students. This group may simultaneously focus its methodology around a particular clinical research activity of general interest to its members and provide a setting for creative thought.

Tape audio and video recorders and rooms with one-way mirrors are useful, although not necessary, adjuncts at various phases of the interview course, inasmuch as they emphasize to the student the need for sticking to the data and for accuracy of description in reviewing and preparing his data for communication. These techniques allow the individual to review his own performance as it actually was, as well as the performances of others. However, the use of any of these is probably best introduced gradually and at specific times, inasmuch as too early and too intensive an awareness of one's performance may initially be intimidating.

METHODS

The instruction in interviewing techniques is an integral part of the course Introduction to Clinical Medicine and is not separated from other observational techniques, including physical examination. This instruction may commence at any time during the student's medical experience and has been inaugurated on a weekly basis at the beginning of the first year at Yale University and the University of Chicago.

Some didactic sessions and some written materials relating specifically to techniques may serve as guides for the student, but the essential features of interviewing are only understood and developed through actual experience. Often a series of demonstrations by experienced interviewers may serve to initiate the course. These may be "performed" before the entire class, using one group of students as the responsible team for discussing what they have observed during the interview. In this way, the broad didactic principles of interviewing can be derived and presented before the entire class with economy. Thereafter, interview instruction is best accomplished in small groups, alternately using a demonstration by the preceptor and "trial and error" exercises by the students, to be followed by group discussion.

The small group exercises may be set up in a stepwise fashion consisting of graduated experiences with different patients in the following manner.

First Session. Each student in the group interviews a different patient at the bedside or in the clinic for 5 minutes, after which the group discusses what has been observed and heard during the interview. A few simple questions—such as: "How are you feeling?"; "What brought you to the hospital?"; "How are things going?" (addressed by the student to the patient)—are often all that is necessary to accomplish the purpose of this exercise, namely, to show how much information may be obtained in a few minutes if the group uses all of its modalities of observation.

Second Session. Interviews of 15 to 20 minutes are suggested. The student is challenged with the task of finding out what is going on with the patient, beginning in the "here and now." In these sessions, the student will invariably become aware of the patient's symptoms and complaints and may begin to identify the setting in which the patient's illness developed, as well as his reaction to the illness and hospitalization.

Third Session. For the third interview, lasting up to 30 minutes, the student is charged with establishing the present illness, clarifying the symptoms, and identifying the setting in which the illness has occurred. During the subsequent discussion, the preceptor begins to direct the group's attention toward the various diagnostic implications of the symptom.

Fourth Session. The interview may be extended to 40 minutes. The student is challenged to synthesize from his data a composite picture of the patient's present illness, namely, the presenting complaint, the setting in which it has occurred, and the patient's response to the illness and hospitalization.

Fifth Session. During this exercise, in which the interview may be expanded to 45 to 50 minutes, emphasis is placed upon relating the present illness to the past medical and life experiences of the patient. This will include an appropriate review of systems as it relates to the patient's complaints and discussion of his previous history and family history.

Sixth Session. This interview of 45 to 60 minutes' duration is a full-dress attempt by the student to perform a complete initial interview, including all that he has been charged with previously. This session may be more expeditiously completed by utilizing preceptors not drawn from the core group but from the faculty as a whole.

Subsequent Sessions. Several additional exercises may be set up to consider special interview techniques necessary for different patient populations, such as children, adolescents, delirious or demented patients,[1] and psychiatric patients.[2] At least once during this sequence, a relative of a patient is interviewed by a student and is asked to meet with the group to discuss the patient. The purpose of this exercise is to demonstrate the frequent need for corroboration of data obtained from the patient, to suggest how the same data may be viewed differently, and to sensitize the student to the fact that the patient's illness occurs in a social milieu contingent upon the family and society of which he is a member.

An alternative approach, useful especially when this method is incorporated in a human development course, is the sequential interviewing of individuals along the life cycle, beginning with the expectant mother and terminating with an elder citizen. In this way, both an overview of life phases and a spectrum of various illnesses associated with them are presented.

HANDLING THE MATERIAL

Following each interview session, the group, including preceptor and students, discusses the data that have been observed and identified from the point of view of the relationship, the information collected, and the therapeutic aspects of the case. The presenting symptom as elicited by the student is examined as to its somatic, social, and psychological meaning and relevance. Discussion of the interplay of these three factors on the relationship of the symptom to the specific diagnosis lends itself to consideration of life stage, personality (see Chapter 4), the setting of illness, and reaction to illness.

At each subsequent session, the student interviewing a particular patient during the previous exercise reports on a follow-up of his experiences with that patient, which may include further interviewing, meetings with family members, discussions with house officers and/or attending physicians, and review of records. This serves to emphasize the value of continuity of patient contact and the need of correlating data, as well as to test the synthesized hypotheses drawn from such data with the observation of others.

At appropriate sessions professional personnel working with the patient—such as nurses, social workers, house officers, and consultants—participate in the discussion of the patient after the interview. By dramatizing the multifaceted approaches to patient care in a modern medical center, this exercise serves to introduce the student to how and when the specific expertise of a particular specialist is valuable in the diagnosis and treatment of a specific patient.

Following the initial discussion of the interview by the group, the student interviewer is charged with writing a summary of the interview with his formulations about the patient and the meaning of the patient's symptoms. The model for presenting this summary is didactically approached by the preceptor with his group and follows traditional medical record models with some of the modifications suggested by Weed.[3] This summary is subsequently reviewed by the preceptor with the student, at which time an attempt is made to bring closure to many of the questions and formulations raised and made about the interview.

CONCLUSION

In this discussion, we have outlined the logistics that are utilized in conveying a method of interviewing, previously reported on. Specifically, it outlines an effective means of communicating interview technique to groups of students working closely with a preceptor by alternating demonstration and didactic instruction with trial and error exercises.

References

1. Engel, G. L., and Romano, J.: Delirium, a syndrome of cerebral insufficiency. J. Chronic Dis. *9*: 260, 1959.
2. Gill, M. M., Newman, R., and Redlich, F. C.: *The Initial Interview in Psychiatric Practice*. New York, International Universities Press, 1954.
3. Weed, L. L.: Medical records that guide and teach. N. Engl. J. Med. *278*: 593, 652, 1968.

The Clinical Case Method in Teaching the Biopsychosocial Approach†

Over the years, those of us who have attempted to teach medical students, residents, specialists, and general practitioners comprehensive approaches to the patient and his symptom have increasingly despaired that didactic methods, with their oftentimes inherent moralisms, fail to convey the message and frequently lose the student in a morass of technical jargon derived from the several conceptual languages with which we attempt to familiarize them. On the basis of our researches, we have attempted to synthesize bridging languages between the conceptual and methodological approaches of biology, sociology, and psychology by using such formulations as the illness onset situation; behavioral patterns and personality styles—the emotions and defenses modifying these in reaction to conflict; the interview method; the patient-physician relationship; phases of illness—premorbid states, acute, convalescent, and rehabilitative; the intensive care unit syndrome; reactions to illness—acute and chronic; delirium and altered states of consciousness; grief processes—denial, ventilatory, defensive, adaptive; therapeutic aspects of interviewing; and modified conversion hypotheses. However, we have found ourselves becoming tedious and losing the interest of our students, who frequently find these formulations esoteric and extraneous to their interest in an approach to the patient and his problem.

The techniques of live and prerecorded audio- and videotaped presentations of interviews of ourselves and students before groups of students, although extremely valuable in semester-long courses, are time consuming and usually attend to only small segments of the interviewer-patient interaction, oftentimes interfering with the very synthesis we are attempting to introduce into the students' thinking.

Believing that the essential challenge facing modern practice and research in medicine is the development of the physician who, despite his major therapeutic orientation, can move with facility in his approaches to the patient and his problem from one conceptual orientation to another, many of us have attempted to devise and utilize innovative approaches by which this may be accomplished. Fundamental to these attempts is a return to the case method presentation.[1] Secondly,

---

† Modified version (and reproduced with permission) of article from Psychosomatic Medicine 37: 454–467, 1975; copyrighted by the American Psychosomatic Society, Elsevier-North Holland.

attempts have been made to return more toward a Socratic method of teaching in which there develops an active dialogue between teacher and students. In this way, the teacher, similar to the therapist, stays with where the student is, attending to his needs and following his lead. At the same time, the teacher's objective is to shape and orchestrate the discussion in such a way as to accomplish his agenda by incorporating both conceptual approaches and substantive content in the course of the seminar. This allows not only for a discussion of didactic material introduced by the case and the instructor, but also for a consideration of affectually determined reactions of the students to the material presented.

An example of one attempt to accomplish these objectives is presented in the cases discussed in Chapters 27 to 30. The instructor presents the material identified in the left-hand column, more or less in the paragraph form indicated, pausing at the end of each paragraph or before, if indicated, to attend to the students' responses. At this point, the instructor elicits the first associations of the students to the material presented, attempting to identify the sources of the students' biases. The instructor objectifies these in order that they be subsequently ruled in or out in light of further data to be supplied. During the discussion, the instructor may move ahead and supply additional information obtained during later phases of the interview, information that students would like to have, which may or may not be available at this point (or later) in the interview, and attend to observations and associations that he had not previously anticipated. In the right-hand column are notes for the instructor suggesting those approaches that he might utilize in directing the discussion. In no sense is it the intention to restrict the free-flowing nature of the discussion by urging the instructor to adhere to either a verbatim presentation of the case or of the discussion. The discussion notes may be further appended by precisely delineating those aspects of the case that the instructor wishes to elaborate by the inclusion of specific references to be suggested to the student for further reading.

The cases presented in this book have been modified for presentation to a number of different audiences. They have been used in working with a small number of psychiatric residents learning consultation-liaison skills. In this context, the presentation and discussion continued over 6 weeks, during which the discussion might deviate into a discussion of conversion reactions at one time, the syndromes of depression at another, etc. In these discussions, the problems encountered in consultation-liaison activities were discussed, and readings on this subject were incorporated into the course.[2–4]

They have also been used as single 1½-hour presentations before groups of general practitioners, social workers, and clinical psychologists, in which, obviously, the discussion was less detailed. When used in this setting, the instructor-large group interaction was especially stimulating, with active exchanges occurring between members of the group. Psychologists were frequently challenged by going beyond the data, whereas social workers were criticized for confining themselves overly with the social field. Physicians, on the other hand, although commencing with a preoccupation with a physical interpretation of the symptom, gradually became absorbed in the social and psychological facets of the problem. When specific subjects came up for discussion, e.g., delirium, the instructor used slides to suggest the stages of delirium and the symptoms and signs relating to them.

In teaching an undergraduate course in the behavioral science department in Determinants of and Integrated Approaches to Human Behavior, the author modified some sections in order to bring into the discussion concepts of learning theory and behavioral therapy. In this course, after having considered a case over several sessions, both instructor and students were able to refer to it throughout the remainder of the course in the discussion of other topics. For this class, expanded versions of the cases with appended references were distributed. This method proved so provocative of discussion for the undergraduate that other case presentations have been prepared for the discussion of the pain-prone patient (as a model for conversion processes), covert depression, and childhood symptoms. The presentations have also been used for a single session discussion with second-year medical students about to embark onto the wards for their Introduction to Clinical Medicine experience. Students in this group, although impressed, indicated that they were not buying the formulations until they had had an opportunity to try them out with their own patients. Feedback later in the course suggested that students indeed were attempting to look for such correlations as the illness onset situation and grief responses in their workup of patients.

In reading these cases, it is advisable to read the left-hand column first, keeping a list of associations and questions. Subsequently, the reader may check these with the comments in the right-hand column, noting areas that he might modify were he to use the case in a teaching session.

References

1. Engel, G. L.: Clinical observation: The neglected basic method of medicine. J.A.M.A. *192:* 849, 1965.
2. Lipowski, Z. J.: Review of consultation psychiatry and psychosomatic medicine. I. General principles. Psychosom. Med. *29:* 153, 1967.
3. Lipowski, Z. J.: Review of consultation psychiatry and psychosomatic medicine. II. Clinical aspects. Psychosom. Med. *29:* 201, 1967.
4. Lipowski, Z. J.: Review of consultation psychiatry and psychosomatic medicine. III. Theoretical issues. Psychosom. Med. *30:* 395, 1968.

CHAPTER

27

Case Method: A Coronary Event[1]

RECORDED HISTORY AND OBSERVATIONS

Mr. S. is a 36-year-old white, recently separated father of three and police sergeant who comes to the emergency department complaining of chest pain.

He tells the triage officer that he thinks it may be indigestion, that he has taken a couple of TUMS and ALKA SELTZERS, but they did not do any good. He says, "I'll be all right. Just let me see the 'doc' to give me something for pain so I can get home to my kids."

The triage officer notes that the sergeant appears tense and pale, is sweating profusely, and is unable to sit still. He records that the pain developed about 10 hours prior to the patient's arrival at the emergency room (ER), that it developed during sexual intercourse, and that it has increased in severity, beginning in the stomach and moving up into the chest. Presently, the pain is radiating to the left shoulder.

FOR DISCUSSION

First impressions
Who is the patient?
(race, age, family, work)
What reactions to expect?
What explanations for symptoms?
(See Chapter 2.)

Patient's rationalization of symptom
Where is patient's preoccupation?

First observations of patient[2]
Development of symptom complex
Illness onset situation[3]
Development of symptom

Modified version (and reproduced with permission) of article from Psychosomatic Medicine 37: 454–467, 1975; copyrighted by The American Psychosomatic Society, Elsevier-North Holland.

The patient says that it is really nothing, probably just indigestion or perhaps pleurisy, that he has never had anything like it before, in fact that he has never been ill before, and that he just needs a chest X-ray and something for pain so that he can get along home before going on to work.

Patient's presentation and rationalization of symptom (denial)
Patient's previous illness history
Patient's preoccupation in "here and now"

The triage officer records a normal temperature, a pulse of 120, a blood pressure of 120/90, and shallow respirations at 20.

Physical observation

Further history indicates that the patient is a Catholic of Irish descent who has worked for the Chicago police force for 13 years.

Further history
Social factors[4]
Professional factors

He has never been hospitalized and has no known medical history. His last physical, a routine police examination, was 6 months ago. He has smoked one pack of cigarettes a day over the past 20 years, increasing this to 1½ to 2 packs a day over the last 3 months "since my wife left." He admitted to drinking several cocktails and a couple of beers daily.

Further medical history[5]
Personal habits

Seen by a physician after admission to the ER, the patient had an electrocardiogram (ECG), which was read as normal, and emergency blood work, the results of which were not immediately reported. The physician's examination corroborated the findings of the triage officer, without substantial new observations.

Further physical observations

Admission to the hospital for further observation was suggested. The patient refused admission, saying that he only wanted something for pain, repeating that he had to get home before the kids left for school and that he could not waste time lying around the hospital when there was not anything really wrong with him, but perhaps a little indigestion. After further cajoling by the ER staff, the patient accepted admission to the hospital and was sent to the coronary care unit (CCU) for further observation with the presumptive diagnosis "myocardial infarction."

Reaction to admission[6]

Upon admission to the CCU, the patient seemed increasingly apprehensive. He said, "This is a lot of nonsense, there's nothing wrong with me; I just have this pain, indigestion, and want

Patient's behavior
Physical factors
Further history
Father's death[7]

something for pain." Shortly after receiving 50 mg of demerol intramuscularly, he seemed somewhat quieter. Vital signs remained stable: BlPr 120/80, P 120, Resp 23 shallow, T 38°C. The CCU house officer took a history, over the continued protests of the patient that there was "Nothing wrong with me; why do you have to ask me all of these questions? I only came in for my chest pain." Further history added that the patient's father had died "around the age of 40, suddenly, maybe his heart"; that a sister and a mother, now 70, were alive and well; that the patient had always been well, "in top-notch shape, never missed a day because of illness." Throughout the interview the patient continued to be preoccupied with being in the hospital and unable to get home to the children. He demanded that he be allowed to call home, to try to "get hold of my wife," whom he said had moved out 3 months before, because "she couldn't take it anymore, wanted to be by herself and figure things out." He said he "didn't blame her, really, she's been depressed for a long time and nothing seemed to please her, maybe it's my fault, but anyway I sure hope she comes the hell back."

Preoccupation of patient
Children/Wife

During the next 8 hours, the patient remained apprehensive and hypervigilant, although he complained of less pain, receiving two subsequent intramuscular injections of demerol. He complained of the noises of the monitors and of being in a "roomful of 'gooks.' " He said, "I'll be ok tomorrow; just call the station and tell them I'll be there tomorrow evening. Call the house and tell the kids I had some business to attend to and I'll see them tomorrow. Tell my mother she'd better look after them, see that they eat and get to bed on time. Try to get hold of that wife of mine; there's money in my wallet if she needs any."

CCU course
Physical
Reaction to environment
Preoccupations
Professional/children/wife

An ECG taken during this period showed developing q waves in III and AVF, a rhythm 120 and regular. Respirations decreased to 18 but remained shallow. T 39°C, BlPr 120/85. Results of laboratory blood work and chest X-ray taken previously were reported as normal.

Additional physical course

The patient was told that he had suffered a heart attack, but was doing well. He responded saying, "Like hell I have! There's nothing wrong

Reaction to diagnosis
Denial
Minimalization

with me, just a little muscle pain, maybe, and I'm getting the hell out of here tomorrow. Right now, just leave me alone and let me get some rest if I can with all the . . . machines going." He tossed and turned, frequently dislodging ECG electrodes, causing alarms to sound which made him, as well as the staff, irritable. When pleaded by the staff to "Take it easy, just relax, try to sleep, don't move around so much," he replied, "Why don't you lie here and see what it's like? Maybe you don't have so much to do, like three kids at home, and two jobs. Where the hell is my wife anyway" At this time he was placed on LIBRIUM, 10 mg intramuscularly.

Reaction to environment
Preoccupations
Job/wife/children
Medication

Over the next 24 hours, he remained restless and apprehensive, sleeping little. He continued to complain about being in the hospital, about the noise, about getting to work. He said the pain was better, he was ok now and was ready to go. He demanded his clothes, said he felt like a prisoner, said he had to call his office and make sure the place was covered, call home and make sure the kids were doing ok. He demanded to see the doctor, so he could get things straight and make sure he got "the hell out of here by tomorrow." He demanded a cigarette. When a nurse attempted to placate him, he told her she was "real cute, maybe we can get together when I get out of here and really make it." He told her she had a "nice bottom," at which point she left him. He yelled after her that she probably was "just like the rest of them." Despite increased amounts of chlordiazepoxide hydrochloride, he continued to remain agitated, sleepless, and hypervigilant, often demanding to know the time and when the doctor was going to come and saying that he felt like a prisoner, that he needed to make a call.

Patient's behavior
Preoccupations
Illness/sexual prowess/environment/children

Repeat physical and laboratory examinations indicated a stable course. The ECG showed a deepening of q waves in III and AVF. Blood work showed elevations of serum glutamic-oxaloacetic transaminase and lactic dehydrogenase. The house officer confirmed his impression to the patient that he had had a myocardial infarction, but was doing well. The patient replied, "Yeah doc, maybe just a little strain, huh; now when are you going to let me out of here?"

Physical course

On the third night, after sleeping fitfully, the patient wakened yelling that he was "being kept a prisoner and being tortured"; that "them Blacks had finally got me" and were going "to do me in unless I get out of here"; that "I really hadn't done anyone any harm, including my wife; she's the one who left, and I just needed another woman." He said, "I'm going to get out of here away from all these machine guns, before they take me out like they did to that guy in the next bed." He began pulling at his bedclothes, taking his johnny off, and rattling the side rails. He threatened to pull out the IV if they did not get the "doc right away." Another time, he said that the Koreans were after him. After the house officer came, he seemed somewhat calmer. He complained that he could not sleep, that there was too much going on, saying, "This is a hell of a place for someone to get some rest. I'd be better off in jail."

CCU course[8]
Intensive care unit syndrome[9–11]
Delirium[12]

Concepts and stages of delirium
Fluctuating and reversible
Electroencephalogram definition
Associated behavioral phenomena

He said he was afraid, "had never been so afraid, even when I was in the marines." He began to cry. He said he missed his wife, that it was all his fault, but that he was going to do better "if I ever get out of here." Physical examination revealed BlPr 130/90, P 140, Resp 26 and shallow; pupils were widely dilated. He was perspiring profusely. The bedclothes were in disarray. After talking with him further, the house officer suggested he talk with the consulting psychiatrist. The patient's response was "So you think I'm crazy; so you're going to call the shrink." After further talking, he reluctantly consented, saying, 'But I'm not going to let them put me away." The house officer agreed. The psychiatrist saw the patient later in the morning. After a ½-hour interview, Mr. S. seemed somewhat calmer. He was able to tell the psychiatrist that he had a lot of problems: he was concerned about his kids and whether he could get his job back; that he felt bad about his wife leaving; that he wondered if he could work again; that maybe he would be put out to pasture; that he felt bad about a relationship he was having with another woman; that he had a lot of thinking to do.

Psychiatric consultation[13]
Ventilation of affect
Talk
Being with where the patient is

The psychiatrist agreed that "Yes, these are important concerns" and that "We shall need to talk about them. But first you need to get some rest and get better; then we can get to

Reassurance

work and try to resolve some of these problems. Now I want you to get some sleep. I am going to give you some medicine that will help, and I'll come back and see you later." The psychiatrist prescribed a butyrophenone after discontinuing the chlordiazepoxide. He talked with the nursing staff and house officer about their concerns, suggesting that they let the patient talk with them and not become upset by what he said, but that they first help him get some rest by controlling his agitation with medication and by reassuring the patient that things were going along smoothly and that he would be out of the CCU in a few days.

Staying with the patient[14, 15]
Medication
Butyrophenone versus hypnotic sedatives
Sleep
Attending to the professional staff[11]

Later in the day, when seen again by the psychiatrist, Mr. S. was much less agitated. He had slept first fitfully and then soundly for 4 hours. He said that he felt better; that he looked forward to getting out of the CCU, out of the hospital, and back home to the kids, work, maybe even his wife; that he was going to take it easy; that he had been working too hard, taking everyone's problems as his own.

Further talks and history
Reactions to illness

Over the next 24 hours his physical course remained stable, without further change in the ECG. He slept soundly much of this time. In talking with the psychiatrist, his concerns were with what he was going to do after he left the hospital; about his kids and wife. He began to talk about his father's death when he was 8; his difficult childhood; his anger about his mother taking over his home and managing the children; how he had always worked hard, at several jobs, in order to give the kids what he had not had as a kid; whether the police force would take him back; how during the past year he had first had his mother move into the house, at his wife's insistence, because she could no longer support herself; how after 13 years he had been promoted to desk sergeant and could only occasionally get out on the "beat, where the action is"; how he had had to give up his second job as a clerk in order to take care of the kids, after his wife left; how broken up he had been when she left; how he had transferred the new car to her name and had given her half of the credit cards; and how he had attempted to woo her back to no avail; how he probably deserved this because he had left her alone for so many years.

Father
Childhood
Mother
Job
Wife

The psychiatrist listened, allowing the patient to express his feelings of anxiety and anger, letting him cry. After ½ hour, Mr. S. said he felt better, that he had never told anyone "any of this stuff before." He apologized for being soft and crying. He vowed he would do better, take better care of himself, get on top of things again, make everything right; if the "old lady" did not come back, he could not help it. It was water over the dam; he would just have to do the best he could, that was all. Maybe he would go back to school, get some college credits.

Grieving[16]
Stages of grieving
Denial
Ventilation
Defenses
Adaptation

Mr. S.'s physical course remained stable. Plans were made for his discharge to a general nursing floor. As the time for transfer approached, he seemed quieter. When the nurses talked with him about this, he said he had a lot on his mind, that they would be glad to see him go, "to get rid of me, because of all the trouble I've caused." Anyway he was not going to let them torture him anymore. Prior to discharge, occasional premature contractions were noted on the ECG associated with a rhythm of 140 at one time. When seen by the psychiatrist, he said "They are trying to get rid of me, throwing me out; now I'll be all alone; those other nurses will know all about me and leave me alone; I won't have any visitors." The psychiatrist suggested that he be visited by several of the floor nurses and that they tell Mr. S. what to expect after transfer. The patient seemed calmer after this. His pulse slowed, and the premature contractions ceased. Transfer to a general nursing floor was accomplished without further incidence.

Separation-anxiety at time of discharge from intensive care unit[17]

After this acute phase of illness, Mr. S.'s convalescent period began. He approached this enthusiastically, determined that everything was going to be all right. Immediately, he began to see that things were ordered. He demanded a telephone and began to call home every 2 hours to find out what was going on. He called the police station at least once during each shift. He tried, without success, to get hold of his wife. He had two newspapers delivered daily. He saw to it that he was attended to first for his morning toilette. He sat up longer than he was supposed to, walked further than suggested, got to know most of the patients on the

Stages of illness
Illness onset—prehospital
Convalescent phase—hospital
Rehabilitation phase—posthospital/home/community/work

Underlying behavior pattern
Pattern type A[18]

floor, talked with them freely, and offered advice as to what they should do. With the psychiatrist, he talked about what he was going to do when he got out. "Maybe I'll begin a garden, dig up some dirt and plant vegetables. I hate to sit still. If I look at television, I got to be doing something, anything, with my hands, fixing something, working on a crossword. Maybe I can fix up the house a bit; it sure needs it. Lacks a woman you know. Not that I don't keep it clean, but a little paint, maybe new chair covers." When the psychiatrist suggested that maybe Mr. S. had other things on his mind, he responded saying, "Oh, you mean work. I figure they'll let me back in 6 weeks or so, if you docs tell them to. They'll probably put me on the bench, but what the hell. I know plenty, and I'm going to go to school part time anyway." When asked if he had other concerns, he said, "Oh yeah, the wife. Well I haven't thought much about that. She's only been to see me once, and it was ok. Not much though; I mean there was a kind of distance between us. Gee it was tough . . . ." At this point, Mr. S. began to sob. After a while, he began to express his fears and anger about his wife and children, later about himself—that he really knew he was not the man he had been; that maybe he would not make it; that maybe they would not let him back to work; that maybe he was all washed up—wife, health, job, money-wise, maybe even sexually—"What good am I to anyone with a bum ticker?"

By the next interview, Mr. S. was his old self again. He had a lot of new plans. "If they don't want me, I can go into business. I know a lot about the liquor business; maybe I could set up a partnership. I got a friend with a bit of cash; maybe I could get him to back me. Anyway I'm not going to worry now. I'm just gonna get better, get out of here, get home and rest, put the kids in order . . . ." He then began to wonder what restrictions were going to be placed on him—diet, smoking, sexual activity, physical activity—saying, "No one's going to make an old lady out of me; why, look at my mother—she's 70 and going strong." The psychiatrist suggested that it sounded like Mr. S. had some real questions to ask the house officers and that maybe he could begin asking them. Mr. S.'s reply was, "Aw, they're too busy. Now that I'm

Concerns over illness[19]

Group counseling[20]

better they just come in in the morning and say 'hello.' Well, maybe I'll try anyway. Hey, doc, how would you like to meet my kids? The other doc says I can go downstairs Saturday and see them. Maybe you could come too?" The psychiatrist assented.

Family counseling

Extension of the contract

Over the next several sessions, the interviews moved back and forth over the regrets of the past, focusing occasionally on the immediate situation and anticipations over the future. As his course continued smoothly and he made preparations for leaving the hospital, Mr. S. allowed as how it sure had helped to have someone to talk with, he was sure going to miss it, maybe he could ring the doc up sometime to chat or maybe even visit. On the basis of this, the psychiatrist and Mr. S. agreed to meet weekly in the clinic to talk over how things were going and to see what kinds of adjustments might be necessary.

At the last interview in the hospital, Mr. S. seemed quite agitated. He greeted the psychiatrist, saying "Hey, you know what they want to do to me now? They want to send me to the pound. I mean, they think maybe they should do surgery on my heart. That's right, do one of those new operations like a graft. What do you think about that, huh?"

New worries

After discharge, Mr. S. and the psychiatrist met weekly over the next 6 weeks and thereafter monthly over the next year, charting Mr. S.'s course, his attempts to resolve some of the conflicts about his marriage, children, illness, jobs, and school. His physical condition remained stable. Surgery was decided against.

Summary
- *Substantiated hypotheses*
- *Unsubstantiated hypotheses*
- *Areas where further information is needed*
- *Speculations as to future course of patient and physician-patient interaction*
- *Problem-oriented review*

References

1. Halberstam, M., and Lesher, S.: *A Coronary Event.* New York, C.B.S. Publications, Popular Library, 1978.

2. Olin, H. S., and Hackett, T. P.: The denial of chest pain in 32 patients with acute myocardial infarction. J.A.M.A. *190:* 977, 1964.
3. Holmes, T. H., and Rahe, R. H.: The social readjustment rating scale. J. Psychosom. Res. *11:* 213, 1967.
4. Zborowski, M.: Cultural components in responses to pain. J. Soc. Issues *8:* 15, 1952.
5. Paffenbarger, R. S., Jr., Wolf, P. A., Notkin, J., and Thorne, M. C.: Chronic disease in former college students. I. Early precursors of fatal coronary heart disease. Am. J. Epidemiol. *83:* 314, 1966.
6. Friedman, M., and Rosenman, R. H.: Association of specific overt behavior pattern with blood and cardiovascular findings. J.A.M.A. *169:* 1286, 1959.
7. Brown, F.: Childhood bereavement and subsequent psychiatric disorder. Br. J. Psychiatry *112:* 1035, 1966.
8. Cassem, N., and Hackett, T. P.: Psychiatric consultation in a coronary care unit. Ann. Intern. Med. *75:* 9, 1971.
9. Kimball, C. P.: ICU syndrome: A new disease of medical progress. Med. Insight *5:* 8, 1973.
10. McKegney, F. P.: The intensive care syndrome: The definition, treatment, and prevention of a new "disease of medical progress." Conn. Med. *30:* 633, 1966.
11. Kornfeld, D. S.: Psychiatric problems of an intensive care unit. Med. Clin. North Am. *55:* 1353, 1971.
12. Engel, G. L., and Romano, J.: Delirium, a syndrome of cerebral insufficiency. J. Chronic Dis. *9:* 260, 1959.
13. Kimball, C. P.: Medical psychotherapy. Psychother. Psychosom. *25:* 193, 1975.
14. Kimball, C. P.: Treatment of delirium. In *Current Therapy,* H. F. Conn, editor, pp. 833–835. Philadelphia, W. B. Saunders, 1974.
15. Kimball, C. P.: Reactions to illness: The acute phase. Psychiatr. Clin. North Am. *2:* 1979.
16. Lindemann, E.: Symptomatology and management of acute grief. Am. J. Psychiatry *101:* 141, 1944.
17. Klein, R. F., Kliner, V. A., Zipes, D. P., et al.: Transfer from a coronary care unit. Arch. Intern. Med. *122:* 104, 1968.
18. Friedman, M., and Rosenman, R. H.: Overt behavior pattern in coronary disease: Detection of overt behavior pattern A in patients with coronary disease by a new psychophysiological procedure. J.A.M.A. *173:* 1320, 1960.
19. Hellerstein, H. K., and Friedman, E. H.: Sexual activity and the post-coronary patient. Arch. Intern. Med. *125:* 987, 1970.
20. Bilodeau, C. B., and Hackett, T. P.: Issues raised in a group setting by patients recovering from myocardial infarction. Am. J. Psychiatry *128:* 73, 1971.

CHAPTER 28

The History of Ms. L.: Conversion

RECORDED HISTORY AND OBSERVATIONS

Ms. L. is a 45-year-old, white, married mother of four daughters, who is referred to a University Hospital for further evaluation of a chronic cough of 2 years'duration and a 1-week history of three asthmatic attacks.

FOR DISCUSSION

In this identifying statement, what further demographic information might help in orienting you to Ms. L.? (See Chapter 2.)
What are some of your immediate speculations regarding some of the psychosocial adjustments Ms. L. might be undergoing?[1]

As the medical student records Ms. L.'s initial history, he records that she has experienced no previous illnesses except the usual childhood diseases. Family history identifies that Ms. L.'s mother is 70. Although she is well according to the family physician, she is known as a hypochondriac. Ms. L.'s father died at age 46 of complications secondary to chronic alcoholism (at that time Ms. L. was 21 and had just graduated from college). A brother 2 years younger than Ms. L. is alive and well.

Consider the significance, if any, of the family history.[2, 3]
Are there specific questions that you would consider asking the patient at this point?

In review of Ms. L.'s early health history, she reported no unusual illnesses or neurotic traits (tics, prolonged thumb sucking, nail biting, school phobias). She reported that she was most attached to her father. It is of interest that Ms. L. has always lived within several blocks of her mother. As an adolescent, she had no unusual problems. Her menses began at age 16.

What other information might be helpful in knowing more about Ms. L.'s development?
- *Specific illnesses*
- *Specific psychosocial development*[4]

Although this was later than many of her friends, it did not really bother her. She was mostly interested in sports and outdoor activities and was known in local circles as a tomboy. After menarche, she experienced severe cramps with each menses and generally felt bad (irritable, crying for no reason at all) for several days. This persisted until after the birth of her first daughter at age 26.

While Ms. L. was giving the history, the student was struck by her vivacious and charming manner. She answered every question with an abundance of other information not directly related to her health history. She recalled trips she used to take with her Daddy and languorous summer afternoons spent fishing from a river bank. While she spoke, she threw back the bedclothes and pulled her legs tightly against her breasts under a negligee. The student pushed his chair away from the bed and began to ask questions more hurriedly. But this was of no avail, as Ms. L. began to describe her two husbands.

How would you conceptualize Ms. L.'s behavior?

What explanations would you give for this behavior in the context of the interview?[5] *(See Chapter 4.)*

How might this modify your approach to the patient?

From what developmental stage would you expect her behavior derived?

At age 25 Ms. L. married a childhood sweetheart, after spending several years in Italy and Spain. From the beginning she argued with her husband, who was a "wealthy playboy" who drank alcoholic beverages excessively and, when inebriated, beat her. Her two oldest daughters were born when she was 26 and 27. After each of these she experienced a several-month period of despondency associated with fatigue, listlessness, lack of energy, and loss of interest.

Are there comments you can make about Ms. L.'s choice of mate?

What would you think about Ms. L.'s period of despondency after childbirth?[6]

What additional questions would you ask her about her despondency?[7]

Were she consulting you when she was 28, what concerns would you have about her becoming pregnant again?

Ms. L. continued to talk about her life with her first husband. When talking about the fights she had with her husband, she became increasingly animated, occasionally tearing. After 5 years of marriage, she divorced her husband, taking her two children to live in Florence for several years. Returning to the small mid-Western town where she had grown up, she began dating a physician, who was a year younger than herself. They were married within a year. He had previously been married and had one daughter, who has lived with the family several

Are there any specific questions you might have for Ms. L. at this point in the interview?

months a year. She is 16. When Ms. L. was 36, another daughter was born, who is now 9. She had four "beautiful" daughters. She and her husband were the socialites of the town, always giving "huge" parties. Everyone liked them. In addition, she was chairperson of the volunteer organization at the local hospital. She liked to garden and take care of her home. She was always busy.

When challenged by the student that this sounded a bit idyllic, Ms. L.'s face clouded and she countered, "What do you mean?" She said she had had a "good life," but now things were "not so good," ever since she had gotten this cough.

What would you do at this point in the interview?[8, 9]

Ms. L. said she had got the cough 2 years ago. She had seen first her family physician, then an allergist, then a pulmonary disease specialist, finally a gastroenterologist. No one could help her. Her husband was unsympathetic. He said he took care of sick people all day long and did not like to come home to take care of a sick wife.

How do you explain Dr. L.'s response?
Do you relate to it?

When asked how Ms. L.'s cough had affected her life, she said, "It's just awful." She no longer slept with her husband "so as not to disturb him." She was often irritable and complaining. When she was this way, her husband would become morose and silent. He was away from home more. They did fewer things together. They could not talk with each other. He was not affectionate. He had never been very affectionate. She always had to approach him. She just wanted to be cared for and held.

How do you assess this part of the interview?
Are there specific questions that you have for Ms. L.?

When asked if there were times when her cough was less prevalent, Ms. L. responded immediately, saying yes. When she had taken her younger daughter to Florida for a week, she did not cough once.

What thoughts do you have about the cough at this point?
How would you go about substantiating these?

When asked if there were times when Ms. L's cough was worse, she said it was at its worst when her oldest daughter had gone off to college the previous fall.

How might you explain this?
How would you respond to this information?

Ms. L. said the cough had gotten increasingly worse. She did less. She stayed home more. Finally it had turned into asthma. When asked

What would you do at this point?
What are your thoughts about Ms. L.'s symptom?

if she could recall when she had had her first asthmatic attack, she said "no" but immediately followed that by saying it was when her husband said he could not stand it anymore. He said she had four choices: (1) to go live in Arizona; (2) to have an operation; (3) to get a divorce or (4)________. She said "do myself in." At this point in the interview, Ms. L. began to cough, then wheeze and exhibit forced expirations.

After Ms. L. had recovered, she recounted how her two closest friends had committed suicide; one, 9 years before, just after her own daughter was born; the other, 4 years ago. She then spoke of the death of her first husband, who had died in prison of carcinoma of the larynx.

Would you do anything at this point?
Does this information influence your thinking about Ms. L.'s complaint?

When asked if Ms. L. had felt angry when her husband had given this ultimatum, she said no—just h-h-hurt. She began coughing and wheezing again. She then said she just wanted things to be right, she just wanted to be cared for, she just wanted to be held. She said she was afraid of dying.

What would you do?

Ms. L. then said she did not like being in the hospital. She wanted to go home, to be in her own bed. It was so strange here and she was afraid of having all those tests again—a bronchoscopy and bronchogram, and esophagoscopy. She could not stand those things being put down her throat. She thought she would sign out and go home.

What would you do?

When Ms. L. was taken to the examining room, she became so agitated that she was heavily medicated for the examinations to proceed on schedule. After 3 hours of examinations, she was returned to her room. Somewhat later, a nurse called the student, saying that Ms. L. seemed to be very upset. When the student appeared, Ms. L. was crying and wheezing. She said she was scared, that her $4,000 diamond ring had been stolen, that all these people in her room (the security guards were there) were persecuting her, that her husband had refused to stay with her and was going to leave her. She said there was nothing wrong with her. It was all a plot by the surgeons who were going to kill her. She said she did not know where she was or what she was doing here.

What is going on here?[10]
What would you consider doing and in what order?
Of what possible value would an electroencephalogram have?

Twenty-four hours later, Ms. L.'s agitation was over. She apologized to the student for causing such a fuss. She did not know how she had lost her ring, but she had found it in the bathroom, even though she was convinced that it had been lost forever. She just felt bad. Everything was lost. All the exams were negative. She just wanted to go home. There was no use. But it was funny, she was no longer coughing or wheezing. If only she could find someone to take care of her. She said she did not know what was going to become of her, what she was going to do, or where she was going. She said that she had never cried like this before. Wasn't she being a big baby! She hurt so much. It felt good to cry, but she could not cry forever. If only she could talk with her husband (he had returned home). She said she did not blame him. She had become old. She was tired. The children did not need her anymore.

What are your thoughts about Ms. L. now?

Based on these, what would you do?

Is there more information (history, examination) you need?

Based upon this information, what are the recommendations you would make?

How would you go about helping Ms. L. to implement these?

As you have followed Ms. L. through this part of her illness, how do you, in your rare moments of reflection, put Ms. L. together?

What speculations do you have, based on the limited data you have, about her:

- *Family history*
- *Development*
- *Personality*
- *Sense of self*
- *Present state*
- *Future life (health) course*

Would you have any advice for her referring family physician?

At what points or situations in her future life do you think Ms. L. would be at risk for illness?

How might these be anticipated?

How might these be prevented?

How might these be managed, if they were to occur?

What questions or observations do you have regarding Ms. L.'s treatment and the medical care "system?"

References

1. Weissman, M. M., and Paykel, E. S.: *The Depressed Woman: A Study of Social Relationships*, parts II and IV. Chicago, University of Chicago Press, 1974.
2. Kenyon, F. E.: Hypochondriasis: A clinical study. Br. J. Psychiatry *110:* 478, 1964.
3. Woodruff, R. A., Jr., Goodwin, D. W., and Guze, S. B.: Affective disorders. In *Psychiatric Diagnosis*, Chapter 1, pp. 3–24. New York, Oxford University Press, 1974.
4. Senn, M. J. E., and Solnit, A. J.: *Problems in Child Behavior and Development.* Philadelphia, Lea & Febiger, 1968.
5. Shapiro, D.: Hysterical style. In *Neurotic Styles*, chapter 4. New York, Basic Books, 1965.
6. Melges, F. T.: Postpartum psychiatric syndromes. Psychosom. Med. *30:* 95, 1968.
7. Akiskal, H. S., and McKinney, W. T.: Depressive disorders: Toward a unified hypothesis. Science *182:* 20, 1973.

8. Engel, G. L.: Conversion symptoms. In *Signs and Symptoms: Applied Physiology and Clinical Interpretation*, C. M. MacBryde, editor, ed. 5, chapter 26. Philadelphia, J. B. Lippincott, 1969.
9. Engel, G. L.: A reconsideration of the role of conversion in somatic disease. Compre. Psychiatry *9:* 316, 1968.
10. Engel, G. L., and Romano, J.: Delirium, a syndrome of cerebral insufficiency. J. Chronic Dis. *9:* 260, 1959.

CHAPTER 29

Hemodialysis and Renal Transplantation: A Personal Account

(Written with Richard Allen Famularo, M.D.)

OVERVIEW

In this chapter is presented a verbatim account of the course of a 23-year-old, single Caucasian male from the onset of his illness through hemodialysis, renal transplantation, possible rejection, and convalescence. A clinical case method for teaching[1] medical students and physicians is presented via the case history (left column) and headlining medical, psychological, and social factors (right column) characteristic of the experience of hemodialysis patients. As stated in Chapter 26, "the teacher's objective is to shape and orchestrate the discussion in such a way as to accomplish his agenda by incorporating both conceptual approaches and substantive content in the course of the seminar. This allows not only for a discussion of didactic material introduced by the case and the instructor, but also a consideration of affectually determined reactions of the students to the dependency, uncertainty, personality factors, loss, frustration, coping and adaptation, effects on family, compliance, denial, ethics, and psychotherapy.

RECORDED HISTORY AND OBSERVATIONS	FOR DISCUSSION
Mr. P., a 23-year-old, single Caucasian man was seen at the time of concern by himself, family, and staff over possible failure and/or rejection of a transplanted kidney received from his fa-	

Modified version (and reproduced with permission) of article from General Hospital Psychiatry 2: 70–80, 1980; copyrighted by Elsevier-North Holland.

ther. He was followed through the acute, convalescent, and early phases of illness. These verbatim reports have been slightly rearranged according to the chronicity of illness in order to present as coherently as possible the patient's experience over the spectrum of illness onset, predialysis, dialysis, transplant, and posttransplant phases.

In the first interview before the conversations with the liaison psychiatrist were taped, the patient identified the historical antecedents of his illness, which seemed to date back to high school when he experienced fevers of unknown origin. Three years before the present hospitalization, he was diagnosed as having focal glomerulonephritis after an abrupt and rapid deterioration of renal functioning. This is described in retrospect in the text.

Interestingly, the first interview commenced with the patient discussing his concern about his sexual functioning.

Premorbid Account

Before I was sick I was sort of carefree, I guess. I was studying something (math) that I really enjoyed. I had a lot of friends and was living in an apartment in New York, going to school, enjoying where I was living, taking walks, going to movies.

Sexual Functioning

Sexual dysfunction (decreased frequency of sexual intercourse, difficulty with erection and ejaculation, difficulty in sexual arousal) occurs in a significant percentage of both male and female dialysis patients. Reportedly as high as 70 per cent of patients have a decrease in frequency of intercourse, 65 per cent of males have difficulty in maintaining erection, and greater than half of female hemodialysis patients have decreased levels of sexual arousal.[2]

Concern about Sex

I'm preoccupied with sex possibly because of the connection of the kidneys with sex organs. Weakness, anemia makes that sort of activity disappear to some extent. You feel weak all the time. And constantly irritated by side effects—you don't particularly feel sexually inclined when you feel lousy, you know, when you're sick with a cold or anything like that...I still haven't regained my old self completely. I notice that I feel sexually impulsive more than I

Sexual Functioning

Sexual dysfunction is multifactorial, not existing as a separate entity but accompanying other physical and psychological disorders, such as inability to work, depression, marital or family discord, organic brain syndromes, and medical complications of renal failure.[2-4]

had when I was on dialysis, so there's an involvement. I'm not worried. Of course when I was a teenager I used to masturbate. I don't have to do that now, though. Sometimes I have a dream where I get an erection, that sort of thing, and I don't do anything, really. I don't have much opportunity to do anything...was afraid I would dry up, my tubes would sort of dry up and get sticky and stick together. I was sort of concerned that my penis would become useless, not only as a sexual organ but as an organ for getting rid of urine as well. That would be disastrous. But I was reassured when every once in a while I would eek out a little urine or fluid, so I knew the passageway was still open. I worried once in a while that I might dry up. I think I asked about it a couple of times and was reassured.

Stress and Coping

Prolonged stress decreases the ability of the chronic renal patient to cope actively. Coping implies the ability to appropriately balance the demands of reality and the demands of the self.[5]

Early Illness

Well, I have been on dialysis for about 2 years, almost to the day that I got my kidney, so the actual symptoms, I suppose, started a couple of months earlier: increased frequency of high fevers, sort of unexplained fevers, headaches, high blood pressure which I had never had before. I was practically blind for a while because of some blood in my retina which didn't allow me to see straight forward, only peripherally; at the time I was living in New York walking around in a funny daze on the streets. It was very strange, this happening to me, and finally I discovered that my kidney was deteriorating. I was sick. It happened suddenly.

Dialysis

I felt a cloud almost immediately upon starting dialysis. I felt weak, I felt that I was essentially deteriorating. I realized that I was going downhill. I didn't think about the end of the road particularly, but there wasn't much chance as far as keeping myself sustained at a certain level, and if anything happened, it would probably be for the worst.

Dialysis Disequilibrium

Typical symptoms of dialysis disequilibrium include headache, nausea, vomiting, twitching, arrhythmias, tremors, and seizures. Preparing the patient for possible difficulties may increase over-all compliance to regimen.[6]

I had a lot of side effects, a lot of difficulty with the medicine, discomfort—itching particularly—constant itching that was the worst discomfort—it was just distracting not to be able to sit down and read a magazine article, to do anything, really, anything that required any amount of concentration, I guess. I'd sit down

Dependency

During dialysis, the patient experiences a transition from an autonomous existence to a state of dependency. The specific nature of the dependency will re-

to start to concentrate and I would just have to start scratching or itching. It was very distracting; I just couldn't concentrate. The most comfortable position for me most times was standing up and pacing. It seemed like standing and moving were the only way I could be reasonably free from a lot of the difficulties that I encountered when I sat down for a long time or when I lay down. I was not sleeping well at all. I'd get maybe 1 or 2 hours sleep. I found myself getting up at three o'clock in the morning, pace around, exhausted, then fall asleep for a few hours. I rarely got more than 3 or 4 hours a day. I also had stomach pain. It's hard to explain, just plain discomfort in that area, due to the high BUN, I guess. The itching that was apparently due to high calcium, high phosphates. I never really got it straight. I really wasn't interested in what it was.

flect early childhood symbiosis and individuation.[7, 8]

Uncertainty

The course of the dialysis patient is unpredictable and fragile. They do not know, nor can they anticipate, when and if they will feel well or sick.[9]

I had very little contact with people. I don't have a lot of close intimate friends, and I would be so uncomfortable that I wouldn't make any attempt at having visitors. If I did have one, I would be so uncomfortable during most of the visit, trying to hide it, pacing around, I am sure I made friends uncomfortable by watching me, so I sort of shied away from contact with people I knew. With doctors and nurses I got along mostly. I don't think I was a particularly nice patient to take care of. I rarely smiled. I think I would go weeks without smiling. I didn't have much of my sense of humor left. It didn't seem appropriate. I didn't really feel any mirth most of the time. The hospital staff thought I was a terrible patient. They constantly told me I was the worst in the group, even though I know objectively that I wasn't.

Personality Factors

The patient's adjustment to hemodialysis obviously is influenced by personality factors. Factors decreasing level of adjustment include inability to delay gratification, acting out of aggression, excessive denial of illness, excessive primary or secondary gain, highly dependent or highly independent individuals, and depressive symptomatology.[10, 11]

Right after the dialysis, I was always itching. That's just miserable. You can't do anything with that. I would be squirming and pacing around, unable to do anything. With a high BUN, I had stomach symptoms. To have an upset stomach is just one of the more affective forms of misery. It would start between one dialysis and the next. It is hard to describe the feeling, sort of not a cramp and not gas pains, just a feeling of something humming down there and causing a lot of pain, mild, subtle discomfort, not violent. I had muscle effects,

Loss and Frustration

The sense of loss and frustration is common among chronic hemodialysis patients. This stems from a loss of body functions, jobs, financial income, and social network. There is a constant frustration of instinctual drives (food, aggression, sex) and a threat of injury from surgery, grafts, and injections.[12]

stiff muscles, funny feelings in my joints, just funny feelings. When all of these were relieved, it was like coming out from under a cloud.

With the itching and stomach pain, I couldn't concentrate. I just had to stop trying to think because I couldn't do anything. You just can't live from day to day for such a long period without much hope of having any immediate relief and still beat your brains out about the things that you can't do any more. I've never been one to mope about things I can't do and regretting things I haven't done. I have all the mechanisms for taking care of that tendency. I would get upset by not being able to do anything to keep myself busy and then I would get in other people's way and bother them. I didn't care; it didn't bother me. Maybe I felt that because I didn't know how they felt. I wasn't particularly interested in loving anybody. I didn't want to become another person just because of the disease. I just wanted to get rid of the disease.

Coping and Adaptation

Successful coping and adaptation to chronic hemodialysis correlate with a less defensive attitude, high intelligence, decreased reliance on somatic defenses (as hypochondriasis) and family emotional support.[13-15]

I was terrible about sticking to my diet, terrible about sticking to my liquid requirements. I was always hungry and thirsty as sort of an escape from the discomfort. I was just so miserable all the time that I felt it wasn't really worthwhile for me to be careful about my diet. Sometimes I overdid it, had to go to the emergency room for emergency dialysis. I was told over and over that I was going to die the next day, but I knew I wasn't. I didn't have an awful lot of confidence in a lot of the facts that I was given. I knew that I could cheat a little and still come out all right. But I was told that if I cheated even a little I would be finished.

Compliance

Factors influencing compliance include (1) psychological (patient's subjective perception of severity); (2) social (concurrent financial, family, marital situation); (3) patient-doctor relationship (including patient's expectations and quality of communication); (4) therapeutic protocol (the more complex and life style alterations, the lower the compliance).[16]

I was feeling miserable all the time. My life had restrictions. I didn't see people. Occasionally, I'd be pretty stable, feel pretty good, manage to take a few trips and to go to a restaurant every once in a while. I could never sit through a movie. I'd take walks, sometimes swim.

Before, a simple conversation was strained after 60 seconds. I'd begin to itch and it would distract me from whatever my thinking was. When I was at my best, I could think about things like a magazine article for a short period of time, but then I would lose interest. Yeah, I was itchy all the time. When I would try to read and concentrate, restlessness would develop... you try to control your tendency to itch, but it seems to just make you itch more. When I would try to sit down and read and concentrate, I was just bound up by this series of distractions like itching or stomach symptoms. This was between dialyses. I wasn't able to do anything, to watch a complete television program or read a whole magazine article. There were times I was well for a couple of days and I would be able to do things, particularly in the beginning of the days. By the end I was probably suffering stomach symptoms and all kinds of things, edema. Then I would not be able to read a whole article. It was just hopeless to start on a novel, although I always depended on a lot of heavy reading to while away my spare time that I would have. All I could really do with myself was to try to make myself as comfortable as possible, which I did by pacing back and forth in the living room and making circles around one floor in the house, eating, drinking and trying to sublimate some of the things I would have thought about had I not realized how hopeless they were.

In the hospital, one of my distractions was raiding the kitchen. That was just challenging myself. I'd see if I could get away with it. It was a mild adventure. I resented institutional rules. When I did feel hungry, I just felt it unimportant that I be particularly strict about these rules. It was just an assertion of my independence. I had become too dependent, babied too much. I've always rebelled against authority occasionally.

Effect on Family

Serious illness may initiate a pattern of family disorganization and disequilibrium. The psychological and physical outcome of the patient is partially determined by the quality of the family reorganization.[17, 18]

I don't really remember when I was home. My memory for that time is spongy. There would be homemakers. I wasn't left alone. My mother feared an emergency, I suppose. I was in almost constant discomfort, unable to sleep, itchy, scratchy, unable to entertain myself, always pacing. It was just a blur. I'd wake up after a few hours, drag myself out of bed, pace around, the sun would come out or wouldn't come out. It was a miserable, blah life, a meaningless one. I didn't have the ability to get out of the house,

Denial of Illness

The use of denial in hemodialysis patients is ubiquitous and provides significant defensive reduction of anxiety arising from the patient's limitations, frustrations, uncertainty, dependency, and medical complications. However, more extreme denial of illness restricts ego function, decreases compliance, and could prevent a had nothing to look forward to. When I couldn't stand it anymore, I would salt my food; I had always enjoyed food, eaten good food. I just didn't enjoy the food I was required to eat. I would rationalize, say this won't make much difference. I convinced myself that some of the things I was eating or drinking weren't that harmful.

Transplant

I don't remember much of it, because I was under the influence of heavy sedation for a long period before and a long period afterwards, and what I know happened during that period is from little anecdotes that I've heard from other people. I understand that I wasn't even conscious enough to sign my name quite well when they asked me for permission to operate, so that part is a total blank. And then I woke up in the ICU room and was told in various stages that I had a new kidney from my father, which I didn't know, that it seemed to be working well, almost too well at first, that I was functioning on new systems actually. I felt pretty well, still groggy for a long period of time, and imagine that I just settled down more and more and started this period of adjustment, which continues. That's about it.... I didn't have any particular elation.... I guess I was gradually coming out from under this cloud... the full impact of what had happened hadn't hit me.... I wasn't told that I was going to have a transplant on this particular day... I had just gone through a 10-hour dialysis right before it and I don't remember anything of that. And then all of a sudden I was operated on. I didn't even know my father had been called until later, so that it was a very slow realization to me; the ability to grasp what had happened came to me very slowly, so it was sort of feeling better and better and realizing very slowly in the midst, that I was sort of a new person. I felt more and more comfortable. For a while, I was on a regular diet, which was strange to me. I just felt very good. Of course, I worried about my father, but I was able to see him very quickly—he looked good, he was cheerful as usual and not affected, so I was relieved at that and sort of comfortable for the first time in a long time.... It's very difficult to share it, be-

patient from seeking attention for an immediate medical complication (i.e., missing hemodialysis).[19, 20]

cause it happens slowly over a period of time. I was surrounded by members of my family and felt very secure and well taken care of, and I think the lack of discomfort that I had experienced for the past 2 years, that all of a sudden it was gone, was the most effective thing at first, because it was such a change. It seemed to dissolve a cloud that had been hanging over me for so long that I could hardly remember anything before.

Not only have I noticed a change in myself, but I have been told by other people that I am sort of a new person, able to communicate with people over an extended period of time. I am able to talk about things that just didn't interest me before, things that were unrelated to my discomfort—pains and aches. There was just a complete change of thoughts after.

The main thing, I didn't have the side effects that I had before. I was much more comfortable; able to enjoy myself a bit, relax, read, sort of content after 2 years of misery.

Ethics
The decision to volunteer for renal donation is made via methods not fully in accordance with American Medical Association ethical guidelines. Consequently, greater responsibility befalls members of the renal transplantation team.[21]

I was pushing them to give it (the transplant to me). I was over at the continuing care unit just getting worse and worse, getting dialyzed three times a week, and each time was worse than last because they had to use my veins so frequently, and my veins were shot, had nothing to look forward to except the transplant. I wanted it done as quickly as possible. Everybody was hesitating—you know, we'll talk about it, we'll talk about, and I have to see this one and we'll have to have a meeting, and that sort of thing. It was very frustrating. There was some question where I would get my kidney. It might have a taken a week or something like that, I don't really remember. I was sure that he (father) would be willing all the time. That any member of my family would be willing, provided, you know, they were compatible. I didn't worry a lot because I knew he (father) was in very good physical condition even though his age might be a consideration. He is a very strong guy. Very dry and wiry, and in very good health. He takes care of himself and always does things in a certain way.... He was in good shape, no heart trouble, no circulatory trouble. I was naturally slightly concerned because this is what they call major surgery, but

Ethics
Significant moral and ethical issues are raised in regard to the live donor who allows his body to be "violated" and deliberately injured for another individual's well-being.[22]

I was told it was a simple operation with a short recovery period and few complications. And I was reassured that the donor is always given the utmost considerations, the first consideration really, in any transplant situation, and if the donor is in any jeopardy they would not do it. So he (father) went for tests and they (doctors) concluded everything was in good enough condition to warrant donating.

My mother would be willing. I think I would have been a lot more worried about her donating a kidney. I know that she would be willing to do it. She would be anxious to do it. Although that's a question, too, really. Sometimes I think I know her, and sometimes I don't. She's changed quite a bit lately, sort of a new person. Her work at school has made her more independent.

He (another patient) had a time when he was feeling very bad about taking a kidney from one of the members of his family. I was surprised at that. I really have no feelings, so far as I can tell, about that sort of thing. I was so reassured that whoever donated a kidney would be almost immediately returned to normal and that one kidney was completely adequate. I know that there are considerations that if the remaining kidney is damaged there is no recourse to use a second kidney. So I just don't feel this is dangerous. It's sort of like giving blood. There's always a possibility. Yet people do it; they're not worried about the sacrifice they might make, the jeopardy they put themselves in, because it is so helpful to another person that in the balance there is no comparison.

Concern over Rejection

Well, we (he and father) joked about it; for example, any time that everything is going all right with the kidney, putting out a lot of urine, and my function is good, he'll say, "Boy, I told you I gave you a good kidney"; and any time I kick out, or one of my functions is not working properly, he'll say, "Well, you are not taking very good care of my kidney, better do something...." I know that his kidney was well taken care of up to the point of operation. I know it's not a defective kidney by any means, so that anything that happens to it is my fault,

Psychotherapy

Recipients often become depressed at certain periods after transplantation. Psychotherapy with recipients is frequently best accomplished by helping patients understand their guilt concerning taking an organ from someone else. The therapist also needs to provide an opportunity for expression of fear of failure.[23]

so to speak. I really doubt that there is any transcendental connection between me and my father, now that I have one of his organs in my body, that he is transmitting his health to me.

I would feel very badly if I rejected the kidney or if this kidney did not turn out to function properly. I guess rejection is the only thing I really feel bad about because here I made him lose a week of work and a couple of weeks of really strong living due to the operation, while he was regaining his strength. On the other hand, if I were a father, I think I would do the same thing. I see it as a really nice opportunity as a person to help a son or a daughter out of a sticky situation. I was really at the end of my rope with dialysis. I was just in a horrible situation as far as being well taken care of on dialysis. It was getting worse and worse.

Well of course, there's a change in the way I react not only to my father, but everyone, because I've just begun to feel better all the time. I can talk and appreciate my family in that way. Much more than when I was on dialysis and uncomfortable all the time. In that way there is a change, but he (father) is still the same. I haven't thanked him or bought him a lot of presents or sent him a letter. He would be embarrassed, and I feel that it is unnecessary. He's my father. It's something he would have automatically done. The fact that he's recovered so soon, almost a record recovery, pleases him. I don't think that being thanked for doing something, making a slight sacrifice, making a sacrifice, I should say, making a sacrifice like that, for him it's just an opportunity, a good feeling. I think that he was as grateful for the opportunity as I was for the kidney, almost. That's the way I'd feel, anyway. I notice that is true of practically anybody who donates a kidney, they're just so willing, so anxious to do it, they feel that they can do tremendous good by just inconveniencing themselves for a week or 2 weeks, which is all it amounts to. I think people that are anxious to do something, particularly members of your family, don't require thanks and gratitude, it's just embarrassing. Thanks, Dad, for the kidney, you know; what do you say? Thanks for saving my life, you know... but how do you express it? It's my progress that really pleases him. He is always enthusiastic.

I realize it's very slim. I don't have any real understanding of what's happening. I know that I have gone through a period of rejection. I'm on high amounts of prednisone and something else. It seems to turn the tide. I know I was watching the output of my kidney, which seemed to be dropping away to nothing, when all of a sudden there was a reverse and now I am sort of leveled off at a particular point. But I'm not really very worried about it. I've been told everybody goes through a period of adjustment, up and down, that I shouldn't be disappointed if things should begin to turn to the worst.... Now I'm a better patient. I haven't stolen anything from the refrigerator, I'm sticking close to my low sodium diet. My attitude just sort of reversed itself. I feel that I am getting better and no matter what I have to go through now, what side effects or things that come up, they are automatically swept by, as I am capable now of being normal, and this is something I didn't feel before. And that makes a world of difference.

Psychotherapy

Effective psychotherapeutic intervention requires decreasing or alleviating the major source of distress or "demoralization" (sense of inability or failure adequately to determine one's own destiny and mastery over the environment). The demoralization decreases during therapy as a function of increasing self-esteem within the patient.[24]

Convalescent Phase

I find that right now I don't feel too much like doing anything. Like concentrating on a book. I've got a lot of little annoying symptoms. I have trouble with my feet. I keep changing the darn bandage. My hands are painful most of the time. I'm required to take care of myself pretty much completely, so I have to bounce around measuring urine, keeping up the input-output charts, changing the dressing myself, keeping track of medications like mycostatin. I don't have much energy, I'm weak. I can only do things slowly and deliberately. It takes me 10 minutes to do what a nurse could do in 5. It tires me. I don't have the muscles to get around and to recover quickly, so that I change the dressing and flop down on the bed and rest. It's a tremendous effort. My hands are shaky. And I don't feel I'm taking care of myself as well as a nurse might.... It's hard for me to stay on my feet too long, and lying in bed I can't read too comfortably. Sitting in a chair interferes with the drainage, and the bandages get uncomfortable. It's a burden and a struggle.

Grief Reaction

Patients may undergo a form of bereavement before an actual (or fantasized) loss. This anticipatory grief conceptually is viewed as a preparation of the grief process and can function in many ways similar to conventional grief.[25]

I was annoyed when all of a sudden they suggested I was ready to go home, what with all of these things bothering me. I can't negotiate stairs. I would just be helpless, like a vegetable, couldn't take care of myself. Our home is not constructed so that things are on one floor. I couldn't manage it. I wasn't ready. I hadn't prepared myself... besides, I can't even wash myself well—this hand is practically useless, no grip. I have to use my left hand and I'm right handed.

I think my physical condition has deteriorated. I haven't really gained any strength. At the same time, I'm asked to do more. I'm not gaining muscle tissue. I'm gaining weight, but not by drinking too much fluid; I'm just not losing fluid as quickly. Now the floor nurses take care of me and I have to wait. There are delays. And having to take care of myself, I can't read. I watch TV, walk up and down the hall, or talk on the phone after I've done that. And few of the floor nurses really know how to change the dressing. It is tedious to have to explain it to them. It's not complicated but is critical at a couple of points. And I like it done right, so it doesn't drip on the floor.

Rehabilitation Outlook

I'm not doing any planning, but I have definite ideas about what will happen in a given circumstance. I really don't know enough about how I am going to do, as far as regaining my strength and my ability to write. I have a lot of trouble with my right hand. I don't know if I'll be able to work right away or to go to school right away. I have several concrete ideas about where I'll be able to work. I would like to go back to work as soon as I regain my strength. It's a job I have done before during summers when I was in high school and college for an engineering and surveying company. The boss is a friend of mine. He said he would be glad to take me back, to get me started again. I know that he is doing a lot of different things now. I think it would be very interesting. I could work and not be taxed beyond my strength, so that I could settle down and adjust myself to the routine at my own pace.

Psychotherapy

Some of the main indications for psychotherapy are significant ego restriction and "personality impoverishment," which are a function of the powerful defenses against the stress of dialysis.[26]

Coping and Adaptation

Successful rehabilitation includes various tasks:

1. Maintaining self-esteem and worth

2. Restoring relations with significant others

3. Holding stress within manageable limits

4. Increasing prospects for restoring body functions

5. Finding and subsequent adaptation to personally valued and socially acceptable life style after maximal recovery[27]

Uncertainty

Appropriate rehabilitation requires acquisition and accomplishment of new and complex psychosocial tasks. The uncertainty is heightened by the limitations of medical understanding and techniques concerning renal transplantation.[22, 27]

References

1. Kimball, C. P.: Teaching medical students psychosomatic medicine: Of substances and approaches. Bibl. Psychiatr. 159: 23, 1979.
2. Levy, N. B. (Guest Editor): Symposium on sexual problems of chronic renal failure patients. Dialysis Transplant. 7: 870, 1978.

3. Holdsworth, S., Atkins, M. B., and deKretser, D. M.: The pituitary testicular axis in men with chronic renal failure. N. Engl. J. Med. *296*: 1245, 1977.
4. Procci, W. R., Hoffman, K. I., and Chatterjee, S. N.: Sexual functioning of renal transplantation recipients. J. Nerv. Ment. Dis. *166:* 402, 1978.
5. Shannan, J., DeNour, A. K., and Aarty, I.: Effects of prolonged stress on coping style in terminal renal failure patients. J. Hum. Stress *2:* 19 1976.
6. Wakim, K. G.: The pathophysiology of the dialysis disequilibrium syndrome. Mayo Clin. Proc. *44:* 406, 1969.
7. Viederman, M.: Adaptive and maladaptive regression in hemodialysis. Psychiatry *37:* 68, 1974.
8. Mahler, M., Pine, F., and Bergman, A.: *The Psychological Birth of the Human Infant.* New York, Basic Books, 1975.
9. Fox, R. C., and Swazey, J. P.: *The Courage to Fail*, pp. 266–301. Chicago, University of Chicago Press, 1978.
10. DeNour, A. K., and Czaczkes, J. W.: Personality factors in chronic hemodialysis patients causing non-compliance with medical regimen. Psychosom. Med. *34:* 333, 1972.
11. Freud, A.: The role of bodily illness in the mental life of the child. Psychoanl. Study Child *7:* 69, 1952.
12. Halper, I.: Psychiatric observations in a chronic hemodialysis program. Med. Clin. North Am. *55:* 177, 1971.
13. Sand, P., Livingston, C., and Wright, R. G.: Psychological assessment of candidates for hemodialysis program. Ann. Intern. Med. *64:* 602, 1966.
14. Abram, H. S.: The psychiatrist, the treatment of chronic renal failure and the prolongation of life. II. Am. J. Psychiatry *125:* 157, 1969.
15. Reichsman, F., and Levy, N. B.: Problems in adaptation to maintainance on hemodialysis: A four year study of 25 patients. In *Living or Dying: Adaptation to Hemodialysis*, N. Levy, editor. Springfield, Ill., Charles C Thomas, 1974.
16. Gillium, R. F., and Barsky, A. J.: Diagnosis and management of patient non-compliance. J.A.M.A. *228:* 1563, 1974.
17. Olsen, E. H.: The impact of serious illness on the family system. Postgrad. Med. *47:* 169, 1970.
18. Anthony, E. J.: The impact of mental and physical illness on the family life. Am. J. Psychiatry *127:* 56, 1970.
19. Short, M. J., and Wilson, W. P.: Roles of denial in chronic hemodialysis. Arch. Gen. Psychiatry *20:* 433, 1969.
20. Kubler-Ross, E.: *On Death and Dying.* New York, Macmillan, 1969.
21. Fellner, C. H., and Marshall, J. R.: Kidney donors: The myth of informed consent. Am. J. Psychiatry *126:* 79, 1970.
22. Fox, R. C.: A sociologic perspective on organ transplantation and hemodialysis. Ann. N. Y. Acad. Sci. *169:* 406, 1970.
23. Kempf, J. P.: Psychotherapy with donors and recipients of kidney transplants. Semin. Psychiatry *3:* 145, 1971.
24. Frank, J.: *Persuasion and Healing.* New York, Schocken Books, 1974.
25. Schoenberg, B., et al., editors: *Anticipatory Grief.* New York, Columbia University Press, 1974.
26. DeNour, A. K.: Psychotherapy with patients on chronic hemodialysis. Br. J. Psychiatry *116:* 207, 1970.
27. Coelho, G., Hamburg, D., and Adams, J., editors: *Coping and Adaptation.* New York, Basic Books, 1974.

CHAPTER 30

Case Method: A New Syndrome: Fibromyositis

INTRODUCTION

The case history presented describes a new syndrome, fibromyositis.[1] The presentation is based on an interview conducted in six sessions over 6 months. Between sessions, there were 20-minute telephone conversations regarding the patient's symptoms, current preoccupations, and medication. The history is arranged chronologically as it took place with a few exceptions. The interview process is viewed, as previously, at the beginning and end of therapy (see Chapters 2 and 27). In this situation, this interview has been taken as prototypical of 12 patients with fibromyositis, referred for more extensive psychological evaluation. The findings of this pilot study are reported and discussed elsewhere.[2]

RECORDED HISTORY AND OBSERVATIONS

Mrs. M. is a 49-year-old white, married mother of three (20-year-old son, 18-year-old daughter, 12-year-old daughter), who is employed as a nursing assistant in a community hospital nursery.

Her chief complaint has been "pain all over my body," commencing about 4 years ago when she was hospitalized for a "viral" infection.

FOR DISCUSSION

Mrs. M. had an extensive workup by the Section on Arthritis and Rheumatology. There were no obvious pathophysiological or pathoanatomical findings. On physical examination, tenderness was found over many of the areas that Mrs. M. had identified. Pain was elicited when pressure was placed over areas where tendons attached to bone. She was given the diagnosis of fibromyositis.[3]

She described her pain as "bones moving out of joints, especially in my fingers, heels, and toes." This is associated with "feelings of helplessness—of not being able to do what I am supposed to do." She says, "Something like this you can't see, but it's there, you can only feel it and you can't do anything. Even in walking from the parking lot, I have to stop four or five times because I just can't move. I feel terrible. It's frightening, like someone pushing a button and you stop moving. Its been going on a long time. I get depressed. I feel like giving up. It's like being in labor without being able to get your breath. I hurt, nobody else knows how it hurts. Sometimes I cry (she begins to weep), but it bothers my children and my husband (she stops crying). But I just can't sit around. Whatever has to be done has to be done now. Life has to go on. There is always someting to be done."

Complaint

Striking are the ways in which Mrs. M. describes her pain. She says it is as if her "bones were moving out of the joints." This is associated with feelings of "not being able to walk or move." She feels "helpless." It is as if "someone pushes a button and you stop moving." She is not in control, but is being controlled by some external source or power. It is autonomous, out of her control, "like being in labor without being able to get your breath." It is also a very private experience: "It hurts, nobody else knows how it hurts." She says, "I'm at the end of my rope. I can't go on. Things are closing in."[4, 5]

A record of her past history reveals the onset of hyperthyroidism at age 29 following the birth of her first son after a difficult pregnancy. After a thyroidectomy, she was placed and has remained on Synthroid. Subsequently, she says all her teeth were removed because of hypoparathyroidism. After her third pregnancy, when she was 37, she had a hysterectomy following a cesarean section. At that time, she first experienced "aches and pains all over." At age 47, she developed gall bladder disease and had a cholecystectomy and an appendectomy. After that, she stopped smoking and put on 35–40 pounds.

Past History

She has had a number of illnesses and operations, each around the time of a significant life event and associated with pain.

Mrs. M. was born and reared on the southside of Chicago. She was the second and oldest girl in the family of four, including two brothers. The father was a security guard. The mother depended on her for much of the management of the home. Parents were of Lithuanian Catholic stock and were rigid and "punitive." The mother was viewed as under the thumb of the father. The mother is presently 81, living with a married sister in Norfolk. She has arthritis and gall bladder disease. "She has always been sick, and I had to take over much responsibility." Her father died 17 years ago (patient 32). Although he "was hard to live with, there was a spark of affection." He was a guard for an

Family Origin and Spouse

These feelings may go back a ways. She was the second oldest child and oldest girl. Her mother was seen as sickly, passive, and dependent. Mrs. M. had much responsibility from an early age. There was not much affection in the family, which was first generation American of Lithuanian Catholic background. The family was strict, especially concerned about her relationships with boys. During high school, she al-

industrial company. Mrs. M. finished high school and went to work. She married at age 24, "because there wasn't anything else to do; everyone else was getting married; I got tired of running around." Her parents felt she was marrying "down." Her father had always frowned on her relationship with boys. Her husband was of Russian stock. She described her husband as "a little boy, who never grew up, given to tantrums." There is little communication. She "can't tell him anything, the truth (she feels she) lives a lie. It (the marriage) was a mistake. He doesn't help, can't do anything for himself. He's a trucker and when he gets home, he just sits and drinks and gets waited on. He hates women. It began in childhood; he had an unaffectionate mother. But he's dependent and hates me because he has to depend on me. I have to work."

ways worked. Afterward, she worked full time at an unskilled job. The little spark she felt was from her father. She married as if in desperation or despair or boredom: "there wasn't anything else to do, I got tired of running around." She married a taciturn man, given to outbursts of violent temper, with whom she has little communication other than conflicts. She senses this is a dishonest relationship, she is living a "lie." She runs the home, manages the children, controls the money. She leaves him alone, but feels "trapped" despite this independent course and cannot leave him: "it would be too much of a hassle."[6, 7]

Of her children, Mrs. M. says they are "my whole life, I live for them." She finds the youngest (Michele) "strong-willed, a constant battle who gets what she wants." Mrs. M. sees herself as "protecting the child from her father." The oldest son is her "pride and joy." He's off to the Navy, on a Mediterranean cruise." The oldest daughter is in a small state college in western Illinois. Mrs. M. drives 300 miles every weekend to visit her and take her food. She sometimes does this with her husband, but they hardly say a word to each other for "6 hours."

She spent much time talking about her "unaffectionate" mother-in-law, who is a "willful, passive-aggressive woman who is a two-time widow." Mrs. M.'s husband never sees her despite her illness. Mrs. M. feels she is the only one who can help the mother-in-law.

Children and Mother-in-law

Her focal point is the children with whom she is very tied in. She is "pushing" her daughter through school, hoping she will be the nurse that she never became herself. She drives 300 miles every weekend to visit the daughter at college and to take her out to lunch. Again, we see the need to keep busy, stay in motion, move around. There is a bit of a vicarious relationship with the son who is in the Navy, off moving around the world. And there are the makings of a constant conflict with the 12-year old, with whom she identifies, who is willful, goes her own way, threatens to leave, and whom she takes the several blocks to and from school daily.

In on-going therapy with Mrs. M., she complained of poor sleep, with difficulty in getting to sleep until 2 to 3:30 a.m. Once asleep, she remains so until 6:30 or 7. She gets up as soon as she wakes up "in order to get going" before the others are up. She "needs (her) coffee and needs to work (her) joints, get them limbered up." She likes "a quiet time." When under pressure, she "gets tension headaches."

On the other hand, she describes a chronic sense of urgency. She says she "just can't sit around, whatever has to be done, has to be done now. Life has to go on." At another time, in a more agitated state, she says, "I'm at the end of my rope. The pain is too much. Things are closing in. I feel a spasm in my chest. It is just too much. I can't get everything done. I've got to take the pressure off. There just isn't time to even tell how I am. There are bills, we owe income tax, a physiotherapy bill, car insurance. I'll have to work an extra day a week. There is just constant pressure. I have to manage the books. I have to protect my little daughter from her father. She threatens to leave. My son is in the Mediterranean. I can't handle anything more. If it would help, I'd leave my husband, but it would be too much of an upheaval. I'll just have to leave him alone. He (husband) doesn't do anything, just sits in a tavern, refuses to see anyone for help."

So Mrs. M. emerges as a driven, pressured, self-sacrificing individual who is heavily burdened with a sense of responsibility for everyone. It has always been so. As a child, she was rigidly controlled by a punitive and harsh father. She had to take over many of the responsibilities for a weak, sickly, dependent mother. She married a man somewhat like her father, but stands up to him, takes away the control, does not buckle under as her mother did. On the other hand, she identifies with the independent, "survivor" mother-in-law, who is hard, strong-willed, and able to make a go of it alone. She will teach her daughters to be independent, even if she has to "lead" them all the way. The oldest daughter is doing college in 3 years. She is partly amused by the growing defiance of her 12 year-old. Her anger is directed at the husband-father, whom she has isolated. Her burdensome victory is the constant battle with the feelings of helplessness that her mother gave in to. Her one respite is sitting in the nursery rocking newborns, giving a warmth she never got and has never been able to give to others. Here, she never experiences pain. It is always outside of the nursery, on the way to or on the way out.[8]

Another time, she says, "this morning I'm under much pressure; I need to talk; I'm going to visit my mother. I have much to do. I avoid my husband all the time. There is nothing there. I go window shopping, to my mother-in-law's, just to get away."

Current History

Despite these feelings, she is driven to go on: "...I can't sit around, what has to be done has to be done now. Life has to go on." There is a chronic sense of urgency. She cannot rest. As soon as she wakes up, she gets up, begins moving around. She stays up until 2 or 3 am., "to get the work done." She gets up early. There is always something to do. She is the only one to do it. No one helps.[9]

There is also a sense of constant defiance and anger. She has great concern about her faith, Roman Catholicism; since the new service was introduced, "I don't like the Apostles' creed; the Church used to mean a lot to me, but I don't know if I even believe any more. I just want to be able to walk, work, get my daughter through school, get my oldest daughter through college."

Commentary

This pain may be viewed as the manifestation of the intense conflict in the patient between underlying, chronically unfulfilled passivity and dependency needs and the defenses attempting to repress and overcome these.[10] *The defense also defends against overt feelings of anxiety, anger, and probably depression, which are generated by the present life stresses but provoke latent conflicts going back to early childhood and the family of origin. The child-adult learned to cope with feelings of impotence, helplessness, and inadequacy through constant activity expressed through the motor system. The pain may be the resultant of the chronic tension in the muscles around the painful joints, whose mechanism in physiological terms is yet to be defined. Can these be explained by a vasospastic theory of disease that results in autoimmune processes?*[11, 12]

References

1. Smythe, H. A.: Non-articular rheumatism and the fibrositis syndrome. In *Arthritis and Allied Conditions*, J. L. Hollander and D. J. McCarty, Jr., editors, ed. 8, pp. 874–884. Philadephia, Lea & Febiger, 1972.
2. Kimball, C. P., Rivers, L., Marks, R., and Medof, E.: Findings in fibromyositis patients. In preparation.
3. Smythe, H. A., and Moldofsky, H.: Two contributions to understanding of the "fibrositis" syndrome. Bull. Rheum. Dis. *28:* 928, 1977–78.
4. Engel, G. L.: "Psychogenic" pain and the pain-prone patient. Am. J. Med. *26:* 899, 1959.
5. Engel, G. L., and Schmale, A. H.: Psychoanalytic theory of somatic disorder: Conversion specificity and the disease-onset situation. J. Am. Psychoanal. Assoc. *15:* 344, 1967.
6. Moldofsky, H.: "Psychogenic rheumatism" or the "fibrositis syndrome." In *Modern Trends in Psychosomatic Medicine*, O. W. Hill, editor. London, Butterworths, 1976.

7. Freud, S.: Inhibitions, Symptoms and Anxiety (1926). In *Standard Edition of the Complete Psychological Works of Sigmund Freud*, vol. 20, pp. 77–174. London, Hogarth Press, 1959.
8. Ruesch, J.: The infantile personality: The core problem of psychosomatic medicine. Psychosom. Med. *10:* 134, 1948.
9. Weiner, H.: *Psychobiology and Human Disease*, pp. 435–464. New York, Elsevier-North Holland, 1977.
10. Dunbar, H. F.: *Psychosomatic Diagnosis*. New York, Hoeber, 1944.
11. Boyd, G. W.: Stress and disease: The missing link: A vasospastic theory. Med. Hypoth. *4:* 432, 1978.
12. Monjon, A. A., and Collector, M. I.: Stress-induced modulation of the immune response. Science *196:* 307, 1977.

Index